The Greatest Gambling Stories Ever Told

The Greatest Gambling Stories Ever Told

EDITED AND WITH INTRODUCTIONS BY
PAUL LYONS

THE LYONS PRESS
Guilford, Connecticut
The Lyons Press is an imprint of The Globe Pequot Press

The Lyons Press is an imprint of The Globe Pequot Press.

Printed in The United States of America

10 9 8 7 6 5 4 3 2 1

ISBN 1–58574–513–8

The Library of Congress Cataloging-in-Publication Data is available on file.

Contents

Introduction:
Edges and Temptations

Go to the gift shop at your favorite casino and try finding a book. Any book! Sure, the casinos would rather have their visitors gambling than reading and reflecting about it. But beyond that they're enforcing and reinforcing a deeply ingrained popular idea that a gambler is one thing and a reader another.

Word is that while gamblers are fabulous talkers (hustlers, fabricators, sob-storyists), they're not much as writers, and they're certainly not readers. Gamblers, it's said, crave immediacy, stimulus, grime or glitter. If they read anything about gambling beyond the Racing Form or morning line they're out for an edge—the skinny on how to beat the slots or their poker game. If they write at all it's in order to recoup losses or splash them therapeutically onto a page and out of their systems. Where the verbal resourcefulness of the gambler is grudgingly granted it's as a kind of creativity wasted, or applied to unfitting subjects. Serious writing and reading, on the other hand, are thought to require a slowing down and a patient looking deeper. Okay for artsy sorts, who'd rather coffee-house about a thing than do it anyway, but not a gambler's cup of tea.

In agreeing to do an anthology like this I'm "making book" against such convenient, erroneous distinctions. I'm betting, bookie-like, that my line-up will be found rewarding to gamblers (at bottom philosophical animals) or people who want to understand more about gambling and like a good story. One hedge against the time I put into assembling this collection was the pleasure I took in reading about an activity that—in its myriad forms—fascinates and often pulverizes me, as any passion submitted to may.

However, gambling *is* proliferating in this country, and others—or rather, it's taking more conspicuous and socially accepted forms. "Judging by the dollars spent," writes Tim O'Brien, "gambling is now more popular in America than baseball, the movies, and Disneyland—*combined*." So I'd be untrue to the speculator in me if there wasn't also a bet (and a hope and a temptation to my reader in the thought) that people will be curious about the impulses and desires behind gambling, the messiness of which are rendered more palpable for me in stories, literary essays, and creative nonfiction than in the accounts written by shrinks and moralists, of which there has never been a shortage.

Insofar as literature is concerned with motivations, actions, consequences—insofar as it is less concerned with routine than with moments when characters chance new courses, lay it on the line, bump against boundaries—literature inclines toward "gamble." Part of what it offers is structured fantasy—a tour of risks we have not risked, or the opportunity to know better, through the lives of characters situated in other times and places, something about the meanings of risks we have taken or considered. Gambling is often, as Larry Merchant has said of boxing matches, a "Theater of the Unexpected." And that which makes gambling gambling elicits an extraordinary, unpredictable range of performances, from the bizarre to the pathological to the sublime. These *have been* brilliantly captured in ways that may entertain and stimulate readers to explore the role of fronting the unexpected in their own lives. The stories and essays in this anthology are a few examples. Before they burst out speaking in their own ways, with their own angles, obsessional musics, and cool or passionate philosophies, a few words more about literature, my selections, and the vexed spirit of gamble.

The first thing to note is that in the literature or oral traditions of *every* culture with which I'm familiar—and I'll bet it's as true of those with which I'm not familiar—you will find some form of wagering. From the earliest times to the present, gambling is a part of the record cultures leave about who they are. Gamblers appear in cosmology, myth, folk and fairy tale, chant, dance, art, song. The varieties of bettors and betting motives or meanings are endless, from dice games for kingdoms (India), to rat-shooting contests (Hawai'i), to deities who bet the sky (Greek) or the rain clouds (Laguna Pueblo), to tycoons who bet on raindrops running down train windows (John Bet-a-Million Gates), to contemporary tracks where emaciated dogs chase mechanical rabbits.

In other words, the "itch for play," as Englishman Charles Cotton (1674) memorably called gambling, is as universal an impulse as any, and one as likely as any to reveal the values, boundaries, excesses, foibles, and eccentricities of particular cultural scenes. For this reason, anthropologist Johann Huzinga concluded that humans might be redesignated from Homo sapiens (man the knower) to Homo ludens (man the player).

Given this pervasiveness of gambling stories, how select a handful? As to "the greatest"? Well, there's only one Muhammad Ali, and there are too many weight classes, divisions, and organizing bodies of written expression to make effective cases that one story would knock another out. My first impulse was to aim for as great a variety as possible, from different cultures and periods, but, for several reasons, I have shifted the emphasis to contemporary, familiar understandings of gambling. For one thing—and the reasons themselves would be interesting—from many cultures I found only fragments related to gambling, paragraphs or anecdotes that while packed with fascinating particulars and characterizations never developed into story, and whose games themselves would require considerable explanation. For another thing, where stories were available, I was not confident that readers would understand cultural contexts enough to do a just reading (as with the Hawaiian rat-shooting story). Additionally, in many cultures there is a telling absence in the literature of what is so strong a cultural feature, and a scarcity of translations of those works on gambling that have made it past the naysayers into print. China, where cab drivers play mah-jongg on every corner, is a notable example.

In choosing the stories, novel excerpts, and essays for this anthology, I have looked first for writing that catches the freshness of gamblers' speech and the specificities of gambling places. I have sought at once to deal with recognizable games and to avoid a sameness in kind (say, too many stories involving showdowns), and to favor those that dramatize or examine the attractions, intensities, and foibles of gambling with edge and insight. For this last reason, I have been drawn to essays and memoir, where writers often achieve a combination of intimacy and critical distance in exploring their own involvement in gamble.

Humor in particular seems a pervasive, redemptive feature that compensates for the loss that is a part of gambling stories. Where gamblers congregate, wit is at a premium. Here, for instance, is the great jazz musician, Jelly Roll Morton, a poolshooter as well, recounting his disastrous foray into the racing game:

> My old friend, Rob Rowe put me onto the horses. Before I knew it, I owned one, a nag named Red Cloud. The owner told me, "Red Cloud is the fastest racehorse in the world. You can blindfold him and he can outrun anything on the tracks, by feeling his way along." The truth was that horse couldn't outrun *me*; he wasn't even a good mule and the officials wouldn't permit him on the track because they claimed I wasn't feeding him.

This humor becomes a natural, instinctive part of the gambler's outlook, patter, and manner of describing places, characters, and actions, as in the following wistful account from the Japanese gangster Junichi Saga's *Gambler's Tale:*

Oyone's father was called Ichizo, and as it happened he was a great gambler, too. Sometimes he played with the laborers, but when he played with the boatmen it was always inside the boat. The police must have known about it, though, as there were raids once or twice a year at least. You should have seen the players when they turned up—they all dived into the river, like so many frogs—they'd be in the air almost before the lookout gave the warning. If somebody had called out "Police" as a joke, I expect they'd have jumped in without bothering to find out if it was true or not.

Beneath the humor, and never quite covered over by it, gambling stories resonate with what Anatole France described as the "fascination with danger at the bottom of all great passions," a sense that there is "no fullness of pleasure unless the precipice is near."

There are those for whom "gamble" is a constant attempt to get an edge over others—to chisel, outfox, or shoot the angles—and there are those for whom "gamble" is bucking the House's edge (the vig, the chop, the rake, seat rental at the table). But what I take as fundamental for both sorts, and for the contemporary spirit of gamble, whatever forms it takes, is a conscious search for the "juice" and vibe of chance experienced as action or "edge."

What that edge is, where that edge is, differs for all of us. But it is a place where you occasionally feel a tingling, vertiginous rush. Once felt—if only for a moment in an evening—you carry it in your insides back to whatever seemingly solid place you came from. There it sits in your gut, a glittering piece of the temptation out of which the edge is made, that temptation to leap, trusting that there is water below, that temptation after letting your stake ride to ride it again.

At the edge restraint fights temptation, or the urge to let go and "tempt fate." In that sense, the edge contains a primal residue of that time when gamble began as a way of risking hard knowledge of the will of the gods. For most, an occasional visit to the edge suffices, and the hard self-knowledge that gambling may or may not afford is not worth it at the price. For edge junkies, life loses sharpness in the safer zones, the senses are less alive. The edge becomes necessary, a place even of calm and stillness clean as casino dice, where complications, responsibilities, and the aspiration for common sense dissolve. If you're not on the edge, such gamblers say, you're taking up too much space.

Gambling places tend to be on the shady edges of society, on the margins of respectability. Boundary spaces, where peoples mix from different walks of life and play together by alternative rules, and by their wits. Thus, in "looking for where the action is," as sociologist Irving Goffman famously described it, "one arrives at a romantic division of the world":

> On one side are the safe and silent places, the home, the well-regulated roles in business, industry and the professions; on the other are all those activities that generate expression, requiring the individual to lay himself on the line and place himself in jeopardy during a passing moment.

This generation of expression would seem to join gambling and writing like pool balls frozen together. In particular because the jeopardy of a "passing moment" can have lasting consequences.

"At its healthiest," writes the poet Stephen Dunn, gambling is "one way of activating the soul, nudging it from its hungry sleep." At its unhealthiest it is a soul-draining, repetitious, and dangerous sickness. This is probably true of most activities about which one might become passionate, but it's especially visible in the literature of gambling, in which there's always the danger, even among the most rational, of "play" getting out of hand.

This temptation to crisis is as evident in eighteenth-century European novels, where heroes lose their patrimonies, as in a Hopi Indian story, which records how, in a game that begins with playing for broom straws, with the loser cooking breakfast, the game got "out of hand . . . when the players began gambling for real possessions. Eventually, they became so addicted that they did not even quit to go to bed." The young man "gambled away his mother's woolen dress and his father's ceremonial kilt and embroidered sash," and since these things are "treasured" and vital to ceremony, he is finally thrown out of the house and set adrift ("The Gambling Boy Who Married a Bear"). The meanings of such stories, while culturally specific, suggest cross-cultural senses in which gambling threatens the loss of things most dear, and social order itself.

Such a latent destructive element, constitutive of gambling writing, can be romanticized, moralized against, or creatively explored. Much of the finest gambling literature, some of which may be found in the pages that follow, does all three.

The
Greatest
Gambling Stories
Ever Told

From The Gambler

BY FYODOR DOSTOEVSKY

translated from the Russian by Constance Garnett

No one has better captured the compulsive aspects of gambling than Dostoevsky in *The Gambler.* As the author wrote to a friend during a gambling bout, "A man can be as wise as Solomon and have an iron character, and still be carried away." Granny in the first selection below is a remarkable case: fresh to the tables, unaware of the rules, she is hooked, "excited," and will run a high gambling fever until something breaks.

Part of the genius of Dostoevsky's portrayal of the gambler attempting to impose his will on the tables against the odds comes from his sense of winning as exhilarating but secondary. In the aftermath of the second selection below, the gambler goes on a pointless spree, as if to confirm for himself that money was never the point. *The Gambler,* that is, enacts deeper dimensions of compulsion. That Dostoevsky in his conflicted way admired aspects of the gambler is clear in a letter proposing to his publisher the novel's theme and explaining its central character:

> all his vital sap, his energies, rebellion, daring, have been channeled into *roulette.* He is a gambler, and not merely an ordinary gambler. . . . He is a poet in his own way, but the fact is that he himself is ashamed of the poetic element in him, because deep down he feels it is despicable, although the need to take risks ennobles him in his own eyes.

The writing of *The Gambler* was itself a gamble. Dostoevsky had three weeks to finish in order to pay off gambling debts, and if he did not deliver the manuscript on time his publisher would assume the rights to earlier books. When it appeared Dostoevsky would finish on time the publisher split town for the weekend, but Dostoevsky's long-suffering wife Anna—to whom it had been dictated—had the manuscript notarized at the police station.

Among the many gambling works influenced by Dostoevsky's novel is the incisive film *The Gambler* (1974), written by James Toback, in which James Caan plays Columbia professor Axel Freed (who of course lectures on Dostoevsky and "freedom"), who burns every bridge in following his search for action to its limit.

Granny's appearance at the roulette table made a profound impression on the public. At the roulette tables and at the other end of the room, where there was a table with *trente et quarante,* there was a crowd of a hundred and fifty or two hundred players, several rows deep. Those who had succeeded in squeezing their way right up to the table, held fast, as they always do, and would not give up their places to anyone until they had lost; for simple spectators were not allowed to stand at the tables and occupy the space. Though there were chairs set round the table, few of the players sat down, especially when there was a great crowd, because standing one could get closer and consequently pick out one's place and put down one's stake more conveniently. The second and the third rows pressed up upon the first, waiting and watching for their turn; but sometimes a hand would be impatiently thrust forward through the first row to put down a stake. Even from the third row people managed to seize chances of poking forward their stakes; consequently every ten or even five minutes there was some "scene" over disputed stakes at one end of the hall or another. The police of the Casino were, however, fairly good. It was, of course, impossible to prevent crowding; on the contrary, the owners were glad of the rush of people because it was profitable, but eight croupiers sitting round the table kept a vigilant watch on the stakes: they even kept count of them, and when disputes arose they could settle them. In extreme cases they called in the police, and the trouble was over in an instant. There were police officers in plain clothes stationed here and there among the players, so that they could not be recognised. They were especially on the look-out for thieves and professional pickpockets, who are very numerous at the roulette tables, as it affords them excellent opportunity for exercising their skill. The fact is, elsewhere thieves must pick pockets or break locks, and such enterprises, when unsuccessful, have a very troublesome ending. But in this case the thief has only to go up to the roulette table, begin playing, and all at once, openly and publicly, take another person's winnings and put them in his pocket. If a dispute arises, the cheat insists loudly that the stake was his. If

the trick is played cleverly and the witnesses hesitate, the thief may often succeed in carrying off the money, if the sum is not a very large one, of course. In
that case the croupiers or some one of the other players are almost certain to
have been keeping an eye on it. But if the sum is not a large one, the real
owner sometimes actually declines to keep up the dispute, and goes away
shrinking from the scandal. But if they succeed in detecting a thief, they turn
him out at once with contumely.

All this Granny watched from a distance with wild curiosity. She was
much delighted at a thief's being turned out. *Trente et quarante* did not interest
her very much; she was more pleased at roulette and the rolling of the little
ball. She evinced a desire at last to get a closer view of the game. I don't know
how it happened, but the attendants and other officious persons (principally
Poles who had lost, and who pressed their services on lucky players and for-
eigners of all sorts) at once, and in spite of the crowd, cleared a place for
Granny in the very middle of the table beside the chief croupier, and wheeled
her chair to it. A number of visitors who were not playing, but watching the
play (chiefly Englishmen with their families), at once crowded round the table
to watch Granny from behind the players. Numbers of lorgnettes were turned
in her direction. The croupiers' expectations rose. Such an eccentric person
certainly seemed to promise something out of the ordinary. An old woman of
seventy, who could not walk, yet wished to play, was, of course, not a sight to
be seen every day. I squeezed my way up to the table too, and took my stand
beside Granny. Potapitch and Maria were left somewhere in the distance
among the crowd. The General, Polina, De Grieux, and Mlle. Blanche stood
aside, too, among the spectators.

At first Granny began looking about at the players. She began in a half
whisper asking me abrupt, jerky questions. Who was that man and who was
this woman? She was particularly delighted by a young man at the end of the
table who was playing for very high stakes, putting down thousands, and had, as
people whispered around, already won as much as forty thousand francs, which
lay before him in heaps of gold and banknotes. He was pale; his eyes glittered
and his hands were shaking; he was staking now without counting, by handfuls, and yet he kept on winning and winning, kept raking in the money. The
attendants hung about him solicitously, set a chair for him, cleared a place
round him that he might have more room, that he might not be crowded—all
this in expectation of a liberal tip. Some players, after they have won, tip the attendants without counting a handful of coins in their joy. A Pole had already
established himself at his side, and was deferentially but continually whispering
to him, probably telling him what to stake on, advising and directing his play—

of course, he, too, expecting a tip later on! But the player scarcely looked at him. He staked at random and kept winning. He evidently did not know what he was doing.

Granny watched him for some minutes.

"Tell him," Granny said suddenly, growing excited and giving me a poke, "tell him to give it up, to take his money quickly and go away. He'll lose it all directly, he'll lose it all!" she urged, almost breathless with agitation. "Where's Potapitch? Send Potapitch to him. Come, tell him, tell him," she went on, poking me. "Where is Potapitch? *Sortez! Sortez!*"—she began herself shouting to the young man.

I bent down to her and whispered resolutely that she must not shout like this here, that even talking aloud was forbidden, because it hindered counting and that we should be turned out directly.

"How vexatious! The man's lost! I suppose it's his own doing. . . . I can't look at him, it quite upsets me. What a dolt!" and Granny made haste to turn in another direction.

On the left, on the other side of the table, there was conspicuous among the players a young lady, and beside her a sort of dwarf. Who this dwarf was, and whether he was a relation or brought by her for the sake of effect, I don't know. I had noticed the lady before; she made her appearance at the gambling table every day, at one o'clock in the afternoon, and went away exactly at two; she always played for an hour. She was already known, and a chair was set for her at once. She took out of her pocket some gold, some thousand-franc notes, and began staking quietly, coolly, prudently, making pencil notes on a bit of paper of the numbers about which the chances grouped themselves, and trying to work out a system. She staked considerable sums. She used to win every day—one, two, or at the most three thousand francs—not more, and instantly went away. Granny scrutinised her for a long time.

"Well, that one won't lose! That one there won't lose! Of what class is she? Do you know? Who is she?"

"She must be a Frenchwoman, of a certain class, you know," I whispered.

"Ah, one can tell the bird by its flight. One can see she has a sharp claw. Explain to me now what every turn means and how one has to bet!"

I explained as far as I could to Granny all the various points on which one could stake: *rouge et noir, pair et impair, manque et passe,* and finally the various subtleties in the system of the numbers. Granny listened attentively, remembered, asked questions, and began to master it. One could point to examples of every kind, so that she very quickly and readily picked up a great deal.

"But what about zéro? You see that croupier, the curly-headed one, the chief one, showed zéro just now? And why did he scoop up everything that was on the table? Such a heap, he took it all for himself. What is the meaning of it?"

"Zéro, Granny, means that the bank wins all. If the little ball falls on zéro, everything on the table goes to the bank. It is true you can stake your money so as to keep it, but the bank pays nothing."

"You don't say so! And shall I get nothing?"

"No, Granny, if before this you had staked on zéro you would have got thirty-five times what you staked."

"What! thirty-five times, and does it often turn up? Why don't they stake on it, the fools."

"There are thirty-six chances against it, Granny."

"What nonsense. Potapitch! Potapitch! Stay, I've money with me— here." She took out of her pocket a tightly packed purse, and picked out of it a friedrich d'or. "Stake it on the zéro at once."

"Granny, zéro has only just turned up," I said; "so now it won't turn up for a long time. You will lose a great deal; wait a little, anyway."

"Oh, nonsense; put it down!"

"As you please, but it may not turn up again till the evening. You may go on staking thousands; it has happened."

"Oh, nonsense, nonsense. If you are afraid of the wolf you shouldn't go into the forest. What? Have I lost? Stake again!"

A second friedrich d'or was lost: she staked a third. Granny could scarcely sit still in her seat. She stared with feverish eyes at the little ball dancing on the spokes of the turning wheel. She lost a third, too. Granny was beside herself, she could not sit still, she even thumped on the table with her fist when the croupier announced "trente-six" instead of the zéro she was expecting.

"There, look at it," said Granny angrily; "isn't that cursed little zéro coming soon? As sure as I'm alive, I'll sit here till zéro does come! It's that cursed curly-headed croupier's doing; he'll never let it come! Alexey Ivanovitch, stake two gold pieces at once! Staking as much as you do, even if zéro does come you'll get nothing by it."

"Granny!"

"Stake, stake! it is not your money."

I staked two friedrichs d'or. The ball flew about the wheel for a long time, at last it began dancing about the spokes. Granny was numb with excitement, and squeezed my fingers, and all at once—

"Zéro!" boomed the croupier.

"You see, you see!"—Granny turned to me quickly, beaming and delighted. "I told you so. The Lord Himself put it into my head to stake those two gold pieces! Well, how much do I get now? Why don't they give it me? Potapitch, Marfa, where are they? Where have all our people got to? Potapitch, Potapitch!"

"Granny, afterwards," I whispered; "Potapitch is at the door, they won't let him in. Look, Granny, they are giving you the money, take it!" A heavy roll of printed blue notes, worth fifty friedrichs d'or, was thrust towards Granny and twenty friedrichs d'or were counted out to her. I scooped it all up in a shovel and handed it to Granny.

"Faites le jeu, messieurs! Faites le jeu, messieurs! Rien ne va plus!" called the croupier, inviting the public to stake, and preparing to turn the wheel.

"Heavens! we are too late. They're just going to turn it. Put it down, put it down!" Granny urged me in a flurry. "Don't dawdle, make haste!" She was beside herself and poked me with all her might.

"What am I to stake it on, Granny?"

"On zéro, on zéro! On zéro again! Stake as much as possible! How much have we got altogether? Seventy friedrichs d'or. There's no need to spare it. Stake twenty friedrichs d'or at once."

"Think what you are doing, Granny! sometimes it does not turn up for two hundred times running! I assure you, you may go on staking your whole fortune."

"Oh, nonsense, nonsense! Put it down! How your tongue does wag! I know what I'm about." Granny was positively quivering with excitement.

"By the regulations it's not allowed to stake more than twelve roubles on zéro at once, Granny; here I have staked that."

"Why is it not allowed? Aren't you lying? Monsieur! Monsieur!"—she nudged the croupier, who was sitting near her on the left, and was about to set the wheel turning. *"Combien zéro? Douze? Douze?"*

I immediately interpreted the question in French.

"Oui, madame," the croupier confirmed politely; "as the winnings from no single stake must exceed four thousand florins by the regulations," he added in explanation.

"Well, there's no help for it, stake twelve."

"Le jeu est fait," cried the croupier. The wheel rotated, and thirty turned up. She had lost.

"Again, again, again! Stake again!" cried Granny. I no longer resisted, and, shrugging my shoulders, staked another twelve friedrichs d'or. The wheel turned a long time. Granny was simply quivering as she watched the wheel.

"Can she really imagine that zéro will win again?" I thought, looking at her with wonder. Her face was beaming with a firm conviction of winning, an unhesitating expectation that in another minute they would shout zéro. The ball jumped into the cage.

"Zéro!" cried the croupier.

"What!!!" Granny turned to me with intense triumph.

I was a gambler myself, I felt that at the moment my arms and legs were trembling, there was a throbbing in my head. Of course, this was a rare chance that zéro should have come up three times in some dozen turns; but there was nothing particularly wonderful about it. I had myself seen zéro turn up three times *running* two days before, and a gambler who had been zealously noting down the lucky numbers, observed aloud that, only the day before, zéro had turned up only once in twenty-four hours.

Granny's winnings were counted out to her with particular attention and deference as she had won such a large sum. She received four hundred and twenty friedrichs d'or, that is, four thousand florins and seventy friedrichs d'or. She was given twenty friedrichs d'or in gold, and four thousand florins in banknotes.

This time Granny did not call Potapitch; she had other preoccupations. She did not even babble or quiver outwardly! She was, if one may so express it, quivering inwardly. She was entirely concentrated on something, absorbed in one aim.

"Alexey Ivanovitch, he said that one could only stake four thousand florins at once, didn't he? Come, take it, stake the whole four thousand on the red," Granny commanded.

It was useless to protest; the wheel began rotating.

"*Rouge,*" the croupier proclaimed.

Again she had won four thousand florins, making eight in all.

"Give me four, and stake four again on red," Granny commanded.

Again I staked four thousand.

"*Rouge,*" the croupier pronounced again.

"Twelve thousand altogether! Give it me all here. Pour the gold here into the purse and put away the notes. That's enough! Home! Wheel my chair out."

Sometimes the wildest idea, the most apparently impossible thought, takes possession of one's mind so strongly that one accepts it at last as something substantial . . . more than that, if the idea is associated with a strong passionate desire, then sometimes one will accept it at last as something fated, inevitable, predestined—as something bound to be, and bound to happen. Perhaps there is something else in it, some combination of presentiments, some extraordinary effort of will, self-poisoning by one's own fancy—or something else—I don't know what, but on that evening (which I shall never in my life forget) something marvellous happened to me. Though it is quite justified by the laws of arithmetic, nevertheless it is a marvel to me to this day. And why, why had that conviction so long before taken such firm and deep root in my mind? I had certainly thought about it—I repeat—not as a chance among others which might or might not come to pass, but as something which was absolutely bound to happen!

It was a quarter-past ten. I went into the Casino with a confident expectation and at the same time with an excitement I had never experienced before. There were still a good many people in the gambling hall, though not half as many as in the morning.

Between ten and eleven there are still to be found in the gambling halls the genuine desperate gamblers for whom nothing exists at a spa but roulette, who have come for that alone, who scarcely notice what is going on around them and take no interest in anything during the whole season, but play from morning till night and would be ready perhaps to play all night till dawn, too, if it were possible. And they always disperse with annoyance when at twelve o'clock the roulette hall is closed. And when the senior croupier announces, just before midnight: *"Les trois derniers coups, messieurs,"* they are ready to stake on those last three strokes all they have in their pockets—and do, in fact, lose most at that time. I went up to the very table where Granny had sat that day. It was not crowded, and so I soon took my place at the table standing. Exactly before me was the word "Passe" scrawled on the green cloth.

"Passe" is the series of numbers from nineteen inclusive to thirty-six.

The first series of numbers from one to eighteen inclusive is called "Manque"; but what was that to me? I was not calculating, I had not even heard what had been the winning number last, and I did not ask about it when I began to play—as every player of any prudence would do. I pulled out all my twenty friedrichs d'or and staked them on "passe", the word which lay before me.

"Vingt deux," cried the croupier.

I had won and again staked all, including my winnings.

"Trente et un," cried the croupier.

I had won again. I had in all eighty friedrichs d'or. I staked the whole of that sum on the twelve middle numbers (my winnings would be three to one, but the chances were two to one against me). The wheel rotated and stopped at twenty-four. I was passed three rolls each of fifty friedrichs d'or in paper and ten gold coins; I had now two hundred friedrichs d'or.

I was as though in delirium and I moved the whole heap of gold to red—and suddenly thought better of it. And for the only time that whole evening, all the time I was playing, I felt chilled with terror and a shudder made my arms and legs tremble. I felt with horror and instantly realised what losing would mean for me now! My whole life was at stake.

"Rouge," cried the croupier, and I drew a breath; fiery pins and needles were tingling all over my body. I was paid in bank-notes. It came to four thousand florins and eighty friedrichs d'or (I could still keep count at that stage).

Then, I remember, I staked two thousand florins on the twelve middle numbers, and lost: I staked my gold, the eighty friedrichs d'or, and lost. I was seized with fury: I snatched up the two thousand florins I had left and staked them on the first twelve numbers—haphazard, at random, without thinking! There was, however, an instant of suspense, like, perhaps, the feeling experienced by Madame Blanchard when she flew from a balloon in Paris to the earth.

"Quatre!" cried the croupier.

Now with my stake I had six thousand florins. I looked triumphant already. I was afraid of nothing—nothing, and staked four thousand florins on black. Nine people followed my example and staked on black. The croupiers exchanged glances and said something to one another. People were talking all round in suspense.

Black won. I don't remember my winnings after, nor what I staked on. I only remember as though in a dream that I won, I believe, sixteen thousand florins; suddenly three unlucky turns took twelve thousand from it; then I staked the last four thousand on "passe" (but I scarcely felt anything as I did so; I simply waited in a mechanical, senseless way)—and again I won; then I won four times running. I only remember that I gathered up money in thousands; I remember, too, that the middle twelve won most often and I kept to it. It turned up with a sort of regularity, certainly three or four times in succession, then it did not turn up twice running and then it followed three or four times in succession. Such astonishing regularity is sometimes met with in streaks, and that is what throws inveterate gamblers who calculate with a pencil in their hands out of their reckoning. And what horrible ironies of fate happen sometimes in such cases!

I believe not more than half an hour had passed since I came into the room, when suddenly the croupier informed me that I had won thirty thousand florins, and as the bank did not meet claims for a larger sum at one time the roulette would be closed till next morning. I snatched up all my gold, dropped it into my pockets, snatched up all my notes, and at once went into the other room where there was another roulette table; the whole crowd streamed after me; there at once a place was cleared for me and I fell to staking again haphazard without reckoning. I don't understand what saved me!

At times, however, a glimmer of prudence began to dawn upon my mind. I clung to certain numbers and combinations, but soon abandoned them and staked almost unconsciously. I must have been very absent-minded; I remember the croupiers several times corrected me. I made several gross mistakes. My temples were soaked with sweat and my hands were shaking. The Poles ran up, too, with offers of their services, but I listened to no one. My luck was unbroken! Suddenly there were sounds of loud talk and laughter, and everyone cried "Bravo, bravo!" some even clapped their hands. Here, too, I collected thirty thousand florins, and the bank closed till next day.

"Go away, go away," a voice whispered on my right.

It was a Frankfurt Jew; he was standing beside me all the time, and I believe sometimes helped me in my play.

"For goodness' sake go," another voice whispered in my left ear.

I took a hurried glance. It was a lady about thirty, very soberly and quietly dressed, with a tired, pale, sickly face which yet bore traces of having once been beautiful. At that moment I was stuffing my pockets with the notes, which I crumpled up anyhow, and gathering up the gold that lay on the table. Snatching up the last roll of notes, I succeeded in putting it into the pale lady's hands quite without attracting notice; I had an intense desire to do so at the time, and I remember her pale slim fingers pressed my hand warmly in token of gratitude. All that took place in one instant.

Having collected quickly all my winnings I went quickly to the trente et quarante.

Trente et quarante is frequented by the aristocratic public. Unlike roulette, it is a game of cards. Here the bank will pay up to a hundred thousand thalers at once. The largest stake is here also four thousand florins. I knew nothing of the game, and scarcely knew how to bet on it, except the red and the black, upon which one can bet in this game too. And I stuck to red and black. The whole Casino crowded round. I don't remember whether I once thought of Polina all this time. I was experiencing an overwhelming enjoyment in scooping up and taking away the notes which grew up in a heap before me.

It seemed as though fate were urging me on. This time, as luck would have it, a circumstance occurred which, however, is fairly frequent in the game. Chance favours red, for instance, ten or even fifteen times in succession. I had heard two days before that in the previous week red had turned up twenty-two times in succession; it was something which had never been remembered in roulette, and it was talked of with amazement. Everyone, of course, abandoned red at once, and after the tenth time, for instance, scarcely anyone dared to stake on it. But none of the experienced players staked on black either. The experienced gambler knows what is meant by this "freak of chance." It would mean that after red had won sixteen times, at the seventeenth time the luck would infallibly fall on black. Novices at play rush to this conclusion in crowds, double and treble their stakes, and lose terribly.

But, noticing that red had turned up seven times running, by strange perversity I staked on it. I am convinced that vanity was half responsible for it; I wanted to impress the spectators by taking a mad risk, and—oh, the strange sensation—I remember distinctly that, quite apart from the promptings of vanity, I was possessed by an intense craving for risk. Perhaps passing through so many sensations my soul was not satisfied but only irritated by them and craved still more sensation—and stronger and stronger ones—till utterly exhausted. And, truly I am not lying, if the regulations had allowed me to stake fifty thousand florins at once, I should certainly have staked them. People around shouted that it was madness—that red had won fourteen times already!

"Monsieur a gagné déjá cent mille florins," I heard a voice say near me.

I suddenly came to myself. What? I had won during that evening a hundred thousand florins! And what more did I want? I fell on my banknotes, crumpled them up in my pockets without counting them, scooped up all my gold, all my rolls of notes, and ran out of the Casino. Everyone was laughing as I went through the room, looking at my bulging pockets and at the way I staggered under the weight of gold. I think it weighed over twenty pounds. Several hands were held out to me; I gave it away in handfuls as I snatched it up. Two Jews stopped me at the outer door.

"You are bold—you are very bold," they said to me, "but be sure to go away to-morrow as soon as possible, or else you will lose it all—you will lose it all . . ."

I didn't listen to them. The avenue was so dark that I could not see my hand before my face. It was half a mile to the hotel. I had never been afraid of thieves or robbers even as a small boy; I did not think of them now either. I don't remember what I thought of on the road; I had no thoughts. I was only aware of an immense enjoyment—success, victory, power—I don't know how to express it. Polina's image hovered before my mind too; I remembered her and was conscious I was going to her; I should be with her in a moment, should be telling her and showing her . . . But I hardly remembered what she had said to me earlier, and why I had gone, and all the sensations I had felt, not more than an hour and a half before, seemed to me something long past, transformed, grown old—something of which we should say no more because everything now would begin anew. Almost at the end of the avenue a sudden panic came upon me. What if I were robbed and murdered at this instant? At every step my panic grew greater. I almost ran. Suddenly, at the end of the avenue there was the glare of our hotel with its many windows lighted up—thank God, home!

I ran up to my storey and rapidly opened the door. Polina was there, sitting on the sofa with her arms crossed, with a lighted candle before her. She looked at me with amazement, and no doubt at that moment I must have looked rather strange. I stood before her and began flinging down all my piles of money on the table.

From The Hustler

BY WALTER TEVIS

No one has illustrated more precisely than Walter Tevis in *The Hustler* (1959) the importance of *character* in gambling. In addition to providing America with several folk-heroes in the persons of Minnesota Fats and Fast Eddie Felson, the book has achieved the status of a gambler's textbook. Its series of matches teaches how, while the poolplayer (like any artist) is defined by his ability to perform what he imagines, talent is never enough.

In the classic showdown—in gambling or any competition—the contestants bring out the best in each other. This is not quite the action of *The Hustler,* where Fats glides around the table as an enormous, graceful obstacle who lacks Fast Eddie Felson's pool imagination, and, crucially, Felson's *gamble.* Felson must realize, in confronting Fats' machinic, grinding, methodical excellence, that wanting to win and having the character to do so are different things, and that a great gambler must have both the restraint to play safe and the nerve to run the risks of creativity.

The first selection below establishes Felson's power over weaker characters—fish who are hooked by their own bug-eyed appetites—and establishes the use of alcohol as misdirection. Against this opening episode, Tevis sets up both Felson and the reader for the second scene, in which Fast Eddie comes up against Fats, who uses his own weapons against him, revealing in the process assorted levels of unreadiness within Felson.

Tevis's versatility as a writer is suggested by *The Man Who Fell to Earth* (played by David Bowie in the film adaptation) and *Queen's Gambit* (a novel about a nine-year-old girl chess phenom). However, he remains best known for *The Hustler* and *The Color of Money* (1984), which, taken as a sequence, show both transformations in the world of pool and poolrooms, and continuities in the essential terms of the game itself. Paul Newman and Jackie Gleason play Fast Eddie and Fats in the film *The Hustler* (1961), and Newman returns

13

(in an Academy Award–winning performance) alongside Tom Cruise, who unfortunately swings his cue in the most improbable ways, in *The Color of Money* (1986).

At about this time two men walked into The Smoker: Pool Hall, Stag Bar, and Grill, in Watkins, Illinois. They seemed to be road weary; both were perspiring although they both wore open-collar sport shirts. They sat at the bar and the younger man—a good-looking, dark-haired fellow—ordered whiskey for them. His voice and manners were very pleasant. He asked for bourbon. The place was quiet, empty except for the bartender and for a young Negro in tight blue jeans who was sweeping the floor.

When they got their drinks the younger man paid the man behind the bar with a twenty-dollar bill, grinned at him and said, "Hot, isn't it?" Now this grin was extraordinary. It did not seem right for him to grin like that; for, although pleasant, he was a tense-looking man, the kind who seems to be wound up very tightly; and his dark eyes were brilliant and serious, almost childishly so. But the grin was broad and relaxed and, paradoxically, natural.

"Yeah," the bartender said. "Someday I'm getting a air conditioner." He got the man his change, and then said, "You boys just passing through, I guess?"

The young man grinned the extraordinary grin again, over the top of his drink. "That's right." He looked to be no more than twenty-five. A nice-looking kid, quietly dressed, pleasant, with bright, serious eyes.

"Chicago?"

"Yes." He set the glass down, only half empty, and began sipping from the water glass, glancing with apparent interest toward the group of four pool tables that filled two-thirds of the room.

The bartender was not normally a garrulous man; but he liked the young fellow. He seemed sharp; but there was something very forthright about him. "Going or coming out?" the bartender said.

"Going in. Got to be there tomorrow," he grinned again. "Sales convention."

"Well, you boys got plenty of time. You can drive in in two, maybe three, hours."

"Say, that's right," the younger man said, pleasantly. Then he looked at his companion. "Come on, Charlie," he said, "let's shoot some pool. Wait out the heat."

Charlie, a balding, chubby-looking little man with the appearance of a straight-faced comedian, shook his head. "Hell, Eddie," he said, "you know you can't beat me."

The younger man laughed. "Okay," he said, "I got ten big dollars says I beat your ass." He fished a ten from his stack of change in front of him on the bar, and held it up, challengingly, grinning.

The other man shook his head, as if very sadly. "Eddie," he said, easing himself up from the bar stool, "it's gonna cost you money. It always does." He pulled a leather cigarette case from his pocket and flipped it open with a stubby, agile thumb. Then he winked gravely at the bartender. "It's a good thing he can afford it," he said, his voice raspy, dry. "Seventeen thousand bucks' worth of druggist's supplies he's sold last month. Fastest boy in our territory. Getting an award at the convention, first thing tomorrow."

The young man, Eddie, had gone to the first of the four tables and was taking the wooden rack from the triangle of colored balls. "Grab a stick, Charlie," he called, his voice light. "Quit stalling."

Charlie waddled over, his face still completely without expression, and took a cue from the rack. It was, as Eddie's had been, a lightweight cue, seventeen ounces. The bartender was something of a player himself, and he noticed these choices. Pool players who know better use heavy cues, invariably.

Eddie broke the balls. When he shot he held the cue stick firmly at the butt with his right hand. The circle of finger and thumb that made his bridge was tight and awkward. His stroke was jerky, and he swooped into the cue ball fiercely, as if trying to stab it. The cue ball hit the rack awry, much of the energy of the break shot was dissipated, the balls did not spread wide. He looked at the spread, grinned at Charlie, and said, "Shoot."

Charlie's game was not much better. He showed all of the signs of being a fair-to-middling player; but he had much of Eddie's awkwardness with the bridge, and the appearance of not knowing exactly what to do with his feet when he stepped up to shoot He would keep adjusting them, as if he were unstable. He stroked very hard, too; but he made a few decent shots. The bartender noticed all of this. Also he watched the exchange of money after each game. Charlie won three in a row, and after each game the two of them had another drink and Eddie gave Charlie a ten-dollar bill from a wallet that bulged.

The game they were playing was rotation pool, also called sixty-one. Also called Boston. Also—mistakenly—called straights. The most widely played pool game of them all, the big favorite of college boys and salesmen. Almost exclusively an amateur's game. There are a few men who play it professionally, but only a few. Nine ball, bank, straight pool, one-pocket are the hustler's games. Any of them is a mortal lock for a smart hustler, while there is too much blind luck in rotation. Except when the best hustlers play it.

But this last was beyond the bartender's scope. He knew the game only as another favorite of amateurs. The serious players around his place were nine-ball men. Why, he had seen one of the players who lived in town run four straight games of nine ball, once, without missing a shot.

The bartender kept watching, interested in the game—for in a small-town poolroom, a ten-dollar bet is a large one—and eventually a few of the town regulars began to drift in. Then after a while the two men were playing for twenty and it was getting late in the afternoon and they were still drinking another one after each game or so and the younger man was getting drunk. And lucky. Or getting hot or getting with it. He was beginning to win, and he was high and strutting, beginning to jeer at the other man in earnest. A crowd had formed around the table, watching.

And then, at the end of the game, the fourteen ball was in a difficult position on the table. Three or four inches from the side rail, between two pockets, it lay with the cue ball almost directly across from it and about two feet away. Eddie stepped up to the shot, drew back, and fired. Now what he obviously should have done was to bank the fourteen ball off the side rail, across the table and into the corner pocket. But instead, his cue ball hit the rail first, and, with just enough English on it to slip behind the colored ball, caught the fourteen squarely and drove it into the corner pocket.

Eddie slammed his cue butt on the floor, jubilantly, turned to Charlie, and said, "Pay me, sucker."

When Charlie handed him the twenty, he said, "You ought to take up crapshooting, Eddie."

Eddie grinned at him. "What do you mean by that?"

"You know what I mean. You were trying to bank that ball." He turned his face away, "And you're so damn blind pig lucky you got to make it coming off the rail."

Eddie's smile disappeared. His face took on an alcoholic frown. "Now wait a minute, Charlie," he said, an edge in his voice, "Now wait a minute." The bartender leaned against the bar, absorbed.

"What do you mean, wait? Rack the balls." Charlie started pulling balls out of the pockets, spinning them down to the foot of the table.

Eddie, suddenly, grabbed his arm, stopping him. He started putting the balls back in the pockets. Then he took the fourteen ball and the cue ball and set them on the table in front of Charlie. "All right," he said. "All right, Charlie. Set 'em up the way they were."

Charlie blinked at him. "Why?"

"Set 'em up," Eddie said. "Put 'em like they were. I'm gonna bet you twenty bucks I can make that shot just like I made it before."

Charlie blinked again. "Don't be stupid, Eddie," he said, gravely. "You're drunk. There's nobody gonna make that shot and you know it. Let's play pool."

Eddie looked at him coldly. He started setting the balls on the table in approximately the same positions as before. Then he looked around him at the crowd, which was very attentive. "How's that?" he said, his voice very serious, his face showing drunken concern. "Is it right?"

There was a general shrugging of shoulders. Then a couple of non-committal "I guess so's." Eddie looked at Charlie. "How is it by you? Is it okay, Charlie?"

Charlie's voice was completely dry. "Sure, it's okay."

"You gonna bet me twenty dollars?"

Charlie shrugged. "It's your money."

"You gonna bet?"

"Yes. Shoot."

Eddie seemed greatly pleased. "Okay," he said. "Watch." He started chalking his cue, overcarefully. Then he went to the talcum powder holder and noisily pumped a great deal too much powder into his hands. He worked this up into a dusty white cloud, wiped his hands on the seat of his pants, came back to the table, picked up his cue, sighted down it, sighted at the shot, bent down, stroked, stood up, sighted down his cue, bent down again, stroked the ball, and missed.

"Son of a bitch," he said.

Somebody in the crowd laughed.

"All right," Eddie said. "Set 'em up again." He pulled a twenty out of his billfold and then, ostentatiously, set the still bulging wallet on the rail of the table.

"Okay, Charlie," he said, "set it up."

Charlie walked over to the rack and put his cue stick away. Then he said, "Eddie, you're drunk. I'm not gonna bet you any more." He began rolling down his sleeves, buttoning the cuffs. "Let's get back on the road. We gotta be at that convention in the morning."

"In the morning's ass. I'm gonna bet you again. My money's still on the table."

Charlie didn't even look at him. "I don't want it," he said.

At this moment another voice broke in. It was the bartender from behind the bar. "I'll try you," he said, softly.

Eddie whirled, his eyes wide. Then he grinned, savagely. "Well," he said. "Well, now."

"Don't be a sap," Charlie said. "Don't bet any more money on that damn fool shot, Eddie. Nobody's gonna make that shot."

Eddie was still staring at the bartender. "Well, now," he said, again, "so you want in? Okay. It was just a friendly little bet, but now you want in it?"

"That's right," the bartender said.

"So you figure I'm drunk and you figure I'm loaded on the hip so you want to get in, real friendly, while all the money's still floating." Eddie looked over the crowd and saw, instantly, that they were on his side. That was very important. Then he said, "Okay, I'll let you in. So first you set up the shot." He set the two balls on the table. "Come on. Set it up."

"All right." The bartender came out and placed the two balls on the table, with some care. Their position was, if anything, more difficult than it had been.

Eddie's billfold was still on the rail. He picked it up. "Okay," he said, "you wanted to get some easy money." He began counting out bills, tens and twenties, counting them onto the middle of the table. "Look," he said, "here's two hundred dollars. That's a week's commission and expenses." He looked at the bartender, grinning. "You bet me two hundred dollars and you get a chance at your easy money. How about?"

The bartender tried to look calm. He glanced around him at the crowd. They were all watching him. Then he thought about the drinks he had served Eddie. It must have been at least five. This thought comforted him. He thought, too, about the games he had watched the men play. This reassured him.

And the young man had an honest face. "I'll get it out of the till," the bartender said.

In a minute he had it, and there were four hundred dollars in bills out on the table, down at the end where they wouldn't affect the shot. Eddie went to the powder dispenser again. Then he got down, sighted, took aim awkwardly, and stroked into the cue ball. Now there was only the slightest difference between that stroke and the stroke he had used all evening—a slight, imperceptible regularity, smoothness, to the motion. But only one man present noticed this. That man was Charlie; and when every other set of eyes in the poolroom was focused in silent attention on the cue ball, an amazing thing happened to the set features on his round face. He smiled, gently and quietly— as a father might smile, watching a talented son.

The cue ball came off the rail and hit the fourteen with a little click. The fourteen ball rolled smoothly across the table and fell softly into the corner pocket. . . .

They had to take an elevator to the eighth floor, an elevator that jerked and had brass doors and held five people. It did not seem at all right to go to a poolroom on an elevator; and he had never figured Bennington's that way. Nobody had ever told him about the elevator. When they stepped off it there was a very high, wide doorway facing them. Over this was written, in small, feeble neon letters, BENNINGTON'S BILLIARD HALL. He looked at Charlie and then they walked in.

Eddie had with him a small, cylindrical leather case. This was as big around as his forearm and about two and a half feet long. In it was an extremely well-made, inlaid, ivory-pointed, French-leather-tipped, delicately balanced pool cue. This was actually in two parts; they could be joined for use by screwing together a two-piece, machined brass joint, fastened to the maple end of each section.

The place was big, bigger, even than he had imagined. It was familiar, because the smell and the feel of a poolroom are the same everywhere; but it was also very much different. Victorian, with heavy, leather-cushioned chairs, big elaborate brass chandeliers, three high windows with heavy curtains, a sense of spaciousness, of elegance.

It was practically empty. No one plays pool late in the afternoon; few people come in at that time except to drink at the bar, make bets on the races or play the pinball machines; and Bennington's had facilities for none of these. This, too, was unique; its business was pool, nothing else.

There was a man practicing on the front table, a big man, smoking a cigar. On another table further back two tall children in blue jeans and jackets were playing nine ball. One of these had long sideburns. In the middle of the room a very big man with heavy, black-rimmed glasses—like an advertising executive—was sitting in an oak swivel chair by the cash register, reading a newspaper. He looked at them a moment after they came in and when he saw the leather case in Eddie's hand he stared for a moment at Eddie's face before going back to the paper. Beyond him, in the back of the room, a stooped black man in formless clothes was pushing a broom, limping.

They picked a table toward the back, several tables down from the nine-ball players, and began to practice. Eddie took a house cue stick from the rack, setting the leather case, unopened, against the wall.

They shot around, loosely, for about forty-five minutes. He was trying to get the feel of the table, to get used to the big four-and-a-half-by-nine-feet size—since the war practically all pool tables were four by eight—and to learn the bounce of the rails. They were a little soft and the nap on the cloth was smooth, making the balls take long angles and making stiffening English difficult. But the table was a good one, level, even, with clean pocket drops, and he liked the sense of it.

The big man with the cigar ambled down, took a chair, and watched them. Then after they had finished the game he took the cigar out of his mouth, looked at Eddie, very hard, looked at the leather case leaning against the wall, looked back at Eddie and said, thoughtfully, "You looking for action?"

Eddie smiled at him. "Maybe. You want to play?"

The big man scowled. "No. Hell, no." Then he said, "You Eddie Felson?"

Eddie grinned, "Who's he?" He took a cigarette out of his shirt pocket.

The man put the cigar back in his mouth. "What's your game? What do you shoot?"

Eddie lit the cigarette. "You name it, mister. We'll play."

The big man jerked the cigar from his mouth. "Look, friend," he said, "I'm not trying to hustle. I don't never hustle people who carry leather satchels in poolrooms." His voice was loud, commanding, and yet it sounded tired, as if he were greatly discouraged. "I ask you a civil question and you play it cute. I come up and watch and think maybe I can help you out, and you want to be cute."

"Okay," Eddie grinned, "no hard feelings. I shoot straight pool. You know any straight pool players around this poolroom?"

"What kind of straight pool games do you like?"

Eddie looked at him a minute, noticing the way the man's eyes blinked. Then he said, "I like the expensive kind."

The man chewed on his cigar a minute. Then he leaned forward in his chair and said, "You come up here to play straight pool with Minnesota Fats?"

Eddie liked this man. He seemed very strange, as if he were going to explode. "Yes," he said.

The man stared at him, chewing the cigar. Then he said, "Don't. Go home."

"Why?"

"I'll tell you why, and you better believe it. Fats don't need your money. And there's no way you can beat him. He's the best in the country." He leaned back in the chair, blowing out smoke.

Eddie kept grinning. "I'll think about that," he said. "Where is he?"

The big man came alive, violently. "For God's sake," he said, loudly, despairingly, "You talk like a real high-class pool hustler. Who do you think you are—Humphrey Bogart? Maybe you carry a rod and wear raincoats and really hold a mean pool stick back in California or Idaho or wherever it is. I bet you already beat every nine-ball shooting farmer from here to the West Coast. Okay. I told you what I wanted about Minnesota Fats. You just go ahead and play him, friend."

Eddie laughed. Not scornfully, but with amusement—amusement at the other man and at himself. "All right," he said, laughing. "Just tell me where I find him."

The big man pulled himself up from the chair with considerable effort. "Just stay where you are," he said. "He comes in, every night, about eight o'clock." He jammed the cigar in his mouth and walked back to the front table.

"Thanks," Eddie called at him. The man didn't reply. He began practicing again, a long rail shot on the three ball.

Eddie and Charlie returned to their game. The talk with the big man could have rattled him but, somehow, it had the effect of making him feel better about the evening. He began concentrating on the game, getting his stroke down to a finer point, running little groups of balls and then missing intentionally—more from long habit than from fear of being identified. They kept shooting, and after a while the other tables began to fill up with men and smoke and the clicking of pool balls and he began to glance toward the massive front door, watching.

And then, after he had finished running a group of balls, he looked up and saw, leaning against the next table, an extremely fat man with black curly hair, watching him shoot—a man with small black eyes.

He picked up the chalk and began stroking his cue tip with it, slowly, looking at the man. It couldn't have been anyone else, not with all of that weight, not with the look of authority, not with those sharp little eyes.

He was wearing a silk sport shirt, chartreuse, open at the neck and loose on his wide, soft-looking belly. His face was like dough, like the face of the full moon on a free calendar, puffed up like an Eskimo's, little ears close to his head, the hair shiny, curly, and carefully trimmed, the complexion clear, pinkish. His hands were clasped over the great belly, above a small, jeweled belt buckle, and there were brightly jeweled rings on four of his fingers. The nails were manicured and polished.

About every ten seconds there was a sudden, convulsive motion of his head, forcing his chins down toward his left collar bone. This was a very sudden movement, and it brought an automatic grimace to that side of his mouth which seemed affected by the tic. Other than this there was no expression on his face.

The man stared back at him. Then he said, "You shoot pretty good straights." His voice had no tone whatever. It was very deep.

Eddie, somehow, did not feel like grinning. "Thanks," he said.

He turned back to the table and finished up the rack of balls. Then when the cashier, the man with the black-rimmed glasses, was racking them up, Eddie turned back to the fat man and said, smiling this time, "You play straight pool, mister?"

The man's chin jerked, abruptly. "Every once in a while," he said. "You know how it is." His voice sounded as though he were talking from the bottom of a well.

Eddie continued chalking his cue. "You're Minnesota Fats, aren't you, mister?"

The man said nothing, but his eyes seemed to flicker, as if he were amused, or trying to be amusing.

Eddie kept smiling, but he felt his fingertips quivering and put one hand in his pocket, holding the cue stick with the other. "They say Minnesota Fats is the best in the country, out where I come from," he said.

"Is that a fact?" The man's face jerked again.

"That's right," Eddie said. "Out where I come from they say Minnesota Fats shoots the eyes right off them balls."

The other man was quiet for a minute. Then he said, "You come from California, don't you?"

"That's right."

"Name of Felson, Eddie Felson?" He pronounced the words carefully, distinctly, with neither warmth nor malice in them.

"That's right too."

There seemed nothing more to say. Eddie went back to his game with Charlie. Knowing Fats was watching him, adding him up, calculating the risks of playing him, he felt nervous; but his hands were steady with the cue and the nervousness was only enough to make him feel alert, springy, to sharpen his sense of the game he was playing, his feel for the balls and for the roll of the balls and the swing of the cue. He laid it on carefully, disregarding his normal practice of making himself look weak, shooting well-controlled, neat shots, until the fifteen colored balls were gone from the table.

Then he turned around and looked at Fats. Fats seemed not to see him. His chin jerked, and then he turned to a small man who had been standing next to him, watching, and said, "He shoots straight. You think maybe he's a hustler?" Then he turned back to Eddie, his face blank but the little eyes sharp, watching. "You a gambler, Eddie?" he said. "You like to gamble money on pool games?"

Eddie looked him full in the face and, abruptly, grinned. "Fats," he said, grinning, feeling good, all the way, "let's you and me play a game of straight pool."

Fats looked at him a moment. Then he said, "Fifty dollars?"

Eddie laughed, looked at Charlie and then back again, "Hell, Fats," he said, "you shoot big-time pool. Everybody says you shoot big-time pool. Let's don't be chicken about this." He looked at the men standing by Fats. Both of them were bugged, astonished. *Probably,* he thought, *nobody's ever talked to their big tin god like this before.* He grinned. "Let's make it a hundred, Fats."

Fats stared at him, his expression unchanging. Then, suddenly, with a great moving of flesh, he smiled. "They call you Fast Eddie, don't they?" he said.

"That's right." Eddie was still grinning.

"Well, Fast Eddie. You talk my kind of talk. You flip a coin so we see who breaks."

Eddie took his leather case from where it was leaning against the wall.

Someone flipped a half dollar. Eddie lost the toss and had to break the balls. He took the standard shot—two balls out from the rack and back again, three rails on the cue ball to the end cushion—and he froze the cue ball on the rail with only a bare edge of a corner ball sticking from behind the rack, to shoot at. Then Fats walked very slowly, ponderously, up to the front of the poolroom, where there was a green metal locker. He opened this and took out a cue stick, one joined at the middle with a brass joint, like Eddie's. He picked a cube of chalk up from the front table and chalked his cue as he walked back.

He did not even appear to look at the position of the balls on the table, but merely said, "Five ball. Corner pocket," and took his position behind the cue ball to shoot.

Eddie watched him closely. He stepped up to the table with short, quick little steps, stepping up to it sideways, bringing his cue up into position as he did so, so that he was holding his cue, standing sideways to the table, out across his great stomach, the left-hand bridge already formed, the right hand holding the butt delicately, much as a violinist holds his bow—gracefully but surely. And then, as if it were an integral, continuous part of his approach to the table, his bridge hand settled down on the green and almost immediately there was a smooth, level motion of the cue stick, effortless, and the cue ball sped down the table and clipped the corner of the five ball and the five ball sped across the table and into the corner pocket. The cue ball darted into the rack, spreading the balls wide.

And then Fats began moving around the table, making balls, all of his former ponderousness gone now, his motions like a ballet, the steps light, sure, and rehearsed; the bridge hand inevitably falling into the right place; the hand on the butt of the cue with its fat, jeweled fingers gently pushing the thin shaft into the cue ball. He never stopped to look at the layout of the balls, never appeared to think or to prepare himself for shooting. About every five shots he stopped long enough to stroke the tip of his cue gently with chalk; but he did not even look at the table as he did this; he merely watched what he was doing at the moment.

He made fourteen out of the fifteen balls on the table very quickly, leaving the remaining ball in excellent position for the break.

Eddie racked the balls. Fats made the break shot, shooting effortlessly but powering the cue ball into the rack so that it scattered balls all over the table. He began punching them in. He was good. He was fantastically good. He ran eighty balls before he got tied up and played Eddie safe. Eddie had seen and made bigger runs, much bigger; but he had never seen anyone shoot with the ease, the unruffled certainty, that this delicate, gross man had.

Eddie looked at Charlie, sitting now in one of the big, high chairs. Charlie's face showed nothing, but he shrugged his shoulders. Then Eddie looked the shot over carefully. It was a good safe, but he was able to return it, freezing the cue ball to the end rail, leaving nothing to be shot at. They played it back and forth, safe, leaving no openings for the other man, until Eddie made a small slip and let Fats get loose. Fats edged up to the table and started shooting. Eddie sat down. He looked around; a crowd of ten or fifteen people had already formed around the table. A neat man with pink cheeks and glasses was moving around in the crowd, making bets. Eddie wondered what on. He looked at the clock on the wall over the door. It was eight-thirty. He took a deep breath, and then let it out slowly.

He had known he would start out losing. That was natural; he was playing a great player and on his own table, in his own poolroom, and he figured to lose for a few hours. But not that badly. Fats beat him two games by one hundred and twenty-five to nothing and in the third game Eddie finally got one open shot and scored fifty on it. It was not pleasant to lose, and yet, somehow, he was not deeply dismayed, did not feel lost in the brilliance of the other man's game, did not feel nervous or confused. He spent most of each game sitting down and each time Fats won a game Eddie grinned and gave him a hundred dollars. Fats had nothing to say.

At eleven o'clock, after he had lost the sixth game, Charlie came over, looked at him, and said, "Quit."

He looked at Charlie, who seemed to be perspiring, and said, "I'll take him. Just wait."

"Don't be too sure." Charlie went back to his chair, on the other side of the table.

Then Eddie started winning. He felt it start in the middle of a game, began to feel the sense he sometimes had of being a part of the table and of the balls and of the cue stick. The stroke of his arm seemed to travel on oiled bearings; and each muscle of his body was alert, sensitive to the game and the movement of the balls, sharply aware of how every ball would roll, of how, exactly, every shot must be made. Fats beat him that game, but he had felt it coming and he won the next.

And the game after that, and the next, and then another. Then someone turned off all the lights except those over the table that they were playing on and the background of Bennington's vanished, leaving only the faces of the crowd around the table, the green of the cloth of the table, and the now sharply etched, clean, black-shadowed balls, brilliant against the green. The balls had sharp, jeweled edges; the cue ball itself was a milk-white jewel and it was a magnificent thing to watch the balls roll and to know beforehand where they were going to roll. Nothing could be so clear or so simple or so excellent to do. And there was no limit to the shots that could be made.

Fats' game did not change. It was brilliant, fantastically good, but Eddie was beating him now, playing an incredible game: a gorgeous, spellbinding game, a game that he felt he had known all of his life, that he would play when the right time came. There was no better time than this.

And then, after a game had ended, there was noise up front and Eddie turned and saw that the clock said midnight and that someone was locking the great oak door, and he looked at Fats and Fats said, "Don't worry, Fast Eddie. We're not going anyplace."

Then he pulled a ten-dollar bill out of his pocket, handed it to a thin nervous man in a black suit, who was watching the game, and said, "Preacher, I want White Horse whiskey. And ice. And a glass. And you get yourself a fix with the change; but you do that after you come back with my whiskey."

Eddie grinned, liking the feel of this, the getting ready for action. He fished out a ten himself. "J. T. S. Brown bourbon," he said to the thin man. Then he leaned his cue stick against the table, unbuttoned his cuffs, and began rolling up his shirt sleeves. Then he stretched out his arms, flexing the muscles, enjoying the good sense of their steadiness, their control, and he said, "Okay, Fats. Your break."

Eddie beat him. The pleasure was exquisite; and when the man brought the whiskey and he mixed himself a highball with water from the cooler and drank it, his whole body and brain seemed to be suffused with pleasure, with alertness and life. He looked at Fats. There was a dark line of sweat and dirt around the back of his collar. His manicured nails were dirty. His face still showed no expression. He, too, was holding a glass of whiskey and sipping it quietly.

Suddenly Eddie grinned at him. "Let's play for a thousand a game, Fats," he said.

There was a murmur in the crowd.

Fats took a sip of whiskey, rolled it around carefully in his mouth, swallowed. His sharp, black eyes were fixed on Eddie, dispassionately, searching. He seemed to see something there that reassured him. Then he glanced, for a moment, at the neat man with glasses, the man who had been taking bets. The man nodded, pursing his lips. "Okay," he said.

Eddie knew it, could feel it, that no one had ever played straight pool like this before. Fats' game, itself, was astonishing, a consistently beautiful, precise game, a deft, quick shooting game with almost no mistakes. And he won games; no power on earth could have stopped him from winning some of them, for pool is a game that gives the man sitting down no earthly way of affecting the shooting of the man he is trying to beat. But Eddie beat him, steadily, making shots that no one had ever made before, knifing balls in, playing hairline position, running rack after rack of balls without his cue ball's touching a cushion, firing ball after ball into the center, the heart of every pocket. His stroking arm was like a conscious thing, and the cue stick was a living extension of it. There were nerves in the wood of it, and he could feel the tapping of the leather tip with the nerves, could feel the balls roll; and the exquisite sound that they made as they hit the bottoms of the pockets was a sound both there, on the table, and in the very center of his own soul.

They played for a long, long time and then he noticed that the shadows of the balls on the green had become softer, had lost their edges. He looked up and saw pale light coming through the window draperies and then looked at the clock. It was seven-thirty. He looked around him, dazed. The crowd had thinned out, but some of the same men were there. Everybody seemed to need a shave. He felt his own face. Sandpaper. He looked down at himself. His shirt was filthy, covered with chalk marks, the tail out, and the front wrinkled as if he had slept in it. He looked at Fats, who looked, if anything, worse.

Charlie came over. He looked like hell, too. He blinked at Eddie. "Breakfast?"

Eddie sat down, in one of the now-empty chairs by the table. "Yeah," he said. "Sure." He fished in his pocket, pulled out a five.

"Thanks," Charlie said. "I don't need it. I been keeping the money, remember?"

Eddie grinned, weakly. "That's right. How much is it now?"

Charlie stared at him. "You don't know?"

"I forgot." He fished a crumpled cigarette from his pocket, lit it. His hands, he noticed, were trembling faintly; but he saw this as if he were looking at someone else. "What is it?" He leaned back, smoking the cigarette, looking at the balls sitting, quiet now, on the table. The cigarette had no taste to it.

"You won eleven thousand four hundred," Charlie said. "Cash. It's in my pocket."

Eddie looked back at him. "Well!" he said. And then, "Go get breakfast. I want a egg sandwich and coffee."

"Now wait a minute," Charlie said. "You're going with me. We eat breakfast at the hotel. The pool game is over."

Eddie looked at him a minute, grinning, wondering, too, why it was that Charlie couldn't see it, never had seen it. Then he leaned forward, looked at him, and said, "No it isn't, Charlie."

"Eddie . . ."

"This pool game ends when Minnesota Fats says it ends."

"You came after ten thousand. You got ten thousand."

Eddie leaned forward again. He wasn't grinning now. He wanted Charlie to see it, to get with it, to feel some of what he was feeling, some of the commitment he was making. "Charlie," he said, "I came here after Minnesota Fats. And I'm gonna get him. I'm gonna stay with him all the way."

Fats was sitting down too, resting. He stood up. His chin jerked, down into the soft flesh of his neck. "Fast Eddie," he said tonelessly, "let's play pool." "Break the balls," Eddie said.

In the middle of the game the food came and Eddie ate his sandwich in bites between shots, setting it on the rail of the table while he was shooting, and washing it down with the coffee, which tasted very bitter. Fats had sent someone out and he was eating from a platter of a great many small sandwiches and link sausages. Instead of coffee he had three bottles of Dutch beer on another platter and these he drank from a pilsner glass, which he held in a fat hand, delicately. He wiped his lips gently with a napkin between bites of the sandwiches and, apparently, paid no attention whatever to the balls that Eddie was methodically pocketing in the thousand-dollar game that he, sitting in the chair and eating his gourmet's breakfast, was playing in.

Eddie won the game; but Fats won the next one, by a narrow margin. And at nine o'clock the poolroom doors were opened again and an ancient colored man limped in and began sweeping the floor and opened the windows, pulling back the draperies. Outside the sky was, absurdly, blue. The sun shone in.

Fats turned his head toward the janitor and said, his voice loud and flat, across the room, "Cut off that goddamn sunshine."

The black man shuffled back to the windows and drew the curtains. Then he went back to his broom.

They played, and Eddie kept winning. In his shoulders, now, and in his back and at the backs of his legs there was a kind of dull pain; but the pain seemed as if it were someone else's and he hardly felt it, hardly knew it was there. He merely kept shooting and the balls kept falling and the grotesque, fat man whom he was playing—the man who was the Best Straight Pool Player in the Country—kept giving large amounts of money to Charlie. Once, he noticed that, while he was shooting and the other man was sitting, Fats was talking with the man with the pink cheeks and with Gordon, the manager. The pink-cheeked man had his billfold in his hand. After that game, Fats paid Charlie with a thousand-dollar bill. The sight of the bill that he had just earned made him feel nothing. He only wished that the rack man would hurry and rack the balls.

The aching and the dullness increased gradually, but these did not affect the way his body played pool. There was a strange, exhilarating feeling that he was really somewhere else in the room, above the table—floating, possibly, with the heavy, bodiless mass of cigarette smoke that hung below the light—

watching his own body, down below, driving small colored balls into holes by poking them with a long, polished stick of wood. And somewhere else in the room, perhaps everywhere in the room, was an incredibly fat man, silent, always in motion, unruffled, a man whose sharp little eyes saw not only the colored balls on the green rectangle, but saw also into all of the million corners in the room, whether or not they were illuminated by the cone of light that circumscribed the bright oblong of the pool table.

At nine o'clock in the evening Charlie told him that he had won eighteen thousand dollars.

Something happened, suddenly, in his stomach when Charlie told him this. A thin steel blade touched against a nerve in his stomach. He tried to look at Fats, but, for a moment, could not.

At ten-thirty, after winning one and then losing one, Minnesota Fats went back to the bathroom and Eddie found himself sitting down and then, in a moment, his head was in his hands and he was staring at the floor, at a little group of flat cigarette butts at his feet. And then Charlie was with him, or he heard his voice; but it seemed to be coming from a distance and when he tried to raise his head he could not. But Charlie was telling him to quit, he knew that without being able to pick out the word. And then the cigarette butts began to shift positions and to sway, in a gentle but confusing motion, and there was a humming in his ears like the humming of a cheap radio and, suddenly, he realized that he was passing out, and he shook his head, weakly at first and then violently, and when he stopped doing this he could see and hear better. But something in his mind was screaming. Something in him was quivering, frightened, cutting at his stomach from the inside, like a small knife.

Charlie was still talking but he broke him off, saying, "Give me a drink, Charlie." He did not look at Charlie, but kept his eyes on the cigarette butts, watching them closely.

"You don't need a drink."

Then he looked up at him, at the round, comic face dirty with beard and said, surprised at the softness of his own voice, "Shut up, Charlie. Give me a drink."

Charlie handed him the bottle.

He turned it up and let the whiskey spill down his throat. It gagged him but he did not feel it burn, hardly felt it in his stomach except as a mild warmness, softening the edges of the knife. Then he looked around him and found that his vision was all right, that he could see clearly the things directly in front of him, although there was a mistiness around the edges.

Fats was standing by the table, cleaning his fingernails. His hands were clean again; he had washed them; and his hair although still greasy, dirty looking, was combed. He seemed no more tired—except for the soiled shirt and a slight squinting of the eyes—than he had when Eddie had first seen him. Eddie looked away, looking back at the pool table. The balls were racked into their neat triangle. The cue ball sat at the head of the table, near the side rail, in position for the break.

Fats was at the side of his vision, in the misty part, and he appeared to be smiling placidly. "Let's play pool, Fast Eddie," he said.

Suddenly, Eddie turned to him and stared. Fats' chin jerked, toward his shoulder, his mouth twisting with the movement. Eddie watched this and it seemed, now, to have some kind of meaning; but he did not know what the meaning was.

And then he leaned back in his chair and said, the words coming almost without volition, "I'll beat you, Fats."

Fats just looked at him.

Eddie was not sure whether or not he was grinning at the fat man, at the huge, ridiculous, effeminate, jeweled ballet dancer of a pool hustler, but he felt as if something were going to make him laugh aloud at any minute. "I'll beat you, Fats," he said. "I beat you all day and I'll beat you all night."

"Let's play pool, Fast Eddie."

And then it came, the laughing. Only it was like someone else laughing, not himself, so that he heard himself as if it were from across the room. And then there were tears in his eyes, misting over his vision, fuzzing together the poolroom, the crowd of people around him, and the fat man, into a meaningless blur of colors, shaded with a dark, dominating green that seemed, now, to be actually being diffused from the surface of the table. And then the laughing stopped and he blinked at Fats.

He said it very slowly, tasting the words thickly as they came on. "I'm the best you ever seen, Fats." That was it. It was very simple. "I'm the best there is." He had known it, of course, all along, for years. But now it was so clear, so simple, that no one—not even Charlie—could mistake it. "I'm the best. Even if you beat me, I'm the best." The mistiness was clearing from his eyes again and he could see Fats standing sideways at the table, laying his hand down toward the green, not even aiming. *Even if you beat me . . .*

Somewhere in Eddie, deep in him, a weight was being lifted away. And, deeper still, there was a tiny, distant voice, a thin, anguished cry that said to him, sighing, *You don't have to win.* For hours there had been the weight, pressing on him, trying to break him, and now these words, this fine and deep and true revelation, had come and were taking the weight from him. The weight of responsibility. And the small steel knife of fear.

He looked back at the great fat man. "I'm the best," he said, "no matter who wins."

"We'll see," Fats said, and he broke the balls.

When Eddie looked at the clock again it was a little past midnight. He lost two in a row. Then he won one, lost one, won another—all of them close scores. The pain in his right upper arm seemed to glow outward from the bone and his shoulder was a lump of heat with swollen blood vessels around it and the cue stick seemed to mush into the cue ball when he hit it. And the balls no longer clicked when they hit one another but seemed to hit as if they were made of balsa wood. But he still could not miss the balls; it was still ridiculous that anyone could miss them; and his eyes saw the balls in sharp, brilliant detail although there seemed to be no longer a range of sensitivity to his vision. He felt he could see in the dark or could look at, stare into, the sun—the brightest sun at full noon—and stare it out of the sky.

He did not miss; but when he played safe, now, the cue ball did not always freeze against the rail or against a cluster of balls as he wanted it to. Once, at a critical time in a game, when he had to play safe, the cue ball rolled an inch too far and left Fats an open shot and Fats ran sixty-odd balls and out. And later, during what should have been a big run, he miscalculated a simple, one-rail position roll and had to play for defense. Fats won that game too. When he did, Eddie said, "You fat son of a bitch, you make mistakes expensive."

But he kept on making them. He would still make large numbers of balls but something would go wrong and he would throw the advantage away. And Fats didn't make mistakes. Not ever. And then Charlie came over after a game, and said, "Eddie, you still got the ten thousand. But that's all. Let's quit and go home. Let's go to bed."

Eddie did not look at him. "No," he said.

"Look, Eddie," he said, his voice soft, tired, "what is it you want to do? You beat him. You beat him bad. You want to kill yourself?"

Eddie looked up at him. "What's the matter, Charlie?" he said, trying to grin at him. "You chicken?"

Charlie looked back at him for a minute before he spoke. "Yeah," he said, "maybe that's it. I'm chicken."

"Okay. Then go home. Give me the money."

"Go to hell."

Eddie held his hand out. "Give me the money, Charlie. It's mine."

Charlie just looked at him. Then he reached in his pocket and pulled out a tremendous roll of money, wrinkled bills rolled up and wrapped with a heavy rubber band.

"Here," he said. "Be a goddamn fool."

Eddie stuffed the roll in his pocket. When he stood up to play he looked down at himself. It seemed grossly funny; one pocket bulging with a whiskey bottle, the other with paper money.

It took a slight effort to pick up his cue and start playing again; but after he was started the playing did not seem to stop. He did not even seem to be aware of the times when he was sitting down and Fats was shooting, seemed always to be at the table himself, stroking with his bruised, screaming arm, watching the bright little balls roll and spin and twist their ways about the table. But, although he was hardly aware that Fats was shooting, he knew that he was losing, that Fats was winning more games than he was. And when the janitor came in to open up the poolroom and sweep the floor and they had to stop playing for a few minutes while he swept the cigarette butts from around the table, Eddie sat down to count his money. He could not count it, could not keep track of what he had counted; but he could see that the roll was much smaller than it had been when Charlie gave it to him. He looked at Fats and said, "You fat bastard. You fat lucky bastard," but Fats said nothing.

And then, after a game, Eddie counted off a thousand dollars to Fats, holding the money on the table, under the light, and when he had counted off the thousand he saw that there were only a few bills left. This did not seem right, and he had to look for a moment before he realized what it meant. Then he counted them. There was a hundred-dollar bill, two fifties, a half-dozen twenties and some tens and ones.

Something happened in his stomach. A fist had clamped on something in his stomach and was twisting it.

"All right," he said. "All right, Fats. We're not through yet. We'll play for two hundred. Two hundred dollars a game." He looked at Fats, blinking now, trying to bring his eyes to focus on the huge man across the table from him. "Two hundred dollars. That's a hustler's game of pool."

Fats was unscrewing his cue, unfastening the brass joint in its center. He looked at Eddie. "The game's over," he said.

Eddie leaned over the table, letting his hand fall on the cue ball. "You can't quit me," he said.

Fats did not even look at him. "Watch," he said.

Eddie looked around. The crowd was beginning to leave the table, men were shuffling away, breaking up into little groups, talking. Charlie was walking toward him, his hands in his pockets. The distance between them seemed very great, as though he were looking down a long hallway.

Abruptly, Eddie pushed himself away from the table, clutching the cue ball in his hand. He felt himself staggering. "Wait!" he said. Somehow, he could not see, and the sounds were all melting into one another. "Wait!" He could barely hear his own voice. Somehow, he swung his arm, his burning, swollen, throbbing right arm, and he heard the cue ball crash against the floor and then he was on the floor himself and could see nothing but a lurching motion around him, unclear patterns of light swinging around his head, and he was vomiting, on the floor and on the front of his shirt. . . .

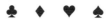

Bennington's had not changed. It was not the kind of place that would change. It was two o'clock in the afternoon when Eddie and Bert stepped from the elevator, walked across the hall and through the huge door. Inside, the room was very quiet. No one was playing pool and there was virtually no one in the place, except for a small crowd of eight or ten men sitting and standing against one wall.

Most of the men seemed familiar to Eddie. One of them, a very big, meaty-looking man with glasses, Eddie recognized as the poolroom manager, Gordon. He did not know any of the others by name, except for one of them. In the middle of the group, sitting, speaking to no one, was Minnesota Fats. He was cleaning his fingernails, with a nail file.

Gordon had looked up when Eddie and Bert walked in, and in a moment they had all stopped talking. Eddie could hear a radio playing, faintly, but nothing else. He looked at Fats. Fats did not look up. There was a very strange sensation in Eddie's stomach; he would not have known what to call it. A polished voice on the radio announced something and then music began to play—a love song.

Bert kept walking and found himself a seat at the edge of the group. Several of the men nodded to him and he nodded back, but no one said anything.

Eddie had stopped beside a table in the middle of the room; he stayed there and began opening his leather case, carefully. While he was doing this he watched Minnesota Fats, not taking his eyes from the moonlike face, the shiny, curly hair, and the massive belly, now covered with tight blue silk—a pale blue shirt that fit so tight across Fats' belly that it clung to it, folding only where the flesh folded, under the narrow belt. On his small feet, Fats was wearing immaculate little brown-and-white shoes, which rested delicately against the foot rail of the chair that held his magnificent, enormous butt.

While Eddie watched him, taking his cue stick from the case and then twisting the two ends together, Fats' face made its regular, jerking grimace, but his eyes did not look up at Eddie.

Then Fats finished what he was doing, slipped the nail file into his breast pocket, and blinked at him. "Hello, Fast Eddie," he said, in the no-tone voice.

The stick was together now, and tight. Eddie walked to Bert, handed him the case, and then, cue in hand, he walked over to Fats, stopping in front of him.

"Well, Fats," he said, "I came to play."

Fats' face made the heavy, ambiguous movement that resembled a smile. "That's good," he said.

Not saying anything, Eddie turned around and began racking the balls on the empty table in front of the sitting men. When he had finished he began chalking his cue quietly and said, "Straight pool, Fats? Two hundred a game?"

From somewhere in the heavy mound of silk- and leather-wrapped flesh in the chair came a kind of short, softly explosive sound, a brief travesty of a laugh. And then, blinking, Fats said, "One thousand, Fast Eddie. One thousand dollars a game."

It figured. It figured immediately; but it was a shock. Fats knew him now. Fats knew his game, and Fats was not going to fool with him, was going to try to put him down fast, on nerve and capital. It was a good move.

Not answering, Eddie bent down and began tapping the cue ball with his cue stick, gently shooting it across the table and back. He kept his hands busy with the cue stick, to keep the fingers from trembling. He kept shooting the cue ball, back and forth across the table, and he thought of the two-and-a-half thousand dollars in his pocket, the dim pain in the fingers of his hands, the stiffness in the joints of his thumbs and in his wrists. And he thought about the money and nerve and experience and skill backing the grotesque and massive man who was sitting behind him now, jerking his chin, watching.

If he played him, he would be bucking the odds. Immediately he thought of Bert again. Bert would never buck the odds. Suddenly he looked up and over at Bert. Bert sat, squat and secure, looking down at him from the high chair, his face clouded, his eyes registering disapproval. No, Bert would never buck the odds.

Eddie stood up from the table and, not looking at anyone, said, "Flip the coin, Fats. Let's see who breaks. . . ."

Fats broke, and he was beautiful. His stroke was lovely; his command of the game miraculous; and the graceful movements of his giant, disgusting body were a compound of impossibility and of genius. He beat Eddie. Fats beat him not just once, but three times in a row.

The scores were close, but it happened so fast that Eddie felt he did not have any control of what happened. Balls had bounced and slipped and rolled and fallen into pockets, and, as before, Fats had seemed to be everywhere, shooting fast, never looking, playing his obscure concerto with his fiddlebow of a cue and his musician's hands with emeralds on the fingers.

For the last twenty minutes of the final game Eddie did nothing but watch while Fats edged and sliced and nursed and coaxed balls to perform for him, making a run of ninety-three and out. When he gave him the thousand, the last thousand, Eddie's hands were sweating and he was still staring fixedly at the table. There was a ringing sound somewhere in his head. Then, still hardly aware of what had happened to him, he looked up.

He was in the middle of a crowd. People were sitting all around the table, all of them watching him. Nobody else was playing pool. It was late afternoon now. There was slanting autumn sunlight in the big room, and everything was very quiet, except for the radio, which seemed to be tinkling and buzzing.

He could not distinguish individual faces in the crowd very well at first, but they began to come into focus. He was looking for Bert; he did not know exactly why. He should not want to see Bert, but he was looking for him. And then he saw Charlie.

He blinked. It was Charlie, no one else, sitting in a chair by the wall, pudgy, bald at the temples, and with no expression on his face. He started to walk to Charlie, to ask him where he had appeared from, what he was doing there; but he stopped, struck in the face by an insight.

Charlie had come to smirk at him, to see him beaten again. Charlie, like Bert, one of the in-turned and self-controlled—one of the cautious, smirking men. Maybe Fats was like that too, maybe the three of them were brothers under the pink flesh, delighting quietly in the downfall of the fast and loose man, finding the weak spot—suddenly it seemed to Eddie that he himself was a Lazarus of sore, weak spots—and then, having found the place where it hurts, gently probing and pushing and twisting until their mutual enemy, the man with all the talent, was lying on the floor vomiting on himself.

Looking at Charlie he could see himself now as a man crucified, and Charlie as his Judas. He could have wept, and he made fists out of his hands and tightened them until he felt that he would scream with the pain. And then the edge of his vision caught sight of Bert, and immediately he came to his senses and saw what he was doing, playing the loser's game with himself, the game of self-pity, the favorite of all the multitude of indoor sports. . . .

Charlie eased himself up from the chair and waddled over. His face was serious, his voice quiet. "Hello, Eddie," he said. "I just got word you were playing up here."

"Why aren't you in Oakland?"

Charlie attempted a smile. The attempt was a failure. "I was. Last week I started getting worried about you and flew back. I been hunting you. Around the rooms."

"What for?" Eddie stared at him; there was something strained about the way Charlie was talking to him. "What do you want me for?"

Not answering at first, Charlie fumbled in his hip pocket and withdrew what looked like a folded-over checkbook and held it out to him. "This is yours," he said.

Eddie took the book and opened it. It was full of traveler's checks, in denominations of two hundred fifty each. "What the hell . . .?" he said.

Charlie's voice was back to its customary lack of expression, like that of a comic miniature of Minnesota Fats. "When you were drunk up here before and hit me for the money, I held out on you. This is what I held out. A little under five thousand." And then, abruptly, his face broke into one of his extremely rare smiles, which lasted only for a moment, "Minus my ten per cent, of course."

Eddie shook his head, letting his thumb run over the thick edges of the blue checks. It figured; it figured, but it was hard to believe: he had just come back from the grave. "So why give it to me now," he said. "So you can watch me lose?"

Charlie's voice was soft. "No," he said. "I been thinking. Maybe you're ready to beat him now. Maybe you were ready before—I don't know. Anyway, you ought to find out."

"Okay," Eddie said. He grinned at Charlie, the old grin, the charm grin, fast and loose. "We'll find out."

He glanced at Fats, who seemed only to be waiting, and then counted the money. There was four thousand five hundred in traveler's checks, and he had about seven hundred in cash. His whole kitty. *Well, here we go. Fast and loose.*

Then he looked at the fat man and said, "Fats," thinking, *you fat bastard,* "let's play a game of pool for five thousand dollars."

Fats blinked at him. His chins jerked, but he said nothing.

"Come on, Fats," he said, "five thousand. That's a hustler's game of pool. It's my whole bankroll, my life's savings." He flipped again through the book of checks, not feeling the pain that doing this caused, and then looked for a moment at Charlie. Charlie's face showed nothing, but his eyes were alert, interested, and Eddie thought, wonderingly, *he's going along with it.* Then he looked at Bert and Bert was smiling thinly, but approvingly; and this too was astonishing and lovely.

"What's the matter, Fats?" he said. "All you got to do is win one game and I'm gone back to California. Just one game. You just beat me three."

Fats blinked at him, his face now very thoughtful, controlled, and his eyes as always a kind of obscene mystery.

"Okay," he said.

Having changed the bet they tossed for the break again, and Fats lost again. He chalked his cue carefully, stepped sideways up to the table, set his hands on the green, the rings flashing, and shot.

The break was good, but not perfect. One ball, the five-ball, was left a few inches out from the rack, unprotected, down at the foot of the table. The cue ball was frozen to the end rail, the table's length from it. It was an odds-off shot, a nowhere shot; and Eddie's first reaction was automatic, play it safe, don't take a chance on leaving the other man in a place where he can score a hundred points. The proper thing to do would be to ease the cue ball down the table, nudge one of the corner balls, and return it to the end rail, letting the other man figure it out from there. That would be the right way to play it—the safe way.

But Eddie stopped before getting ready to shoot and looked at the ball and it occurred to him that although it was a very difficult shot it happened to be one that he could make. You cut it just so, at just such speed and with just so much spin and the ball would fall in the pocket. And the cue ball would split open the rack and the ball game would suddenly be wide open.

It would be smarter to play safe. But to play safe would be to play Bert's game, to play Fats' game, to play the quiet, careful percentage. But, as Bert himself had once said, "There's a lot of percentage players find out they got to work for a living."

He chalked his cue lightly, with three deft strokes. Then he said, "Five ball in the corner," bent down, took careful, dead aim, and shot.

And the cue ball—for a moment an extension of his own will and consciousness sped quickly down the table and clipped the edge of the five-ball, then rebounded off the bottom rail and smacked firmly into the triangle of balls, spreading them softly apart. And while this was happening, the little orange ball with the number 5 in its center rolled evenly across the table, along the rail, and into the corner pocket, hitting the bottom with a sound that was exquisite.

The balls were spread prettily, the cue ball in their center, and Eddie looked at this loose and lovely table before he shot and thought of how pleasant it was going to be to shoot them into the pockets.

And it was a pleasure. He felt as if he had the cue ball on strings and it was his own little white marionette, darting here and there on the green baize as he instructed it by the gentle prodding of his cue. Watching the white ball perform, watching it nudge balls in, ease balls in, slap balls in, and hearing the soft, dark sounds the balls made as they fell into the deep leather pockets gave him a voluptuous, sensitive pleasure. And in operating the white marionette, putting it through its delicate paces, he was aware of a sense of power and strength that was building in him and then resonating, like a drumbeat. He pocketed a rack of balls without missing, and then another and another, and more, until he had lost count.

And then, when he had finished cleaning off the table and was standing, waiting for the rack man to put the fourteen balls back together in their triangle, he realized that the balls should be already racked but they were not, and an absurd idea struck him: he might have already won the game. Fats might never have had a shot.

He looked over to the chair where Bert was sitting. Fats was standing there, beside Bert. He was counting out money—a great many hundred-dollar bills. Fats seemed to be taking an impossible amount of money from his billfold. Eddie looked at Bert's face and Bert peered back at him, through the glasses. Someone in the crowd of people coughed, and the coughing sounded very loud in the room.

Fats walked over and set the money on the edge of the table, his rings flashing under the overhead lights. Then he walked to a chair and sat down, ponderously. His chin jerked down into his collar for a moment, and then he said, "It's your money, Fast Eddie." He was sweating.

He had run the game. He had made a hundred twenty-five balls without missing, and had shot in nine racks of fourteen balls each, making and breaking on the fifteenth ball each time.

Eddie walked to the money, the silent, bulky money. Instinctively, he wiped some of the dust from his hand on the side of his trousers before handling it. Then he took it, rolled up the green paper, pushed it down into his pocket. He looked at Fats. "I was lucky," he said.

Fats' chins dipped quickly. "Maybe," he said. And then, to the rack boy, "Rack the balls."

Out of the next four games Eddie won three, losing the one only when Fats, in a sudden show of brilliance, managed to score a magnificent ninety-ball run—a tricky, contrived run, a run that displayed wit and nerve—and caught Eddie with less than sixty points on the string. But Fats did not sustain this peak; he seemed to fight his way to it by an effort of will and to fall back from it afterward, so that his next game had even less strength than before.

And Fats' one victory did not affect Eddie, for Eddie was in a place now where he could not be affected, where he felt that nothing Fats could do could touch him. Not Eddie Felson, fast and loose—and, now, smart, critical, and rich. Eddie Felson, with the ball bearings in his elbow, with eyes for the green and the colored balls, for the shiny balls, the purple, orange, blue, and red, the stripes and solids, with geometrical rolls and falling, lovely spinning, with whiffs and clicks and tap-tap-taps, with scrapings of chalk, and the fingers embracing the polished shaft, the fingers on felt, the ever and always ready arena, the long, bright rectangle. The rectangle of lovely, mystical green, the color of money.

And then when Eddie had won a game and was lighting his cigarette Fats spoke out grimly with words that Eddie could feel in his stomach. "I'm quitting you, Fast Eddie," he said, "I can't beat you."

From Fool's Die

BY MARIO PUZO

A few years before he wrote *Fool's Die,* Mario Puzo published *Inside Las Vegas* (1976), in which, writing as a self-proclaimed recent ex-"degenerate" gambler, he discussed with street corner wit and savvy his long affair with gambling. The book appreciates the "irresponsible happiness" involved with gambling, and argues that some element of gambling underlies most human achievement: "It is the gambling instinct in man that lifted him up the evolutionary scale, that has led to scientific progress. Why the hell should anyone want to get to the moon?" Puzo's separation from gambling occurred, in part, because, after the massive success of *The Godfather* and other books, Puzo realized that his personal relation to the "ruin factor" that he associated with gambling had necessarily changed: "To gamble," he wrote, "is to risk, to approach 'the ruin factor.' When I was poor the ruin factor was not important. Hell, I was ruined anyway." As the powerful conclusion of this opening section to *Fool's Die* suggests, one can approach the "ruin factor" by winning as well.

O n the luckiest day of Jordan Hawley's life he betrayed his three best friends. But yet unknowing, he wandered through the dice pit of the huge gambling casino in the Hotel Xanadu, wondering what game to try next. Still early afternoon, he was a ten-thousand-dollar winner. But he was tired of the glittering red dice skittering across green felt.

He moved out of the pit, the purple carpet sinking beneath his feet, and moved toward the hissing wheel of a roulette table, pretty with red and black boxes, punishing green zero and double zero. He made some foolhardy bets, lost and moved into the blackjack pit.

The small horseshoe blackjack tables ran down in double rows. He walked between them like a captive through an Indian gauntlet. Blue-backed cards flashed on either side. He made it through safely and came to the huge glass doors that led out into the streets of the city of Las Vegas. From here he could see down the Strip sentineled by luxury hotels.

Under the blazing Nevada sun, a dozen Xanadus glittered with million-watt neon signs. The hotels seemed to be melting down into a steely golden haze, a reachable mirage. Jordan Hawley was trapped inside the air-conditioned casino with his winnings. It would be madness to go out to where only other casinos awaited him, with their strange unknown fortunes. Here he was a winner, and soon he would see his friends. Here he was shielded from the burning yellow desert.

Jordan Hawley turned away from the glass door and sat down at the nearest blackjack table. Black hundred-dollar chips, tiny cindered suns, rattled in his hands. He watched a dealer sliding cards from his freshly made shoe, the oblong wooden box that held the cards.

Jordan bet heavy on each of two small circles, playing two hands. His luck was good. He played until the shoe ran out. The dealer busted often, and when he shuffled up, Jordan moved on. His pockets bulged chips everywhere. But that was no sweat because he was wearing a specially designed Sy Devore Vegas Winner sports coat. It had red crimson trim on sky blue cloth and specially zippered pockets that were optimistically capacious. The inside of the jacket also held special zippered cavities so deep no pickpocket could get at them. Jordan's winnings were safe, and he had plenty of room for more. Nobody had ever filled the pockets of a Vegas Winner jacket.

The casino, lit by many huge chandeliers, had a bluish haze, neon reflected by the deep purple carpeting. Jordan stepped out of this light and into the darkened area of the bar lounge with its lowered ceiling and small platform for performers. Seated at a small table, he could look out on the casino as a spectator looks on a lighted stage.

Mesmerized, he watched afternoon gamblers drift in intricate choreographed patterns from table to table. Like a rainbow flashing across a clear blue sky, a roulette wheel flashed its red, black numbers to match the table layout. Blue-white-backed cards skittered across green felt tables. White-dotted red square dice were dazzling flying fish over the whale-shaped crap tables. Far off, down the rows of blackjack tables, those dealers going off duty washed their hands high in the air to show they were not palming chips.

The casino stage began to fill up with more actors: sun worshipers wandering in from the outdoor pool, others from tennis courts, golf courses, naps and afternoon free and paid lovemaking in Xanadu's thousand rooms. Jordan spotted another Vegas Winner jacket coming across the casino floor. It was Merlyn. Merlyn the Kid. Merlyn wavered as he passed the roulette wheel, his weakness. Though he rarely played because he knew its huge five and a half percent cut like a sharp sword. Jordan from the darkness waved a crimson-striped arm, and Merlyn took up his stride again as if he were passing through flames, stepped off the lighted stage of the casino floor and sat down. Merlyn's zippered pockets did not bulge with chips, nor did he have any in his hands.

They sat there without speaking, easy with each other. Merlyn looked like a burly athlete in his crimson and blue jacket. He was younger than Jordan by at least ten years, and his hair was jet black. He also looked happier, more eager for the coming battle against fate, the night of gambling.

Then from the baccarat pit in the far corner of the casino they saw Cully Cross and Diane step through the elegant royal gray railing and move over the casino floor coming toward them. Cully too was wearing his Vegas Winner jacket. Diane was in a white summer frock, low-cut and cool for her day's work, the top of her breasts dusted pearly white. Merlyn waved, and they came forward through the casino tables without swerving. And when they sat down, Jordan ordered the drinks. He knew what they wanted.

Cully spotted Jordan's bulging pockets. "Hey," he said, "you went and got lucky without us?"

Jordan smiled. "A little." They all looked at him curiously as he paid for the drinks and tipped the cocktail waitress with a red five-dollar chip. He noticed their glances. He did not know why they looked at him so oddly. Jordan had been in Vegas three weeks and had changed fearsomely in that three weeks. He had lost twenty pounds. His ash-blond hair had grown long, whiter. His face, though still handsome, was now haggard; the skin had a grayish tinge. He looked drained. But he was not conscious of this because he felt fine. Innocently, he wondered about these three people, his friends of three weeks and now the best friends he had in the world.

The one Jordan liked best was the Kid. Merlyn. Merlyn prided himself on being an impassive gambler. He tried never to show emotion when he lost or won and usually succeeded. Except that an exceptionally bad losing streak gave him a look of surprised bewilderment that delighted Jordan.

Merlyn the Kid never said much. He just watched everybody. Jordan knew that Merlyn the Kid kept tabs on everything he did, trying to figure him out. Which also amused Jordan. He had the Kid faked out. The Kid was looking for complicated things and never accepted that he, Jordan, was exactly what he presented to the world. But Jordan liked being with him and the others. They relieved his loneliness. And because Merlyn seemed more eager, more passionate, in his gambling, Cully had named him the Kid.

Cully himself was the youngest, only twenty-nine, but oddly enough seemed to be the leader of the group. They had met three weeks ago here in Vegas, in this casino, and they had only one thing in common. They were degenerate gamblers. Their three-week-long debauch was considered extraordinary because the casino percentage should have ground them into the Nevada desert sands in their first few days.

Jordan knew that the others, Cully "Countdown" Cross and Diane, were also curious about him, but he didn't mind. He had very little curiosity about any of them. The Kid seemed young and too intelligent to be a degenerate gambler, but Jordan never tried to nail down why. It was really of no interest to him.

Cully was nothing to wonder about or so it seemed. He was your classical degenerate gambler with skills. He could count down the cards in a four-deck blackjack shoe. He was an expert on all the gambling percentages. The Kid was not. Jordan was a cool, abstracted gambler where the Kid was passionate. And Cully professional. But Jordan had no illusions about himself. At this moment he was in their class. A degenerate gambler. That is, a man who gambled simply to gamble and must lose. As a hero who goes to war must die. Show me a gambler and I'll show you a loser, show me a hero and I'll show you a corpse, Jordan thought.

They were all at the end of their bankrolls, they would all have to move on soon, except maybe Cully. Cully was part pimp and part tout. Always trying to work a con to get an edge on the casinos. Sometimes he got a blackjack dealer to go partners against the house, a dangerous game.

The girl, Diane, was really an outsider. She worked as a shill for the house and she was taking her break from the baccarat table. With them, because these were the only three men in Vegas she felt cared about her.

As a shill she played with casino money, lost and won casino money. She was subject not to fate but to the fixed weekly salary she received from the casino. Her presence was necessary to the baccarat table only in slack hours because gamblers shied away from an empty table. She was the flypaper for the flies. She was, therefore, dressed provocatively. She had long jet black hair she used as a whip, a sensuous full mouth and an almost perfect long-legged body. Her bust was on the small side, but it suited her. And the baccarat pit boss gave her home phone number to big players. Sometimes the pit boss or a ladderman would whisper that one of the players would like to see her in his room. She had the option to refuse, but it was an option to be used carefully. When she complied, she was not paid directly by the customer. The pit boss gave her a special chit for fifty or a hundred dollars that she could cash at the casino cage. This she hated to do. So she would pay one of the other girl shills five dollars to cash her chit for her. When Cully heard this, he became her friend. He liked soft women, he could manipulate them.

Jordan signaled the cocktail waitress for more drinks. He felt relaxed. It gave Jordan a feeling of virtue to be so lucky and so early in the day. As if some strange God had loved him, found him good and was rewarding him for the sacrifices he had offered up to the world he had left behind him. And he had this sense of comradeship with Cully and Merlyn.

They ate breakfast together often. And always had this late-afternoon drink before starting their big gambling action that would destroy the night. Sometimes they had a midnight snack to celebrate a win, the lucky man picking up the tab and buying keno tickets for the table. In the last three weeks they had become buddies, though they had absolutely nothing in common and their friendship would die with their gambling lust. But now, still not busted out, they had a strange affection for each other. Coming off a winning day, Merlyn the Kid had taken the three of them into the hotel clothing store and bought their crimson and blue Vegas Winner jackets. That day all three had been winners and had worn their jackets superstitiously ever since.

Jordan had met Diane on the night of her deepest humiliation, the same night he first met Merlyn. The day after meeting her he had bought her coffee on one of her breaks, and they had talked but he had not heard what she was saying. She sensed his lack of interest and had been offended. So there had been no action. He was sorry afterward, sorry that night in his ornately decorated room, alone and unable to sleep. As he was unable to sleep every night. He had tried sleeping pills, but they gave him nightmares that frightened him.

The jazz combo would be coming on soon, the lounge filled up. Jordan noticed the look they had given him when he had tipped the waitress with a red five-dollar chip. They thought he was generous. But it was simply because he didn't want to be bothered figuring out what the tip should be. It amused him to see how his values had changed. He had always been meticulous and fair but never recklessly generous. At one time his part of the world had been scaled and metered out. Everyone earned rewards. And finally it hadn't worked. He was amazed now at the absurdity of having once based his life on such reasoning.

The combo was rustling through the darkness up to the stage. Soon they would be playing too loud for anyone to talk, and this was always the signal for the three men to start their serious gambling.

"Tonight's my lucky night," Cully said. "I got thirteen passes in my right arm."

Jordan smiled. He always responded to Cully's enthusiasm. Jordan knew him only by the name of Cully Countdown, the name he had earned at the blackjack tables. Jordan liked Cully because the man never stopped talking and his talk rarely required answers. Which made him necessary to the group because Jordan and Merlyn the Kid never talked much. And Diane, the baccarat shill, smiled a lot but didn't talk much either.

Cully's small-featured, dark, neat face was glowing with confidence. "I'm going to hold the dice for an hour," he said. "I'm going to throw a hundred numbers and no sevens. You guys get on me."

The jazz combo gave their opening flourish as if to back Cully up.

Cully loved craps, though his best skill was at blackjack where he could count down the shoe. Jordan loved baccarat because there was absolutely no skill or figuring involved. Merlyn loved roulette because it was to him the most mythical, magical game. But Cully had declared his infallibility tonight at craps and they would all have to play with him, ride his luck. They were his friends, they couldn't jinx him. They rose to go to the dice pit and bet with Cully, Cully flexing his strong right arm that magically concealed thirteen passes.

Diane spoke for the first time. "Jordy had a lucky streak at baccarat. Maybe you should bet on him."

"You don't look lucky to me," Merlyn said to Jordan.

It was against the rules for her to mention Jordan's luck to fellow gamblers. They might tap him for a loan or he might feel jinxed. But by this time Diane knew Jordan well enough to sense he didn't care about any of the usual superstitions gamblers worried about.

Cully Countdown shook his head. "I have the feeling." He brandished his right arm, shaking imaginary dice.

The music blared; they could no longer hear each other speak. It blew them out of their sanctuary of darkness into the blazing stage that was the casino floor. There were many more players now, but they could move fluidly. Diane, her coffee break over, went back to the baccarat table to bet the house money, to fill up space. But without passion. As a house shill, winning and losing house money, she was boringly immortal. And so she walked more slowly than the others.

Cully led the way. They were the Three Musketeers in their crimson and blue Vegas Winner sports jackets. He was eager and confident. Merlyn followed almost as eagerly, his gambling blood up. Jordan followed more slowly, his huge winnings making him appear heavier than the other two. Cully was trying to sniff out a hot table, one of his signposts being if the house racks of chips were low. Finally he led them to an open railing and the three lined up so that Cully would get the dice first coming around the stickman. They made small bets until Cully finally had the red cubes in his loving rubbing hands.

The Kid put twenty on the line. Jordan two hundred. Cully Countdown fifty. He threw a six. They all backed up their bets and bought all the numbers. Cully picked up the dice, passionately confident, and threw them strongly against the far side of the table. Then stared with disbelief. It was the worst of catastrophes. Seven out. Wiped. Without even catching another number. The Kid had lost a hundred and forty, Cully a big three fifty. Jordan had gone down the drain for fourteen hundred dollars.

Cully muttered something and wandered away. Thoroughly shaken, he was now committed to playing very careful blackjack. He had to count every card from the shoe to get an edge on the dealer. Sometimes it worked, but it was a long grind. Sometimes he would remember every card perfectly, figure out what was left in the shoe, get a ten percent edge on the dealer and bet a big stack of chips. And even then sometimes with that big ten percent edge he got unlucky and lost. And then count down another shoe. So now, his fantastic right arm having betrayed him, Cully was down to case money. The night before him was a drudgery. He had to gamble very cleverly and still not get unlucky.

Merlyn the Kid also wandered away, also down to his case money, but with no skills to back up his play. He had to get lucky.

Jordan, alone, prowled around the casino. He loved the feeling of being solitary in the crowd of people and the gambling hum. To be alone without being lonely. To be friends with strangers for an hour and never see them again. Dice clattering.

He wandered through the blackjack pit, the horseshoe tables in straight rows. He listened for the tick of a second carder. Cully had taught him and Merlyn this trick. A crooked dealer with fast hands was impossible to spot with the eye. But if you listened very carefully, you could hear the slight rasping tick when he slid out the second card from beneath the top card of his deck. Because the top card was the card the dealer needed to make his hand good.

A long queue was forming for the dinner show though it was only seven. There was no real action in the casino. No big bettors. No big winners. Jordan clicked the black chips in his hand, deliberating. Then he stepped up to an almost empty crap table and picked up the red glittering dice.

♣ ♦ ♥ ♠

Jordan unzipped the outside pocket of his Vegas Winner sports jacket and heaped black hundred-dollar chips into his table rack. He bet two hundred on the line, backed up his number and then bought all the numbers for five hundred dollars each. He held the dice for almost an hour. After the first fifteen minutes the electricity of his hot hand ran through the casino and the table jammed full. He pressed his bets to the limit of five hundred, and the magical numbers kept rolling out of his hand. In his mind he banished the fatal seven to hell. He forbade it to appear. His table rack filled to overflowing with black chips. His jacket pockets bulged to capacity. Finally his mind could no longer hold its concentration, could no longer banish the fatal seven, and the dice passed from his hands to the next player. The gamblers at the table gave him a cheer. The pit boss gave him metal racks to carry his chips to the casino cage. Merlyn and Cully appeared. Jordan smiled at them.

"Did you get on my roll?" he asked.

Cully shook his head. "I got in on the last ten minutes," he said. "I did a little good."

Merlyn laughed. "I didn't believe in your luck. I stayed off."

Merlyn and Cully escorted Jordan to the cashier's cage to help him cash in. Jordan was astonished when the total of the metal racks came to over fifty thousand dollars. And his pockets bulged with still more chips.

Merlyn and Cully were awestricken. Cully said seriously, "Jordy, now's the time for you to leave town. Stay here and they'll get it back."

Jordan laughed. "The night's young yet." He was amused that his two friends thought it such a big deal. But the strain told on him. He felt enormously tired. He said, "I'm going up to my room for a nap. I'll meet you guys and buy a big dinner maybe about midnight. OK?"

The cage teller had finished counting and said to Jordan, "Sir, would you like cash or a check? Or would you like us to hold it for you here in the cage?"

Merlyn said, "Get a check."

Cully frowned with thoughtful greed, but then noticed that Jordan's secret inner pockets still bulged with chips, and he smiled. "A check is safer," he said.

The three of them waited, Cully and Merlyn flanking Jordan, who looked beyond them to the glittering casino pits. Finally the cashier reappeared with the saw-toothed yellow check and handed it to Jordan.

The three men turned together in an unconscious pirouette; their jackets flashed crimson and blue beneath the keno board lights above them. Then Merlyn and Cully took Jordan by the elbows and thrust him into one of the spokelike corridors toward his room.

♣ ♦ ♥ ♠

A plushy, expensive, garish room. Rich gold curtains, a huge silver quilted bed. Exactly right for gambling. Jordan took a hot bath and then tried to read. He couldn't sleep. Through the windows the neon lights of the Vegas Strip sent flashes of rainbow color, streaking the walls of his room. He drew the curtains tighter, but in his brain he still heard the faint roar that diffused through the huge casino like surf on a distant beach. Then he put out the lights in the room and got into bed. It was a good fake, but his brain refused to be fooled. He could not fall asleep.

Then Jordan felt the familiar fear and terrible anxiety. If he fell asleep, he would die. He desperately wanted to sleep, yet he could not. He was too afraid, too frightened. But he could never understand why he was so terribly frightened.

He was tempted to try the sleeping pills again; he had done so earlier in the month and he had slept, but only with nightmares that he couldn't bear. And left him depressed the next day. He preferred going without sleep. As now.

Jordan snapped on the light, got out of bed and dressed. He emptied out all his pockets and his wallet. He unzipped all the outside and inside pockets of his Vegas Winner sports jacket and shook it upside down so that all the black and green and red chips poured down on the silk coverlet. The hundred-dollar bills formed a huge pile, the black and reds forming curious spirals and checkered patterns. To pass the time he started to count the money and sort out the chips. It took him almost an hour.

He had over five thousand dollars in cash. He had eight thousand dollars in black hundred-dollar chips and another six thousand dollars in twenty-five-dollar greens, almost a thousand dollars in five-dollar reds. He was astonished. He took the big jagged-edged Hotel Xanadu check out of his wallet and studied the black and red script and the numbered amount in green. Fifty thousand dollars. He studied it carefully. There were three different signatures on the check. One of the signatures he particularly noticed because it was so large and the script so clear. Alfred Gronevelt.

And still he was puzzled. He remembered turning in some chips for cash several times during the day, but he hadn't realized it was for more than five thousand. He shifted on the bed and all the carefully stacked piles collapsed into each other.

And now he was pleased. He was glad that he had enough money to stay in Vegas, that he would not have to go on to Los Angeles to start his new job. To start his new career, his new life, maybe a new family. He counted all the money again and added the check. He was worth seventy-one thousand dollars. He could gamble forever.

He switched off the bedside light so that he could lie there in the darkness with his money surrounding and touching his body. He tried to sleep to fight off the terror that always came over him in this darkened room. He could hear his heart beating faster and faster until finally he had to switch the light back on and get up from the bed.

High above the city in his penthouse suite, the hotel owner, Alfred Gronevelt, picked up the phone. He called the dice pit and asked how much Jordan was ahead. He was told that Jordan had killed the table profits for the night. Then he called back the operator and told her to page Xanadu Five. He held on. It would take a few minutes for the page to cover all the areas of the hotel and penetrate the minds of the players. Idly he gazed out the penthouse window and could see the great thick red and green python of neon that wound down the Las Vegas Strip. And farther off, the dark surrounding desert mountains enclosing, with him, thousands of gamblers trying to beat the house, sweating for those millions of dollars of greenbacks lying so mockingly in cashier cages. Over the years these gamblers had left their bones on that gaudy neon Strip.

Then he heard Cully's voice come over the phone. Cully was Xanadu Five. (Gronevelt was Xanadu One.)

"Cully, your buddy hit us big," Gronevelt said. "You sure he's legit?"

Cully's voice was low. "Yeah, Mr. Gronevelt. He's a friend of mine and he's square. He'll drop it back before he leaves."

Gronevelt said, "Anything he wants, lay it on him. Don't let him go wandering down the Strip, giving our money to other joints. Lay a good broad on him."

"Don't worry," Cully said. But Gronevelt caught something funny in his voice. For a moment he wondered about Cully. Cully was his spy, checking the operation of the casino and reporting the blackjack dealers who were going partners with him to beat the house. He had big plans for Cully when this operation was over. But now he wondered.

"What about that other guy in your gang, the Kid?" Gronevelt said. "What's his angle, what the hell is he doing here three weeks?"

"He's small change," Cully said. "But a good kid. Don't worry, Mr. Gronevelt. I know what I got riding with you."

"OK," Gronevelt said. When he hung up the phone, he was smiling. Cully didn't know that pit bosses had complained about Cully's being allowed in the casino because he was a countdown artist. That the hotel manager had complained about Merlyn and Jordan's being allowed to keep desperately needed rooms for so long despite fresh loaded gamblers who came in every weekend. What no one knew was that Gronevelt was intrigued by the friendship of the three men; how it ended would be Cully's true test.

In his room Jordan fought the impulse to go back down into the casino. He sat in one of the stuffed armchairs and lit a cigarette. Everything was OK now. He had friends, he had gotten lucky, he was free. He was just tired. He needed a long rest someplace far away.

He thought, Cully and Diane and Merlyn. Now his three best friends, he smiled at that.

They knew a lot of things about him. They had all spent hours in the casino lounge together, gossiping, resting between bouts of gambling. Jordan was never reticent. He would answer any question, though he never asked any. The Kid always asked questions so seriously, with such obvious interest, that Jordan never took offense.

Just for something to do he took his suitcase out of the closet to pack. The first thing that hit his eye was the small handgun he had bought back home. He had never told his friends about the gun. His wife had left him and taken the children. She had left him for another man, and his first reaction had been to kill the other man. A reaction so alien to his true nature that even now he was constantly surprised. Of course, he had done nothing. The problem was to get rid of the gun. The best thing to do was to take it apart and throw it away piece by piece. He didn't want to be responsible for anybody's getting hurt by it. But right now he put it to one side and threw some clothes in the suitcase, then sat down again.

He wasn't that sure he wanted to leave Vegas, the brightly lit cave of his casino. He was comfortable there. He was safe there. His not caring really about winning or losing was his magic cloak against fate. And most of all, his casino cave closed out all the other pains and traps of life itself.

He smiled again, thinking about Cully's worrying about his winnings. What, after all, would he do with the money? The best thing would be to send it to his wife. She was a good woman, a good mother, a woman of quality and character. The fact that she had left him after twenty years to marry her lover did not, could not, change those facts. For at this moment, now that the months had passed, Jordan saw clearly the justice of her decision. She had a right to be happy. To live her life to its fullest potential. And she had been suffocating living with him. Not that he had been a bad husband. Just an inadequate one. He had been a good father. He had done his duty in every way. His only fault was that after twenty years he no longer made his wife happy.

His friends knew his story. The three weeks he had spent with them in Vegas seemed like years, and he could talk to them as he could never talk to anyone back home. It had come out over drinks in the lounge, after midnight meals in the coffee shop.

He knew they thought him cold-blooded. When Merlyn asked him what the visitation rights were with his children, Jordan shrugged. Merlyn asked if he would ever see his wife and kids again, and Jordan tried to answer honestly. "I don't think so," he said. "They're OK."

And Merlyn the Kid shot back at him, "And you, are you OK?"

And Jordan laughed without faking it, laughing at the way Merlyn the Kid zeroed in on him. Still laughing, he said, "Yeah, I'm OK." And then just once he paid the Kid off for being so nosy. He looked him right in the eye and said coolly, "There's nothing more to see. What you see is it. Nothing complicated. People are not that important to other people. When you get older, that's the way it is."

Merlyn looked back at him and lowered his eyes and then said very softly, "It's just that you can't sleep at night, right?"

Jordan said, "That's right."

Cully said impatiently, "Nobody sleeps in this town. Just get a couple of sleeping pills."

"They give me nightmares," Jordan said.

"No, no," Cully said, "I mean them." He pointed to three hookers seated around a table, having drinks. Jordan laughed. It was the first time he had heard the Vegas idiom. Now he understood why sometimes Cully broke off gambling with the announcement he was going to take on a couple of sleeping pills.

If there was ever a time for walking sleeping pills, it was tonight, but Jordan had tried that the first week in Vegas. He could always make it, but he never really felt the relief from tension afterward. One night a hooker, a friend of Cully's, had talked him into "twins," taking her girlfriend with her. Only another fifty and they would really shoot the works because he was a nice guy. And he'd said OK. It had been sort of cheery and comforting with so many breasts surrounding him. An infantile comfort. One girl finally cradled his head in her breast while the other one rode him astride. And at the final moment of tension, as finally he came, surrendering at least his flesh, he caught the girl astride giving a sly smile to the girl on whose breasts he rested. And he understood that now that he was finally out of the way, finished off, they could get down to what they really wanted. He watched while the girl who had been astride went down on the other girl with a passion far more convincing than

she had shown with him. He wasn't angry. He'd just as soon they got something out of it. It seemed in some way more natural to be so. He had given
them an extra hundred. They thought it was for being so good, but really it was
for that sly secret smile—for that comforting, sweetly confirming betrayal. And
yet the girl lying back in the final exaltation of her Judas climax had reached
out her hand blindly for Jordan to hold, and he had been moved to tears.

And all the walking sleeping pills had tried their best for him. They
were the cream of the country, these girls. They gave you affection, they held
your hand, they went to a dinner and a show, they gambled a little of your
money, never cheated or rolled you. They made believe they truly cared and
they fucked your brains out. All for a solitary hundred-dollar bill, a single
Honeybee in Cully's phrase. They were a bargain. Ah, Christ, they were a bargain. But he could never let himself be faked out even for the tiny bought
moment. They washed him down before leaving him: a sick, sick man on a
hospital bed. Well, they were better than the regular sleeping pills, they didn't
give him nightmares. But they couldn't put him to sleep either. He hadn't
really slept for three weeks.

Wearily Jordan sagged against the headboard of his bed. He didn't remember leaving his chair. He should put out the lights and try to sleep. But the
terror would come back. Not a mental fear, but a physical panic that his body
could not fight off even as his mind stood by and wondered what was happening. There was no choice. He had to go back down into the casino. He threw
the check for fifty thousand into his suitcase. He would just gamble his cash
and chips.

Jordan scooped everything off the bed and stuffed his pockets. He
went out of the room and down the hall into the casino. The real gamblers
were at the tables now, in these early-morning hours. They had made their
business deals, finished their dinners in the gourmet rooms, taken their wives
to the shows and put them to bed or stuck them with dollar chips at the
roulette wheel. Out of traffic. Or they had gotten laid, blown, attended a
necessary civic function. All now free to battle fate. Money in hand, they stood
in the front rank at crap tables. Pit bosses with blank markers waited for them
to run out of chips so they could sign for another grand or two or three. During the coming dark hours men signed away fortunes. Never knowing why.
Jordan looked away to the far end of the casino.

An elegantly royal gray railed enclosure nestled the long oval baccarat
table from the main casino floor. An armed security guard stood at the gate be-

cause the baccarat table dealt mostly in cash, not chips. The green felt table was guarded at each end by high towered chairs. Seated in these chairs were the two laddermen, checking the croupiers and payouts, their hawkish concentration only thinly disguised by the evening dress all casino employees wore inside the baccarat enclosure. The laddermen watched every motion of the three croupiers and pit boss who ran the action. Jordan started walking toward them until he could see the distinct figures of the croupiers in their formal evening dress.

Four Saints in black tie, they sang hosannas to winners, dirges to losers. Handsome men, their motions quick, their charm continental, they graced the game they ruled. But before Jordan could get through the royal gray gate, Cully and Merlyn stepped before him.

Cully said softly, "They only have fifteen minutes to go. Stay out of it." Baccarat closed at 3 A.M.

And then one of the Saints in black tie called out to Jordan, "We're making up the last shoe, Mr. J. A Banker shoe." He laughed. Jordan could see the cards all dumped out on the table, blue-backed, then scooped to be stacked before the shuffle, their inner white pale faces showing.

Jordan said, "How about you two guys coming in with me? I'll put up the money and we'll bet the limit in each chair." Which meant that with the two-thousand limit Jordan would be betting six thousand on each hand.

"Are you crazy?" Cully said. "You can go to hell."

"Just sit there," Jordan said. "I'll give you ten percent of everything your chair wins."

"No," Cully said and walked away from him and leaned against the baccarat railing.

Jordan said, "Merlyn, sit in a chair for me?"

Merlyn the Kid smiled at him and said quietly, "Yeah, I'll sit in the chair."

"You get ten percent," Jordan said.

"Yeah, OK," Merlyn said. They both went through the gate and sat down. Diane had the newly made up shoe, and Jordan sat down in the chair beside her so that he could get the shoe next. Diane bent her head to him.

"Jordy, don't gamble anymore," she said. He didn't bet on her hand as she dealt blue cards out of the shoe. Diane lost, lost her casino's twenty dollars and lost the bank and passed the shoe on to Jordan.

Jordan was busy emptying out all the outside pockets of his Vegas Winner sports jacket. Chips, black and green, hundred-dollar notes. He placed a stack of bills in front of Merlyn's chair six. Then he took the shoe and placed twenty black chips in the Banker's slot. "You too," he said to Merlyn. Merlyn counted twenty hundred-dollar bills from the stack in front of him and placed them on his Banker's slot.

The croupier held up one palm high to halt Jordan's dealing. Looked around the table to see that everyone had made his bet. His palm fell to a beckoning hand, and he sang out to Jordan, "A card for the Player."

Jordan dealt out the cards. One to the croupier, one to himself. Then another one to the croupier and another one to himself. The croupier looked around the table and then threw his two cards to the man betting the highest amount on Player's. The man peeked at his cards cautiously and then smiled and flung his two cards face up. He had a natural, invincible nine. Jordan tossed his cards face up without even looking at them. He had two picture cards. Zero. Bust-out. Jordan passed the shoe to Merlyn. Merlyn passed the shoe on to the next player. For one moment Jordan tried to halt the shoe, but something about Merlyn's face stopped him. Neither of them spoke.

The golden brown box worked itself slowly around the table. It was chopping. Banker won. Then Player. No consecutive wins for either. Jordan riding the Banker all the way, pressing, had lost over ten thousand dollars from his own pile, Merlyn still refusing to bet. Finally Jordan had the shoe once again.

He made his bet, the two-thousand-dollar limit. He reached over into Merlyn's money and stripped off a sheaf of bills and threw them onto the Banker's slot. He noticed briefly that Diane was no longer beside him. Then he was ready. He felt a tremendous surge of power, that he could will the cards to come out of the shoe as he wished them to.

Calmly and without emotion Jordan hit twenty-four straight passes. By the eighth pass the railing around the baccarat table was crowded and every gambler at the table was betting Bank, riding with luck. By the tenth pass the croupier in the money slot reached down and pulled out the special five-hundred-dollar chips. They were a beautiful creamy white threaded with gold.

Cully was pressed against the rail, watching, Diane standing with him. Jordan gave them a little wave. For the first time he was excited. Down at the other end of the table a South American gambler shouted, "Maestro," as Jordan hit his thirteenth pass. And then the table became strangely silent as Jordan pressed on.

He dealt effortlessly from the shoe, his hands seemed to flow. Never once did a card stumble or slip as he passed it out from his hiding place in the wooden box. Never did he accidentally show a card's pale white face. He flipped over his own cards with the same rhythmic movement each time, without looking, letting the head croupier call numbers and hits. When the croupier said, "A card for the Player," Jordan slipped it out easily with no emphasis to make it good or bad. When the croupier called, "A card for the Banker," again Jordan slipped it out smoothly and swiftly, without emotion. Finally going for the twenty-fifth pass, he lost to Player's, the Player's hand being played by the croupier because everyone was betting Bank.

Jordan passed the shoe on to Merlyn, who refused it and passed it on to the next chair. Merlyn, too, had stacks of gold five-hundred-dollar chips in front of him. Since they had won on Bank, they had to pay the five percent house commission. The croupier counted out the commission plaques against their chair numbers. It was over five thousand dollars. Which meant that Jordan had won a hundred thousand dollars on that one hot hand. And every gambler around the table had bailed out.

Both laddermen high up in their chairs were on the phone calling the casino manager and the hotel owner with the bad news. An unlucky night at the baccarat table was one of the few serious dangers to the casino profit margin. Not that it meant anything in the long run, but an eye was always kept on natural disasters. Gronevelt himself came down from his penthouse suite and quietly stepped into the baccarat enclosure, standing in the corner with the pit boss, watching. Jordan saw him out of the corner of his eye and knew who he was, Merlyn had pointed him out one day.

The shoe traveled around the table and remained a coyly Banker's shoe. Jordan made a little money. Then he had the shoe in his hand again.

This time effortlessly and easily, his hands balletic, he accomplished every baccarat player's dream. He ran out the shoe with passes. There were no more cards left. Jordan had stack on stack of white gold chips in front of him.

Jordan threw four of the gold and white chips to the head croupier. "For you, gentlemen," he said.

The baccarat pit boss said, "Mr. Jordan, why don't you just sit here and we'll get all this money turned into a check?"

Jordan stuffed the huge wad of hundred-dollar bills into his jacket, then the black hundred-dollar chips, leaving endless stacks of gold and white five-hundred-dollar chips on the table. "You can count them for me," he said to the pit boss. He stood up to stretch his legs, and then he said casually, "Can you make up another shoe?"

The pit boss hesitated and turned to the casino manager standing with Gronevelt. The casino manager shook his head for a no. He had Jordan tabbed as a degenerate gambler. Jordan would surely stay in Vegas until he lost. But tonight was his hot night. And why buck him on *his* hot night? Tomorrow the cards would fall differently. He could not be lucky forever and then his end would be swift. The casino manager had seen it all before. The house had an infinity of nights and every one of them with the edge, the percentage. "Close the table," the casino manager said.

Jordan bowed his head. He turned to look at Merlyn and said, "Keep track, you get ten percent of your chair's win," and to his surprise he saw a look almost of grief in Merlyn's eyes and Merlyn said, "No."

The money croupiers were counting up Jordan's gold chips and stacking them so that the laddermen, the pit boss and the casino manager could also keep track of their count. Finally they were finished. The pit boss looked up and said with reverence, "You got two hundred and ninety thousand dollars here, Mr. J. You want it all in a check?" Jordan nodded. His inside pockets were still lumpy with other chips, paper money. He didn't want to turn them in.

The other gamblers had left the table and the enclosure when the casino manager said there would not be another shoe. Still the pit boss whispered. Cully had come through the railing and stood beside Jordan, as did Merlyn, the three of them looking like members of some street gang in their Vegas Winner sports coats.

Jordan was really tired now, too tired for the physical exertion of craps and roulette. And blackjack was too slow with its five-hundred-dollar limit. Cully said, "You're not playing anymore. Jesus, I never saw anything like this. You can only go down. You can't get that lucky anymore." Jordan nodded in agreement.

The security guard took trays of Jordan's chips and the signed receipts from the pit boss to the cashier's cage. Diane joined their group and gave Jordan a kiss. They were all tremendously excited. Jordan at that moment felt happy. He really was a hero. And without killing or hurting anyone. So easily. Just by betting a huge amount of money on the turning of cards. And winning.

They had to wait for the check to come back from the cashier's cage. Merlyn said mockingly to Jordan, "You're rich, you can do anything you want."

Cully said, "He has to leave Vegas."

Diane was squeezing Jordan's hand. But Jordan was staring at Gronevelt, standing with the casino manager and the two laddermen, who had come down from their chairs. The four men were whispering together. Jordan said suddenly, "Xanadu Number One, how about dealing up a shoe?"

Gronevelt stepped away from the other men, and his face was suddenly in the full glare of the light. Jordan could see that he was older than he had thought. Maybe about seventy, though ruddy and healthy. He had iron gray hair, thick and neatly combed. His face was redly tanned. His figure was sturdy, not yet willowing away with age. Jordan could see that he had reacted only slightly to being addressed by his telephone code name.

Gronevelt smiled at him. He wasn't angry. But something in him responded to the challenge, brought back his youth, when he had been a degenerate gambler. Now he had made his world safe, his life was under control. He had many pleasures, many duties, some dangers but very rarely a pure thrill. It would be sweet to taste one again, and besides, he wanted to see just how far Jordan would go, what made him tick.

Gronevelt said softly, "You have a check for two hundred ninety grand coming from the cage, right?"

Jordan nodded.

Gronevelt said, "I'll have them make up a shoe. We play one hand. Double or nothing. But you have to bet Player's, not Banker's."

Everyone in the baccarat enclosure seemed stunned. The croupiers looked at Gronevelt in amazement. Not only was he risking a huge sum of money, contrary to all casino laws, he was also risking his casino license if the State Gaming Commission got tough about this bet. Gronevelt smiled at them. "Shuffle those cards," he said. "Make up the shoe."

At that moment the pit boss came through the gate of the enclosure and handed Jordan the yellow oblong ragged-edged piece of paper that was the check. Jordan looked at it for just one moment, then put it down on the Player's slot and said smiling to Gronevelt, "You got a bet."

Jordan saw Merlyn back away and lean up against the royal gray railing. Merlyn again was studying him intently. Diane took a few steps to the side in bewilderment. Jordan was pleased with their astonishment. The only thing he didn't like was betting against his own luck. He hated the idea of dealing the cards out of the shoe and betting against his own hand. He turned to Cully.

"Cully, deal the cards for me," he said.

But Cully shrank away, horrified. Then Cully glanced at the croupier, who had dumped the cards from the canister under the table and was stacking them for the shuffle. Cully seemed to shudder before he turned to face Jordan.

"Jordy, it's a sucker bet," Cully said softly as if he didn't want anyone to hear. He shot a quick glance at Gronevelt, who was staring at him. But he went on. "Listen, Jordy, the Bank has a two and a half percent edge on the Player all the time. Every hand that's dealt. That's why the guy who bets Bank has to pay five percent commission. But now the house has Bank. On a bet like this the commission doesn't mean anything. It's better to have the two and a half percent edge in the odds on how the hand comes out. Do you understand that, Jordy?" Cully kept his voice in an even tone. As if he were reasoning with a child.

But Jordan laughed. "I know that," he said. He almost said that he had counted on that, but it wasn't really true. "How about it, Cully, deal the cards for me. I don't want to go against my luck."

The croupier shuffled the huge deck in sections, put them all together. He held out the blank yellow plastic card for Jordan to cut. Jordan looked at Cully. Cully backed away without another word. Jordan reached out and cut the deck. Everyone now advanced toward the edge of the table. Gamblers outside the enclosure, seeing the new shoe tried to get in and were barred by the security guard. They started to protest. But suddenly they fell silent. They crowded around outside the railing. The croupier turned up the first card he slid out of the shoe. It was a seven. He slid seven cards out of the shoe, burying them in the slot. Then he shoved the shoe across the table to Jordan. Jordan sat down in his chair. Suddenly Gronevelt spoke. "Just one hand," he said.

The croupier held up his arm and said carefully, "Mr. J., you are betting Player's, you understand? The hand I turn up will be the hand you are betting on. The hand you turn up as the Banker will be the hand you are betting against."

Jordan smiled. "I understand."

The croupier hesitated and said, "If you prefer, I can deal from the shoe."

"No," Jordan said. "That's OK." He was really excited. Not only for the money but because of the power flowing from him to cover the people and the casino.

The croupier said, holding up his palm, "One card to me, one card to yourself. Then one card to me and one card to yourself. Please." He paused dramatically, held up his hand nearest Jordan and said, "A card for the Player."

Jordan swiftly and effortlessly slid the blue-backed cards from the slotted shoe. His hands, again extraordinarily graceful, did not falter. They traveled the exact distance across the green felt to the waiting hands of the croupier, who quickly flipped them face up and then stood stunned by the invincible nine. Jordan couldn't lose. Cully behind him let out a roar, "Natural nine."

For the first time Jordan looked at his two cards before turning them over. He was actually playing Gronevelt's hand and so hoping for losing cards. Now he smiled and turned up his Banker's cards. "Natural nine," he said. And so it was. The bet was a standoff. A draw. Jordan laughed. "I'm too lucky," he said.

Jordan looked up at Gronevelt. "Again?" he asked.

Gronevelt shook his head. "No," he said. And then to the croupier and the pit boss and the laddermen. "Close down the table." Gronevelt walked out of the enclosure. He had enjoyed the bet, but he knew enough not to stretch life to a dangerous limit. One thrill at a time. Tomorrow he would have to square the unorthodox bet with the Gaming Commission. And he would have to have a long talk with Cully the next day. Maybe he had been wrong about Cully.

Like bodyguards, Cully, Merlyn and Diane surrounded Jordan and herded him out of the baccarat enclosure. Cully picked up the yellow jagged-edged check from the green felt table and stuffed it into Jordan's left breast pocket and then zipped it up to make it safe. Jordan was laughing with delight. He looked at his watch. It was 4 A.M. The night was almost over. "Let's have coffee and breakfast," he said. He led them all to the coffee shop with its yellow upholstered booths.

When they were seated, Cully said, "OK, he's got close to four hundred grand. We have to get him out of here."

"Jordy, you have to leave Vegas. You're rich. You can do anything you want." Jordan saw that Merlyn was watching him intently. Damn, that was getting irritating.

Diane touched Jordan on his arm and said, "Don't play anymore. Please." Her eyes were shining. And suddenly Jordan realized that they were acting as if he had escaped or been pardoned from some sort of exile. He felt their happiness for him, and to repay it he said, "Now let me stake you guys, you too, Diane. Twenty grand apiece."

They were all a little stunned. Then Merlyn said, "I'll take the money when you get on that plane leaving Vegas."

Diane said, "That's the deal, you have to get on the plane, you have to leave here. Right, Cully?"

Cully was not that enthusiastic. What was wrong with taking the twenty grand now, then putting him on the plane? The gambling was over. They couldn't jinx him. But Cully had a guilty conscience and couldn't speak his mind. And he knew this would probably be the last romantic gesture of his life. To show true friendship, like those two assholes Merlyn and Diane. Didn't they know Jordan was crazy? That he could sneak away from them and lose the whole fortune?

Cully said, "Listen, we have to keep him away from the tables. We got to guard him and hogtie him until that plane leaves tomorrow for LA."

Jordan shook his head, "I'm not going to Los Angeles. It has to be farther away. Anyplace in the world." He smiled at them. "I've never been out of the United States."

"We need a map," Diane said. "I'll call the bell captain. He can get us a map of the world. Bell captains can do anything." She picked up the phone on the ledge of the booth and made the call. The bell captain had once gotten her an abortion on ten minutes' notice.

The table became covered with platters of food, eggs, bacon, pancakes and small breakfast steaks. Cully had ordered like a prince.

While they were eating, Merlyn said, "You sending the checks to your kids?" He didn't look at Jordan, who studied him quietly, then shrugged. He really hadn't thought about it. For some reason he was angry with Merlyn for asking the question, but just for a moment.

"Why should he give the money to his kids?" Cully said. "He took care of them pretty good. Next thing you'll be saying he should send the checks to his wife." He laughed as if it were beyond the realm of possibility, and again Jordan was a little angry. He had given a wrong picture of his wife. She was better than that.

Diane lit a cigarette. She was just drinking coffee, and she had a slight reflective smile on her face. For just one moment her hand brushed Jordan's sleeve in some act of complicity or understanding as if he too were a woman and she were allying herself with him. At that moment the bell captain came personally with an atlas. Jordan reached into a pocket and gave him a hundred-dollar bill. The bell captain almost ran away before Cully, outraged, could say anything. Diane started to unfold the atlas.

Merlyn the Kid was still intent on Jordan. "What does it feel like?" he asked.

"Great," Jordan said. He smiled, amused at their passion.

Cully said, "You go near a crap table and we're gonna climb all over you. No shit." He slammed his hand down on the table. "No more."

Diane had the map spread out over the table, covering the messy dishes of half-eaten food. They pored over it, except Jordan. Merlyn found a town in Africa. Jordan said calmly he didn't want to go to Africa.

Merlyn was leaning back, not studying the map with the others. He was watching Jordan. Cully surprised them all when he said, "Here's a town in Portugal I know, Mercedas." They were surprised because for some reason they had never thought of him as living in any place but Vegas. Now suddenly he knew a town in Portugal.

"Yeah, Mercedas," Cully said. "Nice and warm. Great beach. It has a small casino with a fifty-dollar top limit and the casino is only open six hours a night. You can gamble like a big shot and never even get hurt. How does that sound to you, Jordan? How about Mercedas?"

"OK," Jordan said.

Diane began to plan the itinerary. "Los Angeles over the North Pole to London. Then a flight to Lisbon. Then I guess you go by car to Mercedas."

"No," Cully said. "There's planes to some big towns near there, I forget which. And make sure he gets out of London fast. Their gambling clubs are murder."

Jordan said, "I have to get some sleep."

Cully looked at him. "Jesus, yeah, you look like shit. Go up to your room and conk out. We'll make all the arrangements. We'll wake you up before your plane leaves. And don't try coming back down into the casino. Me and the Kid will be guarding the joint."

Diane said, "Jordan, you'll have to give me some money for the tickets." Jordan took a huge wad of hundred-dollar bills from his pocket and put them on the table. Diane carefully counted out thirty of them.

"It can't cost more than three thousand first class all the way, could it?" she asked. Cully shook his head.

"Tops, two thousand," Cully said. "Book his hotels too." He picked the rest of the bills up from the table and stuffed them back into Jordan's pocket.

Jordan got up and said, trying for the last time, "Can I stake you now?"

Merlyn said quickly, "No, it's bad luck, not until you get on the plane." Jordan saw the look of pity and affection on Merlyn's face. Then Merlyn said, "Get some sleep. When we call you, we'll help you pack."

"OK," Jordan said and left the coffee shop and went down the corridor that led to his room. He knew Cully and Merlyn had followed him to where the corridor started, to make sure that he didn't stop to gamble. He vaguely remembered Diane kissing him good-bye, and even Cully had gripped his shoulder with affection. Who would have thought that a guy like Cully had ever been in Portugal.

When Jordan entered his room, he double bolted the door and put the interior chain on it. Now he was absolutely secure. He sat down on the edge of the bed. And suddenly he was terribly angry. He had a headache and his body was trembling uncontrollably.

How dare they feel affection for him? How dare they show him compassion? They had no reason—no reason. He had never complained. He had never sought their affection. He had never encouraged any love from them. He did not desire it. It disgusted him.

He slumped back against the pillows, so tired he could not undress. The jacket, lumpy with chips and money, was too uncomfortable, and he wriggled out of it and let it drop to the carpeted floor. He closed his eyes and thought he would fall asleep instantly, but again that mysterious terror electrified his body, forcing him upward. He couldn't control the violent trembling of his legs and arms.

The darkness of the room began to run with tiny ghosts of dawn. Jordan thought he might call his wife and tell her of the fortune he had won. But knew he could not. And could not tell his children. Or any of his old friends. In the last gray shreds of this night there was not a person in the world he wished to dazzle with his good luck. There was not one person in the world to share his joy in winning this great fortune.

He got up from the bed to pack. He was rich and must go to Mercedas. He began to weep; an overwhelming grief and rage drowned out everything. He saw the gun lying in the suitcase and then his mind was confused. All the gambling he had done in the last sixteen hours tumbled through his brain, the dice flashing winning numbers, the blackjack tables with their winning hands, the oblong baccarat table strewn with the pale white faces of turned dead cards. Shadowing those cards, a croupier, in black tie and dazzling white shirt, held up a palm, calling softly, "A card for the Player."

In one smooth, swift motion Jordan scooped the gun up in his right hand. His mind icily clear. And then, as surely and swiftly as he had dealt his fabulous twenty-four winning hands in baccarat, he swung the muzzle up into the soft line of his neck and pulled the trigger. In that eternal second he felt a sweet release from terror. And his last conscious thought was that he would never go to Mercedas.

from The Cincinnati Kid

BY RICHARD JESSUP

Author of what is probably regarded as *the* classic poker novel, Richard Jessup was a one-time dealer in a Harlem gambling house who turned to writing after a ten-year period as a merchant seaman. What has given the *Cincinnati Kid* its staying power is its fine portraiture of the "rambling-gambling card-playing life," both of its community of players and of the ritual of the game they follow. The novel's prose is cleanly dealt, with a taut, spare presentation of two exceptional gamblers dedicated to their "pure art" and drawn to a memorable, inevitable showdown.

Cardplayers have chafed a bit about the improbability of the final hand, which, among other things, Lancey would have folded before drawing. For a full account of why see A. Alvarez, *The Biggest Game in Town* (which includes the best written account of the World Series of Poker). However, that scene, particularly as acted by Edward G. Robinson (Lancey) and Steve McQueen (the Kid) in the Norman Jewison film (1965) has a power that goes beyond cards itself, suggesting that, wherever we strive for excellence, there is a nemesis out there, waiting. In his introduction to the 1985 edition, Jerome Charyn captures some of the book's lasting appeal: "We are all players of one sort or another . . . There's always a Lancey out there to steal our pants and destroy our pants and destroy our most secret desires. Defeated like the Cincinnati Kid, we wait, wait, wait until the dream comes back to us, a bit at a time."

In the first selection below Jessup sets up the Kid's introduction to gamble and the progress of his card education: the second takes up the showdown with Lancey as it intensifies.

From thirteen to sixteen he began to *feel* the cards. They became more than just instruments of making money for the movies or a new pair of shoes, which was a very common device used by all of his friends. Out of these quiet, very desperate little penny games in alleys and on the decks of abandoned barges, on wintry street corners, the raw shoeshine boys' poker began to grow and he began to grow with it and when he had grown old enough, he began to hope there was a way open for him; and once he had discovered his feel for cards was real and genuine, an urgency began to rise in him and gain strength.

Out of those volatile games of poker The Kid gleaned by misplay and nerving experience the differences between winning and losing certain basic fundamentals that aid in a winning hand of stud poker. From Jo-Jo, a hulking Negro newspaper route boy, he learned never to stay unless the cards he held, including his hole card, could beat the board; from a bargeman, painfully losing his stake of twenty-seven dollars, he learned never to stay against an open pair, unless he could beat the pair or any possibility of a third card his opponent might have in the hole; from others he learned, sometimes by accident and luck, but mostly because he was growing and remembering every time he would lose, never to raise a pair unless the amount in the pot was at least five or six times the amount of the bet, including the raise; never to stay with two small pairs when there is a pair showing with extra cards higher than yours that can be paired with a hole card, or that can produce three of a kind. He learned about check and raise, and how to avoid it, and how to use it, and how and when to check a cinch; he learned how and when to buy a pot by betting ten and twenty times the amount in the pot; he learned about sticking to patterns of play that might lull his opponent into thinking he was going to stick to that pattern, and then reverse, only to have Bill O'Day spot his scheme and reverse on him and wipe him out. He learned other things too: never to win too much from a stranger who was bigger and stronger and could beat his tail and take all of the money. But this only happened once. The next time it was tried, he left the man half dead in an empty lot.

On his sixteenth birthday he started running himself ragged trying to figure out why there was a chance for him with cards and why it appealed to him; he made a serious effort to find out and it was not too long, because he really pressed this thing, before he discovered that a betting man with an honest dollar to back his judgment on a subject was equal to anyone, anywhere, any time, and that from time immemorial there had been men who would bet, rich men with poor, smart men with stupid men, black men with white men. The size of a man's bet was not a significant factor, nor what he bet on, nor how he bet. It was the idea of a man backing his judgment with something of value and taking the chance of losing. He took his pursuit further and discovered that businessmen were betting on their judgment, and young couples getting married were betting on their judgment, and that a stud game was the same thing, only it was a very narrow fraternity and did not contribute anything to society, or to the economy, or to the development of a town, or a man, or anything at all, except that it was a way for a man to go, and a way a man might have of making his way. He saw, accurately, that there was no difference between the stud man and the stocks and bonds man, and when he saw that he could dedicate his life to learning stocks and bonds, or real estate, and that it would still be his judgment he would be backing with a bet, he turned back to cards because he had been with cards for so long a time and had a head start. And then he recognized that he had this truly fine feeling for them.

On his seventeenth birthday he moved across the river to Kentucky and began learning the difference between playing cards and being a rambling-gambling man. It was still a question of a man backing his judgment and making his bet and winning or losing. But there was more subtlety in the mores and patterns of behavior amongst the professionals than he had ever known with just pick-up games. While he had been playing winning poker on his side of the river, it was strictly social poker and not professional at all. Professional card men, he saw, were really no different from any other card players except in their attitude. It was their whole life and nothing got in the way of it.

Moving into this life The Kid began to learn, first, the rules governing conduct of the rambling-gambling man with his fellows. The most outstanding characteristic The Kid soon discovered was their need for one another. It was never a problem for a rambling-gambling man to locate a game and sit down; it was something else again to find keen competition, honest competition of a standard and excellence of play that astounded The Kid when he first observed it, and touched it.

This need was demonstrated to The Kid in one of his first games across the East River (which is what card men called the Ohio River, with the Missouri being the West River, and the Mississippi called simply, The River) when one of the players had lost everything and made the general statement to the table that he was Tap City. All of the players present gave the loser several dollars, and when The Kid asked why, being a hardhead about money, he was told that Tap City money was for the rambling-gambling man to get on his feet again.

The Kid, moving into this quiet, all-night world of card men who could be found in any city along the banks of the three rivers, learned that card men never loaned money to each other. A man's stake had to be raised outside of the fraternity and sources of supply were the state secrets for each man.

Slowly, adding on, there in the poker parlors of Covington and New-port, Kentucky, in the hall bedroom games, in the kitchen games, moving from the garage games to hotel games, moving from the penny-and-three tables when he had built up his stake, to the nickel-and-dime action, he felt the difference in pressure and learned the difference in play as the stakes grew, from the quarter-and-a-half, to the one dollar no-limit. His resolve hardened, gained muscle, fleshed out, getting firm and strong; and then after several years of this, he began to gain poise with confidence that he might really have found a place for himself. In a little while, before he was twenty, he was to become The Cincinnati Kid.

He went through endless nights and long, long days of cards, and over the years, like many other natural card men, he soon dismissed blackjack as being a game of short bluff and limited scope. He tried faro, but there was not enough in it for him. He gave bridge a try, but didn't like the idea of partners. Once he settled into dominoes, but soon gave it up in raw disgust. He found a heady simplicity in craps, but still there was something in him that wanted a game where there was more personal control, and where it was he and he alone playing cards and not giving it all over to luck, or odds, as it was with horses and craps or roulette. So, finally, instinctively, The Kid gravitated to poker; first to draw poker and then he found stud to be the game that was right as rain.

By the time he was twenty-one, he was a full rambling-gambling man, a three-river man, which was to say that he had been to and played in all of the important places for a card man to play. From Jolly's Omaha Card Club on the Missouri, to Spriigi's Emporium in Wheeling on the Ohio, down to Big Nig's in Memphis on the Mississippi, he was known as The Cincinnati Kid, a comer, with a way about him, and he was welcomed into any game from New Or-leans to the big steel payday games in Pittsburgh.

The Kid was on and off the edge of his stake many times during his early build-up and schooling, and it was noticed that he had begun to get flashy with his card playing. It took Big Nig to teach The Kid a hard lesson, when, as they were playing and The Kid had been getting hot cards all night and betting everything strong, feeling that he could not miss, Big Nig cooled him off with no-stay. Big Nig had sat there and turned over seventy-three hands of cards before he bet, and in that time, The Kid cooled off and Big Nig took him. It was in a sense the last time The Kid took a lesson and it straight-ened him out and he was not so flashy any more, but quiet, and when he did not crybaby about the way Big Nig had taken him, it was forgotten and he was then fully accepted as a member of the fraternity. Then he truly became a three river man.

He had never gone east of Pittsburgh and for the last few years had been using St. Louis as home base. And it was during a game in East St. Louis in the back of Victoria's Bar, with the game moving from there to a St. Louis hotel and then out of the hotel to the drawing room of a millionaire candy manufacturer who was a good stud man and who did not want to break up the game just because he was on his way home to Cincinnati, that The Kid made his first trip back to the bottoms.

And this led him naturally across the river for a visit to the old haunts of Covington and Newport, where, out of action, he had seen Lancey Hodges, and the feeling had settled over him and he knew that Lancey was the man to play. There didn't seem to be any reason for it. It was just there.

Lancey Hodges was a thin man, short, with a banker's look about him, wearing a vest and an iron-gray summer suit, thin wispy hair brushed back over a gleaming skull, dead-white delicate fingers handling cards with the patience of a surgeon and with a surgeon's complete control and knowledge. His stake had been low or he would have sat down then.

Now he knew it was better that he hadn't. Lancey had only been a face to him, a rambling-gambling man who had drifted into the parlor of Miriam's kitchen game and was playing his cards. It did not take him long to learn who he was. This was Lancey Hodges. From Vegas to Brooklyn, Miami Beach to Covington, St. Louis to New Orleans, Lancey Hodges was The Man.

It was Miriam, a woman with a great talent for scolding, and a bitterness about the way life had treated her that made her dippy on the subject of faith and promise, who told The Kid, in a flat, hard way, who Lancey was and what he represented.

"He come nice and clean into the world from a home to Savannah where everything's gotta be cleaned up and smoothed over, because that's the way things is been since they got there in town, with all that money and all, and all he's gotta do is jest sit on it and hold it and what's left of everything will make its way to him, and he don't care for nothing but diddling with cards. I knowed Lancey from back yonder. I see him to Nig's in Memphis and down to Yeller's in Noorlins, back yonder when they was shunting booze inta the country. Him. Sheet! Nothing but a comer like you, Kid, only he liked wimmen too. Always got to feel a leg, that's the kind he is. Oooeeeh! That sonsabitch is cold. I seen him gut a feller with a furth card and rattle him s'bad, the feller quit and got up and pissed red in the john and went square. They ain't but one way to ferk with the kind of man Lancey Hodges is, Kid, and that' to have a tree-mendous stake, and then sit there and wait fer his stomik to get him wild, then gut him. But you won't do nothin' with a little money. You got to be holding *wild* money. An' and I know you busted to the edge. But you growd some, Cincinnata. You kin make his stomik ulcer bleed, but I ain't got much faith in nothin' that will take him. He's liable to bleed to death right on a flush hand before he give up to you. He likes being The Man. But, now you looka here, at this here boy Lancey's sittin' with now, that nigger giving him a run, an ol' field hand up from Tennessee, ain't he got a way with cards? Well, this nigger will go down, but he's got some ride coming to him yit, so if you can raise your stake and get off'n the edge, you kin sit down with him, but you'll have to be quicker than three-four days. Lancey is going to gut this nigger. But I swear, Kid, I like to see that nigger make a deck move. Them hands is like fly-wheels on an old car. Makes me think of The Shooter, way he guns 'em out. Go on, Kid, you got time. Hustle somethin' and raise your load, and come on back."

But there was no time. Lancey reached the Negro field hand from Tennessee the next day and broke him and sent him out into the streets to shine shoes. And in that time, The Kid did something he had never done before and had never done since: he conned his way into a game in a first-class country club, not letting anyone know he was The Cincinnati Kid and a rambling-gambling man, and he got out of the game several thousand dollars clean. When he got back to Miriam's, Lancey had busted the field hand, who had re-fused Tap City money, which made the Negro stand high in the fraternity, and Lancey was gone, down to Big Nig's, Miriam said, and The Kid had gone after him.

"Don' mess 'round with The Man jest yit, Kid," Big Nig had warned him. "Jest learn a little mo' poker. Right now, Lancey'd take skin and leave you dried out like a sucked orange in the sun, juice all gone."

But it had worked on him. And after going on down to Yeller's in New Orleans and learning that Lancey had taken one of the cruise ships and was not in the country, The Kid stood on the levee and looked out over the river and for the first time in his life he began to think further than the hands of cards on the table in a game and he began to try to pierce the inner core of the science of playing stud poker. He had the art. The Shooter told him so when The Kid returned to St. Louis and described his feelings about Lancey to the big man.

"Kid," The Shooter had told him over beer in the Glassways Beer Garden that overlooked the river, "you're one of the truly great artists. Before you was twenty I heard about you even before you knew I was alive. Word comes fast on the three rivers when talent shows. It was all over about the Cincinnati Kid that was playing Miriam's and the parlors in Covey and Newport! Art! Whew! Man, you got the pure art. But you're going to need more than that if you sit down with Lancey Hodges. He's a dead eye, no nerves at all, and steel-minded, and Kid, *he knows.*"

The Kid lacked the depth and he was at a loss as to how he could change that. But he knew he had to. It might have been that The Kid was a fast ball pitcher facing the home run hitter and lacked a curve ball to get him out of the inning. It might have been that The Kid was a natural welter and won-dering if the extra pounds blowing him up to a middle weight would burden him. It might have been that The Kid was a brilliant designer of bridges and lacked the engineering. But he wasn't a fast ball pitcher, or a heavy welter, or a poor engineer. He was a three river man. A stud man. A member of the elite, and for him, Lancey Hodges was the way to go home free.

It didn't take long for the word to get around. They could all see that he was restless and they could see how he was experimenting. It was beyond protocol for them to ask why he was playing in such a probing way, but it didn't take long for them to find out, and they heard it all, his problems, his frustrations, his confusions, his questions, some of the same problems that had bothered them, or they had asked the same questions about themselves, when later they might find The Shooter at the Glassways and listen to his progress report.

The word began to spread beyond St. Louis and traveled down the River to Big Nig's and to Yeller's and west to Vegas. The Cincinnati Kid's itch to sit down with Lancey Hodges became the talk.

Unofficially then, The Shooter had become The Kid's mentor and this too was strictly defined by protocol. No one offered suggestions to The Kid di-rectly, this would have been an affront to The Shooter; protocol demanded they first speak to The Shooter. The Shooter would then rule on their ideas as being sound or unsound for The Kid.

Unofficial too was the relationship between The Kid and The Shooter. The Kid had not asked for and The Shooter had not offered assistance. But it was regarded as high honor and a very great compliment for anyone in The Kid's class to ask The Shooter for help in sitting down with Lancey Hodges. And The Shooter responded, wearing his new role as an elder of the elite gravely.

The Shooter knew. He remembered Whistling Sam Magee and he knew. It was not a small thing.

From then on the game was whispering silent and charged, and the play went rapidly. The Kid began to loosen up and show how far he had come and they all saw this and were secretly proud of him. He began to creep up on Lancey, stealing pots away from him with third and fourth card bets that were shrewd and masterful, never too much to chase Lancey, not enough to show over-confidence, forcing Lancey to bust and then dragging the pot.

Lancey was not the only one who was feeling the pressure The Cincinnati Kid was putting on. Carmody lost it all in three hours of play, a total of seventeen hundred dollars. He backed away from the table refusing Tap City because everyone knew that his woman had plenty. Everyone at the table was a little sorry to see Carmody break out because he had provoked excitement often in a game that was fast becoming a duel of pressure and psychology and that was so pure that the finesse of the playing was lost to all except The Shooter, Lady Fingers, Lancey and The Kid. The Shooter had gained a respectable share of the winnings with over twelve hundred and now, comfortable that he had asserted himself in the game with the big men, began to lay off, buying cards with no-stay, and only coming out when he had them wired.

With Lancey Hodges, The Cincinnati Kid tried no tricks. He felt the urgency of the game rising in him and looking at his stake and remembering the hands, he felt for the first time that he might have a chance. And Lancey was reacting. He could see the difference in Lancey's play and The Kid knew that Lancey was taking him seriously. And there was a change in the way The Shooter was calling the cards. The Kid had an absolutely perfect ear for such things. Win, lose or draw, he knew he would come out of the game with the respect of The Shooter and anyone else who was interested.

They ran through nineteen deals with one or both of them turning their cards over, no-stay, before they both caught hole cards and The Kid opened for a hundred. It was two-thirty. The Kid went in on the third card with a three-hundred-dollar bet and three aces. Lancey folded. He went in once more, five hands later, with a two hundred dollar bet and three tens and Lancey folded again.

The third time they locked horns, The Kid knew that Lancey had four kings and let himself be chased and dropped six hundred. But Lancey knew this too and so did The Shooter and the others, and it did not count. There was a long dry spell when they turned their cards over and played no-stay with either The Kid or Lancey opening for fifty or a hundred and the other one folding.

Then quickly in rapid succession they played honest stud poker for nearly ten hands in a row. They played it straight, no bluffing, no one chasing the other out, and they just played and bet the cards, a slow form of showdown poker, with very large bets and no real interest since there was no real argument about who had what. Out of this The Kid came on very strong and picked up nine hundred. He looked down at his money. He knew that there was about five thousand in his table stake. He was in good position now. He settled with the urgency and began to ease up and felt that it would not be very long now, and with his money, he could go in on any play and stand up to Lancey.

They were both getting tired now, both of them were making frequent trips to the bathroom and they both had taken to their drinks. The Kid sipped his brandy and coffee and Lancey sipped his crème de menthe frappé through a straw and then cracked the ice in his teeth. They had both removed their jackets and shoes and Lancey, who suffered from constipation, was sitting on a pillow.

The Shooter called a halt at seven. "I break," he said. "Sitting here dealing ain't like playing. No real incentive or interest, know what I mean, gents? I gotta eat and sleep. If you wanta go on playing, I'll call Lady Fingers."

"Well, I ain't sleepy," The Kid said. "But I am hungry." He looked up at Lancey for approval.

"I am too, Kid," Lancey said quickly. "Hungry, I mean. Suppose we take a break and see to some breakfast?"

"Good enough," The Kid said.

"Gents," The Shooter said with a formality in his voice that had characterized his behavior all the time of the game, "the food is on me. We can stretch our legs and go over to Victoria's, or we can stay here in the hotel, which has some very fine food."

"Would Victoria be open this early, Shooter?" Lancey asked.

"She told me she would be open anytime we needed anything for the game. Them was her words."

"Wouldn't there be a gang over there?" The Kid asked.

"That wouldn't bother me, Kid," Lancey said.

"Then let's get some air, Lancey, if you want to, I mean? If it's okay with you."

"Fine-fine, Kid. Sure-sure," Lancey said in his usual brisk way, smiling quickly.

"I'll call, get her to have things ready when we get there," The Shooter said, standing and stretching.

"Victoria has a place down to Arkansas that she gets special hams and bacon and sausage," The Kid said pleasantly. "And country fresh eggs."

"I like that," Lancey said. "There isn't anything like fresh eggs and sausage and milk after a night of working."

"I buy that," The Kid said.

"Uh-huh."

While they waited for The Shooter to make the call to Victoria, and while Corrigan and Old Lady Fingers were awakened and invited to come with them for breakfast, Lancey stood at the window looking down into the early morning busy street.

"I hate St. Louis in the summer," Lancey said to The Kid.

"Oh?"

"The heat."

"I don't mind it," The Kid said.

"Cincinnati, huh?" Lancey said.

"Born and raised." The Kid walked over to the second window and stood there, tall, skinny, a little humped over in the shoulders looking down into the street.

"I suppose you know I'm from the South. Savannah. Even so, I can't stand the heat," Lancey said.

The Kid remembered Miriam's description of Lancey, but said nothing. He listened politely as Lancey continued, learning a little more about this brittle little man who played poker with such control and ease and did not ruffle, and who looked so much like a banker or a small-town doctor.

"I like Miami. It's beautiful down there. And they have some beautiful hotels. Beautiful." Lancey turned and looked at The Kid. "You been down?"

"Not yet," The Kid replied. "But I heard a lot about it."

"Lovely," Lancey said. "Really. Ought to try it sometime, Kid. Lot of room down there."

The Kid nodded his head, in acknowledgment of the plain offer that Lancey would not ill consider it if The Kid moved into Miami and the big games that came with the season while Lancey had it staked off.

"I been thinking about Vegas—" The Kid said.

"Now that's nice," Lancey said. "Vegas."

"Uh-huh, I heard."

"A little wearing on the nerves, though. Can't ever get enough sleep in that town. So much going on. Action everywhere you turn. You lose the feel of the cards when you're in so much action day in, day out."

The Kid nodded.

"But the scenery is very calming. Big, great big flats—the desert you know—and mountains. Nights are cool. Wonderful floor shows."

"Is that a fact," The Kid said politely.

"Get all the big Hollywood stars there to entertain. I've seen them all, Danny Thomas, Judy Garland, Bob Hope, Sinatra."

"Sounds good."

"And like I say, lotta action. Anything you want."

"I'm a stud man," The Kid said, stating a fact.

"Well—I am *too*. But I like to lay off once in a while and try craps. Nothing serious—" Lancey said with a quick, fleeting smile.

"Oh, I do *that,*" The Kid said. "But nothing serious. I shoot a little casino."

"Uh-huh."

"Yeah. And sometimes I get careless and buck some twenty-one."

"Uh-huh."

"I dint see Big Nig, did you?"

"No. But he could still come," Lancey said. "Which one was your woman—when we took the break last night?"

"None of them," The Kid said. "We just quit each other."

"Oh."

"Yeah."

"Too bad."

"She wanted it that way."

"I see," Lancey said softly, and then glancing sideways at The Kid. "You burning?"

"Me? Naw! But she was nice," The Kid said with a rare smile and a shrug of his shoulders. "How about yourself?"

"I don't look for a fixed thing any more. I just pick up a nice thing and when I'm away from the cards and the action, I enjoy it and—let it wear itself out."

"That's all right," The Kid said.

"It's a good way," Lancey said.

"Personally," The Kid said, "I always wanted a little more than just something to hold onto, and jazz a little, if you know what I mean."

Lancey looked at him, but did not speak.

"Like I had a little action once down to New Orleans, to Yeller's. There was this big pay off game on a ship—"

Lancey smiled knowingly. "I know them games. They're very nice games."

"So!" The Kid said. "I got to know this mate, that's one of the officers, and he had been a sailor a long time and all, and he told me when he went into a port he never hung around the waterfront with the other sailors, but got up-town, see, and met some woman and moved in with her for as long as he was there, with all the comforts of home and play the radio, come home after each day's work and all. It's like that with me, in a way."

"That's very interesting, Kid," Lancey said, watching The Kid, turned now, to face him.

"Well, that's the way things are."

"Sure-sure, I understand. Well, you're a lot younger than I am, Kid, don't forget that," Lancey said with a truly warm smile.

"A man can't change his nut."

"Nooo, a man can't do that."

"Things work out a certain way."

"They do."

"And you can't mess around with them."

"It is not healthy at all."

"I was hoping Christian would run with me, and wouldn't try to make a big deal out of it."

"Did she try?" Lancey asked after a pause, looking out of the window.

The Kid took a deep breath. "Yeah," he said, letting the air come out slowly. "She tried. But a man can't change his way, because the way I see it a man's lucky he's got something going for him that he can hold onto."

"That's very interesting."

"She dint understand how it was with me and—" The Kid stopped short and did not go on.

"Between us?" Lancey said warmly and very gently.

"There ain't," The Kid said clearly, "but a few people, I guess, that would understand."

"No, not many outside of all who knows us, me and you."

"Yeah, I figure."

"Kid," Lancey said, "you the best stud man I've seen in thirty-five years of action. You know that?"

"I figured I'm good, but—well, thank you, though, Lancey."

"And I'm glad we had this little talk, and all," Lancey said. "So then I know we can be friends regardless what happens and things come out."

"Okay," The Kid said. "I dint think you was coming in at me like a grudge match."

Lancey grinned. "No room for any kind of emotion in a fair game of stud." He jingled a few coins in his pocket and looked out of the window. "I learned that a long time ago, when I was a young guy cutting the deal now and then and making my way. I saw the Dempsey-Tunney fights. That Tunney. He never got mad one time. But Jack was mad all the time. Jack lost the fight, I think, because he was mad and Tunney wasn't."

"Fighters are famous for being cold about it," The Kid said. "That's why using their fists in a street fight is a felony. They're cold and know what to do. A regular person like you or me wouldn't have a chance."

The Kid noticed that Lancey had not once brushed his fingers since they had taken the break, or at any time since they had been talking. And then he wondered if there was some nervous habit to which he was addicted and that he was unaware of, and then he realized that he was presuming that Lancey Hodges was unaware of his brushing his fingers together. He did not think so, but then it wasn't for him to say. He would not take the habit seriously.

"Well, maybe I'll see you down in Miami, Kid," Lancey said, turning to see who had opened the door, and seeing Lady Fingers enter the room, her hair in a handkerchief, her eyes a little red and puffy, wearing a plain skirt and blouse. She went immediately to The Shooter's chair and sat down. Corrigan followed her in with fresh coffee and a double shot of brandy for The Kid and a fresh crème de menthe frappé for Lancey.

"Yeah," The Kid replied. "And maybe I'll see you in Vegas."

Lancey smiled. "Might work out that way."

"Fine," The Kid half nodded and smiled.

They both turned from the windows and returned to the table.

"Where's The Shooter?" Lancey asked Lady Fingers.

"Taking a shower in my room. He'll be right in, Lancey."

The Cincinnati Kid and Lancey Hodges each took a turn in the bathroom where they washed, and The Kid gave himself a quick shave, and then they both sat down at the table, sipping their drinks, and watched Old Lady Fingers pick up the old deck of cards The Shooter had left on the table. She rippled them, shuffled them and displayed her ease with the deck and both Lancey and The Kid knew she was good and appreciated watching her.

"You're still good, Fingers," Lancey said. "Not as good as the old days down to Hattiesburg, and Baton Rouge and New Orleans, but still good."

"Getting crippled up, Lancey," she said in a tired voice.

She played with the cards beautifully and both The Kid and Lancey knew she was not showing off or bragging, but she was playing with the cards and nothing else.

"Yeah!" Lady Fingers said explosively. "There aren't many of the old gang left. Me and you, Shooter, Yeller, Miriam." She stopped. "Did you hear that Sam passed over to the other side?"

Lancey remained perfectly still. "No," he said, watching Old Lady Fingers. "No, I didn't know."

"Year ago or so," she said. "I just happen to be passing through, making a little money playing bridge with Countess von Frankenberg—"

"Is *she* still alive?" Lancey asked.

"And still losing," Lady Fingers said. She looked up at The Kid. "If you're ever on the edge and you're in New Orleans, ask Yeller to set up some bridge with The Countess."

"Thanks, I will," The Kid said.

"Kid," Lancey said, "there is hardly a rambling-gambling man in the country that hasn't played bridge with Countess von Frankenberg at one time or another to get off the edge. You never heard of her?"

"No."

"She is a true Countess," Lady Fingers said, "and she loves cards. She made friends with Yeller a long time ago and they been playing a regular Tuesday and Friday night game as long as I've been around." She looked at Lancey.

He nodded. "I was playing with her and Yeller the night I asked Yeller to set it up with me and old Sam."

"Yeah?" Lady Fingers looked at Lancey. "Is that a fact?"

"I had heard what he did to The Shooter," Lancey said. "And that was when I asked Yeller to set it up for me."

The Kid looked at Lancey. Whistling Sam Magee had taken The Shooter, and Lancey had taken Whistling Sam. The Kid was surprised to learn that Lancey had been The Man so long. There was something about the gambler that made The Kid feel that it was not something he had had a very long time. He looked at Lancey. It was almost as if Lancey had deserted his square job and turned to cards late in life, yet he realized this could not be so and have Lancey take Whistling Sam Magee.

They talked a little more and then The Shooter came into the room, his hair still dripping wet from his shower and rubbing it hard with a towel.

They did not talk cards at all, or discuss the game as they caught a cab and went over to Victoria's. They had a big breakfast which made everybody sleepy, and then all went back to the Dorset Hotel and slept until two o'clock that afternoon.

With Old Lady Fingers dealing in The Shooter's chair, she intoned the words The Shooter, who was sleeping and taking a break until that evening, had used. "This is a game of five card stud poker, gents, and there is no limit. Who was last under the gun?"

"Me," The Kid said.

Lancey Hodges got the first card and the game was resumed.

"A trey and a seven," Lady Fingers said. "Seven bets."

"Fifty dollars," The Kid said, betting his seven, and Lancey turned his cards over, no-stay.

By eight o'clock that night the tension of the game began to flow out of the room and to the halls and the suite of rooms the restaurateur had taken, down to the hotel bar and to the Glassways and Victoria's. Something had to happen, the crowd kept saying, it couldn't go on much longer like this. They had said that at six and then again at seven and now at eight, with the crowds more subdued, they waited. There was good reason for their belief that it could not go on much longer. The Kid and Lancey had been butting heads since two o'clock and it had been a see-saw duel, with Lancey dragging a big pot and The Kid coming right back on the very next deal and taking it all back. They had only played three no-stay hands since they had resumed the game, and at eight o'clock they were exactly where they were when they had started. The Kid had about five thousand dollars before him, and though he had been down to eight hundred once and down to fifteen hundred twice, he was never better, and for that, neither was Lancey, and as the insiders, Yeller, Miriam, Jolly, Spriigi, Wildwood and a few others began to ease through the door, quietly, slipping in behind the players and standing as still as dead people so as not to distract either of them, they saw that something had to give.

At nine o'clock, The Shooter returned, fresh and ready to take over as the dealer. Lady Fingers, who had not even gone to the bathroom since the game had picked up again, was nearly exhausted.

"I break," she said with a gasp of relief that was clearly an expression of pain when she saw The Shooter.

"I don't want no break," The Kid said with irritation.

"Well, I don't either," Lancey said.

"Deal," The Kid said, without looking at The Shooter.

The big man slipped out of his jacket, rolled his sleeves past the elbow and picked up a new deck.

"Same deck's good enough," Lancey snapped, not looking at The Shooter or The Kid, but looking at his money.

"I want a new deck," The Kid said, his voice low and almost sullen.

"All right-all right—a new deck then. Jesus!" Lancey said under his breath.

"Deal," The Kid said.

"Comin' out," The Shooter said. "Down, the dirty hole."

He peeled the cards off. It was as if a window was opened and a breath of fresh air came into the room. Where they had only had three no-stay hands in six hours, they now played for nearly four hours and either it was no-stay or they folded on the third or fourth card.

During this time The Shooter asked every hour on the hour if they wanted a break. Neither man would admit that he wanted to stop. Both of them were red-eyed and hung over from fatigue. The Kid had taken off his shoes and socks, his shirt, and sat in a T shirt with his trousers open at the top. Lancey had removed his jacket, his tie, and opened his vest and unbuttoned his shirt down to his trousers which were open at the belt also. He had taken his shoes off, but not his socks. Jansen came in at midnight with one of his assistants and while Jansen worked on the neck and shoulders and arms of The Kid, the assistant worked on Lancey.

Again and again The Shooter peeled the cards and laid them in before the players and put the deck flat on the table, rested his elbows and called the cards. Again and again it was no-stay or a third card fold. Only once did it ever get to a fourth card and The Kid dragged a nice fourth card pot of six hundred.

At two-thirty, Lancey caught a low heart flush hand, eight high. The Kid had a pair of tens showing on the third card and he bet five hundred, thinking to steal the pot of two hundred fifty. Lancey raised him three hundred.

The Kid did not move. He closed his eyes a moment and then moved his hand as if he were going to call, and then went on past to the cup and the remains of his coffee and brandy. He sipped it, stared down at the seven and eight of hearts. Until then, the bets and the calls, checks and raises had been so automatic that this slight hesitation in his play brought the attention of those in the room up sharply. They were already quiet. Now they did not even breathe.

If he just called, there would be eighteen hundred and fifty in the pot. It was by far the largest third card pot in the entire length of the game.

A seven and an eight. Hearts. The queen he had in the hole was a heart. What would Lancey have in the hole? A kicker? Ace? King? With two cards showing no power, the best a kicker could do would give him three of a kind, and The Kid already had a strong pair.

A third heart? Going for a flush? He had seven and eight, The Kid thought, and he would have to have a six heart card in the hole, because Lancey would not come on so strong in the face of an open pair of tens that could be three of a kind, without a six heart card in the hole. Lancey could build no higher than a jack heart card for a straight flush.

Eighteen fifty in the pot. Lancey would not chase. He had the open pair and the good solid queen in the hole. Solid two ways. Solid in power and solid because it was one less heart for Lancey to snare to make the flush.

And if he got his flush, The Kid would need four tens or a full house with queens. The percentages were in his favor. He felt something icy move up and down his spine as he took another sip of the coffee and brandy and put the cup down very slowly and deliberately, not too showy, but enough so Lancey could see it if he were looking for signs, holding the rim of the bottom of the cup above the saucer long enough for there to be no mistake about his being nervous.

Eighteen fifty in the pot. Lancey would not chase. And he could get a straight, a small straight at that, or a flush, in which case The Kid would have to get a full house, or Lancey could win it all with a straight flush.

Eighteen fifty in the pot. Lancey would not chase.

"Tens," The Shooter said. "Three hundred to the tens."

He's going, The Kid said to himself, for a straight flush. And I've got him.

"I see the three," The Kid said. "And kick it two thousand."

He swept his hand down to his money and without taking his eyes away from Lancey's face, he picked up the stack of fifty-dollar bills and counted them off, dropping them to the table, emptying his hand. Thirty-three fifty-dollar bills covered the middle of the table.

"Sixteen fifty," The Shooter said.

The Kid picked up tens and repeated his move, dropping them to the table in a flutter. Thirty-five ten-dollar bills were laid in an even cover over the fifties.

"And three hundred," The Shooter said.

The Kid dropped three one-hundred-dollar bills into the middle of the small mound of bills.

"Two thou to the seven-eight," The Shooter said.

Lancey had not moved a muscle the entire time The Kid was making his bet. He sighed and leaned back when The Shooter broke the spell of the silence with his chant of the bet.

Lancey picked up his glass of crème de menthe that was now watered down and looking like Pernod before water has been added, and sipped the juice off, staring at the table, then slipped a piece of the ice in his mouth and cracked it with his teeth.

"Two thou," Lancey said in a strong firm voice that everyone could hear and that was perfectly controlled, revealing no quiver or sudden phlegm that fear or nervousness might produce.

Lancey cracked the ice in his teeth and it was the only sound in the room.

"Call," he said lightly, almost abruptly, as simply as if he were asking for a match. He put twenty hundreds together in a neat stack, counting them off so that The Shooter and The Kid could see that he was doing this and put the stack on top of the spread of fifty- and ten-dollar bills.

The Shooter rapped the table lightly one time. The people in the room moved in a step closer to the table.

"Fourth card," The Shooter said, dropping his right hand to the deck and without touching any card except the top card, peeled them off and put them in.

"A queen to the tens," The Shooter said. "And another heart, a ten heart to the seven-eight."

There was a very audible sigh in the room when the ten turned up with the seven and eight. The Shooter had only to turn his head and the room was instantly silent.

"Still tens," The Shooter said.

"Tens are worth one thousand," The Kid said, not hesitating an instant after The Shooter had made the call, and feeling the coldness up and down his spine again, and fighting now to keep anyone from seeing the pounding in his chest. He wondered if he dare put his hand down and scratch his knee which was suddenly itching so badly it was driving him out of his mind. The itch became so violent that his right leg began to jerk convulsively, but he did not move and sat as he had been sitting, motionless, hands on either side of his money, just in back of his cards. The knee was jerking and twitching so steadily now as he waited for Lancey to make his play, that The Kid's heel was tapping the floor. He did not move. He did not grit his teeth. He reached over and picked up his coffee cup and drained it. He put it down slowly and evenly. There was no rattle. He then picked up a cigarette and took his time bringing up a match and he looked at his hands to see if they were shaking and they looked like something not a part of him, and underneath the table his leg continued to jerk.

It showed confidence, that one-thousand-dollar bet, and they all saw that it was the perfect one to make. One thousand dollars was not too much to chase Lancey away from the nearly seven-thousand-dollar pot and it was enough to show at the same time that he had Lancey by the tail and wanted him to stay and was making this hand the big hand.

There were no other hearts showing except those that Lancey had, the seven, the eight and the ten. Catching the ten heart card busted The Kid's go for four tens.

"The bet is one thousand to you, Lancey," The Shooter intoned.

Lancey snapped his eyes up and looked at The Shooter and The Kid caught the expression, which was icy cold; they softened instantly, as Lancey smiled at The Shooter, but The Kid had seen the hard brightness and he knew that Lancey was unsure.

"A thousand is a cheap enough ride," Lancey said, his voice easing back into a friendly quality that had characterized his manner early in the game. He picked up his hundreds and counted off ten bills from the stack. "One thousand for the call," he said.

When Lancey called the bet, those standing around would not be held back. They crowded in on the table and were so close Lady Fingers and Miriam were almost touching the side of the table itself.

The Shooter rapped the table lightly. "Last card comin' out."

The players waited. The Shooter picked up each card, snapped it and put them into the slot.

"A nine to the seven-eight-ten heart hand and a possible straight flush," The Shooter said. He flipped the card over to The Kid, pitching it in perfectly. "And another queen and a pair with the tens."

He leaned over the edge of the table. "Queens bet."

The Kid stared at the seven, eight, nine and ten of hearts and did not believe that Lancey had a jack or a six in the hole. He knew that Lancey was going to bet strong and try and chase him with a bluff of the big bet. But The Kid did not believe there was a straight flush against him, and his full house of three queens over a pair of tens had a simple straight beaten. Lancey was going to try and chase him.

But he didn't want just a showdown. He wanted Lancey to turn over his cards and show how foolish he had been, trying to buck for a straight flush when he had been beaten from the third card on.

The Kid looked down at his money. There was not more than fifteen hundred dollars left.

"Queens," The Shooter said, "is the bettor."

The Kid nodded. He looked down once more and then up at Lancey, who was looking straight at The Kid. The Kid figured Lancey to have about five thousand dollars before him. He was going to be about four thousand dollars shy.

"I'm taking my half hour," The Kid said, "to raise my roll."

The Shooter nodded and looked at Lancey. "Leave the cards and the money on the table, gents. It is now three A.M. The game resumes at three-thirty when the queens bet."

Lancey had not stopped looking at The Kid the whole time The Shooter was speaking.

The Kid started to get up when Lancey spoke.

"I'll take your marker, Kid," he said evenly. "Make your bet."

The Kid hesitated. He looked at Lancey. "I can raise it," The Kid said.

Lancey smiled. "I know you can, Kid."

"As long as you know it."

"I know it."

"Queens bet——" The Kid said, and heard his voice come out strong, and he began to count out his money. "Fourteen hundred twenty dollars."

He dropped the money into the pot. Lancey nodded and then picked up his money. He counted out fourteen hundred twenty dollars and then continued with all he had before him, starting the count all over again and coming to a stop when he was cleaned out. "I see the bet and raise it forty-one hundred even, Kid."

The Kid froze. All he had to do was tap the table to acknowledge that he was calling the bet and it would be over.

Lancey waited. The Shooter waited. Miriam, Lady Fingers and Carey and Wildwood Jones; Yeller and Carmody and Corrigan and the restaurateur and as many as could get into the room, waited and watched The Cincinnati Kid as he stared at the seven, eight, nine, ten of hearts and he could not move his hand.

"Forty-one hundred to the queens," The Shooter said.

The Kid did not move. He stared at his own cards and then at the heart hand opposite him, and he did not move. It was his hand. He had played it exactly the way he wanted to and yet he was considering turning over a full house, queens over tens in the face of what he was convinced could only be a four flush.

"Forty-one hundred to the queens," The Shooter said again. "Kid?"

He was not at all concerned about the mark of forty-one hundred. He had owed more than that, and he was not worried.

"You going to call, Kid?" The Shooter asked, and his voice was firm and businesslike.

The Kid rapped the table once, sharply. "Call," he said.

Lancey turned over his hole card and The Kid stared into the red face of a jack heart, and he did not realize for a moment that he had lost.

"That's forty-one hundred you owe me, Kid," Lancey said easily, with a quick smile, as he pulled the pot.

No one moved, or breathed, or looked or said anything and the only movement in the room was Lancey as he stacked his money. When he was finished, and when all of the fives and tens and twenties and fifties and hundreds were stacked, he turned to The Shooter.

"New deck," he said.

"You playing, Kid?" The Shooter asked. "You got one half hour to raise your roll."

"No," The Kid said quietly. "I'm tapped out."

The Shooter stood. "This game," he announced formally, "is over."

After Lancey had settled up with Lady Fingers for dealing the game, and had settled up with The Shooter for the hotel room and all of the expenses, while The Kid was in the bathroom getting himself cleaned up, he came out and he and Lancey shook hands like gentlemen and made small talk about the game, and how tired they both were and what a good game it was, the room was cleared out and Lancey said good-by, leaving with the police captain and several of the others.

The Shooter said later, after they had gotten The Kid so drunk that he passed out and they put him to bed, that he had gone to pieces. He also told Big Nig in a little note with his payoff bet, that he had never seen Lancey better. When he got hold of it, he never let go.

The Kid slept the clock around and when he woke up he refused to eat anything and turned to the bottle. The Kid and The Shooter got drunk and stayed drunk for five days and went over the poker hands and The Shooter reminded him that he had said The Kid wasn't ready.

The Kid accepted this and said very little.

When both The Kid and The Shooter ran out of money and ran out of their taste for Scotch, The Shooter and his woman sent a telegram to Christian, who came up the next day, with The Shooter and his woman waiting around for her, and then after they had turned The Kid over to her, taking the overnight down to New Orleans.

The Rocking-Horse Winner

BY D. H. LAWRENCE

The role of money in gambling—as opposed to other forms of wagering—is dicey, psychologically complex, reflective of the values, priorities, and often desperate needs of characters who gamble in capitalist societies. A rabbi backgammon-degenerate I know likes to say while gambling, "Money's not the most important thing, but it's way ahead of the second." As "scholars" (or playwrights) have noted, there *are* generally other things involved (status, self-image) in gambling than money. For aristocrats, a grace in ponying up after losing (sometimes intentionally) has been a crucial aspect of gambling, confirming the aristocrat's right to the money! For those who are well enough off, money may be necessary simply to give a sense of action or juice. As the French philosopher Blaise Pascal wrote in *Pensees* of the gambler (1670), "Give him the same amount of money every morning that he is like to win during the day's play on condition that he does not gamble, and you will make him thoroughly unhappy . . . But make him play for nothing; he will not get any excitement out of it all and will merely be bored." For philosophical gambler, Jack Richardson, gambling invests "money with the quality of a medium necessary to the condition of life. It was not that I wanted to *do* anything with it, any more than I wanted to *do* something with oxygen or sunlight; it was simply that cash had become the element I needed for my personal evolution." In contrast, late in *The Color of Money*, Walter Tevis's brilliant sequel to *The Hustler*, Fast Eddie Felson has the frank epiphany: "He could love the game of pool and equipment of the game, the wood and cloth, the phenolic resin of the glossy balls, the finish of his phallic cue stick, and sounds and money of pool. But the thing he loved the most was money."

Lawrence's concern in "The Rocking Horse Winner" is more with the effect of misplaced values and money-madness and with the uncanny costs of willing one's way to "luck." For those who are not well off, and live amongst plenty, the temptations and stakes of gambling take on dire significance. The story was made into a haunting movie in England in 1949, directed by Anthony Pellissier and starring John Howard Davis as Paul.

There was a woman who was beautiful, who started with all the advantages, yet she had no luck. She married for love, and the love turned to dust. She had bonny children, yet she felt they had been thrust upon her, and she could not love them. They looked at her coldly, as if they were finding fault with her. And hurriedly she felt she must cover up some fault in herself. Yet what it was that she must cover up she never knew. Nevertheless, when her children were present, she always felt the centre of her heart go hard. This troubled her, and in her manner she was all the more gentle and anxious for her children, as if she loved them very much. Only she herself knew that at the centre of her heart was a hard little place that could not feel love, no, not for anybody. Everybody else said of her: "She is such a good mother. She adores her children." Only she herself, and her children themselves, knew it was not so. They read it in each other's eyes.

There were a boy and two little girls. They lived in a pleasant house, with a garden, and they had discreet servants, and felt themselves superior to anyone in the neighbourhood.

Although they lived in style, they felt always an anxiety in the house. There was never enough money. The mother had a small income, and the father had a small income, but not nearly enough for the social position which they had to keep up. The father went into town to some office. But though he had good prospects, these prospects never materialised. There was always the grinding sense of the shortage of money, though the style was always kept up.

At last the mother said: "I will see if *I* can't make something." But she did not know where to begin. She racked her brains, and tried this thing and the other, but could not find anything successful. The failure made deep lines come into her face. Her children were growing up, they would have to go to school. There must be more money, there must be more money. The father, who was always very handsome and expensive in his tastes, seemed as if he never *would* be able to do anything worth doing. And the mother, who had a great belief in herself, did not succeed any better, and her tastes were just as expensive.

And so the house came to be haunted by the unspoken phrase: *There must be more money! There must be more money!* The children could hear it all the time, though nobody said it aloud. They heard it at Christmas, when the expensive and splendid toys filled the nursery. Behind the shining modern rocking-horse, behind the smart doll's house, a voice would start whispering: "There *must* be more money! There *must* be more money!" And the children would stop playing, to listen for a moment. They would look into each other's eyes, to see if they had all heard. And each one saw in the eyes of the other two that they too had heard. "There *must* be more money! There *must* be more money!"

It came whispering from the springs of the still-swaying rocking-horse, and even the horse, bending his wooden, champing head, heard it. The big doll, sitting so pink and smirking in her new pram, could hear it quite plainly, and seemed to be smirking all the more self-consciously because of it. The foolish puppy, too, that took the place of the teddy-bear, he was looking so extraordinarily foolish for no other reason but that he heard the secret whisper all over the house: "There *must* be more money!"

Yet nobody ever said it aloud. The whisper was everywhere, and therefore no one spoke it. Just as no one ever says: "We are breathing!" in spite of the fact that breath is coming and going all the time.

"Mother," said the boy Paul one day, "why don't we keep a car of our own? Why do we always use uncle's, or else a taxi?"

"Because we're the poor members of the family," said the mother.

"But why *are* we, mother?"

"Well—I suppose," she said slowly and bitterly, "it's because your father has no luck."

The boy was silent for some time.

"Is luck money, mother?" he asked, rather timidly.

"No, Paul. Not quite. It's what causes you to have money."

"Oh!" said Paul vaguely. "I thought when Uncle Oscar said *filthy lucker,* it meant money."

"*Filthy lucre* does mean money," said the mother. "But it's lucre, not luck."

"Oh!" said the boy. "Then what *is* luck, mother?"

"It's what causes you to have money. If you're lucky you have money. That's why it's better to be born lucky than rich. If you're rich, you may lose your money. But if you're lucky, you will always get more money."

"Oh! Will you? And is father not lucky?"

"Very unlucky, I should say," she said bitterly.

The boy watched her with unsure eyes.

"Why?" he asked.

"I don't know. Nobody ever knows why one person is lucky and another unlucky."

"Don't they? Nobody at all? Does *nobody* know?"

"Perhaps God. But He never tells."

"He ought to, then. And aren't you lucky either, mother?"

"I can't be, if I married an unlucky husband."

"But by yourself, aren't you?"

"I used to think I was, before I married. Now I think I am very unlucky indeed."

"Why?"

"Well—never mind! Perhaps I'm not really," she said.

The child looked at her to see if she meant it. But he saw, by the lines of her mouth, that she was only trying to hide something from him.

"Well, anyhow," he said stoutly, "I'm a lucky person."

"Why?" said his mother, with a sudden laugh.

He stared at her. He didn't even know why he had said it.

"God told me," he asserted, brazening it out.

"I hope He did, dear!" she said, again with a laugh, but rather bitter.

"He did, mother!"

"Excellent!" said the mother, using one of her husband's exclamations.

The boy saw she did not believe him; or rather, that she paid no attention to his assertion. This angered him somewhere, and made him want to compel her attention.

He went off by himself, vaguely, in a childish way, seeking for the clue to 'luck'. Absorbed, taking no heed of other people, he went about with a sort of stealth, seeking inwardly for luck. He wanted luck, he wanted it, he wanted it. When the two girls were playing dolls in the nursery, he would sit on his big rocking-horse, charging madly into space, with a frenzy that made the little girls peer at him uneasily. Wildly the horse careered, the waving dark hair of the boy tossed, his eyes had a strange glare in them. The little girls dared not speak to him.

When he had ridden to the end of his mad little journey, he climbed down and stood in front of his rocking-horse, staring fixedly into its lowered face. Its red mouth was slightly open, its big eye was wide and glassy-bright.

"Now!" he would silently command the snorting steed. "Now, take me to where there is luck! Now take me!"

And he would slash the horse on the neck with the little whip he had asked Uncle Oscar for. He *knew* the horse could take him to where there was luck, if only he forced it. So he would mount again and start on his furious ride, hoping at last to get there. He knew he could get there.

"You'll break your horse, Paul!" said the nurse.

"He's always riding like that! I wish he'd leave off!" said his elder sister Joan.

But he only glared down on them in silence. Nurse gave him up. She could make nothing of him. Anyhow, he was growing beyond her.

One day his mother and his Uncle Oscar came in when he was on one of his furious rides. He did not speak to them.

"Hallo, you young jockey! Riding a winner?" said his uncle.

"Aren't you growing too big for a rocking-horse? You're not a very little boy any longer, you know," said his mother.

But Paul only gave a blue glare from his big, rather close-set eyes. He would speak to nobody when he was in full tilt. His mother watched him with an anxious expression on her face.

At last he suddenly stopped forcing his horse into the mechanical gallop and slid down.

"Well, I got there!" he announced fiercely, his blue eyes still flaring, and his sturdy long legs straddling apart.

"Where did you get to?" asked his mother.

"Where I wanted to go," he flared back at her.

"That's right, son!" said Uncle Oscar. "Don't you stop till you get there. What's the horse's name?"

"He doesn't have a name," said the boy.

"Gets on without all right?" asked the uncle.

"Well, he has different names. He was called Sansovino last week."

"Sansovino, eh? Won the Ascot. How did you know this name?"

"He always talks about horse-races with Bassett," said Joan.

The uncle was delighted to find that his small nephew was posted with all the racing news. Bassett, the young gardener, who had been wounded in the left foot in the war and had got his present job through Oscar Cresswell, whose batman he had been, was a perfect blade of the 'turf'. He lived in the racing events, and the small boy lived with him.

Oscar Cresswell got it all from Bassett.

"Master Paul comes and asks me, so I can't do more than tell him, sir," said Bassett, his face terribly serious, as if he were speaking of religious matters.

"And does he ever put anything on a horse he fancies?"

"Well—I don't want to give him away—he's a young sport, a fine sport, sir. Would you mind asking him himself? He sort of takes a pleasure in it, and perhaps he'd feel I was giving him away, sir, if you don't mind."

Bassett was serious as a church.

The uncle went back to his nephew and took him off for a ride in the car.

"Say, Paul, old man, do you ever put anything on a horse?" the uncle asked.

The boy watched the handsome man closely.

"Why, do you think I oughtn't to?" he parried.

"Not a bit of it! I thought perhaps you might give me a tip for the Lincoln."

The car sped on into the country, going down to Uncle Oscar's place in Hampshire.

"Honour bright?" said the nephew.

"Honour bright, son!" said the uncle.

"Well, then, Daffodil."

"Daffodil! I doubt it, sonny. What about Mirza?"

"I only know the winner," said the boy. "That's Daffodil."

"Daffodil, eh?"

There was a pause. Daffodil was an obscure horse comparatively.

"Uncle!"

"Yes, son?"

"You won't let it go any further, will you? I promised Bassett."

"Bassett be damned, old man! What's he got to do with it?"

"We're partners. We've been partners from the first. Uncle, he lent me my first five shillings, which I lost. I promised him, honour bright, it was only between me and him; only you gave me that ten-shilling note I started winning with, so I thought you were lucky. You won't let it go any further, will you?"

The boy gazed at his uncle from those big, hot, blue eyes, set rather close together. The uncle stirred and laughed uneasily.

"Right you are, son! I'll keep your tip private. Daffodil, eh? How much are you putting on him?"

"All except twenty pounds," said the boy. "I keep that in reserve."

The uncle thought it a good joke.

"You keep twenty pounds in reserve, do you, you young romancer? What are you betting, then?"

"I'm betting three hundred," said the boy gravely. "But it's between you and me, Uncle Oscar! Honour bright?"

The uncle burst into a roar of laughter.

"It's between you and me all right, you young Nat Gould," he said, laughing. "But where's your three hundred?"

"Bassett keeps it for me. We're partners."

"You are, are you! And what is Bassett putting on Daffodil?"

"He won't go quite as high as I do, I expect. Perhaps he'll go a hundred and fifty."

"What, pennies?" laughed the uncle.

"Pounds," said the child, with a surprised look at his uncle. "Bassett keeps a bigger reserve than I do."

Between wonder and amusement Uncle Oscar was silent. He pursued the matter no further, but he determined to take his nephew with him to the Lincoln races.

"Now, son," he said. "I'm putting twenty on Mirza, and I'll put five on for you on any horse you fancy. What's your pick?"

"Daffodil, uncle."

"No, not the fiver on Daffodil!"

"I should if it was my own fiver," said the child.

"Good! Good! Right you are! A fiver for me and a fiver for you on Daffodil."

The child had never been to a race-meeting before, and his eyes were blue fire. He pursed his mouth tight and watched. A Frenchman just in front had put his money on Lancelot. Wild with excitement, he flayed his arms up and down, yelling *"Lancelot! Lancelot!"* in his French accent.

Daffodil came in first, Lancelot second, Mirza third. The child, flushed and with eyes blazing, was curiously serene. His uncle brought him four five-pound notes, four to one.

"What am I to do with these?" he cried, waving them before the boy's eyes.

"I suppose we'll talk to Bassett," said the boy. "I expect I have fifteen hundred now; and twenty in reserve; and this twenty."

His uncle studied him for some moments.

"Look here, son!" he said. "You're not serious about Bassett and that fifteen hundred, are you?"

"Yes, I am. But it's between you and me, uncle. Honour bright?"

"Honour bright all right, son! But I must talk to Bassett."

"If you'd like to be a partner, uncle, with Bassett and me, we could all be partners. Only, you'd have to promise, honour bright, uncle, not to let it go beyond us three. Bassett and I are lucky, and you must be lucky, because it was your ten shillings I started winning with. . . ."

Uncle Oscar took both Bassett and Paul into Richmond Park for an afternoon, and there they talked.

"It's like this, you see, sir," Bassett said. "Master Paul would get me talking about racing events, spinning yarns, you know, sir. And he was always keen on knowing if I'd made or if I'd lost. It's about a year since, now, that I put five shillings on Blush of Dawn for him: and we lost. Then the luck turned, with that ten shillings he had from you: that we put on Singhalese. And since that time, it's been pretty steady, all things considering. What do you say, Master Paul?"

"We're all right when we're sure," said Paul. "It's when we're not quite sure that we go down."

"Oh, but we're careful then," said Bassett.

"But when are you *sure?*" smiled Uncle Oscar.

"It's Master Paul, sir," said Bassett in a secret, religious voice. "It's as if he had it from heaven. Like Daffodil, now, for the Lincoln. That was as sure as eggs."

"Did you put anything on Daffodil?" asked Oscar Cresswell.

"Yes, sir. I made my bit."

"And my nephew?"

Bassett was obstinately silent, looking at Paul.

"I made twelve hundred, didn't I, Bassett? I told uncle I was putting three hundred on Daffodil."

"That's right," said Bassett, nodding.

"But where's the money?" asked the uncle.

"I keep it safe locked up, sir. Master Paul he can have it any minute he likes to ask for it."

"What, fifteen hundred pounds?"

"And twenty! And *forty*, that is, with the twenty he made on the course."

"It's amazing!" said the uncle.

"If Master Paul offers you to be partners, sir, I would, if I were you: if you'll excuse me," said Bassett.

Oscar Cresswell thought about it.

"I'll see the money," he said.

They drove home again, and, sure enough, Bassett came round to the garden-house with fifteen hundred pounds in notes. The twenty pounds reserve was left with Joe Glee, in the Turf Commission deposit.

"You see, it's all right, uncle, when I'm *sure!* Then we go strong, for all we're worth. Don't we, Bassett?"

"We do that, Master Paul."

"And when are you sure?" said the uncle, laughing.

"Oh, well, sometimes I'm *absolutely* sure, like about Daffodil," said the boy; "and sometimes I have an idea; and sometimes I haven't even an idea, have I, Bassett? Then we're careful, because we mostly go down."

"You do, do you! And when you're sure, like about Daffodil, what makes you sure, sonny?"

"Oh, well, I don't know," said the boy uneasily. "I'm sure, you know, uncle; that's all."

"It's as if he had it from heaven, sir," Bassett reiterated.

"I should say so!" said the uncle.

But he became a partner. And when the Leger was coming on Paul was 'sure' about Lively Spark, which was a quite inconsiderable horse. The boy insisted on putting a thousand on the horse, Bassett went for five hundred, and Oscar Cresswell two hundred. Lively Spark came in first, and the betting had been ten to one against him. Paul had made ten thousand.

"You see," he said, "I was absolutely sure of him."

Even Oscar Cresswell had cleared two thousand.

"Look here, son," he said, "this sort of thing makes me nervous."

"It needn't, uncle! Perhaps I shan't be sure again for a long time."

"But what are you going to do with your money?" asked the uncle.

"Of course," said the boy, "I started it for mother. She said she had no luck, because father is unlucky, so I thought if *I* was lucky, it might stop whispering."

"What might stop whispering?"

"Our house. I *hate* our house for whispering."

"What does it whisper?"

"Why—why"—the boy fidgeted—"why, I don't know. But it's always short of money, you know, uncle."

"I know it, son, I know it."

"You know people send mother writs, don't you, uncle?"

"I'm afraid I do," said the uncle.

"And then the house whispers, like people laughing at you behind your back. It's awful, that is! I thought if I was lucky—"

"You might stop it," added the uncle.

The boy watched him with big blue eyes, that had an uncanny cold fire in them, and he said never a word.

"Well, then!" said the uncle. "What are we doing?"

"I shouldn't like mother to know I was lucky," said the boy.

"Why not, son?"

"She'd stop me."

"I don't think she would."

"Oh!"—and the boy writhed in an odd way—"I *don't* want her to know, uncle."

"All right, son! We'll manage it without her knowing."

They managed it very easily. Paul, at the other's suggestion, handed over five thousand pounds to his uncle, who deposited it with the family lawyer, who was then to inform Paul's mother that a relative had put five thousand pounds into his hands, which sum was to be paid out a thousand pounds at a time, on the mother's birthday, for the next five years.

"So she'll have a birthday present of a thousand pounds for five successive years," said Uncle Oscar. "I hope it won't make it all the harder for her later."

Paul's mother had her birthday in November. The house had been 'whispering' worse than ever lately, and, even in spite of his luck, Paul could not bear up against it. He was very anxious to see the effect of the birthday letter, telling his mother about the thousand pounds.

When there were no visitors, Paul now took his meals with his parents, as he was beyond the nursery control. His mother went into town nearly every day. She had discovered that she had an odd knack of sketching furs and dress materials, so she worked secretly in the studio of a friend who was the chief 'artist' for the leading drapers. She drew the figures of ladies in furs and ladies in silk and sequins for the newspaper advertisements. This young woman artist earned several thousand pounds a year, but Paul's mother only made several hundreds, and she was again dissatisfied. She so wanted to be first in something, and she did not succeed, even in making sketches for drapery advertisements.

She was down to breakfast on the morning of her birthday. Paul watched her face as she read her letters. He knew the lawyer's letter. As his mother read it, her face hardened and became more expressionless. Then a cold, determined look came on her mouth. She hid the letter under the pile of others, and said not a word about it.

"Didn't you have anything nice in the post for your birthday, mother?" said Paul.

"Quite moderately nice," she said, her voice cold and absent.

She went away to town without saying more.

But in the afternoon Uncle Oscar appeared. He said Paul's mother had had a long interview with the lawyer, asking if the whole five thousand could not be advanced at once, as she was in debt.

"What do you think, uncle?" said the boy.

"I leave it to you, son."

"Oh, let her have it, then! We can get some more with the other," said the boy.

"A bird in the hand is worth two in the bush, laddie!" said Uncle Oscar.

"But I'm sure to *know* for the Grand National; or the Lincolnshire; or else the Derby. I'm sure to know for *one* of them," said Paul.

So Uncle Oscar signed the agreement, and Paul's mother touched the whole five thousand. Then something very curious happened. The voices in the house suddenly went mad, like a chorus of frogs on a spring evening. There were certain new furnishings, and Paul had a tutor. He was *really* going to Eton, his father's school, in the following autumn. There were flowers in the winter, and a blossoming of the luxury Paul's mother had been used to. And yet the voices in the house, behind the sprays of mimosa and almond-blossom, and from under the piles of iridescent cushions, simply trilled and screamed in a sort of ecstasy: "There *must* be more money! Oh-h-h; there *must* be more money. Oh, now, now-w! Now-w-w—there *must* be more money!—more than ever! More than ever!"

It frightened Paul terribly. He studied away at his Latin and Greek with his tutor. But his intense hours were spent with Bassett. The Grand National had gone by: he had not 'known', and had lost a hundred pounds. Summer was at hand. He was in agony for the Lincoln. But even for the Lincoln he didn't 'know', and he lost fifty pounds. He became wild-eyed and strange, as if something were going to explode in him.

"Let it alone, son! Don't you bother about it!" urged Uncle Oscar. But it was as if the boy couldn't really hear what his uncle was saying.

"I've got to know for the Derby! I've got to know for the Derby!" the child reiterated, his big blue eyes blazing with a sort of madness.

His mother noticed how overwrought he was.

"You'd better go to the seaside. Wouldn't you like to go now to the seaside, instead of waiting? I think you'd better," she said, looking down at him anxiously, her heart curiously heavy because of him.

But the child lifted his uncanny blue eyes.

"I couldn't possibly go before the Derby, mother!" he said. "I couldn't possibly!"

"Why not?" she said, her voice becoming heavy when she was opposed. "Why not? You can still go from the seaside to see the Derby with your Uncle Oscar, if that's what you wish. No need for you to wait here. Besides, I think you care too much about these races. It's a bad sign. My family has been a gambling family, and you won't know till you grow up how much damage it has done. But it has done damage. I shall have to send Bassett away, and ask

Uncle Oscar not to talk racing to you, unless you promise to be reasonable about it: go away to the seaside and forget it. You're all nerves!"

"I'll do what you like, mother, so long as you don't send me away till after the Derby," the boy said.

"Send you away from where? Just from this house?"

"Yes," he said, gazing at her.

"Why, you curious child, what makes you care about this house so much, suddenly? I never knew you loved it."

He gazed at her without speaking. He had a secret within a secret, something he had not divulged, even to Bassett or to his Uncle Oscar.

But his mother, after standing undecided and a little bit sullen for some moments, said:

"Very well, then! Don't go to the seaside till after the Derby, if you don't wish it. But promise me you won't let your nerves go to pieces. Promise you won't think so much about horse-racing and *events*, as you call them!"

"Oh no," said the boy casually, "I won't think much about them, mother. You needn't worry. I wouldn't worry, mother, if I were you."

"If you were me and I were you," said his mother, "I wonder what we *should* do!"

"But you know you needn't worry, mother, don't you?" the boy repeated.

"I should be awfully glad to know it," she said wearily.

"Oh, well, you *can,* you know. I mean, you *ought* to know you needn't worry," he insisted.

"Ought I? Then I'll see about it," she said.

Paul's secret of secrets was his wooden horse, that which had no name. Since he was emancipated from a nurse and a nursery-governess, he had had his rocking-horse removed to his own bedroom at the top of the house.

"Surely you're too big for a rocking-horse!" his mother had remonstrated.

"Well, you see, mother, till I can have a *real* horse, I like to have *some* sort of animal about," had been his quaint answer.

"Do you feel he keeps you company?" she laughed.

"Oh yes! He's very good, he always keeps me company, when I'm there," said Paul.

So the horse, rather shabby, stood in an arrested prance in the boy's bedroom.

The Derby was drawing near, and the boy grew more and more tense. He hardly heard what was spoken to him, he was very frail, and his eyes were really uncanny. His mother had sudden strange seizures of uneasiness about him. Sometimes, for half an hour, she would feel a sudden anxiety about him that was almost anguish. She wanted to rush to him at once, and know he was safe.

Two nights before the Derby, she was at a big party in town, when one of her rushes of anxiety about her boy, her first-born, gripped her heart till she could hardly speak. She fought with the feeling, might and main, for she believed in common sense. But it was too strong. She had to leave the dance and go downstairs to telephone to the country. The children's nursery-governess was terribly surprised and startled at being rung up in the night.

"Are the children all right, Miss Wilmot?"

"Oh yes, they are quite all right."

"Master Paul? Is he all right?"

"He went to bed as right as a trivet. Shall I run up and look at him?"

"No," said Paul's mother reluctantly. "No! Don't trouble. It's all right. Don't sit up. We shall be home fairly soon." She did not want her son's privacy intruded upon.

"Very good," said the governess.

It was about one o'clock when Paul's mother and father drove up to their house. All was still. Paul's mother went to her room and slipped off her white fur cloak. She had told her maid not to wait up for her. She heard her husband downstairs, mixing a whisky and soda.

And then, because of the strange anxiety at her heart, she stole upstairs to her son's room. Noiselessly she went along the upper corridor. Was there a faint noise? What was it?

She stood, with arrested muscles, outside his door, listening. There was a strange, heavy, and yet not loud noise. Her heart stood still. It was a soundless noise, yet rushing and powerful. Something huge, in violent, hushed motion. What was it? What in God's name was it? She ought to know. She felt that she knew the noise. She knew what it was.

Yet she could not place it. She couldn't say what it was. And on and on it went, like a madness.

Softly, frozen with anxiety and fear, she turned the door-handle.

The room was dark. Yet in the space near the window, she heard and saw something plunging to and fro. She gazed in fear and amazement.

Then suddenly she switched on the light, and saw her son, in his green pyjamas, madly surging on the rocking-horse. The blaze of light suddenly lit him up, as he urged the wooden horse, and lit her up, as she stood, blonde, in her dress of pale green and crystal, in the doorway.

"Paul!" she cried. "Whatever are you doing?"

"It's Malabar!" he screamed in a powerful, strange voice. "It's Malabar!"

His eyes blazed at her for one strange and senseless second, as he ceased urging his wooden horse. Then he fell with a crash to the ground, and she, all her tormented motherhood flooding upon her, rushed to gather him up.

But he was unconscious, and unconscious he remained, with some brain-fever. He talked and tossed, and his mother sat stonily by his side.

"Malabar! It's Malabar! Bassett, Bassett, I *know*! It's Malabar!"

So the child cried, trying to get up and urge the rocking-horse that gave him his inspiration.

"What does he mean by Malabar?" asked the heart-frozen mother.

"I don't know," said the father stonily.

"What does he mean by Malabar?" she asked her brother Oscar.

"It's one of the horses running for the Derby," was the answer.

And, in spite of himself, Oscar Cresswell spoke to Bassett, and himself put a thousand on Malabar: at fourteen to one.

The third day of the illness was critical: they were waiting for a change. The boy, with his rather long, curly hair, was tossing ceaselessly on the pillow. He neither slept nor regained consciousness, and his eyes were like blue stones. His mother sat, feeling her heart had gone, turned actually into a stone.

In the evening, Oscar Cresswell did not come, but Bassett sent a message, saying could he come up for one moment, just one moment? Paul's mother was very angry at the intrusion, but on second thoughts she agreed. The boy was the same. Perhaps Bassett might bring him to consciousness.

The gardener, a shortish fellow with a little brown moustache and sharp little brown eyes, tiptoed into the room, touched his imaginary cap to Paul's mother, and stole to the bedside, staring with glittering, smallish eyes at the tossing, dying child.

"Master Paul!" he whispered. "Master Paul! Malabar came in first all right, a clean win. I did as you told me. You've made over seventy thousand pounds, you have; you've got over eighty thousand. Malabar came in all right, Master Paul."

"Malabar! Malabar! Did I say Malabar, mother? Did I say Malabar? Do you think I'm lucky, mother? I knew Malabar, didn't I? Over eighty thousand pounds! I call that lucky, don't you, mother? Over eighty thousand pounds! I knew, didn't I know I knew? Malabar came in all right. If I ride my horse till I'm sure, then I tell you, Bassett, you can go as high as you like. Did you go for all you were worth, Bassett?"

"I went a thousand on it, Master Paul."

"I never told you, mother, that if I can ride my horse, and *get there,* then I'm absolutely sure—oh, absolutely! Mother, did I ever tell you? I *am* lucky!"

"No, you never did," said his mother.

But the boy died in the night.

And even as he lay dead, his mother heard her brother's voice saying to her: "My God, Hester, you're eighty-odd thousand to the good, and a poor devil of a son to the bad. But, poor devil, poor devil, he's best gone out of a life where he rides his rocking-horse to find a winner."

Man from the South

BY ROALD DAHL

Recently I heard from Vegas gambling columnist Mark Pilarski about a man who wagered his toe in a craps game. I did not learn whether the man retained his toe or not, but he does not seem headed, in any event, for an extended career as a ballet dancer. The story was not altogether shocking to me, given the long history of such bets among those who have run out of conventional assets. There is an eighteenth-century British account, for instance, of broke gamblers agreeing that the loser of a bet shall hang himself, in which the loser lives "up" to his end. The sum total of our material possessions in the end, such stories proclaim, is the stuff of our bodies, the pound or so of flesh a twisted adversary may wager, for whatever twisted motive. In the eerie selection below, "Man from the South" (which was made into an episode of *Alfred Hitchcock Presents*), Roald Dahl (author of such delightful children's classics as *Charlie and the Chocolate Factory* and *James and the Giant Peach*), extends what might be considered a tradition of physiological gambling, in which characters wager parts of their own or other people's bodies, whether or not the gambler is in the position to do so.

It was getting on toward six o'clock so I thought I'd buy myself a beer and go out and sit in a deck chair by the swimming pool and have a little evening sun.

       I went to the bar and got the beer and carried it outside and wandered down the garden toward the pool.

       It was a fine garden with lawns and beds of azaleas and tall coconut palms, and the wind was blowing strongly through the tops of the palm trees making the leaves hiss and crackle as though they were on fire. I could see the clusters of big brown nuts hanging down underneath the leaves.

There were plenty of deck chairs around the swimming pool and there were white tables and huge brightly colored umbrellas and sunburned men and women sitting around in bathing suits. In the pool itself there were three or four girls and about a dozen boys, all splashing about and making a lot of noise and throwing a large rubber ball at one another.

I stood watching them. The girls were English girls from the hotel. The boys I didn't know about, but they sounded American and I thought they were probably naval cadets who'd come ashore from the U.S. naval training vessel which had arrived in harbor that morning.

I went over and sat down under a yellow umbrella where there were four empty seats, and I poured my beer and settled back comfortably with a cigarette.

It was very pleasant sitting there in the sunshine with beer and cigarette. It was pleasant to sit and watch the bathers splashing about in the green water.

The American sailors were getting on nicely with the English girls. They'd reached the stage where they were diving under the water and tipping them up by their legs.

Just then I noticed a small, oldish man walking briskly around the edge of the pool. He was immaculately dressed in a white suit and he walked very quickly with little bouncing strides, pushing himself high up onto his toes with each step. He had on a large creamy Panama hat, and he came bouncing along the side of the pool, looking at the people and the chairs.

He stopped beside me and smiled, showing two rows of very small, uneven teeth, slightly tarnished. I smiled back.

"Excuse pleess, but may I sit here?"

"Certainly," I said. "Go ahead."

He bobbed around to the back of the chair and inspected it for safety, then he sat down and crossed his legs. His white buckskin shoes had little holes punched all over them for ventilation.

"A fine evening," he said. "They are all evenings fine here in Jamaica." I couldn't tell if the accent were Italian or Spanish, but I felt fairly sure he was some sort of a South American. And old too, when you saw him close. Probably around sixty-eight or seventy.

"Yes," I said. "It is wonderful here, isn't it."

"And who, might I ask, are all dese? Dese is no hotel people." He was pointing at the bathers in the pool.

ROALD DAHL . 105

"I think they're American sailors," I told him. "They're Americans who are learning to be sailors."

"Of course dey are Americans. Who else in de world is going to make as much noise at dat? You are not American, no?"

"No," I said. "I am not."

Suddenly one of the American cadets was standing in front of us. He was dripping wet from the pool and one of the English girls was standing there with him.

"Are these chairs taken?" he said.

"No," I answered.

"Mind if I sit down?"

"Go ahead."

"Thanks," he said. He had a towel in his hand and when he sat down he unrolled it and produced a pack of cigarettes and a lighter. He offered the cigarettes to the girl and she refused; then he offered them to me and I took one. The little man said, "Tank you, no, but I tink I have a cigar." He pulled out a crocodile case and got himself a cigar, then he produced a knife which had a small scissors in it and he snipped the end off the cigar.

"Here, let me give you a light." The American boy held up his lighter.

"Dat will not work in dis wind."

"Sure, it'll work. It always works."

The little man removed his unlighted cigar from his mouth, cocked his head on one side and looked at the boy.

"*All*-ways?" he said slowly.

"Sure, it never fails. Not with me anyway."

The little man's head was still cocked over on one side and he was still watching the boy. "Well, well. So you say dis famous lighter it never fails. Iss dat you say?"

"Sure," the boy said. "That's right." He was about nineteen or twenty with a long freckled face and a rather sharp birdlike nose. His chest was not very sunburned and there were freckles there too, and a few wisps of pale-reddish hair. He was holding the lighter in his right hand, ready to flip the wheel. "It never fails," he said, smiling now because he was purposely exaggerating his little boast. "I promise you it never fails."

"One momint, pleess." The hand that held the cigar came up high, palm outward, as though it were stopping traffic. "Now juss one momint." He had a curiously soft, toneless voice and he kept looking at the boy all the time.

"Shall we not perhaps make a little bet on dat?" He smiled at the boy. "Shall we not make a little bet on whether your lighter lights?"

"Sure, I'll bet," the boy said. "Why not?"

"You like to bet?"

"Sure, I'll always bet."

The man paused and examined his cigar, and I must say I didn't much like the way he was behaving. It seemed he was already trying to make something out of this, and to embarrass the boy, and at the same time I had the feeling he was relishing a private little secret all his own.

He looked up again at the boy and said slowly, "I like to bet, too. Why we don't have a good bet on dis ting? A good big bet."

"Now wait a minute," the boy said. "I can't do that. But I'll bet you a quarter. I'll even bet you a dollar, or whatever it is over here—some shillings, I guess."

The little man waved his hand again. "Listen to me. Now we have some fun. We make a bet. Den we go up to my room here in de hotel where iss no wind and I bet you you cannot light dis famous lighter of yours ten times running without missing once."

"I'll bet I can," the boy said.

"All right. Good. We make a bet, yes?"

"Sure. I'll bet you a buck."

"No, no. I make you very good bet. I am rich man and I am sporting man also. Listen to me. Outside de hotel iss my car. Iss very fine car. American car from your country. Cadillac—"

"Hey, now. Wait a minute." The boy leaned back in his deck chair and he laughed. "I can't put up that sort of property. This is crazy."

"Not crazy at all. You strike lighter successfully ten times running and Cadillac is yours. You like to have dis Cadillac, yes?"

"Sure, I'd like to have a Cadillac." The boy was still grinning.

"All right. Fine. We make a bet and I put up my Cadillac."

"And what do I put up?"

The little man carefully removed the red band from his still unlighted cigar. "I never ask you, my friend, to bet something you cannot afford. You understand?"

"Then what do I bet?"

"I make it very easy for you, yes?"

"Okay. You make it easy."

"Some small ting you can afford to give away, and if you did happen to lose it you would not feel too bad. Right?"

"Such as what?"

"Such as, perhaps, de little finger of your left hand."

"My *what!*" The boy stopped grinning.

"Yes. Why not? You win, you take de car. You looss, I take de finger."

"I don't get it. How d'you mean, you take the finger?"

"I chop it off."

"Jumping jeepers! That's a crazy bet. I think I'll just make it a dollar."

The little man leaned back, spread out his hands palms upward and gave a tiny contemptuous shrug of the shoulders. "Well, well, well," he said. "I do not understand. You say it lights but you will not bet. Den we forget it, yes?"

The boy sat quite still, staring at the bathers in the pool. Then he remembered suddenly he hadn't lighted his cigarette. He put it between his lips, cupped his hands around the lighter and flipped the wheel. The wick lighted and burned with a small, steady, yellow flame and the way he held his hands the wind didn't get to it at all.

"Could I have a light, too?" I said.

"Gee, I'm sorry. I forgot you didn't have one."

I held out my hand for the lighter, but he stood up and came over to do it for me.

"Thank you," I said, and he returned to his seat.

"You having a good time?" I asked.

"Fine," he answered. "It's pretty nice here."

There was a silence then, and I could see that the little man had succeeded in disturbing the boy with his absurd proposal. He was sitting there very still, and it was obvious that a small tension was beginning to build up inside him. Then he started shifting about in his seat, and rubbing his chest, and stroking the back of his neck, and finally he placed both hands on his knees and began tap-tapping with his fingers against the knee-caps. Soon he was tapping with one of his feet as well.

"Now just let me check up on this bet of yours," he said at last. "You say we go up to your room and if I make this lighter light ten times running I win a Cadillac. If it misses just once then I forfeit the little finger of my left hand. Is that right?"

"Certainly. Dat is de bet. But I tink you are afraid."

"What do we do if I lose? Do I have to hold my finger out while you chop it off?"

"Oh, no! Dat would be no good. And you might be tempted to refuse to hold it out. What I should do I should tie one of your hands to de table before we started and I should stand dere with a knife ready to go *chop* de momint your lighter missed."

"What year is the Cadillac?" the boy asked.

"Excuse. I not understand."

"What year—how old is the Cadillac?"

"Ah! How old? Yes. It is last year. Quite new car. But I see you are not betting man. Americans never are."

The boy paused for just a moment and he glanced first at the English girl, then at me. "Yes," he said sharply. "I'll bet you."

"Good!" The little man clapped his hands together quietly, once. "Fine," he said. "We do it now. And you, sir," he turned to me, "you would perhaps be good enough to, what you call it, to—to referee." He had pale, almost colorless eyes with tiny bright black pupils.

"Well," I said. "I think it's a crazy bet. I don't think I like it very much."

"Nor do I," said the English girl. It was the first time she'd spoken. "I think it's a stupid, ridiculous bet."

"Are you serious about cutting off this boy's finger if he loses?" I said.

"Certainly I am. Also about giving him Cadillac if he win. Come now. We go to my room."

He stood up. "You like to put on some clothes first?" he said.

"No," the boy answered. "I'll come like this." Then he turned to me. "I'd consider it a favor if you'd come along and referee."

"All right," I said. "I'll come along, but I don't like the bet."

"You come too," he said to the girl. "You come and watch."

The little man led the way back through the garden to the hotel. He was animated now, and excited, and that seemed to make him bounce up higher than ever on his toes as he walked along.

"I live in annex," he said. "You like to see car first? Iss just here."

He took us to where we could see the front driveway of the hotel and he stopped and pointed to a sleek pale-green Cadillac parked close by.

"Dere she iss. De green one. You like?"

"Say, that's a nice car," the boy said.

"All right. Now we go up and see if you can win her."

We followed him into the annex and up one flight of stairs. He unlocked his door and we all trooped into what was a large pleasant double bedroom. There was a woman's dressing gown lying across the bottom of one of the beds.

"First," he said, "we 'ave a little Martini."

The drinks were on a small table in the far corner, all ready to be mixed, and there was a shaker and ice and plenty of glasses. He began to make the Martini, but meanwhile he'd rung the bell and now there was a knock on the door and a coloured maid came in.

"Ah!" he said, putting down the bottle of gin, taking a wallet from his pocket and pulling out a pound note. "You will do something for me now, pleess." He gave the maid the pound.

"You keep dat," he said. "And now we are going to play a little game in here and I want you to go off and find for me two—no tree tings. I want some nails; I want a hammer, and I want a chopping knife, a butcher's chopping knife which you can borrow from de kitchen. You can get, yes?"

"A *chopping knife!*" The maid opened her eyes wide and clasped her hands in front of her. "You mean a *real* chopping knife?"

"Yes, yes of course. Come on now, pleess. You can find dose tings surely for me."

"Yes, sir, I'll try, sir. Surely I'll try to get them." And she went.

The little man handed round the Martinis. We stood there and sipped them, the boy with the long freckled face and the pointed nose, bare-bodied except for a pair of faded brown bathing shorts; the English girl, a large-boned, fair-haired girl wearing a pale blue bathing suit, who watched the boy over the top of her glass all the time; the little man with the colourless eyes standing there in his immaculate white suit drinking his Martini and looking at the girl in her pale blue bathing dress. I didn't know what to make of it all. The man seemed serious about the bet and he seemed serious about the business of cutting off the finger. But hell, what if the boy lost? Then we'd have to rush him to the hospital in the Cadillac that he hadn't won. That would be a fine thing. Now wouldn't that be a really fine thing? It would be a damn silly unnecessary thing so far as I could see.

"Don't you think this is rather a silly bet?" I said.

"I think it's a fine bet," the boy answered. He had already downed one large Martini.

"I think it's a stupid, ridiculous bet," the girl said. "What'll happen if you lose?"

"It won't matter. Come to think of it, I can't remember ever in my life having had any use for the little finger on my left hand. Here he is." The boy took hold of the finger. "Here he is and he hasn't ever done a thing for me yet. So why shouldn't I bet him. I think it's a fine bet."

The little man smiled and picked up the shaker and refilled our glasses.

"Before we begin," he said, "I will present to de—to de referee de key of de car." He produced a car key from his pocket and gave it to me. "De papers," he said, "de owning papers and insurance are in de pocket of de car."

Then the colored maid came in again. In one hand she carried a small chopper, the kind used by butchers for chopping meat bones, and in the other a hammer and a bag of nails.

"Good! You get dem all. Tank you, tank you. Now you can go." He waited until the maid had closed the door, then he put the implements on one of the beds and said, "Now we prepare ourselves, yes?" And to the boy "Help me, pleess, with dis table. We carry it out a little."

It was the usual kind of hotel writing desk, just a plain rectangular table about four feet by three with a blotting pad, ink, pens and paper. They carried it out into the room away from the wall, and removed the writing things.

"And now," he said, "a chair." He picked up a chair and placed it beside the table. He was very brisk and very animated, like a person organizing games at a children's party. "And now de nails. I must put in de nails." He fetched the nails and he began to hammer them into the top of the table.

We stood there, the boy, the girl, and I, holding Martinis in our hands, watching the little man at work. We watched him hammer two nails into the table, about six inches apart. He didn't hammer them right home; he allowed a small part of each one to stick up. Then he tested them for firmness with his fingers.

Anyone would think the son of a bitch had done this before, I told myself. He never hesitates. Table, nails, hammer, kitchen chopper. He knows exactly what he needs and how to arrange it.

"And now," he said, "all we want is some string." He found some string. "All right, at last we are ready. Will you pleess to sit here at de table," he said to the boy.

The boy put his glass away and sat down.

"Now place de left hand between dese two nails. De nails are only so I can tie your hand in place. All right, good. Now I tie your hand secure to de table—so."

He wound the string around the boy's wrist, then several times around the wide part of the hand, then he fastened it tight to the nails. He made a good job of it and when he'd finished there wasn't any question about the boy being able to draw his hand away. But he could move his fingers.

"Now pleess, clench de fist, all except for de little finger. You must leave de little finger sticking out, lying on de table."

"*Ex*-cellent! *Ex*-cellent! Now we are ready. Wid your right hand you manipulate de lighter. But one momint, pleess."

He skipped over to the bed and picked up the chopper. He came back and stood beside the table with the chopper in his hand.

"We are all ready?" he said. "Mister referee, you must say to begin."

The English girl was standing there in her pale blue bathing costume right behind the boy's chair. She was just standing there, not saying anything. The boy was sitting quite still, holding the lighter in his right hand, looking at the chopper. The little man was looking at me.

"Are you ready?" I asked the boy.

"I'm ready."

"And you?" to the little man.

"Quite ready," he said and he lifted the chopper up in the air and held it there about two feet above the boy's finger, ready to chop. The boy watched it, but he didn't flinch and his mouth didn't move at all. He merely raised his eyebrows and frowned.

"All right," I said. "Go ahead."

The boy said, "Will you please count aloud the number of times I light it."

"Yes," I said. "I'll do that."

With his thumb he raised the top of the lighter, and again with the thumb he gave the wheel a sharp flick. The flint sparked and the wick caught fire and burned with a small yellow flame.

"One!" I called.

He didn't blow the flame out; he closed the top of the lighter on it and he waited for perhaps five seconds before opening it again.

He flicked the wheel very strongly and once more there was a small flame burning on the wick.

"Two!"

No one else said anything. The boy kept his eyes on the lighter. The little man held the chopper up in the air and he too was watching the lighter.

"Three!"

"Four!"

"Five!"

"Six!"

"Seven!" Obviously it was one of those lighters that worked. The flint gave a big spark and the wick was the right length. I watched the thumb snapping the top down onto the flame. Then a pause. Then the thumb raising the top once more. This was an all-thumb operation. The thumb did everything. I took a breath, ready to say eight. The thumb flicked the wheel. The flint sparked. The little flame appeared.

"Eight!" I said, and as I said it the door opened. We all turned and we saw a woman standing in the doorway, a small, black-haired woman, rather old, who stood there for about two seconds then rushed forward shouting, "Carlos! Carlos!" She grabbed his wrist, took the chopper from him, threw it on the bed, took hold of the little man by the lapels of his white suit and began shaking him very vigorously, talking to him fast and loud and fiercely all the time in some Spanish-sounding language. She shook him so fast you couldn't see him any more. He became a faint, misty, quickly moving outline, like the spokes of a turning wheel.

Then she slowed down and the little man came into view again and she hauled him across the room and pushed him backward onto one of the beds. He sat on the edge of it blinking his eyes and testing his head to see if it would still turn on his neck.

"I am so sorry," the woman said. "I am so terribly sorry that this should happen." She spoke almost perfect English.

"It is too bad," she went on. "I suppose it is really my fault. For ten minutes I leave him alone to go and have my hair washed and I come back and he is at it again." She looked sorry and deeply concerned.

The boy was untying his hand from the table. The English girl and I stood there and said nothing.

"He is a menace," the woman said. "Down where we live at home he has taken altogether forty-seven fingers from different people, and he has lost eleven cars. In the end they threatened to have him put away somewhere. That's why I brought him up here."

"We were only having a little bet," mumbled the little man from the bed.

"I suppose he bet you a car," the woman said.

"Yes," the boy answered. "A Cadillac."

"He has no car. It's mine. And that makes it worse," she said, "that he should bet you when he has nothing to bet with. I am ashamed and very sorry about it all." She seemed an awfully nice woman.

"Well," I said, "then here's the key of your car." I put it on the table.

"We were only having a little bet," mumbled the little man.

"He hasn't anything left to bet with," the woman said. "He hasn't a thing in the world. Not a thing. As a matter of fact I myself won it all from him a long while ago. It took time, a lot of time, and it was hard work, but I won it all in the end." She looked up at the boy and she smiled, a slow sad smile, and she came over and put out a hand to take the key from the table.

I can see it now, that hand of hers; it had only one finger on it, and a thumb.

The Queen of Spades

BY ALEXANDER PUSHKIN

translated by Ethel O. Bronstein

The moment Hermann, the protagonist of "The Queen of Spades," proclaims, "I am in no position to sacrifice the essential in the hope of acquiring the superfluous," the reader is willing to bet that this cautious young man will be drawn in "gamble," against his better judgment and over his head. Pushkin captures, that is, the vertiginous lure of gambling, its potential to peel back prudence, revealing cross-currents within characters who profess one thing while being drawn to do another.

Alexander Pushkin's life and death were full of gamble. "Pushkin fights a duel a day," wrote one of his contemporaries, shortly before this "Shakespeare of Russia" died of pistol wounds. The connection between dueling and gambling is made explicit and dramatic in William Thackery's "action"-full *Barry Lyndon,* as well as in contemporary movies like *The Deerhunter,* where, having been exposed to the most extreme combinations of chance and will, veterans wager huge sums at Russian roulette.

They were playing cards at the home of Narumov, of the Horse Guards. The long winter night went by without their perceiving it; it was going on five in the morning when they sat down to supper. Those who had come out ahead of the game ate with great appetite; the others sat in abstraction before their empty plates. But when champagne appeared, the conversation grew more lively, and everyone took part in it.

"How did you come out, Surin?" asked the host.

113

"I lost, as usual. I must confess I'm unlucky; I systematically refrain from raising my stakes, I never get excited, nothing can make me lose my head—and yet I keep on losing all the time!"

"And you've never been tempted? Never gambled on a flush? I marvel at your firmness."

"But what do you think of Hermann!" remarked one of the guests, indicating a young officer in the uniform of the Engineers. "Never in his life has he picked up a card; never in his life has he doubled a stake; yet he sits with us until five in the morning and watches us play!"

"I find cards most entertaining," said Hermann, "but I am in no position to sacrifice the essential in the hope of acquiring the superfluous."

"Hermann's a German; he's calculating, that's all!" remarked Tomski. "But if there's anybody whom I can't understand it's my grandmother, Countess Anna Fedotovna."

"How? What's that?" clamored the guests.

"I can't conceive," Tomski continued, "why in the world my grandmother doesn't go in for banker or stuss."

"Why," Narumov queried, "what's so remarkable about an old lady of eighty refraining from punting?"

"Then you know nothing about her, I take it?"

"Not a thing, really!"

"Oh? Listen to this, then: you must know that, some sixty years ago, my grandmother went to Paris and became all the rage there. People would run after her just to catch a glimpse of *la Vénus moscovite;* Armand, Duc de Richelieu—grandnephew of the Cardinal, if you'll remember—dangled after her, and grandmother maintains that he all but shot himself because of her hardheartedness. Ladies used to play faro in those days. On one occasion, at Court, she lost—much too much!—to the Duc d'Orléans, on her word. On getting home, as she was peeling the beauty-patches off her face and getting out of her hoop-skirts, she informed my grandfather of her gaming loss and ordered him to pay it. My late grandfather, as far as I remember, was regarded by my grandmother as a sort of major-domo. He dreaded her like fire; just the same, when he heard how staggering the loss was, he lost his temper entirely, fetched his accounts, pointed out to her that in half a year they had run through half a million, that their estates were near Moscow and in Saratov, both of which were nowhere near Paris, and flatly refused to pay this gambling debt. Grandmother slapped his face for him and went to bed alone, as a sign of her disfavor.

"The next day she summoned her husband, hoping that the domestic discipline had had its effect on him, but found that he was not to be moved. For the first time in her life she was reduced to giving him reasons and explanations; she thought she would shame him, condescendingly pointing out that there were debts *and* debts, and that, after all, there was a difference between a prince and a coachmaker. But it was no go! Grandfather was up in arms. No— and that was that! Grandmother didn't know what to do.

"A very remarkable man happened to be one of her closest friends. You've heard of Count St. Germain, of whom so many marvelous things are told. You know that he palmed himself off as the Wandering Jew, as the inventor of the Elixir of Life and the Philosopher's Stone, and so forth. He was ridiculed as a charlatan, while Casanova states, in his *Memoirs,* that he was a spy; be that as it may, St. Germain, despite all the mystery surrounding him, had a most respectable appearance and was a most amiable man in society. Grandmother still loves him madly and becomes angry if anyone speaks of him with disrespect. Grandmother knew that St. Germain had considerable sums of money at his disposal. She decided to have recourse to him and wrote him a note requesting him to come to her without any delay. The queer old stick came at once and found her dreadfully woebegone. She described to him her husband's barbarous behavior, painting it in the blackest hues, and concluded by saying that she placed all her hope in his friendship and amiability. St. Germain grew thoughtful.

"'I could oblige you with such a sum,' said he, 'but I know you wouldn't rest easy till you had repaid me, and I don't want to lead you into fresh difficulties. There's another way: you can win back what you owe.'

"'But, my dear Count,' my grandmother answered, 'I tell you we have no money whatsoever.'

"'There's no money required in this case,' St. Germain countered 'Please deign to hear me out.'

"Thereupon he revealed to her a secret for which everyone of us would be willing to pay dearly—"

The young gamblers redoubled their attention. Tomski lit his pipe, took a deep draw on it, and went on:

"'That same evening my grandmother was in attendance at Versailles, *au jeu de la Reine*—at the Queen's game. The Duc d'Orléans kept the bank, grandmother apologized lightly for not having brought the money to pay her debt, making up some innocent little story to excuse this oversight, and began to punt against him. She picked three cards and played them one after the other: each of the three broke the bank, and grandmother recouped completely everything she had lost."

"Mere chance!" said one of the guests.

"A fairy tale!" remarked Hermann.

"Trick cards, perhaps?" a third chimed in. "An extra spot or so applied in a special light powder—a flick of the finger and it's gone—"

"I don't think so," Tomski replied impressively.

"What!" Narumov cried out. "You have a grandmother who can hit upon three lucky cards in a row, and you haven't yet gotten the cabalistics of it out of her?"

"Hell, no!" answered Tomski. "She had four sons, my father being one of them; all four are desperate gamblers; yet she never revealed her secret to a single one of them, even though it wouldn't have been a bad thing for them, or, for that matter, for me. But here's what my uncle, Count Ivan Ilyich, used to tell me, assuring me on his honor it's all true. The late Chaplitski, the same who died in beggary after squandering millions, once lost something like three hundred thousand when he was a young man—if I remember right it was to Zorich, one of the favorites of Catherine the Great. Chaplitski was desperate. Grandmother, who always looked upon the follies of youth with a stern eye, nevertheless took pity on him. She told him what three cards to pick, stipulating that he play them one after the other, and exacted his word of honor that he would never gamble thereafter. Chaplitski went back to the man who had beaten him; they sat down to play. Chaplitski staked fifty thousand on the first card, and broke the bank; he doubled his stake, and won, then quadrupled the stake and won for the third time, not only recouping his losses but coming out ahead of the game. . . .

"However, it's time to go to bed—it's a quarter to six already."

True enough, dawn was breaking by now; the young men drained their glasses and dispersed.

The old Countess was sitting before the mirror in her boudoir. Three maids hovered around her. One held a rouge pot; another, a box of hairpins; the third, a towering mobcap with flame-colored ribbons. The Countess had not the slightest claim to a beauty long since faded, but she still maintained all the habits of her youth, adhered strictly to the fashions of the seventies, and expended just as much time and care over her dressing as she used to do all of sixty years ago. A young lady, her protégée, was sitting by a window, bent over an embroidery-frame.

"Greetings, *Grand'maman*," said a young officer entering the room. "*Bon jour*, Mademoiselle Lise. *Grand'maman*, I've a favor to ask of you."

"What is it, Paul?"

"Allow me to present one of my friends to you and to bring him to the ball on Friday."

"Bring him along to the ball and you can present him then and there. Were you at ———'s yesterday?"

"Of course! It was a very gay affair; we danced until five. How pretty Yeletskaya looked!"

"Come, dear man! What's so pretty about her? Could she hold up a candle to her grandmother, the Grand Duchess Darya Petrovna? By the way, the Grand Duchess Darya Petrovna must have grown very old, I guess?"

"Grown very old? Why, what do you mean?" Tomski answered without stopping to think. "It's all of seven years by now that she's been dead."

The girl raised her head and made a sign to the young man. He remembered that the death of any of her contemporaries was being kept from the old Countess, and bit his lip. But the Countess heard this news, which was really news to her, with considerable indifference.

"She died!" she said. "Why, I didn't even know that! We were appointed Ladies-in-Waiting together, and as we were being presented, Her Majesty—"

And the Countess, for the hundredth time, told this anecdote to her grandson.

"Well, Paul," she said when she had finished, "you may help me get up now. Lizanka, where's my snuffbox?"

And the Countess, accompanied by her maids, went behind a screen to finish her toilette. Tomski remained with the young lady.

"Who is the gentleman you want to present?" Lizaveta Ivanovna asked quietly.

"Narumov. Do you know him?"

"No. Is he a military man or a civilian?"

"He's a military man."

"In the Engineers?"

"No! In the Cavalry. And what made you think he was in the Engineers?"

The girl burst out laughing—but did not answer a word.

"Paul!" the Countess called out from behind the screen. "Send me some new novel or other, but *please* not a modern one."

"What do you mean, *Grand'maman?*"

"I mean a novel in which the hero doesn't strangle either his father or his mother, and in which there aren't any drowned corpses. I'm horribly afraid of people who drown!"

"There are no novels free from that nowadays. Unless you would like me to send you some Russian ones?"

"Why, *are* there any Russian novels? Send them along, dear man— send them along, please!"

"Excuse me, *Grand'maman*—I must hurry. Excuse me, Lizaveta Ivanovna! Whatever made you think Narumov was in the Engineers?"

And Tomski went out of the boudoir.

Lizaveta Ivanovna was left alone; she dropped her work and began to look out of the window. Presently, on the other side of the street, from behind the house on the corner, a young officer appeared. Her cheeks became mantled with color, she went back to her work, and bent her head so low that it almost touched the embroidery. Just then the Countess came in, fully dressed.

"Order the carriage, Lizanka," she said, "and let's go for a drive."

Lizanka got up from the embroidery-frame and began putting her work away.

"What are you about, my girl? Are you deaf, or what?" the Countess began to shout. "Order them to get the carriage ready as soon as possible."

"Right away!" the young lady answered softly, and ran out into the anteroom.

A manservant entered and handed the Countess some books sent by the Grand Duke Paul Alexandrovich.

"Good! Thank him," said the Countess. "Lizanka, Lizanka! Why, where are you running to?"

"To get dressed."

"You'll have time, my dear girl. Sit here. Open the first volume; read it aloud."

The girl took the book and read several lines.

"Louder!" said the Countess. "What's the matter with you, my girl? Have you lost your voice, or what? Wait a bit; move that footstool closer to me; no, nearer! Well?"

Lizaveta Ivanovna read two pages more. The Countess yawned.

"Drop that book," she said. "What rubbish! Send it back to the Grand Duke Paul, and tell them to thank him. . . . Now, where's that carriage?"

"The carriage is ready," said Lizaveta Ivanovna after a glance into the street.

"But how is it you're not dressed?" asked the Countess. "I always have to wait for you! This is intolerable, my girl!"

Liza ran to her room. No more than two minutes had elapsed when the Countess began to ring with all her might. Three maids ran in through one door and a valet through another.

"Why can't I get you to answer?" the Countess demanded of them. "Tell Lizaveta Ivanovna I'm waiting for her."

Lizaveta Ivanovna entered, in manteau and bonnet.

"At last, my girl!" said the Countess. "What finery! What's it for? To captivate whom? What's the weather like? It seems windy."

"Not at all, Your Ladyship, Ma'am! It's very calm indeed, Ma'am!" the valet informed her.

"You always say the first thing that pops into your head! Open the ventilator. Just as I thought: it's windy! And a very cold wind, at that! Send the carriage back! We're not going, Lizanka; you needn't have dressed yourself up like that."

"And that's my life!" Lizaveta Ivanovna reflected.

Lizaveta Ivanovna was, indeed, a most unfortunate being. "What bitter fare," says Dante, "is others' bread; how hard the path to go upward and downward by another's stair." And who should know the bitterness of dependence if not the poor protégée of an old lady of quality? Countess —— was, to be sure, not cruel at heart, but she was self-willed, as a woman pampered by society would be, miserly, and immersed in chill egotism, as are all old people who have had their fill of love in their day and are out of touch with the present. She took part in all the vanities of high society; dragged herself to balls, where she would sit in the corner, bedizened in old-fashioned finery and berouged, like a hideous yet indispensable ornament of the ballroom; the guests as they arrived would walk up to her with low bows, as if in accordance with an established rite, and after that not a soul paid any attention to her. At home, she received the whole town, observing the strictest etiquette, but without recognizing a single face. Her numerous house serfs, grown fat and gray in her anteroom and maids' quarters, did as they pleased, vying with one another in robbing the moribund old woman.

Lizaveta Ivanovna was the martyr of the household. She poured the tea—and received reprimands for the excessive consumption of sugar; she read novels aloud—and was held accountable for all the faults of each author; she accompanied the Countess on her outings—and had to answer for the weather and the state of the cobbled roadway. She was assigned a salary which was never paid her in full, yet at the same time it was demanded of her that she dress like everyone else—that is, that she dress like the very few. Out in society she played the most pathetic of roles. Everybody knew her and nobody noticed her; at balls she danced only when there was a partner short in the quadrille, and the ladies would take her by the arm whenever they had to go to the powder-room to put something to rights about their attire. She had self-esteem, felt her position keenly, and looked about her in impatient expectancy of a deliverer; but the young men, calculating even in their fickle vanity, would not deign to notice her, even though Lizaveta Ivanovna was a hundred times more charming than the barefaced and coldhearted prospective brides on whom they danced attendance. How many times, quietly leaving the boring, sumptuous drawing room, would she go off to cry in her miserable room, which contained a screen covered with wallpaper, a bureau, a small mirror, and a painted bedstead, and where a tallow candle burned in a brass candlestick!

One day—this happened two days after the evening of cards described at the beginning of this tale, and a week previous to the scene we have just left—one day Lizaveta Ivanovna, as she sat at the window over her embroidery-frame, chanced to look out into the street—and saw a young officer in the uniform of the Engineers standing there motionless and with his eyes directed toward her window. She lowered her head and resumed her work; five minutes later she looked again: the young officer was still standing on the same spot. Since she was not in the habit of flirting with passing officers, she stopped looking into the street and went on with her embroidery for nearly two hours, without once raising her head. Dinner was served. She got up, began putting away her embroidery-frame and, chancing to look out into the street once more, again caught sight of the officer. This struck her as rather odd. After dinner she went up to the window with a somewhat uneasy feeling, but the officer was no longer there—and she did not give him any further thought.

Two days later, as she was going out to the carriage with the Countess, she caught sight of him again. He was standing by the very entrance, his face masked by his beaver collar; his black eyes glittered from under his hat. Lizaveta Ivanovna grew frightened without herself knowing why, and entered the carriage in inexplicable agitation.

On her return home she ran over to the window: the officer was standing in his former place, his eyes fixed upon her. She left the window, tortured by curiosity and troubled by a feeling completely new to her.

From that time forth not a day passed without the young man's putting in an appearance at a certain hour under the windows of the house. Without any prearrangement, certain relations were established between them. As she sat at her work in her place, she could sense his approach; lifting her head, she would watch him longer and longer each day. The young man, it seemed, felt grateful to her for this: she perceived, with the keen vision of youth, how quickly a flush mantled his pale cheeks each time their glances met. A week more, and she gave him a smile. . . .

When Tomski had asked the Countess for permission to present his friend, the poor girl's heart had begun to beat fast. But when she learned that Narumov was not in the Engineers but the Horse Guards, she regretted having betrayed her secret to the frivolous Tomski by her indiscreet question.

Hermann was the son of a Russianized German who had left him a very small patrimony. Firmly convinced of the necessity for making his independence secure, Hermann refrained from touching even his interest and lived entirely on his salary, without permitting himself the slightest indulgence. However, he was secretive and ambitious, and his associates rarely had an opportunity to laugh at his excessive thrift. He had strong passions and an ardent imagination, but his firmness of character saved him from the usual vagaries of youth. Thus, for instance, although a gambler at heart, he never touched cards, for he had coldly calculated that his circumstances did not permit him (as he put it) *to sacrifice the essential in the hope of acquiring the superfluous*—yet for all that, he would pass night after night sitting at card tables, and follow, with a feverish agitation, the various turns of the game.

The anecdote of the three cards affected his imagination deeply and would not leave his mind all night long.

"What would happen," he kept thinking all evening on the following day, as he wandered about Petersburg, "what would happen if the old Countess were to reveal her secret to me? If she were to designate those three unfailing cards to me! Why shouldn't I try my luck? I ought to get an introduction to her, worm my way into her good graces—become her lover, perhaps; but all that demands time, whereas she's all of eighty-seven; she can die in a week—in a couple of days! And then there's the story itself—can anyone believe it? No: Calculation, Moderation, and Industry: there are my three unfailing cards; there's what will increase my fortune threefold and even sevenfold, and bring me security and independence!"

Meditating in this fashion, he found himself on one of the principal streets of Petersburg, before a house of old-fashioned architecture. The street was blocked with vehicles, as carriage after carriage rolled up to the brightly lit entrance. At every minute the carriage doors opened, and the shapely foot of some belle would emerge, or a high boot with jingling spur, or the clocked stocking and patent-leather pump of a diplomat. Capes and fur coats flitted past the majestic doorman. Hermann stopped.

"Whose house is that?" he asked the policeman in a striped sentry-box at the corner.

"Countess ——'s," answered the policeman.

Hermann felt his pulse quicken. The amazing anecdote came to his imagination again. He began pacing to and fro near the house, thinking of its mistress and her wonderful faculty. It was late when he came back to his own modest quarters; it was long before he could fall asleep; and when sleep did overcome him, he dreamt of cards, of the gaming table covered with green baize, of heaped-up bank notes and mounds of gold pieces. He played card after card, placed his stakes without the least hesitation, and won with never a break, raking in the gold and stuffing the notes in his pockets.

When he awoke, quite late, he sighed at the loss of his imaginary wealth, went out to roam about the city again, and again found himself before the house of Countess ——. An unknown force, it seemed, was drawing him to it. He stopped, and fixed his eyes upon its windows. In one of them he caught sight of a little dark head apparently bent over a book or some work. The pretty head lifted. Hermann glimpsed a rosy little face and a pair of dark eyes.

That moment decided his fate.

No sooner had Lizaveta Ivanovna taken off her manteau and bonnet than the Countess sent for her again and ordered the carriage once more. They went down to it. Just as two footmen had lifted the old woman and thrust her in through the carriage door, Lizaveta Ivanovna saw her young Engineer standing by the very wheel. He seized her hand. She was beside herself with fright; the young man vanished—and she found a letter in her hand. She hid it inside her glove and throughout the entire drive neither heard nor saw anything. The Countess was in the habit of asking questions every minute while they were in the carriage: Who was that they had met?—What was the name of that bridge?—What did that sign say? On this occasion Lizaveta Ivanovna answered at random and so very wide of the mark that she provoked the Countess.

"What's come over you, my girl? Are you in a daze, or what? Either you aren't listening to me, or you don't understand me! Thank heaven, I don't lisp, and I'm not so old that I haven't my wits about me!"

Lizaveta Ivanovna was not listening to her. When they returned home, she ran to her room and took the letter (it was not sealed) out of her glove. She read it. The letter contained a declaration of love: it was tender, deferential—and taken word for word out of a sentimental German novel. But Lizaveta Ivanovna knew no German and was very pleased with the epistle.

Nevertheless, the letter she had accepted troubled her exceedingly. It was the first time she had ever entered into secret, close relations with a young man. His presumption horrified her. She reproached herself with imprudent behavior and did not know what to do: should she stop sitting at the window and, by her indifference, cool the young officer's inclination to pursue her further? Should she send the letter back to him? Should she answer him coldly and in positive terms? She had no one with whom to take counsel; she had no friend or preceptress. At last Lizaveta Ivanovna decided to answer the letter.

She sat down at her small desk, got out quill and paper, and sank into thought. She began her letter several times—and tore it up each time: her expressions seemed to her either too condescending or too severe. Finally, she succeeded in writing a few lines with which she remained satisfied.

"I am sure," she wrote, "that your intentions are honorable and that you would not wish to offend me by an unconsidered action, but our acquaintance must not begin in such fashion. I am returning your letter to you, and I hope that, hereafter, I shall have no reason to complain of a lack of respect which I do not merit."

The next day, seeing Hermann approaching, Lizaveta Ivanovna rose from her embroidery frame, went out into the drawing room, opened the ventilator, and tossed the letter out into the street, trusting to the young officer's adroitness. Hermann darted forward, picked up the letter, and stepped into a confectioner's shop. On breaking the seal, he found his own letter and Lizaveta Ivanovna's answer. He had expected as much, and returned home very much fascinated by his intrigue.

Three days later a young, bright-eyed miss brought Lizaveta Ivanovna a note from a fashionable shop. Lizaveta Ivanovna opened it with misgivings, anticipating a dun, but suddenly recognized Hermann's handwriting.

"My dear, you've made a mistake," she said. "This note isn't for me."

"Oh, but it is for you, sure enough!" answered the pert girl without concealing a sly smile. "Be kind enough to read it."

Lizaveta Ivanovna ran her eyes over the note. Hermann requested a meeting.

"Impossible!" said Lizaveta Ivanovna, frightened both at the urgency of his request and the means he had taken for its delivery. "This is certainly not for me!" And she tore the letter into tiny pieces.

"If the letter isn't for you, then why did you tear it up?" asked the shopgirl. "I'd have taken it back to the party who sent it."

"Please, my dear," said Lizaveta Ivanovna, flaring up at her remark, "from now on don't bring me any notes! And as for the one who sent you, tell him he ought to be ashamed of himself!"

But Hermann would not desist. She received a letter from him every day, transmitted in one way or another. No longer were these letters translations from the German. Hermann wrote them inspired by passion, and spoke in his own language: both the inflexibility of his desires and the disordered state of an unbridled imagination were expressed in them. Lizaveta Ivanovna no longer thought of sending them back; she drank them in; she began to answer them—and her notes were becoming longer and more tender from hour to hour. At last she threw the following letter to him from the window:

"There's a ball tonight at the A—— an Ambassador's. The Countess is going. We shall be there until about two. This is your opportunity to see me alone. As soon as the Countess has left, her servants will probably disperse. The doorman will be left in the vestibule, but he usually goes off to his own cubbyhole. Come at half-past eleven. Go right up the steps. If you should find anyone in the hall, just ask whether the Countess is home. They will tell you she isn't, and there won't be much left for you to do but to come back and try again. But probably you won't meet anyone. The maids will be sitting in their own room. From the vestibule turn left and go straight to the Countess's bedroom. There, behind a screen, you will see two small doors; the one at the right leads to the study, which the Countess never enters; the one at the left into a corridor, and there you will find a narrow winding stairway: it leads to my room."

Hermann quivered like a tiger as he waited for the appointed time. At ten that evening he was already standing outside the Countess's house. The weather was frightful; the wind howled, the snow fell in large wet flakes; the lanterns burned dimly; the streets were deserted. Occasionally a jehu would amble by with his gaunt nag, on the lookout for a belated fare. Hermann stood there, in his light tunic, feeling neither the wind nor the snow. At last the Countess's carriage drew up. Hermann saw how the bent old woman, wrapped in a sable cloak, was practically carried out under the arms by flunkies, and how, in a wrap that did not give much warmth, with fresh flowers adorning her head, her protégée flitted behind the Countess. The doors of the carriage slammed; it lumbered off over the powdery snow. The doorman closed the doors. The windows grew dark. Hermann began to walk up and down beside the house that now seemed deserted; he walked up to a street lamp and looked at his watch: it was twenty minutes past eleven. He remained under the street lamp, his eyes fixed on the hands of his watch as he waited for the remaining minutes to pass.

At exactly half-past eleven Hermann went up the steps of the Countess's mansion and entered the brightly lit vestibule. The doorman was not around. Hermann ran up the stairs, opened the door into an anteroom, and saw a servant asleep under the lamp, seated in an ancient, soiled armchair. With a light firm step Hermann walked past him. The drawing room and the parlor were dark, the lamp from the anteroom lighting them but feebly.

Hermann entered the bedroom. Before an ark filled with ancient images a golden lampad glowed warmly. Armchairs and sofas, most of their gilt worn off, upholstered in faded silk, their cushions stuffed with down, were ranged in depressing symmetry against walls covered with Chinese wallpaper. Two portraits painted in Paris by Mme. Lebrun hung on a wall. One depicted a man about forty, ruddy and stout, in a light green uniform with a star of some order; the other, a young aquiline-nosed beauty with a rose in her powdered hair, done into ringlets at the temples. Every nook and corner was cluttered with porcelain shepherds and shepherdesses, clocks made by the celebrated Leroy, little boxes, diavolos, fans and all sorts of feminine knickknacks, invented at the end of the eighteenth century together with Montgolfier's balloon and Mesmer's magnetism.

Hermann went behind the screen. There stood a small iron cot; at the right was a door leading into the study; at the left another, leading into a corridor. Hermann opened it; he saw a narrow winding stairway which led to the room of the poor protégée. . . . But he turned back and entered the dark study.

Time dragged by. All was still. Twelve o'clock struck in the parlor; one after another, the clocks in all the rooms struck midnight—and everything grew still again. Hermann stood leaning against the cold tile stove. He was calm; his heart beat evenly, like that of a man who has decided on a course of action that is hazardous but inevitable. The clocks struck the first, then the second hour of the morning—and he heard the distant rattle of a carriage. He was overcome by an excitement beyond his control. The carriage drove up and stopped. He heard the clatter of the carriage-step being let down. Commotion sprang up throughout the house. People started running about, voices were heard, and the house was lighted up. Three elderly chambermaids ran into the bedroom, and the Countess, more dead than alive, came in and sank into a deep, high-backed leather wing-chair. Hermann peeked through the keyhole: Lizaveta Ivanovna went past him. He heard her hurried steps on the treads of her stairs. Something resembling the gnawing of conscience stirred in his heart, but was stilled again. He was petrified.

The Countess began to undress before her mirror. Her maids unpinned her mobcap trimmed with roses; they took the powdered wig off her gray, closely-cropped head. Hairpins rained about her. The yellow dress, embroidered with silver, fell down about her swollen feet. Hermann was witness to the revolting mysteries of her toilette. Finally, the Countess remained in her nightgown and nightcap; in that costume, more suitable to her old age, she seemed less horrible and outrageous.

Like old people in general, the Countess suffered from insomnia. After undressing she sat down by the window in the wing chair and dismissed the chambermaids. The candles were carried out and the room was again lit only by the solitary icon-lamp. The Countess sat there, all yellow, moving her pendulous lips, her body rocking from side to side. Her turbid eyes expressed nothing but complete absence of thought; looking at her, one might have thought that the rocking of the frightful old woman proceeded not from her will but from the action of secret galvanism.

Suddenly that dead face altered indescribably. Her lips ceased moving, her eyes became animated: a strange man was standing before the Countess.

"Don't be frightened; for God's sake don't be frightened!" he said in a clear and quiet voice. "I have no intention of harming you; I have come to implore a certain favor of you."

The old woman was looking at him in silence and, it seemed, without hearing him. Hermann surmised that she was deaf and, bending to her very ear, he repeated what he had just said. The old woman remained as silent as before.

"You have it in your power," Hermann went on, "to bring about my life's happiness, and it would entail no cost to you: I know that you can guess three winning cards in a row—"

Hermann paused. The Countess, apparently, had grasped what was being demanded of her; she seemed to be groping for words with which to answer.

"It was a jest," she said at last. "I swear to you it was a jest!"

"This is not a matter to jest about," Hermann retorted angrily. "Remember Chaplitski, whom you helped to win back his losses."

The Countess became visibly embarrassed. Her features betrayed a powerful agitation of the soul, but she soon sank back into her former insensibility.

"Can you," Hermann persisted, "designate to me those three infallible cards?"

The Countess remained silent; Hermann resumed:

"For whom should you guard your secret? For your grandchildren? They're rich even without that; why, they're actually unaware of the value of money. Your three cards would be of no avail to a profligate. He who cannot guard his patrimony will die a beggar in the end, even if all the demons exerted themselves in his behalf. I am no profligate; I know the value of money. Your three cards will not be wasted on me. Well? . . ."

He stopped and awaited her answer with trepidation. The Countess maintained her silence; Hermann got down on his knees.

"If ever," he said, "your heart has known the feeling of love, if you remember its raptures, if you even once smiled at the cry of a newborn son, if anything human ever throbbed in your breast, then I implore you, by the feelings of a wife, a mistress, a mother—by all that is held holy in life—do not deny my plea! Reveal your secret to me! Of what good is it to you? Perhaps it is bound up with some horrible sin, with the loss of eternal bliss, with some diabolical compact. . . . Reflect: you are old, you have not long to live—I am ready to take your sin upon my soul. Do but reveal your secret to me. Consider that a man's happiness lies in your hands; that not only I but my children, my grandchildren and great-grandchildren will bless your memory and hold it sacred. . . ."

The old woman did not answer a word.

Hermann got up from his knees.

"You old witch!" said he, clenching his teeth. "In that case I'll make you answer—"

With these words he drew a pistol out of his pocket.

At sight of the pistol the Countess evinced strong emotion for the second time. She began to nod her head and raised an arm, as if to shield herself from the shot. . . . Then she rolled backward—and remained motionless.

"Stop acting childishly," said Hermann, taking her hand. "I am asking you for the last time: do you want to designate your three cards to me? Yes or no?"

The Countess made no answer. Hermann perceived that she had died.

Lizaveta Ivanovna, still in her ballroom finery, was sitting in her room, plunged in thought. On arriving home she had hastened to dismiss the sleepy wench who had grudgingly offered her services, telling her that she would undress herself, and had entered her room in trepidation, hoping to find Hermann there—and wishing she might not find him. At first glance she was convinced of his absence and thanked fate for whatever obstacle had hindered their meeting. Without undressing, she sat down and fell to recalling all the circumstances which, in so short a time, had seduced her to such lengths. Not even three weeks had passed since the first time she had noticed the young man from her window—and here she was already carrying on a correspondence with him, and he had already succeeded in inducing her to grant him a tryst at night! She knew his name only because some of his letters had been signed; she had never spoken with him, had never heard his voice, had never even heard of him until that very evening. A strange thing! That very evening at the ball Tomski, angry with the young Duchess Pauline—because she, contrary to her custom, flirted not with him but someone else—had wanted to pay her back by a show of indifference: he had sought out Lizaveta Ivanovna and danced an endless mazurka with her. During all that time he twitted her about her partiality for officers in the Engineers, assuring her that he knew much more than she could suppose, and some of his jokes were so close to the mark that several times Lizaveta Ivanovna thought her secret was known to him.

"From whom did you find out all this?" she asked, laughing.

"From a friend of the person you know," answered Tomski. "From a very remarkable man!"

"And who may this remarkable man be?"

"His name is Hermann."

Lizaveta Ivanovna said nothing in reply, but her hands and feet turned to ice.

"This Hermann," Tomski went on, "is truly a character out of a romantic novel; he has the profile of Napoleon—and the soul of Mephistopheles. I think this man must have at least three malefactions on his soul. . . . How pale you've become!"

"I've a headache. But what was it this Hermann—or whatever his name is—told you?"

"Hermann is very much displeased with his friend: he says that, in his place, he would have acted altogether differently. I even surmise that Hermann himself has designs upon you; at any rate, he listens to the infatuated exclamations of his friend with anything but indifference."

"But where did he see me?"

"At church, or perhaps when you were out on a drive! God alone knows what Hermann is up to! Perhaps in your room, while you were asleep; he is capable of it—"

Three ladies, coming up to Tomski and offering him his choice of a partner under the mask-words of *"Oubli ou regret?"* interrupted the conversation, which was becoming excruciatingly tantalizing for Lizaveta Ivanovna. The lady chosen by Tomski was none other than the Duchess Pauline. She contrived to clear things up with him, after having made an extra turn around the room and still another near her chair. Tomski on coming back to his own place gave no further thought either to Hermann or Lizaveta Ivanovna. She felt it imperative to renew the interrupted conversation, but the mazurka ended, and shortly after the old Countess made her departure.

Tomski's words were nothing more than the badinage appropriate to a mazurka, but they sank deeply into the soul of the young dreamer. The portrait sketched by Tomski bore a resemblance to the picture she herself had formed, and such a character, by now vulgarized through the latest novels, both frightened and captivated her imagination. She sat, with her bared arms crossed, her head, still bedecked with flowers, sunk forward on her décolletée bosom. . . . Suddenly the door opened and Hermann entered. She began to tremble.

"Where have you been?" she asked in a frightened whisper.

"In the bedroom of the old Countess," Hermann replied. "I've just come away from her. The Countess is dead."

"My God! What are you saying?"

"And it seems," Hermann continued, "I am the cause of her death."

Lizaveta Ivanovna glanced at him, and Tomski's words resounded in her heart: *This man must have at least three malefactions on his soul!*

Hermann sat down on the window sill near her and told her everything that had happened.

Lizaveta Ivanovna heard him out with horror. And so those passionate letters, those flaming demands, this audacious, determined pursuit—all this had not been love! Money—that was what his soul had hungered after! It was not she who could allay his desires and make him happy! The poor protégée had been nothing but the blind accomplice of the brigand, the murderer of her aged benefactress! . . . She burst into bitter tears in her belated, agonizing repentance.

Hermann watched her in silence; his heart, too, was in torture, but neither the poor girl's tears nor her striking loveliness in her grief troubled his obdurate soul. He felt no remorse at the thought of the dead old woman. Only one thing horrified him: the irretrievable loss of the secret which he had expected to enrich him.

"You're a monster!" Lizaveta Ivanovna uttered at last.

"I did not desire her death," Hermann retorted. "My pistol is unloaded."

They fell silent.

Morning was at hand. Lizaveta Ivanovna extinguished the dying candle; a wan light was diffused through her room. She dried her tear-stained eyes and raised them to look at Hermann: he sat on the window sill, his hands folded and his brows knit in a sinister frown. In this attitude there was something about him amazingly reminiscent of portraits of Napoleon. This resemblance overwhelmed even Lizaveta Ivanovna.

"How will you get out of the house?" she asked at last. "I was thinking of taking you down the secret staircase, but it would be necessary to go past the bedroom, and I'm afraid."

"Tell me how to find this secret staircase; I'll find my way out."

Lizaveta Ivanovna rose, took a key out of the bureau, put it into Hermann's hand, and gave him detailed directions. Hermann pressed her cold, unresponsive hand, kissed her bowed head, and went out.

He descended the winding stairway and once more entered the Countess' bedroom. The dead old woman sat there, rigid as stone: her face wore an expression of profound calm. Hermann stopped in front of her; he gazed at her a long time, as if wishing to assure himself of the horrible truth. Finally he went into the study, groped for and found the door concealed by wallpaper, and began to descend the dark staircase, agitated by strange sensations. Up this same stairway, he mused, perhaps all of sixty years ago, into that same bedroom, at just such an hour, his hair dressed à l'oiseau royal,[1] pressing his three-cornered hat to a heart beating fast under an embroidered long coat, some fortunate youth, now long turned to dust in his grave, had been making his stealthy way—and this night the heart of his most ancient mistress had ceased to beat. . . .

Hermann found the door at the foot of the staircase, which he opened with the same key, and found himself in an open passageway which let him out into the street.

At nine in the morning, three days after the fatal night, Hermann went to the celebrated monastery of V———, where a requiem mass was to be sung over the remains of the departed Countess. Though he felt no repentance, he nevertheless could not completely still the voice of conscience that kept repeating to

---

[1]After the style of the royal bird—that is, the heron.

him: "You are the murderer of the old woman!" Having but little real faith, he was hagridden by a host of superstitions. He believed that the dead Countess could exercise a baneful influence on his life—and decided to attend her funeral in order to beg for and obtain her forgiveness.

The church was full. Hermann could barely force his way through the throng. The coffin rested on a sumptuous catafalque under a baldachin of velvet. The woman now gone to her long rest lay with her hands crossed on her breast, in lace cap and gown of white satin. Round about stood the members of her household: the servants in black caftans, with armorial ribbons over their shoulders and candles in their hands; her relatives—her children, grandchildren, and great-grandchildren—all in deep mourning. Nobody wept; tears would have been *une affectation*. The Countess was so old that her death could not stun anyone, and her relatives had long regarded her as one who had lived beyond her time. A youthful prelate delivered the funeral oration. In simple and moving terms he described the peaceful passing away of this righteous woman, whose long years had been a quiet, touching preparation for an end befitting a Christian.

"The Angel of Death came upon her," said the orator, "as she was keeping vigil amid pious meditations and awaiting the Bridegroom that cometh at midnight."

The service concluded with sad decorum. The relatives were the first to come forward to bid the body farewell. Then followed the multitudinous guests, who had come to pay their last homage to one who had ever so many years ago been a participant in their frivolous diversions. And after them came all the domestics. The last to approach was the ancient "lady's lady" or housekeeper, a serf-woman of the same age as the deceased. Two young girls supported her under the arms as they led her along. It was beyond her strength to bow down to the ground—yet she was the only one to shed a few tears as she kissed the cold hand of her mistress.

After she had turned away, Hermann summoned up the resolution to approach the casket. He prostrated himself, and lay without moving for several minutes on the cold floor strewn with fir needles. Finally he rose, pale as the dead woman herself, went up the steps of the catafalque, and bent over the casket. . . . At that moment it appeared to him that the dead woman gave him a mocking glance, puckering up one eye. Hastily drawing back, Hermann missed a step and crashed to the ground, falling flat on his back. They picked him up. At the very same time, Lizaveta Ivanovna was carried out in a faint to the church porch. This incident disturbed for several minutes the solemn pomp of the somber ceremonial. A subdued murmur arose among the onlookers, and a gaunt Court Chamberlain, a near relative of the deceased, whispered into the ear of an Englishman standing next to him that the young officer was her son on the wrong side of the blanket, to which the Englishman replied with a chill "Oh?"

Hermann was extremely upset all that day. Dining in an obscure tavern, he drank a great deal, contrary to his custom, in the hope of silencing his inner disquietude. But the wine merely enfevered his imagination still more. When he returned home he threw himself on his bed without undressing and fell fast asleep.

When he awoke it was already night. His room was flooded with moonlight. He glanced at his watch; it was a quarter to three. Sleep had left him; he sat down on the bed and meditated on the funeral of the old Countess.

At that moment someone peered in from the street through the window—and immediately stepped back. Hermann paid not the least attention to this occurrence. A minute later he heard someone opening the door in the entry. Hermann thought it was his orderly, drunk as usual, returning from a nocturnal prowl. But the step he heard was an unfamiliar one: someone was softly shuffling along in slippers. The door opened; a white-garbed woman entered. Hermann took her for his old wet-nurse, and wondered what could have brought her at such an hour. But the woman in white, gliding along, suddenly confronted him—and Hermann recognized the Countess.

"I have come to you against my will," she said in a firm voice, "but I am under a command to fulfill your request. The trey, the seven, and the ace will win for you in that order—but only under these conditions: that you stake on only one card in twenty-four hours, and never play again in your life thereafter. As for my death, I forgive you—provided you marry my protégée, Lizaveta Ivanovna."

With the last word she turned quietly, went to the door, and disappeared, her slippers shuffling. Hermann heard the outer door slam in the entry and saw someone again peer in at his window.

It was a long time before Hermann could come back to himself. He went out into the other room. His orderly was sleeping on the floor; it was all Hermann could do to rouse him. As usual, the orderly was drunk; there was no getting anything sensible out of him. The door into the entry was locked. Hermann went back to his room, lit the candle, and wrote down an account of his apparition.

Two fixed ideas can no more co-exist in the nature of morality than two bodies can occupy one and the same space in the physical world. *Trey, seven, ace*—these soon obscured the image of the dead old woman in Hermann's imagination. *Trey, seven, ace*—they never left his mind and were perpetually on his lips. If he laid eyes on a young woman, he would say:"How shapely she is! . . . Nothing short of a trey of hearts!" If he was asked:"What time is it?" he would answer:"Five minutes to a seven of—" Every paunchy man called up an ace in his mind. *Trey, seven, ace* haunted him in his sleep, taking on every guise possible. The trey bloomed before him in the shape of a magnificent, luxuriant flower; the seven presented itself as a Gothic portal; the ace, as an enormous spider. All his thoughts coalesced into one: to avail himself of the secret which had cost him so dear. He began thinking of resigning and traveling. He wanted to wrest a treasure-trove from the bewitched goddess Fortune in the open gambling hells of Paris. But chance relieved him of going to any trouble.

A syndicate of wealthy gamblers was organized in Moscow under the chairmanship of the celebrated Chekalinski, who had spent all his life at cards, and who had at one time amassed millions by accepting IOU's when he won and by paying in cold cash when he lost. His experience of many years had earned for him the confidence of his associates, while the open house he kept, his famous chef, and his own geniality and affability had gained him the respect of the public. He came to Petersburg. The young people flocked to him, neglecting dances for cards and preferring the temptations of faro to the fascinations of gallantry. Narumov took Hermann with him to Chekalinski's.

They passed through a succession of magnificent rooms, with obsequious flunkies at every step. Several generals and privy councilors were playing whist; young men were lounging and sprawling on the divans upholstered in brocaded silks, eating ice cream or smoking pipes. In the main room, at a long table with a score or so of gamblers crowded around it, sat the host, keeping the bank. He was a man of about sixty, of the most respectable appearance: his head was silvery gray; his full, rosy face wore an expression of geniality; his eyes twinkled, animated by a never-failing smile. Narumov presented Hermann to him. Chekalinski shook hands with him cordially, begged him to make himself at home, and went on dealing.

The game lasted a long time. There were more than thirty cards on the table. Chekalinski stopped after every deal to give the players time to arrange their hands, tallied the losses, listened attentively to the players' demands, and even more attentively straightened out the extra corner turned down by the hand of some gambler too absent-minded to put up the additional stake signified thereby. But at last the game came to an end. Chekalinski shuffled the cards and prepared to deal again.

"Let me stake on a card," said Hermann, stretching out his hand from behind a stout man who was also about to punt. Chekalinski smiled and bowed in silence in token of courteous acquiescence. Narumov laughingly congratulated Hermann on breaking his long abstention at last, and wished him beginner's luck.

"Here goes!" said Hermann, writing his stake in chalk above his card.

"How much, Sir?" asked the banker, screwing up his eyes. "I can't quite make it out, Sir."

"Forty-seven thousand," answered Hermann.

At these words every head in the room turned instantaneously, and all eyes were directed at him.

"He's gone out of his mind!" thought Narumov.

"Allow me to point out to you," Chekalinski said with his unfailing smile, "that you're playing a very high game—nobody here has ever yet staked more than two hundred and seventy-five on a single card."

"Well, what is it to be?" retorted Hermann. "Are you covering my card or not?"

Chekalinski bowed with the same air of submissive acquiescence.

"I merely wanted to inform you that, since I am honored by the confidence of my associates, I cannot play except for spot cash. For my own part, of course, I'm convinced that your word is enough, but, for the sake of keeping the game and tallies straight, I must ask you to put up money on your card."

The young Engineer took a bank note out of his pocket and handed it to Chekalinski, who, after a cursory glance at it, placed it on Hermann's card. Chekalinski began to deal for stuss. A nine lay to the right of Hermann's card and, to its left, a trey.

"My card won!" said Hermann, showing his card.

A murmur arose among the players. Chekalinski frowned, but the smile immediately came back to his face.

"Would you care to have your winnings now?"

"If you will be so good."

Chekalinski took several bank notes out of his pocket and settled on the spot. Hermann took his money and left the table. Narumov was in a daze. Hermann drank a glass of lemonade and went home.

On the evening of the following day he again appeared at Chekalinski's. The host was dealing. Hermann walked up to the table; the players immediately made room for him. Chekalinski bowed to him affably.

Hermann waited for a new game, picked his card, and staked thereon his own forty-seven thousand and his winnings of the evening before.

Chekalinski began to deal. A jack turned up to the right of Hermann's card, a seven to its left.

Hermann showed his seven.

The cry of astonishment was general. Chekalinski was obviously disconcerted. He counted out ninety-four thousand and passed the sum over to Hermann. The latter accepted it with *sang-froid* and instantly withdrew.

On the following evening Hermann appeared at the gaming-table again. Everyone had been expecting him. The Generals and Privy Councilors dropped their whist in order to watch such extraordinary play. The young officers jumped up from their divans; all the flunkies gathered in the main salon. Everybody surrounded Hermann. The other players did not pick any cards, impatiently waiting to see how he would wind up. Hermann stood by the table, preparing to play alone against the pale yet still smiling Chekalinski. Each broke the seal on a fresh deck of cards. Chekalinski shuffled his deck. Hermann picked a card from his and placed his stake, snowing under the card with a heap of bank notes. The situation resembled a duel. A profound silence reigned throughout the room.

Chekalinski began to deal; his hands were shaking. A queen came up to the right, an ace to the left.

"The ace has won!" said Hermann, and turned up his card.

"Your queen is done for," said Chekalinski amiably.

Hermann shuddered: true enough, instead of an ace he held the queen of spades. He could not believe his own eyes, unable to understand how he could have missed.

At that moment it seemed to him that the queen of spades puckered up her eye and smiled mockingly. The extraordinary resemblance stunned him.

"The old woman!" he screamed in horror.

Chekalinski drew the forfeited bank notes toward him. Hermann was still standing motionless. When he at last left the table, noisy discussion sprang up throughout the room.

"He played splendidly!" the players commented.

Chekalinski shuffled the cards anew; the game resumed its ordinary course.

Hermann went out of his mind. He is now confined in the Obuhov Hospital, in cell No. 17; he never responds to any questions, but mutters with remarkable rapidity: "Trey, seven, ace! Trey, seven, queen! . . ."

Lizaveta Ivanovna married a very agreeable young man; he has some sort of post and is possessed of considerable means—he is the son of a former steward to the old Countess. She is bringing up a girl, a poor relation of hers.

Tomski has been promoted to a captaincy, and is engaged to be married to the Duchess Pauline.

From Memoir of a Gambler

BY JACK RICHARDSON

There is a strand in gambling literature—one that literalizes and dramatizes the senses in which every gambling act involves temptation—in which the gambler is offered (through supernatural arts, talismans, or techniques of cheating) the means of triumphing over other gamblers. In classical formulations—as with the selling of the soul for knowledge or riches—the gambler must not misuse such talents for fear of having them withdrawn with ruinous consequences, as in E. T. A. Hoffman's "Gambler's Luck." In the following selection, Jack Richardson is faced with a contemporary version of temptation through an unlikely, suitably quirky character.

Richardson's *Memoir of a Gambler* (1979) is a suave, carnal, existential picaresque through the underside of the gambling world from Las Vegas to Gardenia to Macao to Hong Kong, where, in a sketchy Hong Kong neighborhood, he bets on various amphibians, insects, and annelids, and finally on which snake out of a group will eat a rodent first, and watches "with horror and amazement as [his] snake, when placed on the ground among its brothers, slithered with ominous purpose toward the caged rodent, struck lethally between the bars, and won, with great appetite, the wager [he] had put on him." An acclaimed playwright and gambling columnist for *Esquire,* Richardson is a scholar of squalor, brilliant self-diagnostician, and memorable storyteller.

"Can I buy you a drink, young fellow?"

It had been so long since anyone except a casino dealer had talked to me, that I didn't answer, certain that the man was addressing someone else. I kept staring at my reflection in the giant mirror behind the Lucky Horseshoe's bar, marveling how, in slightly over a week, I had become a study in genteel decline. Expensive suit, but un-

137

pressed and spotted; rumpled shirt with collar open and twisted over the jacket's lapels; face washed but unshaven; hair neat in appearance but really made rigid by sweat; expression, that of dignified hysteria, with eyes reflecting exhaustion.

"You don't look that good that you should pass up a drink."

This time I knew I was being spoken to. I looked at the man and said that I agreed with him.

"Blake's the name," he said. "Boris Blake, the last of a breed. Take a good look at me, young man, for I'm vanishing quickly."

I did and saw a comically malevolent face whose most impressive feature was a widow's peak that dropped across the width of his forehead almost to the bridge of the nose. The rest of his ink-black hair was slicked down on either side of a gleaming part that seemed made with a ruler. His eyes were slightly slanted, as were the brows above them. A thin mustache formed a neat triangle with his upper lip, and needed only a curl at each end to complete the standard portrait of a melodrama villain.

"So, are you taking out any money?" he asked when the drinks arrived. "You look like you've been working hard."

Even his voice had a twang of theatrical evil to it, a mixture of sinister cackles and greasy whines. His hands, however, were not those of a heartless landlord or riverboat sharper, not tapered and diabolically delicate. They were gruesomely large, with giant spatulate fingers into which the nails were crushed and embedded. They seemed deformed, yet they manipulated the drink and cigarette they held with unusual grace.

"This town is tough, I'm telling you. You don't get an inch from anyone here," Boris complained when I told him that things had not been going too well. "You look like a nice, gentlemanly person, if you know what I'm saying. And there's nothing around here but a bunch of thieves."

"All the thieves are on the house side of the table," I said, hoping that Boris was off on a loser's lament. To coax someone else who has lost into a display of chagrin is one of the lowest forms of comfort available to a losing gambler, but I was not above making use of it.

"You understand me," Boris said, a bit of amazement in his voice, as if he'd said something terribly complex. "You come here for a little honest gambling and you have to make yourself a sucker, turn yourself into a mark before they let you play. You gotta walk around carrying their vig on your back like some sort of coolie. Everyone's supposed to be equal in this country, so how come the house gets a five percent edge at blackjack and only pays thirty-to-one on double sixes?"

"That's the entertainment tax," I answered.

Boris reared back, his features arched in shock.

"And you're being entertained?" he asked.

At this point we suddenly were joined by the chief of the casino guards, a huge man who wore a gun and a serious expression.

"You're not thinking of doing any gambling here, are you, Boris?" he said softly. Boris put his glass down and asked why he was always being picked on every time he came into the Lucky Horseshoe, especially since he had lost thousands over the years at its tables.

When the guard answered with a blank expression, Boris demanded once and for all that it be explained to him why he should be hounded and harassed when he had the urge to make a five-dollar bet or just sniff around the games a little. Had he ever been offensive or slowed down the play at the tables? Was his money counterfeit, his breath bad, his racial origins not suited to the clientele's tastes? Was he, and he used this word with obvious pride in having learned it, a pariah? It seemed Boris could have continued his offended performance forever, but then he had to pause for breath and the hiatus in his complaint was filled by a drawled order to finish his drink and leave. Then the guardian of the casino patted him heavily on the back, stared at me for several seconds, and wandered off.

"I am *not* going to fool with crazy Texans," Boris said and drained his glass. "They're worse than the Wops up on the Strip. Up there they don't want to hurt anybody because of their image. Around here, they don't have any image that doesn't go with shooting people. It's their goddamn tradition, so I'm leaving."

During the next few days, as I waited for my luck to change, I kept glimpsing Boris prowling about the gambling rooms. Although he never bet or even mixed with the other players, he invariably was invited to leave by someone of menacing dimensions, and, after a brief argument, would quickly vanish.

I wondered vaguely why he was an outcast in a world open to anyone disposed to make a one-dollar bet, but I was too concerned with my own persecution to make any inquiries about his. The move to downtown Las Vegas was proving ineffective. In between bursts of luck, I still suffered long series of losses, and each morning I returned to my room three or four hundred dollars poorer than I'd been when the day began. With a brain filled with sour memories and sad financial calculations, it was impossible to sleep deeply, and I often simply forced myself to stay in bed until enough time had passed for me to believe that I must have rested. Then I'd jump up, splash water on my face, make a half-hearted effort to dry-shave—I was too impatient to be out of the room to bother with lathering—pick out my most presentable shirt, and head for the streets and another day at the tables.

I was eating lunch at a chili stand when I spoke to Boris the second time. For a day or so I had been unable to keep my hands from trembling whenever they closed in a gripping position, and I was having a difficult time trying to lead a huge, dripping taco into my mouth.

"Appearance is man's greatest asset, so said my uncle the tailor."

Boris was looking at a rivulet of rust-colored sauce oozing down my sleeve. I dabbed at it with a paper napkin and sent more of the taco splattering on the floor.

"They still grinding you out, young man?" he asked, taking a small but pointed step back from my droppings.

"Why do you keep calling me 'young fellow' and 'young man'?" I asked, trying to rise above my run-down condition.

"Just a manner of speaking," Boris protested. "Just a little friendly patter."

He paused and looked around him, his head throbbing forward and back like a lizard's.

"One of the few joints they don't throw me out of," he said approvingly. "Because it's one of the few joints that don't even have a slot machine on the premises."

I gave him a moment to savor his bitterness and then asked why he was so coolly received everywhere he went.

"Because I'm not a sucker," he answered proudly; then ruefully, "and because I've got too much heat. That's what I want to talk to you about, before they suck so much out of you that you start turning into a lush or shooting a little consolation up into your veins."

"I'm not so simple," I answered, and threw what remained of my Mexican lunch into a trashcan.

"I know you're not," Boris said, moving a little closer to me now that there was no danger of his being spattered. "I've got a good eye for class, and you look like you could move in any circles you wanted to. But let's face it, it don't look like you're doing too great at the moment."

"What if I'm not? Why should that interest you?"

"So you can tell I'm not an eccentric millionaire looking for people to help," Boris laughed. "The fact is, I've got a proposition for you if you can spare a little time. And in a way I am going to give you something for nothing. I am going to make you my heir."

We walked a block or so together and then got into a large station wagon. In a few minutes we were driving outside of Las Vegas, along a highway, through the desert.

"I mean this is bleak land, isn't it?" Boris sighed as we drove through a landscape of scrub cactus, dried clay, dust-covered rocks and tumbleweeds. "I was driving along a highway through country like this in New Mexico once, and I kept seeing signs that read 'Beware of Gusts.' I've no idea what the hell a gust's supposed to be, so I figure you've got to be pretty hard luck to run into one. So don't you know one of those goddamn gusts comes up behind me when I'm doing seventy an hour, and flips my car right off the road. One lousy gust cost me three months in a hospital. I tell you, nature can be a mean son-of-a-bitch. Don't fool with it."

"Where are we going?" I asked, as Las Vegas began to recede behind us.

"Somewhere where I can make you my offer in private," Boris said, and after chuckling and muttering to himself for a few miles, he suddenly answered the question I'd put to him at the lunch counter.

"So you want to know why they don't let me play in the gambling capital of the world? It's because they know I'm gonna rob them. Walk right out with their money, and they gotta just stand there and watch me."

"And how do you do that?"

"With these," Boris said, lifting his hands from the wheel for inspection. "With these mashed-up beauties I make cards and dice do weird, wonderful things. Do you understand what I'm tellin' you?"

"So you cheat."

"My friend," Boris answered, after weighing my statement with a few nods of meditation, "there was a time when I would have objected to that word. I would have put in a claim that I was an artist, or a Robin Hood who only stole from those who wanted to steal from me. But now I accept the word 'cheat.' Boris Blake at your service, the best dice and card mechanic in the world. No more, certainly no less."

"How good can you be if everyone knows your profession?" I asked. It was a question that made Boris wince.

"I've been at this for twenty years," he said in his best injured tone. "All over the world I've busted out games that no one thought could be taken. I've spotted cards with cream cheese in poker sessions in the Catskills and switched in shapes right under the nose of the toughest greaseballs in Brooklyn. I mean I took their money, friend. Right out of their goddamn pockets. I ... took ... their ... money! Hell, once when I was in jail I threw in a cooler against four Muslims in one game. I had no fear, that's why I was the best."

Suddenly Boris turned off the highway and headed up a side road that seemed to lead nowhere.

"But now, I've just been around too much. Even though no one's caught me in the act, there's just too much suspicion, too much heavy heat. I can't even do a little light work now and then without someone starting a beef. Fame has been thrust upon me, and I can't do anything about it."

"Why don't you retire?" I asked. "You must have made enough by now."

"Young man—after that remark I get to call you 'young man'—what the hell is enough? Come on, you're a gambler, you tell me what's your limit."

It was a good question, one which I had always known I would have to answer.

Suddenly Boris stopped. There was nothing around us for miles, which is exactly what he seemed to want as he scanned the area. When we got out of the car, we were almost knocked down by the desert heat, and for a minute both of us were afraid to breathe or speak. Slowly, I began to slide back into the air-conditioned wagon.

"No!" Boris finally gasped. "You've got to get out. I can't show you anything in there."

"We'll get a stroke if we stand out in the sun," I said, and tried to close the door past the wedge Boris had made with his body against it.

"Just ten minutes. I'll show you my work in ten minutes. Everything that I can teach, but enough for you to walk away with that whole goddamn town over there."

I looked at where Boris was pointing and saw, shimmering in the heat, a Las Vegas of vague, liquid colors and undulate forms.

Boris opened the rear door, took out a folding table, and set it on the hard, baked ground. Then he brought forth a small trunk, which he placed under the table, and two folding chairs. He asked me to sit in one, then took a deck of cards from the trunk and began shuffling them.

"You can understand," he said while performing neat, tight riffles with the deck, "why I wouldn't want to display all this in a hotel room. One nosy bellboy who tells a few stories and all those crazy cowboys who think they've gotta kill somebody once a week got me with the goods. Then they just don't ask me to leave, they do a little job on my body while I'm going."

Boris set the cards down on the table and motioned to me to cut them. Then he began his performance, speaking only to explain the precise nature of each manipulation or to exhort me to look closely at his large, mangled hands. For a few minutes, in that cooked wasteland, I watched him work his magic. Bottoms, seconds, annulment cuts, deck switches, holdouts, palmings, waving—all were displayed in swirls of easy movement that made a mockery of the senses. The demonstration ended with my dealing him hands of blackjack which he converted each time into the jack of clubs and ace of diamonds.

"Well, what do you think?" Boris asked, sweeping the cards from the table in a quick, single-handed movement.

"An impressive display," I said.

"Only part of my repertoire," he beamed. He then returned to the car and, from under a tarpaulin, removed what looked like a small, topless coffin and placed it on the table. When I peered into it, I saw that it was a scaled-down craps table, correct in every detail, even to its sides being covered by tiny rubber spikes to insure that dice would carom in a manner that can't be predetermined. Boris knelt down at one end of the long box, rolled a pair of ruby-colored dice along the length of the shooting surface, and asked me to examine them. I counted the number of spots on each side, made sure they were cubes, and let the sun flash through them to reveal any impurities.

"All right, toss them back, if you think they're legitimate."

I did, Boris picked them up, rattled them for several seconds, and then sent them crashing against my end of the table. When they came to rest, I saw that their color was now a deep emerald, and on closer inspection I discovered that the dotted sides contained only three numbers instead of six, that there was no possibility of their forming a combination that totaled seven. They could therefore be rolled forever and always make the shooter's point.

"How's that for a switch?" Boris asked.

"Magical," I answered.

"No, just work motivated by a love of larceny. Of course I don't switch in a pair of shapes like that except when I'm playing with some retards."

He then produced the red dice from a hollow in his hand that had been covered by a lump of muscle at the base of the thumb.

"All right," he said, "now I'm going to hold up a six, five times in a row. Keep your eyes on the little red squares."

Dizzy from the sun, I struggled to focus on the dice as they careened and bounced about the table. As Boris predicted, one of them always came to rest with a six-spotted side upward. Boris said nothing after the rolls were over, as if he divined my thoughts and had no wish to interrupt speculation on what it would mean to master such an art.

As we drove back to Las Vegas, Boris still avoided the subject of my becoming his pupil. Instead he told me about the event that had started his decline as a mechanic.

"I mean I had done real well for over fifteen years. Movin' from Miami to Vegas, from San Juan to London—anywhere there was action. And I never had no heat. I mean any time I wanted to I could drop into a joint and pick up five or ten large and slip away like a thief, like I'm Boris the Invisible. Then I go to Greece 'cause I hear they've opened up some new casinos there, and it figures that the joints oughtta be pretty soft, with dealers who don't even know how to count chips yet. Well, I walk into this place outside of Athens, a beautiful, plush layout with a view of some ruins up on a hill, and it looks just like a piece of cake. The dealers can't even peek at a hand without flashing their hole card and the guys at the dice table, half the time, forget to pick up a losing bet. I mean I could have played on the upsky and beaten that joint *all* the money. But I gotta do what I've taught myself to do, right? Which meant a little holding out at the blackjack table. Nothing too strong. Maybe three times an hour I come in with a twenty-one from my pocket, and nobody even thinks of blinking when I do. I'm not lookin' to make an impression, so after I've won about two thou I tip the dealer real nice and head for the cash-in window, thinking it's all been sweet and easy, and that maybe I'll drop back in a few days and hit for the same number. Then, just as I'm being paid off, this guy in a uniform walks up to me. He tells me he's Captain something-or-other and points to a nameplate and a badge he's got pinned on his uniform. Right away I know there's gonna be a beef and that the best way to handle that is to come on strong, start shouting about how much money you've dropped in their joint, how they've got some nerve to get nasty when you finally have a little run of luck, and in general make them want to get you out of there before you start scaring away all their customers. But for some reason I don't want to get this guy angry. It was hard to figure what he was gonna do. I mean, for Chrissake, how do you take a reading on a guy with triangles in his name. So, *schmuck* that I am, I let him take me back into his office, where we are joined by two sullen gorillas, also wearing badges and a lot of geometry on their chests, and I resign myself to getting bruised or giving back the money. However, the Captain offers me a chair and starts chatting with me real nice, asking me if I'm enjoying my stay in Athens and why I'd chosen Greece for a vacation. I answer him soft and polite, and for a minute I think maybe he's just some guy from the tourist bureau assigned to find out what kind of clientele the casino's attracting. Then he goes and opens the window and he stares at whatever you call those ruins at the top of the hill and very softly he asks me, 'Mr. Blake, why do you cheat?' just like that. Like he was asking what hotel I was stayin' at. Well, I say, 'I beg your pardon?' and he, with his back still to me, he sort of sighs and says again, 'Mr. Blake, I would like to know very much why you cheat.' Well, I'm forced to make a little protest at this you understand, so I give him my offended act and start to get up from the chair. This stirs up the gorillas, however, and so I sit down, and very calmly demand an apology. But he just turns around, smiles, and asks me the same question again. Did he see me cheat? I ask. Did anybody see me do anything wrong? He shrugs and wags his head like it didn't matter if anyone actually saw me making a move or two, like all he had to do was stare at my ears to tell that I'm a swindler. Then he starts a spiel about how cheating is really no more than robbery, and when you rob you make society a little worse than it was, and since you're a part of society you've made yourself also a little worse. Now, I'm listening to this—with two grand of the joint's money in my pocket, I feel I can afford to listen even if the guy is coming on like a mental case—and nodding like it's makin' sense. So he goes on and on, tellin' me that by palming an ace in his joint I'm really holdin' out on myself since I'm swindling what I'm a part of and no sane man is gonna do that, right? Right. But I say to him that I, Boris Blake, was robbing nobody. Only passing a little time. He shakes his head at this, like he's more disappointed than steamed up over the way I stick to my story. Then he picks up this little broken statue that's on his desk, you know one of those goddesses with drapery on them that you find in every junk shop in Athens. He gives it to me and asks me to look at it. It's about a foot high and real heavy, and as I'm running it down, thinking the lady's shoulders are a little broad for my taste, the Captain tells me who the goddess was and what she was supposed to have done and all sorts of things like he was a museum guide. Then suddenly right out he asks me if I think she's beautiful. Of course, I give him what I think he wants to hear, and tell him yes. He takes the statue back, nods at it—I'm getting an uneasy feeling that the guy is pure crazy by now—and then he asks me what I would think if I saw somebody relievin' himself on this beautiful statue. I start to laugh, but I gulp it right down when I see how serious the Captain's face is. I tell him it would be terrible, and he says, yes, it would be terrible because it would show ignorance. I go along with that, and then he makes a quick mental move back to me robbin' the joint. I'm ignorant of what I'm really doin', because I don't understand it. How can I understand what I didn't do? I shoot back at him. But if I had done it, would I understand it? And if I didn't do it, would it matter, if I didn't understand what I didn't do? I mean that was his ploy. Every time I answer a question, he's got another one, and I feel like a job's being done on me, but I can't figure where the con is. I just keep answerin' yes and no, no and yes, until I don't know what I'm talking about. I mean all I can get is that this guy is tryin' to prove that I'm some kind of moron or a thief, and I'm not buyin' either one of them. But it's like I'm standing on two chairs that are being pulled further and further apart. Finally I say no when I should have said yes or vice versa. He gives me a nice big smile and says, 'So, you did cheat us, Mr. Blake.' I give it one more shot at sayin' no, but he goes over everything we've said, all the questions and answers which to him, and to the two gorillas, prove that not only am I a bandit, but I'm a dumb bandit as well. Then he sort of pats my shoulder and says that you can't blame ignorance too much, so if I'll just return the money there'll be no official action taken. I figure okay, it's a standoff, so let's be civilized about it. I take out the cash and put it on the desk. This guy looks at it for a while and then he shoots a little sly look at the gorillas and suddenly each one grabs onto an arm so that my hands are stretched out flat on the desk. And this Greek bastard sort of shrugs, and brings that square-shouldered lady down on my left hand, then on my right, and then twice more on each of them. I won't even try to tell you what the pain was like. I mean I just kept whimpering all the time they dragged me off to some doctor, who doesn't do nothing but wrap some bandages around them so the bleeding doesn't show, and then to the airport where my bags are waiting for me along with a ticket out of the country. Then the Captain has my picture taken just in case, even with the banged-up hands he's given me, I come up with some way to beat the gambling joints, because, as he says, still talking soft and reasonable, it's hard to learn to be an honest man, even when you've really had a good teacher. Every casino in the world is gonna get a copy of my picture just in case I get confused about things again. Then he puts the statue next to me on the waiting bench and walks off."

When we stopped in front of my hotel, Boris told me that I didn't have to make my mind up right away. Then he held his hands out in front of me.

"In one year I had them working again. But the pictures ruined me. And to tell the truth, I never could've really made it in class joints. I got a bad face. I mean it's pretty easy to read me for larceny. But you, no one could ever take you for an outright weasel. You could bring what I know into places that don't let me through the door."

I told Boris that I would let him know my decision, but I really considered his proposal to teach me his craft no more than a fairy-tale boon, like a cloak of invisibility or a golden touch. It had its fantastic appeal, but I was still confident that I needed no wiles in order to gamble successfully, that I would naturally find my way to good fortune.

However, during the next few days, this confidence in myself began to fade. As my money dwindled, anxious swells passed over me, cold intimations of failure and permanent dishevelment, of a lifetime spent in a casino mob that scurries pointlessly from promise to promise. I kept demanding to win, but could still not find the courage needed to make winning possible, and so I went on changing games and tables, betting five or ten dollars at a time, waiting for an impossible run of luck that would, in an unbroken string of right choices, retrieve all the thousands I'd lost.

During this time, Boris did not talk to me again, but everywhere I gambled, he made a brief, pointed appearance. As a defense against immediate ejection, he had taken to wearing ridiculous disguises—beards, wigs and glasses, behind which it was absurdly easy to recognize his condemned features and detect his soul's devotion to chicanery. We of course didn't acknowledge each other, and I would continue gambling as though I'd never considered making a pact between us.

One morning, at about five o'clock, I believed my luck had finally changed. All night I had been losing, and I now had nothing left of the money I'd brought to Las Vegas except two thousand-dollar traveler's checks. The evening's long series of defeats had left me too exhausted to go through the procedure of cashing one, a process that had naturally become more difficult as my appearance deteriorated, and I began a slow retreat from the casino's center tables. On the way, I stopped for a second at all the slot machines, hoping to find one that had been left primed by an absent-minded player. This was indeed a low ritual, indulged in by the most debased victims of bad luck who milled about the downtown casinos. But for the last few nights, I had tried the handles without shame, unembarrassed even when I knew I was being contemptuously watched by employees and players alike.

Somewhere in the middle of a row of dollar machines, I drew down a handle and felt it slip past the locking gears. I took a breath, continued to pull, and indeed the machine sprang to life, its strips of colored symbols humming into a single blur that, after three separate clicking stops, would resolve into a trio of bells, fruit and golden bars.

However, when the whirring stopped, it was not these usual symbols I saw in front of me. Instead, one, then another, and then a third small red heart appeared behind the glass covering, and before I could check its diagram of winning combinations, the machine began to buzz, brighten and pulsate with colored lights. I rushed to snatch a cup from a nearby table just as a long metallic retch was followed by a clanging spew of silver dollars from the mouth of the machine. I filled the cup, my pockets and my hands, and still the flood continued, coins dropping around me on the floor, adding their clatter to the noise the machine still made to advertise its generosity. Other players stopped to help me retrieve them, and even those who had been uneasily entertained by the sight of my attempting to coax free chances from the slots, joined in the search and brought me, with congratulations, my silver dollars.

When all had been found, a guard escorted me to a change booth, where a smiling lady presented me with a large, round pin that had the casino's name and "Jackpot Winner" stamped on it. Then she counted my coins and changed them into a form I could more conveniently carry—a single hundred-dollar bill.

Naturally, it was not the amount, but the way of obtaining it, that made me feel certain I'd been given the sign I'd waited for during the weeks of slow, grinding descent. I sensed I was again part of a formal drama that was constructed from the beginning with a just resolution in view. Not to act decisively after such *ex machina* intercession would mean that one should forfeit the right to gamble forever, and, so, wearing my winner's badge, with the vision of three tiny red hearts held in my mind for triple courage, I went to the craps table, and bet the hundred dollars when the dice were passed to me.

I lost on the first roll, which caused no stir among the stickmen and players at the table, but which took me several horrible minutes to comprehend. And even when I understood that an event had indeed just taken place that put an end to dramatics, I could not accept that I'd been used with such cruelty. I had not expected gambling to create for me a world of honorable coherence, but neither had I expected a malicious one. To have tricked me with a false sign, a sign that no one who nostalgically wishes for meanings in things would not trust in and follow, meant that gambling was as perverse as any of the old philosophies I'd abandoned; that it was no more than raw and raucous data. I watched the dice bounce upon the table, the chips and money pass back and forth between those who ran the game and those who played in it, and rage began to swell inside me. Never had I been so toyed with, so beguiled by apparent meaning, and when I was calm enough to leave the table, I'd decided to accept everything Boris had offered me.

For the next hour I searched for him in the casinos and all-night bars along the streets and avenues of lower Las Vegas. By now it was well into morning, but there were no social signs around me of a day's beginning. Instead, I saw all the activities of night perpetuating themselves, and the people caught up in them, whether just wakened or driven past sleep by fear or amusement, appeared unconcerned with ordinary notions of time. They were used to conducting life's business according to schedules of private noons and midnights, and they filled bars at eight in the morning as comfortably as they did supermarkets at eleven at night.

Instead of the unease I usually felt when I found myself drifting from one day into another without the traditional pause for sleep and ablutions, I enjoyed the disordered morning. The mixture of di- and nocturnal attitudes helped strengthen my resolve to give up all desire for a design to life, and as I'd freed myself in Munich from an addiction to pure thought, so I now was ready, in lower Las Vegas, to abandon my gambler's superstitions.

Since it was proving difficult to find a disguised Boris among the early-morning rabble, I decided to let him seek me, certain that it would not take very long before he sensed my readiness to come to terms. To make his search easier, I entered a casino I played in often, and walked slowly and conspicuously about the tables, distinctly remembering how I'd lost at almost all of them. I could even discern my old auras at the chairs I'd sat in; sad, unkempt penumbras of energy that faded a little with each losing bet. All that expense of spirit, I thought, for nothing; all that care and calculation wasted.

As I moved toward the room's entrance, my way was suddenly blocked by a file of tourists behind a guide who announced he was leading them to one of Las Vegas' most famous sights. I waited as they passed, and then watched them form an adoring crescent around the promised wonder—a large glass rectangular case that held, in cash, a total of one million dollars.

"Here, ladies and gentlemen," the guard droned in a voice struggling with early morning phlegm, "is probably your first and last sight of one million United States dollars."

The tourists made appreciative noises, and then quickly fell into mute reverence, transfixed by the sight of neat rows of ten-thousand-dollar bills seemingly suspended in the air. Some moved their lips in silent counting; others blinked and wagged their heads in a manner that suggested a desire to disbelieve what they were seeing, as though they wished there were no reality to the number they so often invoked whenever they defined a perfect life. A boy, whose attention wandered for a moment to the pistol worn by the display's guard, had his head firmly turned by his mother until he again directly faced the goal she was quietly setting for him. A young man and woman, who were dressed in a way that revealed they'd come directly from one of the town's twenty-four-hour wedding chapels, clasped each other around the waist, as if to reassure themselves that love doesn't need so much common currency, and that the life they'd planned was still a wonderful ambition.

Finally the guide decided it was time to dissolve the solemn mood that had settled over his tour. Clearing his throat for attention, he began in a quiet, soothing voice to tell a joke about a Texas millionaire who kept his rolls of hundred-dollar bills in his bathroom to be used as toilet paper. When asked why, the Texan had answered: "If somethin' didn't cost a hundred dollars, it's no fun doin' it." There were sputters of laugher, enough at least to break the million-dollar spell. Then after the guide further amused them by smothering the glass-covered money with passionate kisses, they went away content to have put another item on the tour behind them, one which, several were bold enough to say, had proved, after all, a little disappointing.

I, however, was impressed, for I knew if I accepted Boris' tutelage, I would have a seven-figured answer to the question, "How much is enough?" If my fate were now to be reckoned in numbers, then one million would be a proper premium for my having learned that there was nothing more to life than the counting of its parts, the gathering of bits and pieces of experience which, in sufficient number, can deaden the mind's passion for a systematic world. The money before me meant an easeful passing of time. If it was not enough to blot out seizures of fright in the manner of an emperor, to divert myself with games, grottoes and executions, it was sufficient for a comfortable retirement. Looking deeply into the glass of the million-dollar display, I could even see the garden in which I would cultivate my resignation, a place of fountains and cypresses, of shade mixed with meridional sunlight, of bleached gravel paths and sloping terraces, a setting designed for wry thought and doleful memories. I looked again and saw the villa I would own and, in its one unshuttered window, myself looking exactly as I did in reflected superimposition on the rows of ten-thousand-dollar bills. I wore pajamas, a soft straw hat, and a look that expressed no interest in keeping up appearances.

But then this picture of genteel seclusion faded, and only the money remained. The cold thought struck me that in order to acquire the necessary real estate for my retirement I was going to have to go to work. There would be no single moment of revenge in which, masked in innocence, I pillaged the halls of gambling. Rather, there would be long hours of modest thefts, days and days of pleasureless travel, months, perhaps years, of slow, disciplined cheating that would cause no suspicion. Work was the only description for the wage-earner's time I saw stretched before me, for the long sessions of rudimentary exercises I'd have to master before my hands could perform the most simple devious maneuvers. After a life of dramatic reflection, I was accepting the fact that my purpose lay in the learning of a trade, that I must labor in order to achieve nothing more than a comfortable old age.

This, however, would be the price for that certainty that was lacking in the symbols of logic and slot machines. Once a few mechanical skills had been mastered, everything would be inevitable, and I could shape my fortune like a careful potter. Only an immature mind would balk at the boredom in this order of things or feel shame over the manual labor involved.

But whether immature or nobly childlike, my mind did reject this outline of the future. Aching with fatigue, it still managed to rouse itself into remembrance of old duties and imperatives that had no reason for being except that they were mine and formed the private definition of myself.

I turned from the case of treasury notes, and went to the cashier's window. I pushed one of my thousand-dollar traveler's checks and a passport toward two suspicious clerks. They scrutinized me carefully and studied my signature and photographs. Finally, I was verified to their satisfaction and the money was counted and delivered to me.

I took a seat at the roulette table, made a small bet on the even numbers, and spun my mind with the wheel. The cycles of thought whirled into a single argument against the small strategies of life that promise certain compensation. But to refute certainty requires a logic that finally turns its sting upon itself, and dies gasping "There is no greatest number," or that "'How much is enough?' is a meaningless question." And yet if a man wishes to excuse a life lived at random, then he must first exhaust all of philosophy in order to justify idly waiting for a pleasant surprise or a graceful windfall. And when there's nothing left of thought, then must there be silence? Not in the least. We simply return to the beginning, to the alternative that was always present in the lighter Platonic moments. Which is to say, we make up marvelous stories about ourselves.

When I returned to my hotel, I found my luggage had been moved to the lobby. In my abstracted state, I'd not paid the rent for the last two days, an oversight that had caused my eviction. The dour young bellboy who had welcomed me was at the desk, and he informed me as I paid him that my room was now occupied. Then in a tone that both offered advice and anticipated its refusal, he mentioned that a bus stopped at the hotel in a few minutes that went all the way to San Diego for less than twenty dollars. What he could see, I already knew; Las Vegas and I had worn each other out.

The bus, filled with tired Las Vegas refugees, was just about to leave when, from my window, I saw Boris waving at me frantically. He was in a padded cowboy suit, and wore a henna-colored wig and a short matching beard. With an exaggerated fat man's waddle, he moved alongside the bus until I shook my head several times in emphatic refusal. He stopped then and threw up his arms in a gesture of bafflement. I waved to him and thought how simple it is to resist temptation when submission entails a greater effort.

Gambling:
Remembrances and Assertions

BY STEPHEN DUNN

Many musicians capture the grimy lyricism of gambling places, like Jelly Roll Morton or B. B. King or Willie Nelson. Last year's Pulitzer Prize winner for poetry, Stephen Dunn is among the handful of poets, including Diane Wakoski and Charles Bukowski, who writes with the authority of one who's been there:

> Yesterday at the blackjack table,
>
> a few hundred yards from the shore,
> I doubled-down with eleven
> and drew a three. That was it.
>
> I walked up North Carolina to Arctic
> all alone. The wind suggested
> wonderful movement at sea.
>
> I didn't care. I didn't care if
> the waves were high and white
> or if the seagulls
>
> were dropping clam shells from the sky.
> I had a loser's thought: how wise I was
> for not paying to park.

—from "Atlantic City" in *Not Dancing* (1984)

Dunn thinks of the essayist as one who "believes there's value in being over-heard clarifying things for himself." In the following essay, he begins his at-tempt at clarifying his lifelong fascination with gambling with remembrances of early gambling in his household, before moving on to measured assertions about the great gambler's mixtures of knowing and daring. For Dunn the gambler, imaginatively seen, emerges finally as someone willing to accept the inevitable costs of gambling for the occasional chances it affords him to be "startled or enlarged."

M y father had a small romance with danger. He followed sirens, for one. Even if we were eating dinner, he'd get in his car and pursue a police car or fire engine. And he was a gambler, though he wasn't at the racetrack or the poker table when he lost everything.

In his early forties, he gave all the family savings, five thousand dollars, to my grandfather (his father-in-law) to help pay the hospital bills for Grandfather's secret mistress. My grandfather died soon thereafter, the debt unpaid. When my mother asked where the savings went, Father said, "The track," and lived with that lie for fourteen years until his death. He was thought of as a wastrel, and drank, I think, in order not to speak. Nobility? Stupidity? I have my opinions, none of them certain.

Our family myth was that gambling destroyed my father and placed us in a financial situation from which we never fully recovered. It had its degree of truth. Though I know it was some blend of circumstance, propriety, and male camaraderie that caused his downfall, a part of me always has felt he made a gambler's decision when he loaned Grandfather that money. Even if he'd been paid back, there still would have been a sizable period of time when he wouldn't have been able to account for the zeros in the bank book. Whatever else it may have been, this was high-stakes gambling.

I suppose if I were rational about my legacy, I'd play everything straight. Yet I drift to the casinos on boring afternoons, sometimes unboring afternoons. I play in a weekly poker game. I love to handicap and bet on the horses. And I continue to be fascinated with the various ways in which one can ruin or vivify one's life.

In many ways, I may replicate my father's behavior, though I've never gone as far as he did. That is, past the balance that reasonable poker players maintain: where something higher (like nobility) or lower (like greed) could cast you into the abyss. To some degree I consider this a failure on my part. Great gambling may involve the uncommon next step.

Good high-stakes poker players are neither noble nor greedy. They've sized up their fellow players, know a good deal about probabilities and tendencies, and wish like poets that their most audacious moves be perceived as part of a series of credible gestures. In big-stakes poker games, as A. Alvarez has pointed out, they need to think that the fifty thousand dollars they've raised, say, on four diamonds showing is leverage, not money that might go toward a new house. To the extent that they translate money into commodities or security it's likely they'll give something away at crunch time. A hesitation. A tic. The great gamblers, and there are not many, don't need anything. They simply wish to prevail. And we know how dangerous people are who don't need anything. The purity of leverage. I raise you fifty thousand dollars. I'm saying I have a flush. I'm neither smiling nor shaking. See me if you dare.

I'm not that kind of gambler. I'm full of commonplace desire mixed with modest means. Though occasionally I've taken relatively large chances, I mostly think of gambling as fun, an evening's diversion. Worst of all, I do think of what money can buy. At crunch time, my astute poker-playing friend says, I reveal something, though of course he won't tell me what. But I *am* calculating, I have some sense of when to push the action, when to withdraw. I only flirt with being my father.

Early on, though, the signs weren't good. One year after my father, drunk, told me his secret (it was unmistakably—the way pain is—true), I got into a neighborhood card game. Acey-deucey, a game that requires only boldness, no skill. I was seventeen, working as a checkout boy at Food Fair earning very little money, and I had with me only thirty dollars. The pot kept increasing. It was my turn; the two cards dealt were a king and a three. I could bet any portion of the pot, wagering on the probability that the next card would fall in between those two cards. I'd been counting the cards already played. The odds were immensely in my favor. I told the other players I didn't have the money, but could get it if I lost. The pot was $216; I called it. The next card was a three. It was my grandmother to whom I appealed, who lovingly gave me the money. Our secret, in a family of secrets. It took the entire school year to pay her back.

This was my introduction to gambler's guilt, carried around in silence. For days after, I'd look at my mother to see if she knew. No, Grandmother didn't tell her. I felt that strange mixture of relief and desire-to-be-punished, a sensation which gamblers experience when their concealments are successful. Paying back Grandmother was a kind of punishment, but the privacy of our pact kept guilt from tripping over into shame. I lived in limbo, a somewhat livable place.

Such gambling failures didn't occur often. Neither did such titillations. I learned more intimately than ever that there's a relationship between heartbeat and pleasure, heartbeat and fear. Around this time I met a girl who became my girlfriend, a different kind of rush. She slowed me down, taught me new options for free time. Lady luck.

Some things I know: If you go to the casino with one hundred dollars, don't expect to win a thousand. If you approach poetry writing without reading great poetry, you will reach, at best, the level of your ignorance.

When to be bold? A gambler's question, to be sure. But perhaps an important question for anyone. The gambler's sense of it is instructive. You go on what you know and can intuit. A mixture of knowledge and daring. The fool knows little and thinks he knows more. The great gambler knows something about himself, and everything about his territory. I was once in a poker game with Donald Justice, a very good player. In seven-card stud he had two jacks showing, and even though no one raised him, he folded. He was happy to say why. The likelihood was that he'd end up with two pair, jacks up, and jacks up seldom won in seven-card stud. A measured decision. A measured poet, one of our best. Yet one imagines someone like Walt Whitman thinking, "Jacks up, Jesus Christ, I'd risk America on that." If you're not a Walt Whitman, you end up in debtor's prison.

It's wiser for some people to be bolder than others. It's often a matter of temperament, secondarily a matter of nerve, and somewhat a matter, to borrow William Matthews's phrase, of the degree to which we can "metabolize loss." Good gamblers trust their ability to correctly read situations, yet what one *does* with what he knows and feels is what separates one gambler from another. Great gamblers trust their knowledge *and* possess the equipoise necessary to go out on that edge where the gods and demons live. Failure lives out there on that edge. So does luck, and a sensation that's richer than satisfaction, though not as sufficient. I wish I could say I've been there more often.

Short of the edge, there are different, quieter pleasures. The banter and table talk at friendly poker games. The arc and sway of luck over a long evening, and all the little moves one must keep to himself. Or a good blackjack table, everyone playing smart, all rooting against the dealer. And the dealer, if he or she has personality, rooting for the table. Every gambler could extend this list according to the game and its niceties.

A nicety: the Racing Form—that poor man's anthology of histories, equine and human—provides the kind of information that instructs us about the insufficiency of certain knowledge. Yet I've always been pleased by the talk, gambler's talk, that emanates from such information. I especially love the talk about why a particular horse can't lose. When that horse loses we're left sometimes with pure intelligence, a fine mind that we've been privileged to overhear, however wrong.

Several years ago I went to Vegas to meet a childhood friend, the kid picked on for being clumsy and boorish. He was now a psychotherapist in Los Angeles. I'd kept in touch with him for twenty years, through many difficulties. I was the last remnant of his humiliating childhood, and he needed to remind me of that every time we saw each other, usually through some perverse behavior.

We met at the Stardust Hotel. It was 1979. He was stoned when I arrived, wearing buckskin from shoulder to foot. This allowed him to make fun of my sports jacket, professorial, conservative. I let him get away with it, out of guilt, I suppose. I, too, had picked on him when we were kids.

He wanted to leave the Stardust and go to Circus-Circus. In the carnival-like area above the gaming tables he knew there was a test-your-accuracy basketball game, a difficult one—a very small hoop and a regular-size basketball. He said he wanted to win a prize for his son. You had to make three out of three to win a prize. Stoned as he was, he was able to make three out of three a few times. The best I managed was two out of three. He collected some prize coupons, not enough to win the giant stuffed bear he desired. *Many* coupons were needed for that. Next we went to the break-the-balloon-with-the-dart game, where he proceeded to fail. But we'd come to Vegas to gamble, and I guess he decided to start. He leapt over the counter, a forty-year-old psychotherapist with a forty-year-old poet sidekick, grabbed all the coupons from the waist of the girl in charge, said, "Let's run, let's get out of here," and we ran like the criminals we were while she screamed for Security.

He had given me no choice, and I was furious with him as we ran. I was also terrified, could see jail and ruin ahead of me, or a bullet in the back. Somehow, we got away. Safely in our room at the Stardust we laughed for what seemed like hours. When we stopped I told him I thought he was crazy, and if he kept doing things like this we couldn't be friends. He was not apologetic. It would be two years and one other aberration later before I fully got the message.

That next morning, different shift, different personnel, we returned to Circus-Circus and he got that bear. We did gamble at the tables that weekend, won a little, lost a little, but there was no doubt about what had been the real gambling.

Clearly, he had been a dumb gambler, and I a not wholly unwitting pal to self-destructiveness. The stakes were much too high, the reward not worth the risk. That we got away with it is often the spur that sends bad gamblers back to the original scene: the primal success. Such gamblers always are in pursuit of the once-achieved giant stuffed bear. The metaphorical police are frequently waiting.

It's interesting to note that probably an old wound was at the heart of my friend's actions. It pushed him out of conventional behavior, led him to the giant stuffed bear. Drivenness. The poet in me took note of it.

When I'm served a plate and the server says, "This is very hot, don't touch it," I always touch it. Just a tap with one finger, a quick withdrawal. I love how my wife shakes her head when I do this. It's sure-thing gambling. No chance of getting burned, and an audience that pretends to believe otherwise.

I still remember the horse's name, Dancer. Dancer in the fifth at Aqueduct. My father had gotten a tip that Dancer, a first-time starter, had been training exceptionally well and was a lock. There was even a hint that a fix was in. I'm not sure how old I was at the time, fifteen or sixteen. I'm only sure that it was before Father gave all our money to Grandfather, and before acey-deucey, because nothing needed to be concealed. He announced in the morning he had a tip and was going to Aqueduct, just eight miles from our house. I told several of my friends, who in turn told their fathers. There must have been twelve of us, true believers, easy-money Algers, American down to the depths of our dreams, who went that day.

The inside word must have gotten out. Dancer went off at six to one, though there was nothing visible in the Racing Form to warrant such betting support. My father was still happy with the possible payoff. He bet a hundred dollars, a lot of money for him, for us. It was a six-furlong race, a sprint. Dancer broke from the gate so fast he had a five-length lead in the first furlong. He led easily to the head of the stretch.

There's a moment in a race when you know your horse isn't going to win. Dancer started to go backwards, or so it seemed. In fact, "going backwards" is a familiar description for a horse that starts to fade. "C'mon, Dancer," which we'd been screaming, was replaced by "Shit" and "Goddamn" (heavy accent on last syllable), and then silence when every other horse, the swift and the untouted, passed him. Eleven of us looked at my father. He had that smile you often see on gamblers' faces, part resignation, part bemusement that once again the sure thing wasn't. "It was a good tip," he said, by which he meant that the horse showed speed and *was* ready, albeit for a three-furlong race instead of a six. "It'll be interesting to see what he does next time," my father said. Already, he was metabolizing loss, getting beyond it.

A gambler, like a good hitter in baseball, knows he'll fail more than succeed, even though he expects to succeed each time in the singular instance. A part of him is prepared for loss. Thus, the gambler's smile.

If other aspects of our lives—our love life, our work life—are satisfactory, we can manage to live with loss. However, when our lives are going bad or have gone bad, that's when the demons rise up and won't be appeased. Dostoyevsky perhaps was the first to suggest that the gambler, by which he meant the compulsive gambler, secretly wishes to lose. The demons, as in D. H. Lawrence's "The Rocking-Horse Winner," are always demonically chanting "more." The compulsive gambler wants something like love or quiescence, and in his best moments only gets money. He wants to fill some emptiness, and he pushes his bets so far he ends up with a greater emptiness, perhaps an emptiness that has an odd measure of solace in it: he can delude himself that he knows its source.

After my father became known as a wastrel, after he lost respect at home, he lost that gambler's smile forever.

Some things I know: When I've had a fight with my wife, walked out of the house, and gone to the casino, I've always lost. I stay too long, could be one explanation. More likely I'm seeking to deepen my mood, to let sullenness feed on sullenness, to enter that cocoon state of the wronged where everything corroborates misery. The needy person should never gamble. The needy person wants to.

Sports gamblers (basketball, football) are an especially needy breed, and I'm happy to say I've never been one of them. Usually they are the gamblers who require regular or even constant action—the bulimics of bettors—perpetuating a cycle of fullness (new bets) then emptiness (wins *or* losses). There's never closure.

Robert Frost felt that without theme you wouldn't be able to properly slow down a poem. Certainly you wouldn't know where to end it. Theme could be a synonym for having a center, a place both nourishing and nourishable. The sports bettor, more than most gamblers I know, has no such place.

The opposite of these bettors is the fan, the lover (*ama*teur), who finds a sufficiency in the game itself and/or in the performance of one particular team. In the middle are the fans who, now and then, for fun, wager with friends that their favorite team will win. Those people, of course, you can bear to be around.

But sports bettors depress me. Often they're like the kind of stock market players openly pleased when General Motors streamlines operations by laying off thousands. They talk point spreads instead of people, cumulative points (among two teams) instead of, say, a player's excellence or brilliance. I've heard them cheer when a quarterback has been injured. At their best, values aside, they're too fidgety to savor a fine moment. And they're not capable of the gambler's smile.

Clearly, I reveal my prejudices here, and one should know when he's become moralistic that he has little more to say on his subject. I should admit that all of us who gamble are, importantly, fellow gamblers. Perhaps the ones I've criticized didn't have, way back when it counted, a lucky grandmother or girlfriend or, for that matter, an unlucky father who was an emblem of decency. A small turn here or there, and I could be them.

My resolution for the New Year is to work on my soul. I used to think that first you had to locate it, but now believe it makes itself invisibly palpable when it's been tended to. I wish there was more talk about soul. We've largely given up such talk. Commerce, politics, the talk of people who expect answers, results. I've said in a poem, "the normal condition of the soul is to be starved." If this is true, those of us who are vigilant about our souls are trying to feed them. *Save* them? Faust gambled with his soul, which suggests that we should be using different currency when we gamble. But it seems to me that gambling, at its healthiest, is one way of activating the soul, nudging it from its hungry sleep. I'm speaking about gambling in its most reductive form: taking a chance. The *act* of taking a chance is energizing. The *art* of the act of taking a chance can lead to the sublime. Like the time I saw Paco Camino exhibit perfect grace—a series of slow, exact moves—with an erratic bull in Madrid. Or Miles Davis, years ago at a club, riding an impulse beyond himself. Surely those folks who play their lives and their work eminently safe don't often put themselves in the position where they can be startled or enlarged. Don't put themselves near enough to the realm of the unknown where discovery resides, and joy has been rumored to appear. The realm of the unknown is contiguous to the realm of failure. The gambler, deep down, has made a pact with failure. He'll accept it because it has interesting neighbors. In such realms the soul, I think, is fed, not to mention exercised.

But those of us who gamble for pleasure mostly know more level moments. The small loss, or win. The perfect bluff that when successful precludes joy because the satisfaction must be kept to oneself. (Here some of us know the virtues of suppression.) Or the breaking even. I suspect that the spouses of gamblers have heard "I broke even" more than any other lie. To literally break even, of course, isn't bad. If we love to gamble it means we've had some free entertainment. But only the existentially terrified *play* to break even. Aren't we after what dailiness seldom provides? The edge. We're betting we're smart and talented and/or lucky enough to lean but not to fall. Sometimes we are.

The Notorious Jumping Frog
of Calaveras County

One could fill an anthology with stories from the Anglo-American West, a region that saw itself as one gigantic gamble, one GLITTER GULCH. My Western anthology would include characters like Johnson Jones Hooper's slip-jacks-off-the-bottom-of-the-deck-dealing hero Simon Suggs, with his oft repeated motto, IT'S GOOD TO BE SHIFTY IN A NEW COUNTRY and Bret Harte's unflappable John Oakhurst, who appears in stories like "The Outcasts of Poker Flat." There would be lady gamblers, like Poker Alice, who claimed she would "rather play poker with five or six experts than to eat." And there would be riverboat gamblers, like those in Mark Twain's *Life on the Mississippi* (which includes mule and steamboat racing, along with cockfighting) or George Devol's *Forty Years a Gambler on the Mississippi,* who act as prototypes for all the Bret Mavericks and Kenny Rogerses you see wearing cowboy boots and hats at the table.

But pride of place in my anthology would go to the Jim Smileys, the imaginative scamps who seemingly populated every mining camp or saloon. With his "trained" pet frog Dan'l Webster, Twain's Smiley expresses the spirit of that great congregation of flim-flam men, sharpers, raconteurs who depend upon the greed of the sucker to lubricate a bet. As a general rule there's art or angle behind the willingness to accept any side of any wager, and when you hear a fast-talker laying out a proposition bet you'd do well to keep in mind the advice given in Damon Runyon's "Idyll's of Miss Sarah Brown":

> Son, no matter how far you travel, or how smart you get, always remember this: Some day, somewhere, a guy is going to come to you and show you a nice brand-new deck of cards on which the seal is never broken, and this guy is going to offer to bet you that the jack of spades will jump out of the deck

and squirt cider in your ear. But, son, do not bet him, for as sure as you do you are going to get an ear full of cider.

Mark Twain's literary career began as a reporter in the West, and he never forgot his literary roots in "the Territories." In his disastrous "Whittier Birthday Speech," he presented the Eastern literary establishment as drunk miners around a campfire who "pretty soon got out a greasy old deck and went to playing cutthroat euchre at ten cents a corner—on trust," a game which ends with Ralph Waldo Emerson reaching for his bowie knife.

I n compliance with the request of a friend of mine, who wrote me from the East, I called on good-natured, garrulous old Simon Wheeler, and inquired after my friend's friend, Leonidas W. Smiley, as requested to do, and I hereunto append the result. I have a lurking suspicion that *Leonidas W.* Smiley is a myth; that my friend never knew such a personage; and that he only conjectured that if I asked old Wheeler about him, it would remind him of his infamous *Jim* Smiley, and he would go to work and bore me to death with some exasperating reminiscence of him as long and as tedious as it should be useless to me. If that was the design, it succeeded.

I found Simon Wheeler dozing comfortably by the bar-room stove of the dilapidated tavern in the decayed mining camp of Angel's, and I noticed that he was fat and bald-headed, and had an expression of winning gentleness and simplicity upon his tranquil countenance. He roused up and gave me good-day. I told him a friend of mine had commissioned me to make some inquiries about a cherished companion of his boyhood named *Leondias W.* Smiley—*Rev. Leondias W.* Smiley, a young minister of the Gospel, who he had heard was at once time a resident of Angel's Camp. I added that if Mr. Wheeler could tell me anything about this Rev. Leonidas W. Smiley, I would feel under many obligations to him.

Simon Wheeler backed me into a corner and blockaded me there with his chair, and then sat down and reeled off the monotonous narrative which follows this paragraph. He never smiled, he never frowned, he never changed his voice from the gentle-flowing key to which he tuned his initial sentence, he never betrayed the slightest suspicion of enthusiasm; but all through the interminable narrative there ran a vein of impressive earnestness and sincerity, which showed me plainly that, so far from his imagining that there was anything ridiculous or funny about his story, he regarded it as a really important

matter, and admired its two heroes as men of transcendent genius in *finesse*. I
let him go on in his own way, and never interrupted him once.

"Rev. Leonidas W. H'm, Reverend Le—well, there was a feller here
once by the name of *Jim* Smiley, in the winter of '49—or may be it was the
spring of '50—I don't recollect exactly, somehow, though what makes me
think it was one or the other is because I remember the big flume warn't finished when he first come to the camp; but any way, he was the curiosest man
about always betting on anything that turned up you ever see, if he could get
anybody to bet on the other side; and if he couldn't he'd change sides. Any way
that suited the other man would suit *him*—any way just so's he got a bet, *he* was
satisfied. But still he was lucky, uncommon lucky; he most always come out
winner. He was always ready and laying for a chance; there couldn't be no
solit'ry thing mentioned but that feller'd offer to bet on it, and take ary side
you please, as I was just telling you, If there was a horse-race, you'd find him
flush or you'd find him busted at the end of it; if there was a dog fight, he'd bet
on it; if there was a cat-fight, he'd bet on it; if there was a chicken-fight, he'd
bet on it; why, if there was two birds setting on a fence, he would bet you
which one would fly first; or if there was a camp-meeting, he would be there
reg'lar to bet on Parson Walker, which he judged to be the best exhorter about
here, and so he was too, and a good man. If he even see a straddle-bug start to
go anywheres, he would bet you how long it would take him to get to—to
wherever he was going to, and if you took him up, he would foller that
straddle-bug to Mexico but what he would find out where he was bound for
and how long he was on the road. Lots of the boys here has seen that Smiley,
and can tell you about him. Why, it never made no difference to *him*—he'd bet
on *any* thing—the dangdest feller. Parson Walker's wife laid very sick once, for
a good while, and it seemed as if they warn't going to save her; but one morning he come in, and Smiley up and asked him how she was, and he said she was
considerable better—thank the Lord for his inf'nit mercy—and coming on so
smart that with the blessing of Prov'dence she'd get well yet; and Smiley, before
he thought says, "Well, I'll resk two-and-a-half she don't anyway."

Thish-yer Smiley had a mare—the boys called her the fifteen-minute
nag, but that was only in fun, you know, because of course she was faster than
that—and he used to win money on that horse, for all she was so slow and always had the asthma, or the distemper, or the consumption, or something of
that kind. They used to give her two or three hundred yards' start, and then pass
her under way; but always at the fag-end of the race she'd get excited and
desperate-like, and come cavorting and straddling up, and scattering her legs
around limber, sometimes in the air, and sometimes out to one side amongst

the fences, and kicking up m-o-r-e dust and raising m-o-r-e racket with her coughing and sneezing and blowing her nose—and *always* fetch up at the stand just about a neck ahead, as near as you could cipher it down.

And he had a little small bull-pup, that to look at him you'd think he warn't worth a cent but to set around and look ornery and lay for a chance to steal something. But as soon as money was up on him he was a different dog; his under-jaw'd begin to stick out like the fo'castle of a steamboat, and his teeth would uncover and shine like the furnaces. And a dog might tackle him and bully-rag him, and bite him, and throw him over his shoulder two or three times, and Andrew Jackson—which was the name of the pup—Andrew Jackson would never let on but what *he* was satisfied, and hadn't expected nothing else—and the bets being doubled and doubled on the other side all the time, till the money was all up; and then all of a sudden he would grab that other dog jest by the j'int of his hind leg and freeze to it—not chaw, you understand, but only just grip and hang on till they throwed up the sponge, if it was a year. Smiley always come out winner on that pup, till he harnessed a dog once that didn't have no hind legs, because they'd been sawed off in a circular saw, and when the thing had gone along far enough, and the money was all up, and he come to make a snatch for his pet holt, he see in a minute how he'd been im-posed on, and how the other dog had him in the door, so to speak, and he 'peared surprised, and then he looked sorter discouraged-like, and didn't try no more to win the fight, and so he got shucked out bad. He give Smiley a look, as much as to say his heart was broke, and it was *his* fault, for putting up a dog that hadn't no hind legs for him to take holt of, which was his main depen-dence in a fight, and then he limped off a piece and laid down and died. It was a good pup, was that Andrew Jackson, and would have made a name for hisself if he'd lived, for the stuff was in him and he had genius—I know it, because he hadn't no opportunities to speak of, and it don't stand to reason that a dog could make such a fight as he could under them circumstances if he hadn't no talent. It always makes me feel sorry when I think of that last fight of his'n, and the way it turned out.

Well, thish-yer Smiley had rat-tarriers, and chicken cocks, and tom-cats and all them kind of things, till you couldn't rest, and you couldn't fetch nothing for him to bet on but he'd match you. He ketched a frog one day, and took him home, and said he cal'lated to educate him; and so he never done nothing for three months but set in his back-yard and learn that frog to jump. And you bet you he *did* learn him, too. He'd give him a little punch behind, and the next minute you'd see that frog whirling in the air like a doughnut—see him turn one summerset, or may be a couple, if he got a good start, and

come down flat-footed and all right, like a cat. He got him up so in the ma'ter
of ketching flies, and kep' him in practice so constant, that he'd nail a fly every
time as fur as he could see him. Smiley said all a frog wanted was education,
and he could do 'most anything—and I believe him. Why, I've seen him set
Dan'l Webster down here on this floor—Dan'l Webster was the name of the
frog—and sing out, "Flies, Dan'l, flies!" and quicker'n you could wink he'd
spring straight up and snake a fly off 'n the counter there, and flop down on the
floor ag'in as solid as a gob of mud, and fall to scratching the side of his head
with his hind foot as indifferent as if he hadn't no idea he'd been doin' any
more'n any frog might do. You never see a frog so modest and straightfor'ard as
he was, for all he was so gifted. And when it come to fair and square jumping
on a dead level, he could get over more ground at one straddle than any animal
of his breed you ever see. Jumping on a dead level was his strong suit, you
understand, and when it come to that, Smiley would ante up money on him as
long as he had a red. Smiley was monstrous proud of his frog, and well he might
be, for fellers that had traveled and been everywheres, all said he laid over any
frog that ever *they* see.

Well, Smiley kep' the beast in a little lattice box, and he used to fetch
him down town sometimes and lay for a bet. One day a feller—a stranger in
the camp, he was—come acrost him with his box, and says:

"What might it be that you've got in the box?"

And Smiley says, sorter indifferent-like, "It might be a parrot, or it
might be a canary, maybe, but it ain't—it's only just a frog."

And the feller took it, and looked at it careful, and turned it round this
way and that, and says, "H'm—so 'tis. Well, what's *he* good for?"

"Well," Smiley says, easy and careless, "he's good enough for *one* thing,
I should judge—he can outjump any frog in Calaveras county."

The feller took the box again, and took another long, particular look,
and give it back to Smiley, and says, very deliberate, "Well," he says, "I don't see
no p'ints about that frog that's any better'n any other frog."

"Maybe you don't," Smiley says. "Maybe you understand frogs and
maybe you don't understand 'em; maybe you've had experience, and maybe
you ain't only a amature, as it were. Anyways, I've got *my* opinion and I'll resk
forty dollars that he can outjump any frog in Calaveras county."

And the feller studied a minute, and then says, kinder sad like, "Well,
I'm only a stranger here, and I ain't got no frog; but if I had a frog, I'd bet you."

And then Smiley says, "That's all right—that's all right—if you'll hold
my box a minute, I'll go and get you a frog." And so the feller took the box, and
put up his forty dollars along with Smiley's, and set down to wait.

So he set there a good while thinking and thinking to hisself, and then he got the frog out and prized his mouth open and took a teaspoon and filled him full of quail shot—filled him pretty near up to his chin—and set him on the floor. Smiley he went to the swamp and slopped around in the mud for a long time, and finally he ketched a frog, and fetched him in, and give him to this feller, and says:

"Now, if you're ready, set him alongside of Dan'l, with his fore-paws just even with Dan'l's, and I'll give the word." Then he says, "One—two—three—*git!*" and him and the feller touched up the frogs from behind, and the new frog hopped off lively, but Dan'l give a heave, and hysted up his shoulders—so—like a Frenchman, but it warn't no use—he couldn't budge; he was planted as solid as a church, and he couldn't no more stir than if he was anchored out. Smiley was a good deal surprised, and he was disgusted too, but he didn't have no idea what the matter was, of course.

The feller took the money and started away; and when he was going out at the door, he sorter jerked his thumb over his shoulder—so—at Dan'l, and says again, very deliberate, "Well," he says, "*I* don't see no p'ints about that frog that's any better'n any other frog."

Smiley he stood scratching his head and looking down at Dan'l a long time, and at last he says, "I do wonder what in the nation that frog throw'd off for—I wonder if there ain't something the matter with him—he 'pears to look mighty baggy, somehow." And he ketched Dan'l by the nap of the neck, and hefted him, and say, "Why blame my cats if he don't weigh five pound!" and turned him upside down and he belched out a double handful of shot. And then he see how it was, and he was the maddest man—he set the frog down and took out after that feller, but he never ketched him. And—"

(Here Simon Wheeler heard his name called from the front yard, and got up to see what was wanted.) And turning to me as he moved away, he said: "Just set where you are, stranger, and rest easy—I ain't going to be gone a second."

But, by your leave, I did not think that a continuation of the history of the enterprising vagabond *Jim* Smiley would be likely to afford me much information concerning the Rev. *Leonidas W.* Smiley, and so I started away.

At the door I met the sociable Wheeler returning, and he buttonholed me and re-commenced:

"Well, thish-yer Smiley had a yaller one-eyed cow that didn't have no tail, only jest a short stump like a bannanner, and—"

However, lacking both time and inclination, I did not wait to hear about the afflicted cow, but took my leave.

From The National Football Lottery

BY LARRY MERCHANT

How do they do it? Larry Merchant talked a publisher into giving him $30,000 dollars to write an account of pro football and gambling. He could pocket the money, or if he bet it keep whatever he won. Journalist David McCumber got a monster advance that allowed him to stake and accompany pool hustler Tony Annigoni on the road around America, taking a cut of whatever Annigoni won without lifting more than his pen. The account became *Off the Rail,* which brilliantly catches the rhythm of contemporary road action, quick-developing risk, and ego clashes from dives to tournaments. In other words, how they do it is that they write brilliantly. I don't know how the publisher's made out off the books, but they were right to bet on both authors delivering.

    Cigar in mouth, beer in hand, I have found Larry Merchant erudite, sometimes nutty, always entertaining company for watching pay-per-view boxing matches over the years. He has a way of identifying when a fighter "commits" to a punch that seems to extend meaningfully to other endeavors. To commit is to risk. And in the aftermath of an intense fight, coming down off involvement in other people's commitments, there's always Merchant's audacious, jaw-dropping questions to exhausted, damaged, demoralized fighters to ease you back into your skin, your living room. The opening sections of Merchant's sadly out-of-print memoir of a season of football betting, reprinted below, are an engaging (if not committed) attempt to understand America's "gambling rage" with pro football—one as pronounced today as ever.

Suddenly Respectable

A bank president became aware of a man with a savings account who deposited $500 a day every day for two years. Astonished, the banker left word for the man that he would like to meet him.

Shortly thereafter the man appeared in the banker's office. "I've been with this bank for 30 years," the banker said, "and I've never come across anything quite like this. If you don't mind my asking, what business are you in?"

"I'm a gambler," the man said.

"That's very interesting," the banker said. "But don't gamblers lose sometime?"

"Not if you know what you're doing," the gambler said.

"Why, that's extraordinary," the banker said. "Even the smartest businessmen don't win all the time."

"I'll prove it to you," the gambler said. "I'll bet you $500 that at noon tomorrow I'll show up here and you'll have square balls."

The banker stammered, fingered a letter opener nervously, and was surprised to hear himself say, "It's a bet."

Next day the gambler arrived on schedule, trailed by a horny dwarf. "I see you made it," the banker said, appearing a bit flushed.

The gambler nodded.

Without a word the banker stepped around his desk and dropped his pants.

The horny dwarf's jaw dropped to his waist.

The gambler reached between the banker's thighs and felt his balls.

The horny dwarf fainted.

"What happened?" the banker asked.

"I bet him," the gambler said, "$1,000 that at noon today I'd have a bank president's balls in my hands."

You may search for your own moral in this story. For me it raises some intriguing questions.

Like: Do professional gamblers win all the time or just most of the time, and why? Do amateur gamblers lose all the time or just some of the time, and why? Are bookmakers really illegal bankers, merely skimming the interest off bets?

And, crucially, am I the horny dwarf?

There are other questions that intrigue me as well, because the gambling rage of our times is pro football. Betting and pro football is a marriage made in heaven. The ceremony was performed without benefit of clergy, but it is one of the few fads of the tumultuous sixties to endure and flourish.

How widespread is the phenomenon of pro football betting? What are its implications? Why and how do people bet? Who makes the betting line? Can it be beaten? How does betting affect one's head, one's life—socially, sexually, spiritually, financially? Should betting on football be legalized? How do bookies operate? Are there fixes? What is a Jimmy the Greek?

Also, can I, Larry Merchant, sportswriter, bet on National Football League games, win money, have fun, and find God and true love? And other fantasies.

There are several reasons why I chose to investigate gambling, NFL style. Not the least of them was the fact that I have been betting on the pros for ten years and—gamblers are congenital liars but this is petrified truth—have never had what I consider a losing season. A losing season being a season in which I lost enough (as I once did in baseball) to cut down on taxi rides; I may have lost a few dollars in a season when the winnings and losings were so minimal that I didn't even keep casual track of them. One season I won $1,500. Another season I won $7,000. I've never started a season betting more than $100 a game, which is in my league, which means I can afford to blow a few hundred and shrug it off as an entertainment expense. Arnold Rothstein the legendary plunger I'm not, but look what all his betting coups got him. Rich, famous and murdered.

It occurred to me along the way that my involvement paralleled a lot of people's, that not many people who were involved understood the first thing about football or betting, and that, zounds, a book structured around my betting experiences might outsell the Bible. It would, too, confirm my prowess as a handicapper, for me if no one else, or expose me under pressure as a fraud, likewise. Either possibility had its charm. I envisioned myself betting $100,000 on the Super Bowl or winding up as a tragic Dostoevskian figure cleaning car windshields with greasy rags on the Bowery.

It also occurred to me that pro football bettors included vast numbers of the kind of upstanding citizens who used to think that a bookmaker was a fellow who made books. (I knew a fellow who got a job on an army newspaper because he listed his civilian occupation as bookmaker.) Before the pro football boom they bet only on the World Series, the Kentucky Derby and a heavyweight championship fight. I have a theory about that. I have more theories than George Allen has game balls. Call this Theory No. 1.

The theory is that there is a symbiotic relationship between pro football and betting. Like lovers, they turn each other on.

The popularity of the game obviously is a turn-on for the degenerate with a compulsion to bet on everything that moves. It's always there on the telly, an overexposed goddess, beckoning and daring.

But there's something about the game that twitches the betting instinct in the ordinary fan too. That makes it fashionable to bet a dollar or two socially. That has transformed the NFL into a National Football Lottery.

A Louis Harris poll last year found that nearly one out of every four fans bets regularly; the percentage must be much higher in the population centers that have teams. This means that twelve to fifteen million fans break the law on any given Sunday or Monday.

These fans are NFL's best friends, because pro football basically is a television sport—a small fraction of the fans who support the game actually go to games—and nothing short of the Second Coming or the Flood will uproot them from the 50-yard-line seats in their homes. A fan who has bet will sit there to the bitter or boring end, cheering and squirming for his money while getting his brain plugged into the sponsors' products. Small wonder that Merrill Lynch, Pierce, Fenner, and Whatshisface are so "Bullish on America."

It is implicit then that betting—social or serious—is a factor in the high TV ratings that yield an ever-expanding cornucopia of riches for the NFL.

Bookies furnish further proof. They report that an average televised game that doesn't feature the home team attracts as much or more betting than a nontelevised game of the home team, and two or three times as much as a game of above-average interest that isn't televised. Monday night games, with no competition, attract still-larger sums. One bookie I spoke to said that five of the top ten betting events of 1972, in all sports, were Monday night games.

All this feverish activity is good for pro football in another, important, way. It keeps the pot boiling for the six days of the week when nothing is going on.

Baseball, in contrast to football, is played every day. It thrives on vivid personalities whose exploits and antics can be closely identified with, strategy that a ten-year-old can fathom, and statistics that provide a meaningful reference. A world of fact and fantasy can be constructed from these elements—without necessarily seeing the games—shifting and portending with every home run, every final score. For those who care this world is fully contained, circular, like a baseball. Betting has no function in its mystique (although, because of the long schedule, there is a greater volume bet on baseball, with bookies, than on any other game).

Caring about a game or a team on a day-to-day basis, or even on a weekend-to-weekend basis, is difficult if not impossible for many adults. "Betting," says a priest in Boston who bets $10 a game on football, "adds to my enjoyment of the event." It stimulates the caring glands. That is why there is so much caring at a race track. Rooting for the home team is, for the bettor, kid stuff; he's rooting for a worthier entity—himself. Professional gamblers call themselves "players."

Football, in contrast to baseball, is an impersonal game with few vivid personalities poking out from under all that armor, with strategy that frequently is unfathomable, and with statistics that as often as not are misleading. Football compels us primarily with its explosive choreography, its tense blend of skill pirouetting on a field mined with danger. It is a game of action that must be seen to be enjoyed. Once seen, the focus changes, sometimes within hours, usually within a day, to the next game. Enter, smiling seductively, bosom heaving, the point spread.

Like the weight handicap in horse racing, the point spread is designed, and divined, to neutralize the advantage of one team over another, in the mind of the betting public. Part of my purpose is to demonstrate that it often does no such thing, but for now the point is that the spread becomes the reference, the yardstick, for the center of football's between-games existence: the next game.

The point spread becomes the official common denominator on Tuesday when favorites and underdogs are established. Speculation in the media and conversation over drinks revolve around these roles. As Wednesday becomes Thursday and Thursday Friday, the buildup becomes a challenge to red-blooded aficionados. Fans have opinions, and opinions backed by cash are convictions. Or hunches. The weekend hysteria begins.

Allowing for a margin of error in the Harris poll, anywhere from one out of every fifteen to twenty people in this country answer the challenge weekly.

That's a heap of folks, folks.

A heap of money too.

The impact on the society of this massive involvement is enormous, clearly, but how can it be measured? One way is the infiltration of gambling attitudes and jargon into the consciousness and language, suggesting not that the work ethic is going to hell but that psychologically we are fessing up to homo sap's need to take chances.

In the process gambling, like aggression, has gained an air of respectability as one of those traits that makes homo sap such a wonderful lunatic, that adds zest to life when kept under control. Ambrose Bierce's observation that "The gambling known as business looks with disfavor on the business known as gambling" is losing relevancy as Damon Runyon's cynical "All life is 6–5 against" looms on the outside as a rallying cry of optimism.

Acknowledging the gambling imperative, businessmen–legislators are eager to raise tax revenues through pari-mutuel betting and lotteries; legal betting on football, baseball and basketball, as in Nevada, may not be far behind. Breathes there a governor with soul so dead that he hasn't bet a bushel of his state's fruit against another governor's alfalfa on the outcome of a game? And that was President Nixon himself commenting upon the appointment of George Allen as coach of the Redskins, "I'll bet they win a championship in a year or two."

One could hear, faintly, in the wind, the cooing response, "Er, how much, Prez?"

Consider this sampling of newspaper clippings: Advertising copy from a financial management service that propositions, "If you bet 8 cents on yourself, we'll bet $2 on you. Good odds?" An executive for an oil company noting of a big strike, "We're playing poker." Paul Simon regarding his first single recording after his breakup with Art Garfunkel, "It was time to take a gamble."

An artist is a cosmic gambler, and none gambled as outrageously as Fëdor Dostoevski. He gambled at the gaming tables, but his biggest gamble was a contract he signed with a publisher to produce a novel on a certain date or else forfeit the royalties on it and anything else he would write in the future. Three weeks before the deadline he hadn't written a word. On the due date he turned in his mini-classic, *The Gambler.*

This book represents a gamble for several upstanding citizens, myself among them.

My agent is gambling that I am not compelled by poor sales to put out a different, and deadlier, contract on him.

Early on in this project, when it was just a bright idea romancing investors, he broached it to business acquaintances. Said acquaintances flipped out and offered $100,000, take it or leave it, for all rights. Meaning that the book, as a property, would belong to them totally: Any monies generated beyond $100,000 (from, if any, a movie sale, paperback, reprint, book clubs, etc.) would be theirs, all theirs.

I thought they were stark raving mad.

But not as mad as my agent. He rejected it. I thought he should be committed.

His acquaintances were willing to gamble that this would be one out of, at a guess, every thousand books that earns $100,000 or more. They were not stupid men, or they wouldn't have that kind of money to bet. But I liked my chances a lot better than theirs.

Trouble was, my agent did not tell me about the offer until he had rejected it. Presumably he is not a stupid man either. It's just that he gambles too.

My initial reaction to the news of this wheeling-and-no-dealing was nausea With $100,000 I could acquire some of the feeble amenities I deserved. I could start eating cherries again even though they cost $1.29 a pound. I could move out of my eleventh-floor garret overlooking Sheridan Square in Greenwich Village and overhearing the stereophonic clattering of garbage trucks every morning. I might even be able to make a down payment on a cottage in Sagaponack, Long Island, an enclave of potato fields and sand dunes where a city rat can get stoned on fresh air during the summer.

My second reaction was violent. I wanted to blind-side my agent. But he is eight inches taller and fifty pounds heavier than me, and a squash racquets champion.

Lastly it dawned on me that he was right, although not because I thought we could make a million, as he did.

If I am to conduct an unchartered odyssey through the cement jungles and crazed minds of pro football betting, I would lose all credibility if I had a sure thing going for me.

Besides that, Joseph Kennedy, father of the Kennedy clan, once said, "Journalists are the last of the talented poor." Three-hundred-dollar-a-week sportswriters aren't supposed to have $100,000. I accept that. It probably wouldn't be worth living on a planet where sportswriters had $100,000.

The bright idea then was submitted to four publishers. One bid, i.e., bet, $20,000. Three went to $25,000. One of the three raised to $27,500. Holt, Rinehart & Winston won me for $30,000. That's gambling.

The $30,000 was mine to do with as I saw fit. None of it was designated as a stake. I could bet moderately or immoderately. I could take the money and run. I had only to write a book on pro football and gambling. But no one was playing for as much as I was playing for.

I am playing for that worthiest of entities. I am putting myself on the line, as any author or self-styled expert does when he exposes himself.

Thirty big ones is not sliced eggplant either. I have never had $30,000. I have never had half of it, which I will be lucky to have after expenses, a leave of absence from my job and various bloody cuts (by the government, my agent, and former first lady). If I lose $5,000 I will be sick. If I lose $10,000 I will be inconsolable. If I lose $15,000 I will be a heathen in my own eyes because I will have worked for nothing, and that's against my religion.

Yet I must bet meaningfully, bet enough to feel it in my gut. I may not be risking suicidal ruin, but I am not playing for toothpicks. As William Saroyan cried, leaping onto a dice table that was breaking him, "I don't care what Freud says, I want to win!"

I should note, before embarking on this odyssey, that being a sportswriter gives me no special advantage. Quite the opposite. As a breed we are, like players and coaches and others in the animal kingdom, notoriously bad handicappers.

Nor do I have access to so-called inside information. For which I am grateful. I don't believe in inside information. Show me a bettor who needs inside information and I'll show you a loser. My entire approach to betting on pro football is based on outside information, information available to anyone who wants it.

The trick is knowing what to do with it. If you know the trick you have a license to steal, tax free.

This approach may seem odd, but wait until you see where I take my preseason practice. In Monte Carlo.

Monte Carlo?

Gentlemen, I'll bet $500 you have square balls.

Ladies, I'll be with you in a moment.

The Red and the Black

Why not Monte Carlo?

Would truth, beauty and profit better be served in Tampa or Memphis or Birmingham or some such tropical furnace where NFL exhibitions are played?

I would just as soon spend the summer reading play books in the Gobi Desert. I would rather go to Transylvania, put on a low-cut gown and take a walk in the mist with Count Dracula.

I can do without exhibition games.

There are reasons. Esthetic reasons and grubby money-making reasons.

One: The summer is when I bury my head in sand and baseball and other summer things. I have a linear head. It rejects for as long as possible the next season until the current one is over. It absolutely banishes exhibitions of the next season while the current one is wending toward its climax. I go sockless and wear my seersucker jacket and drink gin and tonic until the leaves change color.

On Labor Day or thereabouts an alarm clock goes off in my uncluttered head, waking me to the new season and its possibilities. In midseason I'll be fresh and enthusiastic, and the guy who started in July will be confused, tired, poor, and into the next season. The seasons, betting or otherwise, should be savored as fully as a watermelon eaten to the rind. Mix at your own peril.

Two: Granted, exhibitions can be entertaining, in the manner, say, that a band rehearsal can be entertaining. It's still a clothesline of jocks running and jumping, throwing and catching, rocking and socking. But essentially exhibitions are bloodless charades, lacking intensity and drama. Worse for the bettor, they are deceiving. They will, in the long run and pass of the season, be counterproductive.

A contradiction illuminates the deception. Professional gamblers are more successful betting on exhibitions than on regular games. Because they make it their business to know: which coaches experiment and which go all out to win, how much key veterans are going to play, whether a team is trying hard because management wants to sell season tickets. Anyone really tuned in can get the messages, but it is a tedious, professional chore to keep abreast of such developments on all games, and generally they will be reflected in the point spread anyway. Where the linemaker slips up, the professional pounces. The got-to-have-action amateur flounders. Fortunately for him, bookies limit bets on exhibitions.

The deception is twofold. When one wins and loses real money on fake games, one is likely to take them seriously and incorrectly evaluate the teams for games that count. This is like winning or losing in Monopoly and then buying or selling stock in the Reading Railroad. More fatal, when one wins with the kind of inside information that is valid for exhibitions, or loses because such information wasn't general knowledge, an attitude is encouraged that the road to everlasting happiness is paved with inside information. It isn't.

So I never bet on exhibitions. I like the summer, and I like football too much.

Three: Football isn't that mysterious. Picking winners isn't that tough. Picking winners is the easy part. Managing your money—your emotions—is the hard part.

I went to Monte Carlo to test myself in management, in discipline. If you're going to suffer for your art you might as well suffer first class.

Additionally I hoped that through the prism of a concentrated period of gambling, a week or so, I would collect some clues to its fascination and some insights into my own motivations. So if I blew my advance and found myself contemplating a flying leap into Sheridan Square, I might be comforted by knowing why.

I was curious too about the relationship of sex and gambling. Partly because I am curious about the relationship of sex and anything and partly because I had a bad experience in gambling once. It was too painful, and I was too dense and preoccupied with the spastic frug of my daily rhythms, to ask myself or anyone else what it was about.

What happened of course was that I lost a bundle. Lost control, terrifyingly. And it shattered me. The sheer stupidity of it. A snake in the garden of self-esteem, exposing unsuspected vulnerability.

The bundle had $8,000 in it. I had to borrow from a bank, lying through the borrowing ritual, to pay it. The $7,000 I had won a year before was gone, invested in furniture and paintings before I could squander it. But the objects testified to my genius—in my mind's eye each was adorned by a bronze medallion with the legend of its origin, like "Green Bay minus 7 over Giants, November 18, 1965"—and convinced me of my omnipotence. I bet basketball and survived. I bet baseball and, on one long lost try-to-catch-up weekend, got knocked on my ass. I don't bet basketball or baseball anymore.

The monthly check to the bank irritated me mainly as a reminder of my stupidity, which after a while I rationalized into a blessing-in-disguise-because-I-won't-ever-let-that-happen-again, as I once did after losing $20 in the shell game on a troop ship. Using subways instead of taxis seemed to be poetic penance; they actually got me to where I was going faster. It was the sixteen-pound shot that materialized in my chest that bothered me.

Sometimes it pulsed. Sometimes it burned. Sometimes it pressed against my sternum as though a heavy-handed masseur were working on me, air escaping from my lungs in gasps. Musing to myself about my next column, walking to the corner for a paper, drinking with the gang at the Lion's Head, eating dinner with Gail, pulling the covers over me, awaking, the sixteen-pound shot was my constant and closest companion.

It probably began to dissolve after I told Gail about it late one night in the darkness after months of holding it in, months when we communicated and touched even less than usual. The stupidity, the guilt, the shame trickled out like tears, with tears. It was a humiliating confession of weakness to me. A window into the dark secret heart I wanted to keep secret from myself. The confession was incomplete. I still couldn't be completely open. She asked me how much I lost, borrowed. "A lot. Too much." My lips would not form the numbers. I never told her.

Which brings us back to sex and gambling. The trauma, as traumas will, dehorned the horny dwarf.

I was prepared to cope with losing, to exorcise my demons, somehow. That was, in the end, fairly simple. But I was not prepared to cope with deeper man-woman complexities, complexities of myself. Games and other obsessions can be magnificent escapes.

The south of France is not bad in the escape department. Before Monte Carlo I sunned myself for three weeks at Saint-Tropez, a nipple on the bountiful breast of Provence, where the landscape is sensual, the food French, the women both. On my first afternoon in Monte Carlo I realized that I hadn't once thought of gambling in Saint-Tropez. I realized this when I saw a dowager, strangling in jewels, trussed in blue silk stockings and a brocade bathing suit. A relic of fading elegance, like Monte Carlo. I thought about gambling.

My plan of attack was as follows: I would play roulette exclusively. (One doesn't eat crepes in Yazoo City, Mississippi, and one doesn't shoot craps in Monte Carlo.) I would limit myself to 300 francs (about $60) nightly. I would use an international medley of systems. I would play 0 and 26, as recommended by a fashion photographer I met in Copenhagen who swore he never lost. I would play colors (black or red) as did Dostoevski's wealthy grand-mamma in *The Gambler,* but only after one of them came up three times in a row, in which case I would let the money ride as long as I dared. (This was an adaptation of a baseball betting system I once read about: keep betting on a team that wins three games in a row, on the theory that you will catch some long winning streaks.)

A word about gambling systems: I don't believe in them. Systems substitute mathematical equations for human equations, a fatal flaw because humans must operate them. They would turn an essentially romantic pastime into a grind. On the other end of the scale they imply submission to a higher authority. Who? Why? The odds should be respected, but they don't have to be held in awe. What I did at Monte Carlo was pure whimsy. It would, I trusted, enable me to stretch out my investment of time and money. I did not expect to win.

I had had two previous experiences with roulette. Nineteen years before, as a sportswriter on leave from *Stars & Stripes* in Germany, I went to Monte Carlo with $30. I played 17 because it was the first two-digited number

I picked up in French (*dix-sept*). On my last franc it hit. I put a few more francs on it and it hit again. I walked out with about $60. Two days after the 1969 Super Bowl, the Joe Namath Super Bowl, I put a $10 bill on 12 (Namath's number) in San Juan (at the standard 35–1 odds). The croupier handed the bill back to me because, he said, in a ruling that still mystifies me, I had to have a seat to play. Yes, 12 came up.

(One horse racing tale of woe. A day before the Super Bowl I went to Hialeah Race Track, determined to bet the 1–2 daily double, because of the zany week Namath was having. The driver of the borrowed limousine I was in got lost, incredibly, and we didn't arrive until the second race. The 1–2 won and paid $1,100.)

(Gamblers are selective in their memories. Few of us recall the incidents of games, horses or numbers that dropped dead after we almost bet them.)

Systems and numerology, whimsical or not, provide a hopeful framework, I suppose, for what we recognize as a streak of insanity. They resemble ethical or moral systems, religions, that try to hold things together, impose a discipline from without, make order out of chaos. If systems were any good the casinos wouldn't be so big and we wouldn't be so small.

On the first night, a Monday, I sallied forth from my hotel, the Metropole, a four-star Sidney Greenstreet of a hotel with its garden bar and birdcage elevator, and entered the big casino. I thought, "Bet nobody else is here for preseason practice." I thought, "George Allen, you don't go any first classer than me."

I expected Arabian princes with princely piles of chips in front of them. There were four wheels surrounded by peasants like myself. I sat down at a 10-franc-minimum table, exchanged 200 francs for chips, leaving 100 in reserve. I was ready to scrimmage, to do grass drills, to take laps.

I was not ready for the opportunity that came and went immediately, like a hole at tackle that opens and closes in a flash. I was not ready for what-might-have-been: a run to moonlight with a bag of gold crooked under my arm.

I won hundreds. I should have won thousands.

Zero came up on the third spin. Twenty-six came up on the eighth spin. I was ahead 14–0 in the first quarter. My eye began to roam, like a bench-warmer checking out the cheerleaders. I made mental notes of the pink marble columns and gaudy chandeliers and nineteenth-century palace decor. I sized up my playmates: a young couple out of a primitive painting of a French wedding party; an old couple playing clusters of numbers (at smaller odds than

35–1) with passionless prudence; an old man sitting next to me, charting every spin in quest of the wheel's glandular cycle; a Burgess Meredith type, directly across from me, playing with style and abandon, scattering 20-franc reds hither and yon.

My stack of 10-franc blues was depleting when I noticed the color red seemed to be repeating. There, another one. Another. I put a 100-franc greenie on red. Red. I hadn't been paying attention. I picked up one greenie, leaving one greenie on red. Red again. I picked up a greenie. Again.

I was stricken with a sense of panic. Not panic itself. The sense of being disoriented, missing the train in a crowded foreign depot, being at an uptown cocktail party and waiting for a girl to free herself and then, after scanning the etchings, watching another dude moving in.

I had blown it.

Black.

"Fourteen times," the old man next to me whispered, his pencil making jagged arthritic moves. "Red, fourteen times."

I felt warm, my insides percolating. Counted my money: 560 francs. Imagined that the people standing behind me could see my neck reddening. (When the sun rose and set on Joe DiMaggio I saw his neck redden, standing in the batter's box at Yankee Stadium, 0-for-7 in a doubleheader, getting booed. He tripled.) I played my numbers three more futile times. I was ahead 300 francs. The clock read 11:30; I had been there exactly an hour. I knew I would blow it all if I hung on. I felt hot. (DiMaggio was out trying to steal home.) I left.

Trying to compose myself at a café, I calculated that had I bet 20 francs on red after it had come up three times I could have won 20,240 francs. (There was a 10,000-franc limit.) It seemed like such a ridiculous figure—I mean I had never even won a bag of marbles at the Saturday matinee—that I cooled off.

Coolly, I had a meeting with myself.

"Fucked up again."

"Sure did. But what would I have done for an encore?"

"Don't rationalize."

"Rookies make mistakes."

"You didn't make a mistake. You lost the championship."

"Still walked out a winner."

"Three hundred francs. A three-yard gain. Some romantic you are."

"Paid for the day, plus. Let's be realistic: I'm trying to beat the house, not break the bank. I'm trying to have fun, not get rich."

"Twenty thousand francs would have been fun. Ten thousand would have been worth a few laughs. Three hundred is a bloody cop-out."

"Look, I'm in training. I had the control to get out while I was ahead. Inner discipline. It's a long season. I'll get them tomorrow."

"Bullshit."

"It's one o'clock. Curfew. Good night, George Allen, wherever you are."

Tuesday I got them.

Zero hit on the fifth spin. It is a thing of beauty and a joy, for a while at least, to score early when the odds are against you and you have bet on the underdog. Anxiety drains into relief as the prospect of instantly being wiped out is put to rest. What we all want if we can't have the money is a run for the money, evidence that we aren't ciphers.

My lead dwindled, without protest, to a handful of chips, and I have small hands. But I was into the game, concentrating, summoning, and when black came up for the third straight time I reached into my pocket for the last 100-franc note and placed it on black.

Black hit. I let the 200 ride. Black—400. Black—800. Heart, be still. Black.

I had found my price. I fetched 1,500 francs, leaving 100. Black hit again—200. Again—400. Red.

Zero came up in another few spins. I fondled a large rectangular 1,000-franc chip. I felt myself levitating, wanting to fly out. I threw 40 francs each on 0 and 26—nothing. It was 10:00 P.M., I had played for a half hour. I flew.

Fleeing through the great rooms of the casino after cashing in, I was lit up by an electric current. Was my nose blinking, my ears semaphoring? I had chills. My body was having an orgasm. It subsided, then returned as I hit the steps. Fantasmagoric. A multiple orgasm.

I once won $2,000 on a football game. I glowed inside for days. Winning this 1,500 francs, this measly $300, twanged an undiscovered chord in my ganglia. I was a Fourth of July sparkler, sizzling.

Over dinner I discussed it.

"Jesus, you're terrific."

"I know."

"I didn't think you had it in you to play black. Isn't it always red that has the streaks in novels and movies?"

"Black is beautiful. Have to keep an open mind."

"I have to admit that, in retrospect, you handled last night's situation the way you should have."

"I have to admit you're right."

"Remember that time in high school, playing against Jefferson, when the lineman said in the huddle they couldn't move that 320-pound guard, run thirty-six to the left? You ran right into the big bastard the first time, but the second time you veered left and found the hole."

"I'm a slow learner."

"Slow runner. There was a hole big enough for the First Division to go through, and you made about seven. But I love you."

"Love you too. Night."

Wednesday I lost.

Zero and 26 performed nobly but indecisively. Up and down, down and up. Three reds came up once, and I played red and, because I had an odd chip and thought I might save 10 francs on one spin, I didn't play 0. It hit. My stomach flinched, as though steeling itself for a punch. The eyes of strangers condemned me. Discombobulated, I played colors indiscriminately, won some, lost some. I needed action. After two hours I was glad to come to any decision. The numbers seemed like random hieroglyphics. I was disappointed that I was not afflicted by vertigo instead of boredom.

"Now what was that all about?"

"I was about to ask you."

"Man, you have to hang in there."

"Gene Mauch once told me that young players lose their concentration quickly. Two hours is a long time to look at numbers, numbers, numbers. Nothing was happening. It was a grind. I didn't come here to grind."

"It's a long season. You came here to get ready for a long season."

"But there's no control, or illusion of control, as in football. No opinion to be right about. I feel no connection to roulette, even though I'm playing it, while in football I feel that I'm a part of it, even though I have nothing to do with the game."

"Crazy American, the bottom line is that you lost control of yourself, not the game."

"I'm still 1,500 francs to the good. I just got careless."

"They don't get careless when they have your money. They keep taking it. They're counting on you to get careless with their money. Don't."

"Just my humanity shining through. Let's mark it down as a good lesson."

"What are you drinking?"

"How do you say gin and tonic in French?"

"Gin and tonic."

"Perrier and Creme de Menthe. Sidney Greenstreet would drink Perrier and Creme de Menthe in Monte Carlo."

Thursday I won.

For variety and pizazz, and to broaden my vocabulary and horizons, I refined the system. I continued to play 0 and went to 25–26 and 26–27 instead of 26 alone, putting 10 francs on 26 and five each on 25 and 27, adding up to a 30-franc investment per spin, allotting me just 10 spins before the nightly stake could expire.

Twenty-six proceeded to mock my lapse of faith by scoring four times in a dozen or so spins. I was ahead 1,000 francs. Twenty-six, it dawned on me, was the number worn by Jack Mitchell, the original split-T quarterback at Oklahoma. As a sophomore last-string halfback I was given jersey 26 for the first game of the season after he graduated. Somebody thought better of it. For the second game I was 21.

Zero struck again and then, in succession, 26 and two 25s. It was a rout. I had an urge to punch the air triumphantly, to shout whoopee, something, but the stuffy decorum was intimidating. I searched for recognition or applause among my playmates. Unmindful, or resentful, of the great drama unfolding in their midst, they continued to root for their own money, the philistines.

Playing with the casino's money, 1,800 francs of it, I made my move. I doubled and tripled my bets, put 100 francs on 8, my daughter's age. In ten deliberately frenzied minutes I went through 1,200 francs. I took 600 in profit and fled.

"That was lovely. You took your shot and got out while you were ahead."

"I have 2,100 francs of their money. There's no way they'll get it all back."

"If you beat this silly game you ought to be able to murder football."

"I'm hip."

"You're fantastic."

"I'm horny. Got to share all these vibes."

At a discotheque a young German told me about The Sporting Club, an annex of the main casino where the high rollers roll. So that's what that Rolls-Royce motor pool was all about on Avenue Princess Grace.

♣ ♦ ♥ ♠

Friday night I ambled into The Sporting Club with all the insouciance I could muster. The musky odor of power and the thick scent of sexcitement hit me the way Mike Curtis, the linebacker, forearmed a Baltimore fan who ran onto the field. I was stunned.

I have been around the very rich while they have their fun and games, and I have found them only more uptight than you and I. Here, playing out fantasies on an exotic Super Bowl grid, they seemed less uptight than you and I. There were men, princes of industry, most of them much past their prime, in the barely concealed frenzy of lions at feeding time. There were women, great beauties, diamonds cascading from every public part, lionesses in heat. There was a primal growl in the air.

My own fortunes interested me less than the real fortunes of others. Twenty francs was the minimum, so I raised my stake to 500. Zero and 25–26–27 rose to the occasion, steadily building a 700-franc lead. Then a bouncy little old man, animated as a chimpanzee, won 240,000 francs on four turns of the wheel. My 1,200 francs seemed puny. I decided I needed a bigger stake and went to the dice table. I pressed it to 2,300 and depressed it back to 600. Back at roulette I depressed it to minus 200, dug into my pockets for 500 more, and accepted a total loss of 700. I had gone 400 over my limit. The growl had jumped into my throat.

I had already caught a dizzying whiff of a card game called 30–40, where a man was playing for the limit, 40,000 francs (about $8,000) per hand. He was losing heavily; markers on the table counted up to 600,000 francs. His eyes were glassy with resignation, his mouth expressionless, waxy with death. As his losses mounted to 800,000 his body seemed to sag. I wondered what the autopsy would show.

Then, gradually, he reduced the row of markers. As he did his mask of tragedy transformed through stages of aliveness to hope to anticipation to victory, and finally to celebration. Marcel Marceau, the mime, couldn't have done it any better. When the last marker was wiped out the man toured the room jubilantly, hugging and kissing women.

I felt that I had seen a man dig his own grave and climb out.

I was sure that he had an electric current sizzling through him.

Psychiatrists tell us that tempting fate—engaging in a life-death struggle—is one of the subconscious forces egging on the compulsive or pathological gambler. It could also be, they say, a desire to expiate guilt or seek love or return to the infantile state of being at the center of the universe. I don't know how guilt-ridden, love-starved, or well-diapered this man was, or whether he was even a case for the couch, but he certainly managed to stir himself viscerally by dying and being reborn.

Which, thankfully, brings us back to sex. On another level, psychiatrists tell us, gambling is a surrogate sexual experience. Whether it is a substitute or a supplementary entry for the real thing is up to the individual. Whatever, the heart-pounding risk of gambling is an erotic quick release that simulates the intensity of sex.

Those of us who gamble only from time to time are not, by the psychiatric definition, gambling at all. A clinical gambler is a screeching-with-anxiety neurotic who can't relax until he loses. The rest of us are getting a cheap thrill by creating an easy gut involvement.

My involvement in betting on football, particularly in how I handicap games, is, I began to understand in Monte Carlo, an extension of misspent youth as a player and high school backfield coach. The competition. The planning. The tension. Winning and losing.

But gambling for fun has its risks too, no less than social drinking. I've suffered a lapse gambling. A time or two I've gotten smashed drinking. Getting smashed is cheaper.

"You got manic in there, stud."

"No use gambling if you can't lose your head once in a while."

"Forget the book?"

"When you get into it, there's no book. First you live it, then you write it."

"Is that what you got out of your preseason practice?"

"That, and 1,400 francs, and a dynamite suntan."

"Lots of luck."

"Rather be good."

"Better be good, or you'll be good and broke. What's that ringing?"

"The alarm clock in our head, shmuck. Football season."

A Jolly Game

BY MIKHAIL ZOSHCHENKO

Gambling places almost always include laughter, humorous banter, at least early in the evening. This can take the form of crowing. Jesse May writes of an Indian poker player at the Taj Mahal in Atlantic City who would say after winning a big pot, "On behalf of my country, let me welcome you to the Taj Mahal." But humor has an aggressive, belittling side, and carries with it the risks of becoming something uglier. In gambling places there's a premium on verbal resourcefulness, a kind of "dozens." If a man never says a word, someone's sure in mid-stroke to stop, walk over to him, and yell, "Stop talking so much while I'm shooting"; if you call someone a "fish," another chimes in, "I hear he brings his own tartar sauce." I have seen exceptional insulters, for the merriment of kibbitzers, utterly degrade opponents, even while losing. A measure of creative taunting, that is, sweetens the pot, activates the "caring glands" (as Larry Merchant phrases it). Among a number of Russian billiard players, as Robert Bryne has noted, "apparently, beating a man at billiards and taking his money didn't sufficiently humiliate him." Sociologist Irving Goffman talks about how losers in gambling often receive a "status bloodbath." This sort of dousing is what the winner in the following selection from popular Russian writer Mikhail Zoshchenko tries to administer.

A short time ago I had dinner in a restaurant and then looked in at a poolroom. I felt like seeing, as they say, how the balls were rolling.

There's no question that it's an interesting game. It's absorbing and can distract a man from any kind of misfortune. Some even find that the game of billiards develops courage, a sharp and steady eye, and good aim, and doctors assert that this game is extremely beneficial to unbalanced men.

I don't know. I don't think so. Some unbalanced man might fill himself so full of beer while playing billiards that he could hardly crawl home after the game. So I doubt that this would be beneficial to the nervous and distraught. And as for its giving you a sharp eye, that all depends. A fellow from our house got both his eyes blackened with the cue when his partner was taking aim, and even though he wasn't blinded, he did go slightly blind in one eye. There's your development of a sharp eye for you. If someone should give him a workout in the other eye now, the man will be completely deprived of any vision at all, let alone aim.

So that in the sense of usefulness, it's all, as they say, old wives' tales.

But the game is certainly amusing. Especially when they're playing "for keeps"—very absorbing to watch.

Of course, they rarely play for money nowadays. But they think up something original instead. Some of them make the loser crawl under the table. Others make him buy a round of beer. Or have him pay for the game.

When I went to the poolroom this time, I saw a very mirth-provoking scene.

A winner was ordering his bewhiskered partner to crawl under the table carrying all the balls. He stuffed some balls in his pockets, put a ball in each hand, and on top of that tucked one under his chin. And in this state the loser crawled under the table to the accompaniment of general laughter.

After the next game the winner once again loaded down the be-whiskered fellow with balls and on top of that made him carry the cue between his teeth. And the poor fellow crawled again, to the Homeric laughter of the assembled company.

For the next game, they had trouble thinking up anything.

The bewhiskered one says, "Let's make it something easier, you've done me in as it is."

And really, even his mustache was drooping, he was so dragged out.

The winner says, "Don't be a fool—with such penalties I'll give you a marvelous lesson in how to play billiards."

An acquaintance of the winner's was there. He said, "I've thought of something. If he loses, let's do this: have him crawl under the table loaded down with the balls and we'll tie a case of beer to his foot. Let him crawl through like that."

The winner, laughing, says, "Bravo! That'll really be some trick!"

The bewhiskered one said in a hurt way, "If there's going to be beer in the case, I won't play. It'll be hard enough to crawl with an empty case."

In a word, he lost, and amid general laughter they again loaded him down with the balls, put the cue between his teeth, and tied a case to his foot. The winner's friend also started poking him with a cue to hasten his journey under the billiard table.

The winner laughed so hard that he fell into a chair and grunted from exhaustion.

The bewhiskered one emerged from under the table in a state of stupefaction. He gazed dully at the company and did not move for a while. Then he dug the balls out of his pockets and began untying the case of beer from his foot, saying that he wasn't playing anymore.

The winner was laughing so hard he shed tears. He said, "Come on, Egorov, old pal, let's play one more game. I've thought up another funny trick."

The other says, "Well, what else have you thought up?"

The winner, choking with laughter, says, "Let's play for your mustache, Egorov! That fluffy mustache of yours has bothered me for a long time. If I win, I'll cut off your mustache. Okay?"

The bewhiskered one says, "No, for my mustache I won't play, not unless you give me a forty-point handicap."

In a word, he lost again. And before anyone could catch his breath, the winner grabbed a table knife and began sawing off one side of his unlucky partner's fluffy mustache.

Everyone in the room was dying of laughter.

Suddenly one of those present goes over to the winner and says to him, "Your partner must be a fool, agreeing to such forfeits. And you take advantage of this and make fun of a man in a public place."

The winner's friend says, "What damn business is it of yours? After all, he agreed of his own free will."

The winner says to his partner in a tired voice, "Egorov, come here. Tell the assembled multitudes that you agreed to all the forfeits of your own free will."

The partner, supporting his half-severed mustache with his hand, says, "Obviously it was of my own free will, Ivan Borisovich."

The winner says, turning to the company, "Some people make their chauffeur wait in the freezing cold for three hours. But I treat people humanely. This is the chauffeur from our office, and I always bring him inside where it's warm. I don't patronize him but play a friendly game of billiards with him. I teach him, and I punish him a little. And why they're picking on me now, I just can't understand."

The chauffeur says, "Perhaps there's a barber in the house. I'd like my mustache evened off."

A man comes out of the crowd and says, taking a pair of scissors from his pocket, "I will be sincerely happy to even off your mustache. If you like, I'll make you one like Charlie Chaplin's."

While the barber was fussing with the chauffeur, I went up to the winner and said to him, "I didn't know that was your chauffeur. I thought it was your friend. I wouldn't have let you pull such tricks."

The winner, a bit shaken, says, "And what sort of a bird are you?"

I say, "I'll write an article about you."

The winner, really frightened, says, "But I won't tell you my name."

I say, "I'll just describe the actual event and add that it was a fairly stout, reddish-haired man named Ivan Borisovich. Of course, you may even get away with it, but if you do I hope your rotten soul will tremble before the lines of print."

The winner's friend, hearing something about an article, instantly made himself scarce and disappeared from the premises.

The winner drank beer and talked big for a long time, shouting that he didn't give a damn for anyone.

They trimmed the chauffeur's whiskers, and he became somewhat younger looking and handsomer. So that I even decided to tone down my feuilleton.

After I came home, as you see, I wrote it up. And now you're reading it and probably feeling amazed that such passionate gamblers exist and that you can run into such unattractive reddish-haired men.

Goodbye Watson

"The racetrack tells me where I am weak and where I am strong," Charles
Bukowski writes in the following selection. Bukowski went to the track
almost every day for thirty years. Gambling scenes, particularly related to
"horseplay," appear in much of his fiction and poetry with a mix of lyricism
and grittiness:

> we are betting on the miracle again
> there before the purple mountains,
> as the horses parade past
> so much more beautiful than
> our lives.
>
> —"12 minutes to post"

For Bukowski the track was, at some level, a way of confirming his aversion to
and connection with the masses whose sickness he regarded as the measure of
their humanity. Part of the draw was, as he put it in one of his last works, *The
Captain Is Out to Lunch and the Sailors Have Taken Over the Ship:*

> the faces of the horseplayers, cardboard faces, horrible, evil, blank, greedy,
> dying faces, day after day. Tearing up their tickets, reading their various papers,
> watching the changes on the toteboard as they are being ground away to less
> and less, as I stand there with them, as I am one with them. We are sick, the
> suckerfish of hope. Our poor clothing, our old cars. We move toward the mi-
> rage, our lives wasted like everybody else's.

The image of Bukowski as randy wino-brawler is much influenced by
the film *Barfly,* modeled on his life, with Mickey O'Rourke playing the
hoarse-voiced poet. The following selection suggests the relation of gambling

and other activities to Bukowski's writing, and the advice to prospective creative writers is priceless.

    it's after a bad day at the track that you realize that you will never make it, coming in stinking at the socks, a few wrinkled dollars in your wallet, you know that the miracle will never arrive, and worse, thinking about the really bad bet you made on the last race on the eleven horse, knowing it couldn't win, the biggest sucker bet on the board at 9/2, all the knowledge of your years ignored, you going up to the ten buck window and saying, "eleven twice!" and the old grey-haired boy at the window, asking again: "eleven?" he always asks again when I pick a real bad one. he may not know the actual winner but he knows the sucker bets, and he gives me the saddest of looks and takes the twenty. then to go out and watch that dog run last all the way, not even working at it, just loafing as your brain starts saying, "what the fuck, I gotta be crazy."

    I've discussed this thing with a friend of mine who has many years at the track. he's often done the same thing and he calls it the "death-wish," which is old stuff. we yawn at the term now, but strangely, there's still some basis in it yet. a man does get tired as the races progress and there IS this tendency to throw the whole game overboard. the feeling can come upon one whether he is winning or losing and then the bad bets begin. But, I feel, a more real problem is that you ACTUALLY want to be somewhere else—sitting in a chair reading Faulkner or making drawings with your child's crayons. the racetrack is just another JOB, finally, and a hard one too. when I sense this and I am at my best, I simply leave the track; when I sense this and I am not at my best I go on making bad bets. another thing that one should realize is that it is HARD to win at anything; losing is easy. it's grand to be The Great American Loser—anybody can do it; almost everybody does.

    a man who can beat the horses can do almost anything he makes up his mind to do. he doesn't belong at the racetrack. he should be on the Left Bank with his mother easel or in the East Village writing an avant-garde symphony. or making some woman happy, or living in a cave in the hills.

    but to go to the racetrack helps you realize yourself and the mob too. there's a lot of murky downgrading of Hemingway now by critics who can't write, and old ratbeard wrote some bad things from the middle to the end, but his head was becoming unscrewed, and even then he made the others look like schoolboys raising their hands for permission to make a little literary peepee. I know why Ernie went to the bull-fights—it was simple: it helped his writing.

Ernie was a mechanic: he liked to fix things on paper. the bullfights were a drawingboard of everything: Hannibal slapping elephant ass over mountain or some wino slugging his woman in a cheap hotel room. and when Hem got in to the typer he wrote standing up. he used it like a gun. a weapon. the bull-fights were everything attached to anything. it was all in his head like a fat but-ter sun: he wrote it down.

with me, the racetrack tells me quickly where I am weak and where I am strong, and it tells me how I feel that day and it tells me how much we keep changing, changing ALL the time, and how little we know of this.

and the stripping of the mob is the horror movie of the century. ALL of them lose. look at them. if you are able. one day at a racetrack can teach you more than four years at any university. if I ever taught a class in creative writ-ing, one of my prerequisites would be that each student must attend a racetrack once a week and place at least a 2 dollar win wager on each race. no show bet-ting. people who bet to show REALLY want to stay home but don't know how.

my students would automatically become better writers, although most of them would begin to dress badly and might have to walk to school.

I can see myself teaching Creative Writing now.

"well, how did you do Miss Thompson?"

"I lost $18."

"who did you bet in the feature race?"

"One-Eyed Jack."

"sucker bet. the horse was dropping 5 pounds which draws the crowd in but also means a step-up in class within allowance conditions. the only time a class-jump wins is when he looks bad on paper. One-Eyed Jack showed the highest speed-rating, another crowd draw, but the speed rating was for 6 fur-longs and 6 furlong speed ratings are always higher, on a comparative basis, than speed ratings for route races. furthermore, the horse closed at 6 so the crowd figured he would be there at a mile and a sixteenth. One-Eyed Jack has now shown a race around in 2 curves in 2 years. this is no accident. the horse is a sprinter and only a sprinter. that he came in last at 3 to one should not have been a surprise."

"how did you do?"

"I lost one hundred and forty dollars."

"who did you bet in the feature race?"

"One-Eyed Jack. class dismissed."—

before the racetrack and before the sterilized unreal existence of the t.v. brain-suck, I was working as a packer in a huge factory that turned out thousands of overhead lighting fixtures to blind the world, and knowing the libraries useless and the poets carefully complaining fakes, I did my studying at the bars and boxing matches.

those were the nights, the old days at the Olympic. they had a bald little Irishman making the announcements (was his name Dan Tobey?), and he had *style,* he'd seen things happen, maybe even on the riverboats when he was a kid, and if he wasn't *that* old, maybe Dempsey-Firpo anyhow. I can still see him reaching up for that cord and pulling the mike down slowly, and most of us were drunk before the first fight, but we were easy drunk, smoking cigars, feeling the light of life, waiting for them to put 2 boys in there, cruel but that was the way it worked, that is what they did to us and we were still alive, and, yes, most with a dyed redhead or blonde. even me. her name was Jane and we had many a good ten-rounder between us, one of them ending in a k.o. of me. and I was proud when she'd come back from the lady's room and the whole gallery would begin to pound and whistle and howl as she wiggled that big magic marvelous ass in that tight skirt—and it *was* a magic ass: she could lay a man stone cold and gasping, screaming love-words to a cement sky. then she'd come down and sit beside me and I'd lift that pint like a coronet, pass it to her, she'd take her nip, hand it back, and I'd say about the boys in the galley: "those screaming jackoff bastards, I'll kill them."

and she'd look at her program and say, "who do you want in the first?"

I picked them good—about 90 percent—but I had to see them first. I always chose the guy who moved around the least, who looked like he didn't want to fight, and if one guy gave the Sign of the Cross before the bell and the other guy didn't you had a winner—you took the guy who didn't. but it usually worked together. the guy who did all the shadow boxing and dancing around usually was the one who gave the Sign of the Cross and got his ass whipped.

there weren't many bad fights in those days and if there were it was the same as now—mostly between the heavyweights. but we let them know about it in those days—we tore the ring down or set the place on fire, busted up the seats. they just couldn't afford to give us too many bad ones. the Hollywood Legion ran the bad ones and we stayed away from the Legion. even the Hollywood boys knew the action was at the Olympic. Raft came, and the others, and all the starlets, hugging those front row seats. the gallery boys went ape and the fighters fought like fighters and the place was blue with cigar smoke, and how we screamed, baby baby, and threw money and drank our whiskey, and when it was over, there was the drive in, the old lovebed with our dyed and vicious women. you slammed it home, then slept like a drunk angel. who needed the public library? who needed Ezra? T.S.? E.E.? D.H.? H.D.? any of the Eliots? any of the Sitwells?

I'll never forget the first night I saw young Enrique Balanos. at the time, I had me a good colored boy. he used to bring a little white lamb into the ring with him before the fight and hug it, and that's corny but he was tough and good and a tough and good man is allowed certain leeways, right?

anyway, he was my hero, and his name might have been something like Watson Jones. Watson had good class and the flair—swift, quick quick quick, and the PUNCH, and he *enjoyed* his work. but then, one night, unannounced, somebody slipped this young Balanos in against him, and Balanos had it, took his time, slowly worked Watson down and took him over, busted him up good near the end. my hero. I couldn't believe it. if I remember, Watson was kayoed which made it a very bitter night, indeed. me with my pint screaming for mercy, screaming for a victory that simply would *not* happen. Balanos certainly had it—the fucker had a couple of snakes for arms, and he didn't *move*—he slid, slipped, jerked like some type of evil spider, always getting there, doing the thing. I knew that night that it would take a very excellent man to beat him and that Watson might as well take his little lamb and go home.

it wasn't until much later that night, the whiskey pouring into me like the sea, fighting with my woman, cursing her sitting there showing me all that fine leg, that I admitted that the better man had won.

"Balanos. good legs. he doesn't think. just reacts. better not to think. tonight the body beat the soul. it usually does. goodbye Watson, goodbye Central Avenue, it's all over."

I smashed the glass against the wall and went over and grabbed me some woman. I was wounded. she was beautiful. we went to bed. I remember a light rain came through the window, we let it rain on us. it was good. it was so good we made love twice and when we went to sleep we slept with our faces toward the window and it rained all over us and in the morning the sheets were all wet and we both got up sneezing and laughing, "jesus christ! jesus christ!" it was funny and poor Watson laying somewhere, his face slugged and pulpy, facing the Eternal Truth, facing the 6 rounders, the 4 rounders, then back to the factory with me, murdering 8 or ten hours a day for pennies, getting nowhere, waiting on Papa Death, getting your mind kicked to hell and your spirit kicked to hell, we sneezed, "jesus christ!" it was funny and she said, "you're blue all over, you've turned all BLUE! jesus, look at yourself in the mirror!" and I was freezing and dying and I stood in front of the mirror and I was all BLUE! ridiculous! a skull and shit of bones! I began to laugh, I laughed so hard I fell down on the rug and she fell down on top of me and we both laughed laughed laughed, jesus christ we laughed until I thought we were crazy, and then I had to get up, get dressed, comb my hair, brush my teeth, too sick to eat, heaved when I brushed my teeth, I went outside and walked toward the overhead lighting factory, just the sun feeling good but you had to take what you could get.

The Babylon Stakes

BY MICHAEL ONDAATJE

I recently came across a colonial document from nineteenth-century India with about five hundred pages of legal code establishing governmental ways of clamping down on all of the known forms of gambling. What always emerges from such comprehensive documents is the need to regulate a gambling that has become rampant to the point of threatening social order. In this sense Ondaatje's comment that in India "only the aristocracy gambled" seems to me to represent a Sri Lankan perspective! Only the aristocracy gambled in the country that invented dice, whose sacred scriptures are filled with stories of extravagant gamblers? Whatever the truth about gambling in India, Ondaatje's terrific short section on gambling in Ceylon (now Sri Lanka), taken from his memoir *Running in the Family,* captures the passion a whole society can have for forms of gambling, and the degree to which such passion spills into everyday life. Ondaatje won the 1992 Booker Prize for his novel *The English Patient,* the screen version of which won the Oscar for Best Picture in 1996.

The only occupation that could hope to avert one from drink and romance was gambling. In India only the aristocracy gambled; in Ceylon the bankers and lime-burners and fishmongers and the leisured class would spend their afternoons, shoulder to shoulder, betting compulsively. The rulers of the country genuinely believed that betting eliminated strikes; men had to work in order to gamble.

If it was not horses it was crows. A crippled aunt, who could not get to the track, began the fashion of betting on which crow would leave a wall first. This proved so popular that the government considered putting a bounty on crows. In any case, soon after the time Gertie Garvin trained a pet crow, bird-

gambling proved to be untrustworthy. But the real stars were involved with racing: horses such as "Mordenis," jockeys like "Fordyce," the trainer "Captain Fenwick." There were racetracks all over the island. If you sat in the grandstand all bets were five rupees. Then there was the two-rupee enclosure and finally, in the middle of the track, the 'gandhi enclosure' where the poorest stood. "From the grandstand you could watch them leaving like ants a good hour before the last race, having lost all their money."

The most dangerous track profession was starter of the race, and one of the few who survived was Clarence de Fonseka, who was famous for knowing every horse in the country by sight. As starter, he positioned himself at the far end of the track. And to forestall threats of death from the crowd in the gandhi enclosure, Clarence kept his fastest horse near him at all times. If a popular horse lost, the mob would race across the field to the starting post to tear him apart. Clarence would then leap onto his horse and gallop down the track in solitary splendour.

Racing concerned everyone. During the whole month of August my mother would close down her dancing school and go to the races. So would my grandmother, Lalla. Her figure at the races is ingrained in several people's memories: a large hat at a rakish angle that she wore with no consideration for anyone behind her, one hand on her hip, one hand on her hat, and a blue jacaranda blossom pinned to the shoulder of her dusty black dress, looking off into the drama of the one-hundred-yard stretch with the intensity of one preparing for the coming of the Magi. When the races were over, groups would depart for dinner, dance till early morning, go swimming and have a breakfast at the Mount Lavinia Hotel. Then to bed till noon when it was time for the races once more. The culmination of the season was the Governor's Cup stakes. Even during the war the August races were not to be postponed. Ceylon could have been invaded during the late afternoon as most of the Light Infantry was at the race track during these hours.

Many of my relatives owned a horse or two, which languished in comfort for much of the year and got trotted out for the August race meet. My grandmother's horse, 'Dickman Delight,' refused to step out of the stable if it was at all muddy. She would bet vast sums on her horse knowing that one day he would surprise everyone and win. The day this eventually happened, my grandmother was up north. She received a telegram in the early morning which read: "Rain over Colombo" so she put her money on another horse. Dickman Delight galloped to victory on dry turf. Japanese planes had attacked Galle Face Green in Colombo and the telegram should have read: "Raid over Colombo." Dickman Delight never won again.

Most people tried to own a horse, some even pooled their money, each "owning a leg." The desire was not so much to have horse-sense but to be involved with the ceremonial trappings. Percy Lewis de Soysa, for instance, took great care selecting his colours, which were gold and green. In his youth, while successfully entertaining a woman at a Cambridge restaurant, he had ordered a bottle of champagne and at the end of the evening whispered to her that when he eventually owned a horse his racing colours would be taken from the label of the bottle. 'Searchlight Gomez' chose his colours, pink and black, after a certain lady's underwear and was proud of it.

There were races all year long. The Monsoon Meet in May, the Hakgalle Stakes in February, the Nuwara Eliya Cup in August. Some of the horses had become so inbred that jockeys could no longer insure themselves. The Babylon Stakes was banned after one horse, 'Forced Potato,' managed to bite a jockey and then leapt the fence to attack as many as it could in the jeering gandhi enclosure. But the jockeys had their perks. Gambling was so crucial to the economy of certain households that semi-respectable women slept with jockeys to get closer to "the horse's mouth."

If the crowd or the horses did not cause trouble, *The Searchlight,* a magazine published by the notorious Mr. Gomez, did. "One of those scurrilous things," it attacked starters and trainers and owners and provided gossip to be carefully read between races. Nobody wished to appear in it and everyone bought it. It sold for five cents but remained solvent, as the worst material could be toned down only with bribes to the editor. 'Searchlight Gomez' went to jail once, and that for too good a joke. Every January issue featured the upcoming events for the year. One year he listed, under October 3rd, Hayley and Kenny's Annual Fire. This blatant but accurate reference to the way fire insurance was used to compensate for sagging trade was not appreciated and he was sued.

The Gasanawa group tried to take in all the races. In December they drove down to the Galle Gymkhana, stopping on the way to order oysters and have a swim at Ambalangoda. "Sissy," Francis' sister, "was always drowning herself because she was an exhibitionist." The men wore tweed, the women wore their best crinolines. After the races they would return to Ambalangoda, pick up the oysters "which we swallowed with wine if we lost or champagne if we won." Couples then paired off casually or with great complexity and danced in a half-hearted manner to the portable gramophone beside the cars. Ambalangoda was the centre for devil dances and exorcism rites, but this charmed group was part of another lost world. The men leaned their chins against the serene necks of the women, danced a waltz or two, slid oysters into their partner's mouths. The waves on the beach collected champagne corks. Men who had lost fortunes laughed frantically into the night. A woman from the village who was encountered carrying a basket of pineapples was persuaded to trade that for a watch removed from a wrist. Deeper inland at midnight, the devil dances began, drums portioned the night. Trucks carrying horses to the next meet glared their headlights as they passed the group by the side of the road. The horses, drummers, everyone else, seemed to have a purpose. The devil dances cured sickness, catarrh, deafness, aloneness. Here the gramophone accompanied a seduction or an arousal, it spoke of meadows and "little Spanish towns" or "a small hotel," a "blue room."

A hand cupped the heel of a woman who wished to climb a tree to see the stars more clearly. The men laughed into their tumblers. They all went swimming again with just the modesty of the night. An arm touched a face. A foot touched a stomach. They could have almost drowned or fallen in love and their lives would have been totally changed during any one of those evenings.

Then, everyone very drunk, the convoy of cars would race back to Gasanawa in the moonlight crashing into frangipani, almond trees, or slipping off the road to sink slowly up to the door handles in a paddy field.

From Tracks

BY LOUISE ERDRICH

Native American gambling, traditionally, was ritual and contest connected with the sacred, and used for a great variety of individual and social functions. As it emerges in cosmological stories, it suggests indigenous ways of thinking about risk and uncertainty. It is within such contexts that the enormous variety of gambling games that Europeans found among "Indians" at the time of "contact" have to be understood. In contemporary Native American fiction, authors often layer the traditional senses and values of gambling contests against scenes involving introduced games. This makes such scenes difficult to read without a knowledge of the older mythologies of the sacred. At the same time, gambling has become a part of Native American society in new ways, and writers like Erdrich are marvelous at revealing character through gambling scenes. In *Love Medicine* (1984), Erdrich has three characters playing for a Pontiac Firebird, among them one (Lipsha) is card-shark, having inherited from several generations of card players, and having learned to cheat as "an attendant at the Senior Citizens":

> It wasn't cheating to them, anyway, just second nature. The games were cheer-fully cutthroat vicious, and the meanest player of them all was Lulu. She'd learned to crimp, that is, to mark your cards with little scratches and folds as you play, when she started losing her eyesight. It was just supposed to keep her even in the game, she said. I learned to crimp from her before I ever knew she was my grandmother, which might explain why I took to it with such enormous ease. The blood tells. I suppose there is a gene for crimping in your string of cells.

Fleur Pillager in Erdrich's *Tracks* is Lipsha's great-grandmother. In the following selection she systematically beats four white men at poker, her skill unmanning them, their anger building into violence in the brutal aftermath of the game.

Her cheeks were wide and flat, her hands large, chapped, muscular. Fleur's shoulders were broad and curved as a yoke, her hips fishlike, slippery, narrow. An old green dress clung to her waist, worn thin where she sat. Her glossy braids were like the tails of animals, and swung against her when she moved, deliberately, slowly in her work, held in and half-tamed. But only half. I could tell, but the others never noticed. They never looked into her sly brown eyes or noticed her teeth, strong and sharp and very white. Her legs were bare, and since she padded in beadworked moccasins they never saw that her fifth toes were missing. They never knew she'd drowned. They were blinded, they were stupid, they only saw her in the flesh.

And yet it wasn't just that she was a Chippewa, or even that she was a woman, it wasn't that she was good-looking or even that she was alone that made their brains hum. It was how she played cards.

Women didn't usually play with men, so the evening that Fleur drew a chair to the men's table there was a shock of surprise.

"What's this," said Lily. He was fat, with a snake's pale eyes and precious skin, smooth and lily-white, which is how he got his name. Lily had a dog, a stumpy mean little bull of a thing with a belly drum-tight from eating pork rinds. The dog was as fond of the cards as Lily, and straddled his barrel thighs through games of stud, rum poker, *vingt-un*. The dog snapped at Fleur's arm that first night, but cringed back, its snarl frozen, when she took her place.

"I thought," she said, her voice soft and stroking, "you might deal me in."

There was a space between the lead bin of spiced flour and the wall where Russell and I just fit. He tried to inch toward Fleur's skirt, to fit against her. Who knew but that he might have brought her luck like Lily's dog, except I sensed we'd be driven away if the men noticed us and so I pulled him back by the suspenders. We hunkered down, my arm around his neck. Russell smelled of caraway and pepper, of dust and sour dirt. He watched the game with tense interest for a minute or so, then went limp, leaned against me, and dropped his mouth wide. I kept my eyes open, saw Fleur's black hair swing over the chair, her feet solid on the boards of the floor. I couldn't see on the table where the cards slapped, so after they were deep in their game I pressed Russell down and raised myself in the shadows, crouched on a sill of wood.

I watched Fleur's hands stack and riffle, divide the cards, spill them to each player in a blur, rake and shuffle again. Tor, short and scrappy, shut one eye and squinted the other at Fleur. Dutch screwed his lips around a wet cigar.

"Gotta see a man," he mumbled, getting up to go out back to the privy. The others broke, left their cards, and Fleur sat alone in the lamplight that glowed in a sheen across the push of her breasts. I watched her closely, then she paid me a beam of notice for the first time. She turned, looked straight at me, and grinned the white wolf grin a Pillager turns on its victims, except that she wasn't after me.

"Pauline there," she said. "How much money you got?"

We had all been paid for the week that day. Eight cents was in my pocket.

"Stake me." She held out her long fingers. I put the coins on her palm and then I melted back to nothing, part of the walls and tables, twined close with Russell. It wasn't long before I understood something that I didn't know then. The men would not have seen me no matter what I did, how I moved. For my dress hung loose and my back was already stooped, an old woman's. Work had roughened me, reading made my eyes sore, forgetting my family had hardened my face, and scrubbing down bare boards had given me big, red-dened knuckles.

When the men came back and sat around the table, they had drawn together. They shot each other small glances, stuck their tongues in their cheeks, burst out laughing at odd moments, to rattle Fleur. But she never minded. They played their *vingt-un,* staying even as Fleur slowly gained. Those pennies I had given her drew nickels and attracted dimes until there was a small pile in front of her.

Then she hooked them with five card draw, nothing wild. She dealt, discarded, drew, and then she sighed and her cards gave a little shiver. Tor's eye gleamed, and Dutch straightened in his seat.

"I'll pay to see that hand," said Lily Veddar.

Fleur showed, and she had nothing there, nothing at all.

Tor's thin smile cracked open, and he threw in his hand too.

"Well, we know one thing," he said, leaning back in his chair, "the squaw can't bluff."

With that I lowered myself into a mound of swept sawdust and slept. I woke during the night, but none of them had moved yet so I couldn't either. Still later, the men must have gone out again, or Fritzie come to break the game, because I was lifted, soothed, cradled in a woman's arms and rocked so quiet that I kept my eyes shut while Fleur rolled first me, then Russell, into a closet of grimy ledgers, oiled paper, balls of string, and thick files that fit be-neath us like a mattress.

The game went on after work the next evening. Russell slept, I got my eight cents back five times over, and Fleur kept the rest of the dollar she'd won for a stake. This time they didn't play so late, but they played regular, and then kept going at it. They stuck with poker, or variations, for one solid week and each time Fleur won exactly one dollar, no more and no less, too consistent for luck.

By this time, Lily and the other men were so lit with suspense that they got Pete to join the game. They concentrated, the fat dog tense in Lily Veddar's lap, Tor suspicious, Dutch stroking his huge square brow, Pete steady. It wasn't that Fleur won that hooked them in so, because she lost hands too. It was rather that she never had a freak deal or even anything above a straight. She only took on her low cards, which didn't sit right. By chance, Fleur should have gotten a full or a flush by now. The irritating thing was she beat with pairs and never bluffed, because she couldn't, and still she ended each night with exactly one dollar. Lily couldn't believe, first of all, that a woman could be smart enough to play cards, but even if she was, that she would then be stupid enough to cheat for a dollar a night. By day I watched him turn the problem over, his lard-white face dull, small fingers probing at his knuckles, until he finally thought he had Fleur figured as a bit-time player, caution her game. Raising the stakes would throw her.

More than anything now, he wanted Fleur to come away with something but a dollar. Two bits less or ten more, the sum didn't matter just so he broke her streak.

Night after night she played, won her dollar, and left to stay in a place that only Russell and I knew about. Fritzie had done two things of value for Fleur. She had given her a black umbrella with a stout handle and material made to shed water, and also let her board on the premises. Every night, Fleur bathed in the slaughtering tub, then slept in the unused brick smokehouse behind the lockers, a windowless place tarred on the inside with scorched fats. When I brushed against her skin I noticed that she smelled of the walls, rich and woody, slightly burnt. Since that night she put me in the closet, I was no longer jealous or afraid of her, but followed her close as Russell, closer, stayed with her, became her moving shadow that the men never noticed, the shadow that could have saved her.

August, the month that bears fruit, closed around the shop and Pete and Fritzie left for Minnesota to escape the heat. A month running, Fleur had won thirty dollars and only Pete's presence had kept Lily at bay. But Pete was gone now, and one payday, with the heat so bad no one could move but Fleur, the men sat and played and waited while she finished work. The cards sweat, limp in their fingers, the table was slick with grease, and even the walls were warm to the touch. The air was motionless. Fleur was in the next room boiling heads.

Her green dress, drenched, wrapped her like a transparent sheet. A skin of lakeweed. Black snarls of veining clung to her arms. Her braids were loose, half unraveled, tied behind her neck in a thick loop. She stood in steam, turning skulls through a vat with a wooden paddle. When scraps boiled to the surface, she bent with a round tin sieve and scooped them out. She'd filled two dishpans.

"Ain't that enough now?" called Lily. "We're waiting." The stump of a dog trembled in his lap, alive with rage. It never smelled me or noticed me above Fleur's smoky skin. The air was heavy in the corner, and pressed Russell and me down. Fleur sat with the men.

"Now what do you say?" Lily asked the dog. It barked. That was the signal for the real game to start.

"Let's up the ante," said Lily, who had been stalking this night for weeks. He had a roll of money in his pocket. Fleur had five bills in her dress. Each man had saved his full pay that the bank officer had drawn from the Kozkas' account.

"Ante a dollar then," said Fleur, and pitched hers in. She lost, but they let her scrape along, a cent at a time. And then she won some. She played unevenly, as if chance were all she had. She reeled them in. The game went on. The dog was stiff now, poised on Lily's knees, a ball of vicious muscle with its yellow eyes slit in concentration. It gave advice, seemed to sniff the lay of Fleur's cards, twitched and nudged. Fleur was up, then down, saved by a scratch. Tor dealt seven cards, three down. The pot grew, round by round, until it held all the money. Nobody folded. Then it all rode on one last card and they went silent. Fleur picked hers up and drew a long breath. The heat lowered like a bell. Her card shook, but she stayed in.

Lily smiled and took the dog's head tenderly between his palms.

"Say Fatso," he said, crooning the words. "You reckon that girl's bluffing?"

The dog whined and Lily laughed. "Me too," he said. "Let's show." He tossed his bills and coins into the pot and then they turned their cards over.

Lily looked once, looked again, then he squeezed the dog like a fist of dough and slammed it on the table.

Fleur threw out her arms and swept the money close, grinning that same wolf grin that she'd used on me, the grin that had them. She jammed the bills inside her dress, scooped the coins in waxed white paper that she tied with string.

From The Man with the $100,000 Breasts

BY MICHAEL KONIK

Konik has that gambler's sense of being surprised by nothing, of being at home around what some would consider eccentric behavior, along with the nose for incident and eye for detail of the born profiler. Konik knows gambling from the inside out, and his short introductions to individual gamblers are windows into a "culture" where the bets seem incredible, or incredibly stupid, but the stakes are real. Konik accepts people doing what they do, going to ludicrous lengths to back what they've said with actions. In the selection that follows, Konik begins with a man who has bet 14 grand that he can live in a bathroom for a month, a seemingly minimal bet compared to that in Russian writer Anton Chekhov's short story, "The Bet," in which a banker bets a young man a million dollars that he won't stay in solitary confinement for five years. The structure of the bets is similar, suggesting some juvenile, impulsive spirit of gamble that works through motives as different as moral conviction and goofy opportunism—something in the land of "put up or shut up" that makes humanoids susceptible to being carried away.

♣ ♦ ♥ ♠

When I first meet Brian Zembic, he is living in a bathroom.
This is not because he can't afford a place that has all the amenities, like a bedroom. It's because a couple of his degenerate gambling buddies bet him $14,000 he couldn't stay in a bathroom for 30 straight days.

Several gambler friends playing the poker tournament circuit had told me about some psychopath they knew who would do anything to win a bet. "The guy's an animal," they opined. "You gotta meet him." But my pals neglected to mention that Brian doesn't really have a permanent address, save for a cheap motel he often stays in when he comes to Las Vegas. Tracking him down is like hunting a fugitive; he seems to jump to another motel, another apartment, another country, every time I try to get him on the phone. That he is confined to a bathroom for a month is my best opportunity yet to actually confirm this cipher's existence.

When I arrive in Las Vegas, he's six days into the bathroom bet, and already he's going a little stir-crazy. As far as bathrooms go, it's a nice bathroom: carpeted, brightly lighted, bordering on spacious. But it's still a bathroom. The terms of Brian's bet allow him to keep the door open, but prohibit him from crossing the threshold into the adjoining hallway. Since Brian lives in the bathroom by himself—a $50-a-day housekeeper brings him sandwiches whenever he yells for her—most of his time is spent reading and practicing magic tricks. Rows of $100 bills are taped to the mirror to remind Brian what he's earning each day he serves his self-imposed sentence but, he confesses, his resolve is weakening. "Joey, one of the guys who made the wager with me, he owns the apartment and he's been sending people over here to take a dump," Brian tells me, reclining on the floor. "It's brutal."

Six days later his buddies cave in and buy Brian out of the bet for $7,000.

"I didn't think he'd do it, to tell you the truth," Joey admits, shortly after paying Brian off with a thick stack of hundreds. "*I* wouldn't do it. *You* wouldn't do it, right? I couldn't imagine myself or anybody else with half a brain staying in a bathroom for a month. I thought it was a good bet. I was wrong."

Anyone who knows Brian Zembic well understands the guy will do just about anything to put money in his pocket—as long as it doesn't require punching a clock. Ironically, Brian's a top Las Vegas blackjack player, one of the world's best at "shuffle tracking," a complex method of following cards through the mixing process. He could be earning thousands of dollars a day plying his trade. But he doesn't do it regularly because that would feel too much like *working,* a concept that Brian despises. Working, he believes, means somebody owns him, owns his time, his freedom. When he needs to earn some money, which happens occasionally, he gambles. Backgammon mostly, a little poker, ping-pong when he can find a sucker—anything where his skill gives him the edge. Anything where his superior talent or knowledge makes him a favorite to win. This includes taking insane proposition bets. Like walking around for a year with a nice pair of womanly breasts.

When I meet him at his bathroom prison cell that summer afternoon, he's had them for close to a year. He's wearing a baggy sweatshirt, so his business isn't obvious. But you can tell there's something lurking under all that cotton. I ask Brian if the past 10 months have been humiliating. He laughs. "No. Not at all. It's been great. I've probably never had more fun in my life."

Fun? Playing with big beautiful breasts every day of the year I can see. But *possessing* them?

"Let me put it this way," Brian says, smiling conspiratorially, as his housekeeper shuffles past the doorway. "I've never gotten so much pussy in my life. I mean, I've never done bad. But since I got these," he says, giving his bosom an absentminded poke, "it's been like one woman after another."

For Brian Zembic, 37, from Winnipeg, Manitoba, life has not always been so busty. He's always been an attention-getter, a fast-talking high-energy maniac who usually reduces everyone around him to a chuckling mess. Even though he's notorious for never picking up a check—Brian's possibly the cheapest bastard on the planet—his buddies love taking him out to dinner and nightclubs, because he's a total chick magnet. Friends call him "the Wiz," short for Wizard. Brian's like a sorcerer. He does magic tricks and tells jokes and makes women you would be too scared to talk to giggle like teenagers at an Antonio Sabato Jr. underwear signing.

Brian the Wiz does not look like what you might imagine a hard-core gambler to look like. No gold chains. No pinkie rings. No dark sunglasses. He's got a boyish face and an easy grin. (And large breasts.) In terms of physique and looks and presence, you would probably call Brian average. Average height and weight. Average build. Nondescript. Indeed, a little more than a year ago, Brian was, like any other guy, flat-chested—and perfectly happy that way.

But one night a couple of years ago, Brian was playing backgammon at the Ace Point Club in New York City. It's a quasi-legal dingy little place in midtown Manhattan that looks like someone's living room, except that it's filled with backgammon tables and a cast of shady characters you probably wouldn't want hanging around if it were *your* living room. This is Brian's world. On this particular night he's playing for $300 a point with his high-rolling pals, a gang of action junkies escaped from the pages of a Damon Runyon story: magicians, card cheats, sports bettors. Guys who are prone to bet on which raindrop will get to the bottom of a window pane first. The conversations in this crowd tend toward the deeply philosophical.

"What would you play Russian Roulette for?"

"I dunno. A million, maybe."

"Yeah? How much for two bullets in the gun?"

Tonight, a cold desperate winter night in 1996, Brian is engaged in a passionate debate with his cohort JoBo, one of the biggest backgammon play

208 . The Greatest Gambling Stories Ever Told

ers on the planet. Like the stakes he plays for, JoBo is a large man, a stout man, a man with thick forearms and a powerful chest. He tends to express his opinions with a stolid certainty that does not invite contradiction. JoBo's saying it's crazy how women get implants, how in hopes of attracting men, they actually jam a bag of saltwater in their chest.

Brian suggests that getting implants probably isn't so bad. "Look at Maggie," he says, referring to a mutual friend with a substantial breast job. "She seems pretty happy with her boobs."

"You think so?" JoBo asks. "How'd you like it if you had to walk around with those things all day?"

Brian leans back in his chair and laughs. JoBo is not a man who likes to be laughed at. He's the kind of guy who frequently challenges those who contradict him to put their money where their mouth is.

"Tell you what, pal," JoBo says. "I'll give you a hundred thousand if *you* get tits."

Now, a hundred grand to JoBo isn't going to change his life one way or another. He plays backgammon matches against Saudi sheiks for stakes nearly that big. So Brian knows JoBo isn't fooling. JoBo really *would* pay $100,000 just to see one of his friends sporting a set of perky breasts. And $100,000 to Brian Zembic—$100,000 for not working—is a serious matter.

"How large would they have to be?" Brian asks.

"As big as Maggie's, of course."

They discuss the wager's fine points: Brian's responsible for the surgery costs; JoBo will put the $100,000 prize in escrow; Brian collects the money only if he keeps his breasts for a year.

"Okay," Brian says. "You're locked into it."

Sure, whatever. JoBo knows Brian is the kind of goofball who likes to talk a good game. It's part of his life-of-the-party shtick.

"And you know I'm fucked up enough to do it," Brian warns.

"No you're not," JoBo says. "Nobody's that fucked up."

For the next three months, JoBo and Brian play a lot of backgammon together. Every time they see a woman with attractive shapely breasts, they joke about their crazy bet.

After one long night of rolling the cubes, Brian confides in JoBo that he's going to put a lot of money in the stock market. Seems his pal Fat Steve, another Vegas wiseguy, has a can't-miss tip. "And if it does miss," Brian tells JoBo, "I figure I've got your hundred-thousand-dollar insurance policy."

During the summer of '96, Brian, on Steve's advice, buys stock in some company that makes heart-scanning equipment. Coincidentally, JoBo already owns a bunch of shares, and also assures him it's the stock of the century. So Brian plunges a huge chunk of his savings, a total of $125,000, into the deal. Meanwhile, JoBo's unloading his shares as quickly as his broker can find some sucker to buy them. In one week the stock goes from 6½ to 5.

Brian finds out he's been duped by his buddy. He unleashes a vitriolic monologue at JoBo, alternately calling him a scumbag-cocksucking-ass-licking-motherfucker and hanging up on him. This is how Brian typically deals with anger: call, scream, swear, hang up. His friends know this. The bitterness passes and Brian goes back to being the Wiz.

This time, though, the ranting doesn't bring Brian any satisfaction. He's still steamed. So, a week after his stock debacle, pissed off and stuck, he threatens to get breasts.

"No," JoBo says, "you waited too long. Bet's off."

Brian disagrees. So the two gamblers do what most gamblers do when confronted with an intractable difference of opinion: They convene an arbitration panel of fellow gamblers—in this case, three allegedly impartial jurists who happen to be JoBo's high-rolling friends. These are fellows whose combined weight would probably eclipse that of the Packers' offensive line, guys who have mastered the art of consuming 6,000 calories a day while doing nothing but playing cards and backgammon and the occasional video game. They look like a trio of Buddhas.

In a big booth at a Chinese restaurant off the Vegas Strip, Brian and JoBo make their case before the panel, which has dubbed itself the Titty Tribunal. After five minutes of solemn deliberation, over plates of moo shu pork, Mongolian beef, and most everything else on the menu, the tribunal issues its ruling: The bet's on.

Brian's little joke is no longer a joke. He's got a deal. But now he's got to figure out how to hold up his end of it—if he truly *wants* to hold up his end. Any doubts he might harbor pass quickly, thanks to a profound analytical technique Brian often resorts to when confronted with tough decisions. "I don't think about things too much," he explains. "Once I make up my mind, it's over."

Brian knows a plastic surgeon, a scalpel-wielding casino junkie he and his cohorts sometimes gamble with. "Would you give me breast implants?" Brian asks the doctor. "In a heartbeat," Doc says. "I work on transsexuals all the time."

Thinking maybe his gambling doctor buddy isn't necessarily the most responsible member of the medical community—the guy spends at least half his waking hours playing backgammon—Brian seeks a second and third opinion. Every surgeon says yes. "Not one of them had a single ethical or legal or moral qualm," Brian recalls. "They were all, like, 'Sure, I'll give you tits!'"

Doc's fee is $4,000 to put them in, $500 to take them out. Now, Brian, being about the stingiest miser to ever roll a pair of dice, balks at the price. Oh, he has the money. He just doesn't want to spend 4.5% of his expected profit.

So Brian makes the surgeon a proposition. They'll play a little backgammon. A $5,000 match. Brian has the operation paid for in two hours.

Now Brian the Wiz realizes the surgery is really going to occur. That he's only hours away from going under the knife. That he's going to have *tits.* At this point, most men would be queasy at the thought of getting their nipples sliced open. But Doc assures him the operation isn't really out of the ordinary. Putting implants in a man, he says, is virtually no different than in a woman. Brian has nothing to worry about. A little nip, a little tuck—sew it up and out the door. Simple.

Sure, except for the two big mounds he's going to be carrying around for a year. After all, if our balls, our testosterone-filled testicles, are the nexus of our manhood, then breasts—protruding insistent mammaries—are surely one of the hallmarks of womanhood. But Brian is calm. Eerily calm.

You or I would be wondering and worrying, allowing visions of embarrassment and unwanted femininity and, God forbid, impotence, to dance in our muddled heads. What's going to happen when my poker buddies see me built like a centerfold? How am I going to explain this to the first woman I coax into bed? What the fuck is wrong with me?

That's why we're not the Wiz.

On a gray Manhattan winter afternoon, Brian Zembic has clear plastic pouches inserted through his nipples (over the pectoral muscles) and filled with 14 ounces of saline. After a routine two-hour procedure, he is the proud owner of two 38C breasts.

"I was in a serious motorcycle accident a few years ago," Brian says. "I went through fifteen different operations to put my body back together. Compared to having your jaw reconstructed and your skull held together by pins, getting a boob job is nothing."

He recalls feeling vaguely heavy—top-heavy—when he wakes. "Everything went smoothly," Brian says. "I just couldn't get out of bed for two weeks." He remembers being interminably groggy, with a chronically sore back. And a lingering fear of touching his new breasts.

"I was afraid of popping them," he says. "I thought if I touched them they might fall out."

Instead, Brian looks. He ogles his breasts, just as some guys might slather over a stripper. Most of the time that he's in bed, he keeps his tits hidden under a sweatshirt. But whenever he gets the urge, he takes a peek. And he's got to admit, they look pretty damn good. Finally, about two weeks after his surgery, after everything has "settled," Brian has his first squeeze.

His new breasts feel hard, as though the doctor implanted two regulation softballs. (Eventually they soften.) Every time he touches his breasts Brian wants to laugh—"I've got tits!" he's thinking—so he has to stop touching them. Laughing hurts his scars too much.

Men joke that if they had tits of their own, they could quit chasing women. Brian Zembic proves otherwise. "I was hoping it would be a turn-on to squeeze my tits," Brian admits. "But I never had much feeling in that area before the operation and I didn't have any afterward. I was a little disappointed."

Shortly after his initial grope, as soon as he's mobile, Brian calls his buddy JoBo. "For Christ sake, take 'em out! I was bluffing," JoBo says. "I didn't think you'd actually do it." JoBo offers to settle the bet for $50,000. Brian tells him the breasts are staying right where they are—he intends to collect his $100,000.

JoBo is sick. He thinks he might vomit. What sort of twisted lunatic would actually go through with this? "You cheap, ugly, little cocksucker!" he screams. "You've got to be kidding me!"

Brian isn't kidding.

"Then I'm going to get my money's worth," JoBo vows. "Get your ass over to the club, you little prick. It's time for a show."

For his "debut," Brian briefly considers wearing the baggiest trench coat he can find. "But then I think, I should be proud of my tits," Brian says. "Not many guys would have the balls to walk around with a pair of hooters."

No, indeed they would not. You can grow a ponytail or wear an earring or, if you're really a "rebel," smear on some eye shadow. But how "different" does that make you from every other guy in the world seeking an anchor of individuality in a sea of matching ties and nicely creased Dockers? Brian has breasts, 38C breasts. *That's* different.

It's nearly midnight, but the Ace Point is still full of gamblers. When Brian appears at the backgammon club, dressed as he always dresses, in a T-shirt and bomber jacket, a small crowd forms at JoBo's beckoning. "You could tell some people were almost scared to look, like at a murder scene," Brian recalls. When he lifts his shirt to reveal two round protuberant mounds peeking over his hairy belly, JoBo laughs so hard he almost pukes. "You keep these for a year, and it'll be worth every penny."

Mikey Large, a regular at the high-stakes backgammon games, keeps begging Brian for another peek. He likes the breasts. A lot. Brian calls him a pervert, a sick twisted lowlife. And flashes him anyway. At this point, his breasts are a new toy, like a flashy watch or a graphite-shafted oversize driver: Hey, boys, look what I got!

"It was like seeing a beautiful long-haired girl from behind," JoBo recalls. "You're falling in love, and then she turns around and you see it's some rocker dude with a moustache. Most men find that disturbing. I found Brian's tits disturbing. But funny, too."

Proving to your buddies you have titanium testes is fine. Winning a $100,000 bet is fantastic. But no sex for a year? That's a torturous proposition. Initially Brian thinks that when he's around women he'll have to try to hide his breasts, that his year will be filled with ingenious subterfuges and concealments. He learns quickly that, dressed in baggy clothes and a jacket, almost no one can tell he's stacked. Within a few weeks, after sharing his secret with several female friends, it becomes clear to Brian that most women do not regard him as a nauseating freak. They *like* his breasts.

"I was getting 'chi-chi' three weeks after the surgery," Brian claims.

He says that having breasts forges a bond between him and womankind. "Women feel closer to me now. My female friends, we walk around topless together. We compare our cleavage and talk about bras, like I'm one of the girls."

His first post-operation lover is a jeweler from New York City. Brian meets her at a party, where he tells her about his unique accessories, demurely hidden under a loose-fitting jacket. She smiles and says matter-of-factly, "That arouses me. I want to see them." A half-hour later they're in her apartment.

"She attacked me!" Brian says, still in awe at the memory. "She wouldn't stop sucking on them."

This, according to Brian, is standard procedure. "A few of the girls I've met have been extremely turned on by them," he reports. "They want to suck on them and play with them. All the stuff guys like to do."

I ask Brian if *he's* grown to like his breasts. "I'm really a tit man. I'm totally fixated on breasts. Unfortunately," Brian Zembic says, jostling his boobs, "these don't turn me on. I wish they did, but they just don't. I guess I want all the other tits out there, not mine."

Most men, as JoBo asserts, find Brian's breasts rather unattractive, if not downright weird. "I guess it's because they tend to have chest hair growing on them, even though I shave them once in a while," Brian says. "But the women!

I'm telling you, I don't know if it's like a latent lesbian thing or what. Seriously, the chicks are nuts for them."

Incredulous, I track down a couple of the women Brian claims to have slept with. One of them, Jeannie, a leggy stripper who works at one of the top-less joints off Las Vegas Boulevard, says she's bisexual, and that Brian and his breasts fulfill all her fantasies at once.

"It's just awesome to get fucked *and* have nice tits to suck on," Jeannie explains. I tell her I understand completely.

Sharon, a smashing redhead who might pass for Geena Davis—if only Geena Davis worked as a blackjack dealer at a major Vegas casino—is a woman Brian had pursued for months, to no avail. "I thought he was funny. Kind of silly and harmless," she says. "Well, one day he left me a little love note with a naked picture of him, with his boobs. I could hardly stop laughing. If you know him, you realize only Brian would do that."

Sharon initially resisted Brian's attributes. "At first I told him, 'Too bad, I'm not looking for a guy with tits.' But then I got curious."

Brian, for his part, has no regrets about taking up JoBo's bet. He hasn't sworn off gambling; he hasn't stopped carousing; he's not treated like a leprous outcast. "Everything is just like before. Only I can't jog." Fact is, most strangers can't tell that Brian Zembic has breasts. I meet him one afternoon at a casino coffee shop, where hundreds of tourists congregate for cheap steak and a sympathetic ear. Nobody notices Brian's bosom. Thanks to his unflattering ensemble—untucked sweatshirt, windbreaker—even I can't tell the Wiz is lugging around a set of bodacious ta-tas. It's only when he wants the world to know that his secret becomes a public spectacle.

What about his family? Can he keep his rack from them? Sure, but he doesn't have to. His family, back in Canada, thinks his saline-pouch adventure is a big hoot. "It hasn't fazed them a bit," Brian says. "My brothers laugh their asses off." Brian hasn't talked to his mom in several years, but he has told his dad about the breasts, and his dad says, hell yeah, if someone gave him $100,000, he would do it too.

Of everyone who knows him, Brian insists, not one person disapproves of his decision. Some have been more shocked than others, but no one has condemned him for taking a silly joke too far. One day Brian walks into the cardroom at a Strip casino, where he encounters Herbie, an old friend who hasn't seen him in a few years. They've talked on the phone, and Brian has told his friend about getting the breasts. But Herbie thought the Wiz was joking. Like he always jokes. When Herbie sees Brian in the cardroom, he claps Brian on the back and says, "Hey, man, what's up?" Brian shrugs, pulls up his shirt, and says, "These."

Herbie freaks out a little. But only because he's surprised. He says, after calming down, that he actually likes Brian's breasts, though he wouldn't mind them slightly bigger.

"Guy's a pervert," Brian says.

Life with breasts is sweet. In fact, Brian Zembic insists he's already a richer man for his troubles—besides the money. "This has been very educational for me," Brian says. "I feel I understand women a lot better. Having breasts gives you insight. You see what life is like for women. Taking hours to dress, worrying about how your breasts look. And you start to see what pigs we men are, the way we talk about breasts, like they're jewelry or a hat or something." The Wiz doesn't use words like *objectification,* but he knows now how it feels to have a part of your body talked about as though it weren't a part of you.

Brian and I are at Joey's apartment in Vegas, down the street from the Desert Inn. The Wiz is showing me some sleight-of-hand magic tricks. He's astoundingly good at them. But my mind keeps wandering.

In the interest of investigative journalism—and because I'm going insane with curiosity—I ask Brian if I can feel his breasts. "Oh, man!" he says, grimacing. "Do you have to?" I tell him I do.

He sighs heavily. Most guys don't ask for a squeeze, because they're afraid the Wiz will think they're a fag or a pervert. He giggles nervously, like a teenaged girl letting her high-school boyfriend get his first grope. These are his tits, for God's sake!

Brian lifts his T-shirt and peels up his sports bra. There they are: breasts, round and womanly and appealing. I reach over and give the breast closest to me a perfunctory squeeze. It feels pretty good, almost natural. I'm thinking I might even enjoy a breast such as this, if only it didn't have razor stubble all over it. "Not bad," I say, relieved to have discharged my reportorial duties without any messy psychosexual complications.

Brian seems pleased. Maybe even proud. He knows these implants aren't really an organic part of him. They're a synthetic miracle concocted by a plastics company, and temporarily joined to him because of a $100,000 bet. He knows one day soon they'll be gone, disposed of in a medical waste bin. Still, Brian, you can tell, is far from ashamed of his breasts; he's got pride in them as though they were pretty eyes or graceful hands or sculpted abs. They are the crowning feature that makes him unique, that completes the legend of the Wiz. One day I'm talking with him on the phone, and I jokingly refer to his breasts as "those ugly-ass tits." He hangs up on me.

This is when I start to suspect that Brian Zembic, Mr. Do Anything For a Bet, isn't counting the minutes until he can lose his breasts and find another wager to conquer. He's had them nearly a year, but I haven't heard any impending plans for surgical reversal. So when I see him next a few weeks later back in Vegas, at the Mirage, where he's ensconced in a poker game, I ask him, "Are you going to get your tits removed when time's up?"

He smiles bashfully. "I thought I would. I mean, I *know* I will eventually," Brian says, adjusting his bra. "But to tell you the truth, I'm in no hurry to lose them." He exchanges grins with a long-legged cocktail waitress passing by. "No hurry at all."

A month later, late in 1997, Brian is in Monte Carlo, playing in a monster backgammon match. JoBo's there, too. So is Joey. They're all sharing a hotel suite, chasing down "chi-chi" and running up a $10,000 room-service bill.

Over the phone I ask the boys if they've come up with another can't-miss wager to enliven their time on the continent. Riding a unicycle in the nude, perhaps. "No," JoBo snarls. "I've learned my lesson. I won't make any more stupid bets with that cheap, ugly motherfucker."

And thus the one-year deadline comes and goes. The Wiz wins.

Brian gets his money, deposited into a Swiss bank account. The chi-chi flows freely. And still the ersatz breasts remain firmly implanted in his hairy chest.

They're still there, 18 months after he had his $100,000 operation.

Brian is chronically lazy. He admits it. But sloth doesn't explain why he doesn't have—why to this day he hasn't had—his breasts removed. Why he doesn't return to his former life as a decidedly flat-chested cleavage-less man.

"I don't know. It's kind of fun to have them," Brian mumbles over the international phone line.

He won't admit it: He *loves* his breasts. He loves that he's the only guy currently walking the Earth who has the nerve to do what he has done. He loves that he's the Wiz. And nobody will ever forget him.

"Who knows, maybe I'll keep them for another three months," he equivocates. "Maybe I'll keep them for six months, a year. I don't know. I don't want to do the operation over here. I'll probably wait until I get home. You know, I'm thinking of using the money to buy a house—no more stock market. I might buy a place in Vegas, or maybe Montreal. Maybe I'll buy something here in Europe. I don't know."

I reckon Brian Zembic might never have his breasts removed. Maybe he thinks he's starting a trend. Maybe he thinks history will remember him as an innovator, the guy who brought new and unimagined meaning to the phrase "tit man." I try to get the Wiz to give me a straight answer, to tell me when exactly he's going to face the scalpel and lose the breasts.

But he says he can't stay on the phone any longer. He's got to run. Seems there's this hot 19-year-old he met on the beach who's crazy for his tits, and he's got to meet her for dinner, where, if all goes as planned, she'll give him a hand job in the restaurant.

"And she better do it!" Brian the Wiz says. "I bet JoBo a thousand she would."

From Shut Up and Deal

BY JESSE MAY

There is writing that uses gambling as a metaphor or as a means of exploring aspects of life, and there is writing about gambling that comes from the perspective of those immersed in it, that seems written to fellow obsessives, that reeks of the tables. It is the rarest thing to find writing, like Jesse May's, that's both without being heavy-handed. In *Shut Up and Deal,* the poker world emerges through a cycle of tight vignettes that, while conveying the joy, drain, swings, slides, and strategies of games themselves, profile gamblers in the process of reading, bushwhacking, or backing each other. May did several stints in the philosophy department at the University of Chicago before being called to the tables, having found plenty in their streaky chances and loyalties to philosophize about. May's most recent book is *The Gambler's Guide to the World: The Insider Scoop from a Professional Player on Finding the Action, Beating the Odds, and Living It Up around the Globe* (2000), which provides an underview of gambling circuits from Argentina to Helsinki to Moscow. Filled with smart, sometimes hilarious asides about the gambler's edgy life, it can be enjoyed by those with no plans of going anywhere, but read it and you run the risk of making a new plan, Stan, quitting your job.

♣ ♦ ♥ ♠

Foxwoods, 50–100 Hold'em. It's the Christmas tournament, I'm just back into poker after four months in Europe, and I have a foolhardy desire to test myself against prime competition and gamble with my bankroll. So here I am—stuck—at three o'clock in the morning and it's a purple rope game.

Because of too many spectators crowding the big games during the tournament, the two high-limit games are cordoned off. It's completely super-

fluous now because there are no spectators. None. In fact, the casino is almost deserted. Our poker table is roped off with the things they use in movie theaters and shows, thick, furry, purple rope attached to gold stands, and now because the game is full and there's no spectators it looks like maybe the purple ropes are to keep the players in rather than the spectators out. It seems that way, too, because no one has moved from their seat in five hours and no one looks in a hurry to go anywhere except maybe New Castle Ted. There's something else, however, that accounts for the fact that no one's left this game and that the casino is deserted, and it's not the fact that it's three in the morning.

It's snowing. Hard. Like a blizzard. Rumor has it that the roads are impassable, so nobody's leaving. The ultimate poker game. Like a slow boat to China.

And like I said, Foxwoods doesn't even have a hotel yet—they've only been open ten months—so nobody can even duck away to get a room. And it is a rocking game. There are guys in it who haven't played much Hold'em before. But I'm stuck, losing in the game, and Frank who is sitting next to me is stuck and New Castle Ted is stuck and swearing and calling everyone saps and the saps are getting lucky and the game is at a lightning pace. Everybody knows they can't leave, so they might as well gamble.

Afterward, Ted always says to me when we're in a really good game, They oughta get the purple rope out for this one. And it's funny, you know, because those ropes are purple velvet, like material for royalty, make you feel special, and inside the ropes is dirty gambling. So that you wish the ropes really are there to keep people in—to hold them or tie them up while you take their money and their watch. But right now those purple ropes with the gold stands are just around the table, about two feet behind all the chairs, and the game is hopping and humming with at least four or five guys in every hand and ten at the table plus the dealer and there's one other big game going at a table not far from ours, but it's definitely not full and they're playing Stud, 200–400. And there's Bart Stone and the Iceman, who won the World Series of Poker one year and a lot of tournaments since then, and maybe one or two other people who I don't know real well, but I do know, even from my position at the table so that my back is to him, that Bart Stone is losing.

Bart Stone. I can hear his motherfuckers and this and that and cursing the dealer from over here. But our game is humming and I don't pay it much attention because I'm stuck and tired and not really playing that well. Now New Castle Ted loses two or three hands in a row and he throws down his cards, picks up his chips and money, says "Lucky fucking saps," stalks over to the bigger game and takes an empty seat. New Castle is like that—he can't tolerate losing and he figures that if he's stuck a few thousand at 50–100 it'll be much easier to win it back quick at 200–400 than stay here . . . or else go broke. But he figures that he's such a good player that he's supposed to beat anybody as long as they're not too lucky.

Anyway, Ted's over there playing with the big boys now and I'm thinking his bankroll isn't really comfortable for even 50–100 but it doesn't really matter. The rules state that all you need to sit down in a game is the minimum buy-in, and in a 200–400 game that's only two thousand dollars, I think. But it can all be gone on the first hand—or not. That's New Castle Ted, always looking at the small picture, how he's doing right now, rather than at the game. I mean how could you leave a game like this? Not that I am doing any great shakes either because I'm sitting on Frank's right and we're bullshitting and talking between hands and he's always asking me what I had and every time that I raise he reraises right behind me and tries to isolate me and some of the hands I'm raising with are shit and some of the hands that aren't shit I'm missing the flops and maybe getting bluffed out, usually by Frank.

Frank, he's got my number and he seems to be winning a lot of pots lately, and every time I call him he's got enough and every time I fold he's got shit, but this is before I learned to freeze someone out and so it just seems like I'm giving Frank a lot of money. This is mainly on my mind and I'm thinking about how much I'm down and whether or not I should have played that ten-jack, or raised with it, and I'm not paying attention to much of anything outside the game and when New Castle Ted comes back over and takes the seat he recently vacated I almost don't notice him.

I almost don't notice him, but I do because the change in his personality and temperament is so profound that you have to notice the guy, along with all the chips that he definitely didn't have when he left the 50–100 game thirty minutes ago and now comes plopping back down for all to see. And he's practically whistling he's so full of gaiety and himself so that there's no reason to ask how he did. This time he got even—and better.

He's doing the eye-catching thing, which is what some people do when they have something that they want to say or tell to the whole poker table but know that nobody really wants to listen or they feel stupid talking to no one. You catch somebody's attention and then you can talk to them. Maybe I'm just easy. Guys are always talking to me at the poker table. Probably because I just sit there with a stupid smile on my face while they blabber away. There are some guys who I think play poker mainly because they want people to talk to, and the poker table is a good place for that. Ten people sitting around a table, unable to change seats and with no option but to be some sort of audience for whatever drivel a lonely bastard wants to spew. But Ted's also doing the chuckling thing, where he shakes his head as if in wonderment to himself and laughs softly, like he's just seen or heard something which is more funny or exciting than you can imagine and he can't wait to tell. But you have to ask.

So I say, "What's up, Ted," me the sucker, and he says, "You'll never believe what Bart Stone just did in that game. This has to be the all-time craziest fucking thing I've ever seen." So now I'm listening and a couple of other guys at the table prick their ears up and New Castle Ted has an audience, which is what he really wanted in the first place. Now he's made his little score for the day and he's feeling like chirping. Chirping chips, we say. A guy gets some chips and he starts to chirp. Now that Ted's ahead he's happy, doesn't really care about winning or losing so much and is in that winner's mode where everything is so funny and the poker room is filled with exciting characters and stories and interesting things besides the actual action itself. That's when you're winning. Ted tells us what he witnessed in the other game just five minutes before.

Bart Stone is losing. And he's mad. Real mad. After losing a brutal pot he looks like he's finally had enough. Bart jumps out of his seat hurling curses, picks chips and money up in one giant armful, and then throws chips and money back down on the table and hisses, "Deal me in!" just in time to receive his first card down from the dealer. Bart picks the card up and slams it back on the table face up for all to see—king of diamonds. Even the professionals at the table raise their eyebrows in mild surprise and amusement—they've been playing with Bart all night. Bart gets his next card down from the dealer and flips that over also without looking at it—eight of diamonds. His third card is a two, also diamonds, which I guess is a good start in Stud—three suited cards—but in Stud your first two cards are supposed to remain hidden to the end. Bart's whole hand is exposed. Stupid!

Since Bart's low with the deuce he's forced to bet fifty dollars, which he wings into the pot like he's trying to stone the dealer, who says deuce of diamonds is low. The Iceman, sitting across the table from Bart behind a mountain of chips and every hair in place, takes a sip of his mineral water and raises with an ace up. Bart reraises. Everybody else folds. The Iceman reraises, making the bet six hundred to go, and now Bart calls. The Iceman's representing aces, but does it matter? I mean he's playing a pot against a man who's showing him his cards. But Iceman does have aces and when the next card comes and the Iceman catches a blank and Bart catches the four of spades, which is also a blank, a nothing card, Iceman bets two hundred dollars and Bart calls, throwing his money in while still bending over behind his chair with a sneering snarling kill mask of rage, which is why nobody asks him why his hand is exposed. Everyone's just watching.

Bart's fifth card is the four of diamonds, which gives him a four flush and a pair. The Iceman catches what appears to be a blank, but if he's got aces then he's still the favorite, but a slight one, or so I'm told, depending on what cards he has in the hole and which cards have been exposed, which is something that I don't know. But I'm sure the Iceman does and what happens next is just way out for anything, way out, because now the lights are shining down on this poker table and there's green twenty-five-dollar and black hundred-dollar chips and lots of hundred-dollar bills in front of the players but there's only four or five people at the table plus the dealer and nobody watching and empty tables all around except for a 50–100 Hold'em game going on a few tables away. And on the other side of the room there are four or five lower-limit games going on, but they are quiet too, and it feels very empty in that big poker room with about forty tables and only six games going and the whole place sort of empty and hushed. Everyone's thinking snowed in and gamble and no one's railbirding, not even the big game where they're playing 200–400, and Bart Stone's putting on a show or something. But he's standing at the table and playing this hand and his cards are all face up, which is ridiculous because why would he want everyone to know what he has, the crazy motherfucker? I mean there's already two thousand dollars in the pot what with the antes and bets and raises up until the fifth card, but Bart ain't looking like he thinks there's anything wrong with showing everyone his hand, he just looks tall and mean and he's standing there and not talking, just looking like an ax murderer. But when the Iceman bets four hundred dollars with ace-ten-nine showing and two cards down, Bart just rasps one thing—"Raise." But he doesn't say it, he hurls the words out of his mouth and puts the money in and then they both become machines. The Iceman raises four hundred. Bart raises four hundred. And back. And forth. The Iceman sitting there tan, short hair, impeccably cut, groomed, manicured, cool, ready, casually dressed in a polo shirt and slacks and loafers and sipping from a bottle of Poland Springs mineral water, separating eight black chips off one of the stacks in front of him and placing them in two neat stacks of four, signifying a raise. And Bart, tall, gaunt, dressed in all black and smoking hard on his Pall Mall cigarette, all explosive motions as his fingers quickly count eight hundred dollars from a pile of bills he holds tightly in the other hand. And he throws the money toward the pot and the dealer. Raise.

The pile of money and chips in the center of the table that is the pot gets bigger and bigger, the dealer frantically trying to keep up with the action, until he realizes that something weird is going on here. So he just stops and waits and watches. Back and forth, Bart Stone then the Iceman—raise, raise . . .

Ted says they raised eighteen times until the Iceman finally called because Bart just wouldn't stop and they each had put like eight thousand dollars in just on that one card so there is about eighteen thousand dollars in a big pile in the middle of the table and there are still two cards to come.

Bart wins the pot. He makes a king on sixth street for two pair, now he has the best hand. Bart bets and the Iceman just calls and says wryly, "Aren't you going to turn this one over too?" to which Bart grates four hundred dollars and bets before seeing his last card. But the Iceman can't beat Bart's open two pair so he mucks his hand and Bart rakes a pot, which is like all the chips at the table, or at least all the Iceman's chips. Bart standing there like the Tasmanian devil, everything moving, wild, flailing, huffing, snarling, mean, lean, smoking, mass of anger. Except that his cards are face up, which in baseball is kind of like pitching to the guy underhand. Ted is laughing as he tells it and says Bart is one crazy man. I think it's wild.

It's still dark when I wake up—no, not dark—just dark gray. I go straight into the poker room. Don't pass go, don't collect two hundred dollars. It's not even seven yet and I didn't have much of a sleep, just jumped awake out of a dream and thought, What's happening in the poker room? Time to try and get some money back, time to keep an eye on the guy who I lent five dimes to, the guy I got 10 percent of.

The worst part is from my door down the steps to my car. No winter jacket, not for the poker room. Just jeans, velour shirt, orange plaid sport coat, cap, and sunglasses, and it's freezin' fuckin' cold as I'm hopping around trying to get my door open—frozen stuck. And then my fingers, numb on the steering wheel or pressed up against the vent during most of the drive before the heat gets working. And then about three minutes before I get to the Taj Mahal I'm comfortably warm and one minute later I got the heat off and the window open and cold is the last thing on my mind as I slip into the almost empty valet area. I get out, get my ticket, go through the revolving door, and turn to my right to walk into the poker room.

As I turn toward the high-limit section I see a black hat on a man, long and lean. Bart, unmistakable even with his back to me. As I get closer, I see John. He's sitting back in his chair watching the dealer shuffle. From about twenty feet away I can't tell if John has his eyes closed or not. I guess it doesn't matter—zombie stare is zombie stare. He's not moving.

I get up to the table. There's two cigarettes burning in John Smiley's ashtray. DB sees me coming. He has a piece of Bart. He's sitting in the two seat next to Bart, sweating him. Bart's in the five seat just opposite the dealer and John's in the eight seat, facing DB.

"Hey, Mickey, your man needs some help over here!"

"What's up, DB? How is it, Bart?"

"Mickey." That's all Bart says. And he nods his head one time. Ain't no reason for him to ever wear sunglasses. His eyes just look all mean all the time.

"How's it going, John?"

"Well, I'm losing . . ." That I could tell. Look at all the chips that Bart's got.

"What uh . . . What are you guys playing?" It's everyone has gotta draw the line somewhere. Actually, a lot of people manage to go through life without having to draw a line at all, but if you play poker, if you gamble, if you do drugs, you better draw that line because sure enough you're gonna be slammed up against it often enough, and one step over—well, it's just over.

"Mind if I sit here, John?"

"No, it's fine."

I pull a chair over from the next table and sit on John's left, slightly behind him where I can see his cards when he lifts them up off the table. He doesn't take any pains to conceal them. Heads-up play is not a cramped undertaking. A waitress swings by and I order my usual insta-wake-up, black coffee and a grapefruit juice. She replaces John and Bart's ashtrays. Both are filled to overflowing.

Bart Stone and John Smiley are finally playing head up and I got a ringside seat. It's seven in the morning and there ain't no way I'm gonna miss this one because John's my hero and also because he owes me five thousand dollars and I got 10 percent of him. The poker room is really quite empty and besides me the only guy watching the game is Ken, the floorman, who's more interested in looking at my crossword puzzle.

Just another poker game, just another poker game. This one is three and six hundred and there's about fourteen thousand dollars in black hundred-dollar chips on the table and it's easy to see who's won the last big pot because right now Bart has all those black chips in front of him in three towering stacks. And Bart, Bart's just so tall and sits way up high and jerks all around and bends his head down and when he reaches down to make a raise he grabs so that he has more than twelve chips in one hand and then snakes his hand out around the stacks. "Raise!" The voice of death. And then thunk-thunk-thwept, three piles of four chips all in a row, twelve hundred dollars. Call and raise. Yeah, Bart's got all the chips in front of him.

For every cigarette that John smokes, there's another one that he absent-mindedly lights and leaves burning in the ashtray. Two mostly empty coffee cups on coffee-stained paper napkins are on the table next to the ashtray, and three packs of Marlboro Reds. One pack is empty and one is less than half full. John's shoes are off and his feet, clad in dirty white socks, are stretched out and propped up on an unused chair at the side of the table. They've been here awhile. John never even leans forward in his chair anymore except maybe to get the last card in a big pot. Craig, the dealer, is doing a good job of keeping the game moving, stacking both their bets and pushing the cards close in front of the players.

I watch them play for a while—three minutes and they've both completely bowled me over. Holy cow. They're playing so good. Neither player gives an inch. John has got nerves of . . . John hasn't got any nerves at all.

So Bart Stone and John Smiley are finally playing head up, 300–600 half and half. Half Stud and half Hold'em. Generally, Bart's game is Stud and John's is Hold'em. At least those are their MOs. But John once told me, "Everybody calls me a Hold'em player, but I don't care so much. When you get short-handed, poker is poker, one and the same."

They're playing Hold'em right now and John needs some help. His chips are shrinking. They go back and forth awhile, John trying to make some headway into Bart's pile. A big hand builds. John's got king-ten and the flop is ten eight four and John check raises Bart on the turn, but when an ace hits on the river John raps down his hand in disgust, he knows he's beat. Bart bets and turns over ace-eight . . . ace or eight was his only out.

"Lucky shit." That hand hurt John.

"You fucking cocksucker. Your mother's a fucking whore!"

"Just shut up about my mother, asshole."

Bart's head is down low near the table and he swings it up in a half circle so everything's moving and the words get hurled out of his mouth in that dry hiss, extra loud. "I said she's a fucking whore!"

Silence. John's hand goes white around the coffee cup and I swear he's gonna throw it at him. Bart's fuckin' there in his face and John, John is just so tense I don't know what the fuck is gonna happen. What a fuckin' asshole this Bart is. And his whole game is just to get John off his. And it's working.

Two hands later, John's all in. Bart doesn't waste any time. "You still playing?" You evil motherfucker, Bart.

John looks up at me. "Can I talk to you a second?"

We both walk two tables down and outside the glass door. Now we're in the hallway. Separated from Bart by a glass wall. Well, actually a long glass picture window, we can see in and they can see out. On my right side is Bart and the poker room. On my left side is the valet window. In front of me is John. He's hooked and he knows it. He ain't got time for much.

"So what's up, John?"

"Well, I'm losing."

"How uh . . . How do you think you're playing?"

"I don't know." John's fidgety. He's fidgeting his hands and shuffling his feet. And looking up and down and at me and at the guy passing us on his way to go to the bathroom.

Bart's back at the table, watching us, bullshitting with DB. Acting like he don't care or don't know, but he knows the whole score. Knows that right now I got the bullets and I'm the guy he's gonna get the money from. He's gonna try and win it from John, but he knows what the bulges mean in my front jeans' pockets, double barreled. Don't carry money around unless you expect that you might lose it. Not in a casino. Not around gamblers. Or be stupid like me and a million other guys.

John has already lost ten thousand, five from me and five from Jimmy. I had 10 percent of him, so he only owes me four.

"Look, Mickey, he's got me hooked ten and it's personal. I want to keep playing. I don't want you to do something you don't want to do and gosh, I mean you've been a real friend already. Yeah, it's just up to you. I mean, I want to play."

"So, hold it. How much you want? Ten more?"

"Yeah. I can either call my friend or I can drive home and get the money."

"Look, John, I mean if you say you got it, then you got it. I'm not really worried about getting paid back." Yeah, sure. "I don't really know what I should do. . . ." Famous last words.

"Look, you don't have to take a piece of me anymore. This is just personal. If you don't want to do it, it's no problem, I understand and I appreciate everything you've done for me. But I mean I got the money, y'know, I got thirty thousand sitting with my friend . . ."

"Yeah, pffhytt, I don't know, John, I mean, are you sure you want it? I don't want you to do anything that you're gonna regret. I mean you're my friend, and I don't know, y'know you might feel different about it later." Like when you're straight.

"Look, I just really want to beat that asshole bad."

Of course I gave him the ten thousand. I can't really say no to John. I just want him to win so bad, I want Bart to go down, I want to see Bart break. Like Bart breaks. "But look, John, you definitely have the money, right? And I need it back right away, no matter what happens."

Oh shit, oh shit.

We walk back in. John gets up to the table holding a five-thousand roll in each hand. One he tosses in front of Bart. The other he puts behind his piddly pile of chips, more like a scattering. Bart looks up. "How much is it?"

"It should be five," I say.

DB pipes in, "Here, give it to me. I'll count it." Bart hands him the roll and DB starts riffling through it.

"You want to change both of 'em?" Bart directs himself toward the other one. "Mickey, you count it." Like Bart knows, 100 percent for sure, that even when I'm getting robbed for my last few dollars by a fuckin' snake in the woods, I don't have what it takes to cheat on the count. He's right.

They start playing again, Stud. Then the new dealer comes in and John says, "It's Hold'em." And Bart moves up and down and hisses, "No more Hold'em! Stud."

"No, it's time for Hold'em."

"Fuck Hold'em. I ain't playing no more fuckin' Hold'em."

"We made a deal."

"Fuck the fuckin' deal!"

"Wow, you're not . . . tthh, you're not even worth talking to. . . . All right, deal Stud. I can't believe this."

Wow, Bart is a fuckin' evil guy. Now he's got John hooked and he's gonna squeeze him, take away Hold'em, make him grovel, drive him into the ground.

But John, John Smiley's playing hard, man. He plays so good, I'm boggled by what he does, what he knows during the hands. But Bart's right there, he's no fucking slouchy player, and he's getting the cards too, and he's grinding him, grinding him down.

Two floor people come over for the daily counting of the dealer's box. "I'm sorry, guys, but we're gonna have to stop the game for a few minutes."

John's got about six thousand in chips left. He says, "I'm going up to the room for a second. You wanna come?"

There's not much to say in the ride up to John and Jimmy's room. "Whhirrr" says the elevator in a high-pitched hum. It's one of the elevators on the end, and as it rises way above the casino we can see Atlantic City through the big glass wall.

John leads the way into the room. He walks straight to an open dresser drawer and pulls out a pair of socks, a Baggy of pot, and a pipe. He puts the socks back. I walk in past the bathroom, past the bed where Jimmy's asleep in a tangle of sheets and blankets, and across to the round table under a hanging lamp. I sit down on a chair with a shirt hanging on the arm.

"Here you go. I don't have any papers, but you can use this pipe."

"Yeah, it's fine, John." Jimmy sits up for about three noncomprehending seconds and falls back down. He's out. "Sorry, Jimmy. Oh, you been playing all night, huh?"

"Mmm . . ." he says and rolls over to the other side of the pillow.

John sits down at the table across from me. He lifts up a magazine and the cocaine is right there on the table and he cuts off a line and snorts some and I'm packing some pot into a pipe and Jimmy's motionless on the far bed and John starts talking fast and I have to tell you he don't sound good. He's saying, "Look. I'm finished. I just wanna get fifteen thousand down there so I can give five to Jimmy and ten to you and then just go home and owe you four and get my money. He's just outplaying me."

"Whoah. He's really fuckin' playing good right now, John. He just ain't giving nothing away."

"I wasn't exactly catching any cards either. But I mean I just can't seem to catch when I need it."

"Yeah, I know. It's unbelievable. He's such a fucking jerk!"

"I'm just sick of this whole thing," he says and he's snorting another line and he says, "Are you ready? I gotta get back down quick. Just take your time, let yourself out. I'll see you down there." And I say, "Play good, John," and he says, "Yeah," and he's out the door. And the door shuts behind him and it's silence, and then just the sound of me taking a big hit of pot. I breathe out and I look around and I'm like, shit! He owes me fourteen thousand dollars and he's doing cocaine and Bart is fuckin', I never seen such a cold-blooded evil guy and he's playing so good and he got John off his game and holy fuck! I hope he just gets lucky, what the hell am I doing? Oh, man, this is messed up. All right, so let's see . . . John owes me fourteen and I got about two in my Vegas account and five in Connecticut and four in Natwest and whoah! What if he doesn't send me the money? No, he's gonna pay me back. Just concentrate on yourself.

And Jimmy, a lost soul in the corner. He's just trying to stay in action—like me—like the rest of us. Grateful for small moments of sleep, no matter how fitful, when there's no up and no down and no one wants anything from you and life will remain suspended as long as you can stay in your dream world. Jimmy doesn't have to fight too hard to ignore me. He's been up too long and his body is just about broken from living six months inside this hotel room and the poker room. And when I think about John, about what I'm doing, it's just hell, man.

When I got downstairs, it was all over. I had a million billion hopes and dreams, but what I wanted more than anything was for John to go down there and beat that fucker. I don't care how lucky or skill or whatever and then John would win and the bad guy would lose and I would get my money and John would be a new man and just like a goddamn fairy tale. I've given a guy like most of my money to gamble with and I'm sitting in a casino hotel room stoned and my best-case scenario is that the whole shebang has a fairy-tale ending. And this is how I make my living.

I come into the poker room to find John alone at the table. "Where's Bart?"

"I guess he quit. His chips were gone when I got down here. Shit. All right, look . . . I just wanna get out of here." I guess Bart knew John was fin-ished. I guess he knew John was just gonna try and pull a hit and run on him. I guess he didn't give a fuck about anything but the money. I guess it wasn't very personal with him. He ended up beating John Smiley for fourteen thousand that night. John's finished. He paid off what he could and left town the next day.

Everybody knows I'm lending John money and they all think I'm crazy, stupid, and that John is a broke crack addict who will never pay me back and think how much money I have if I can lend John twenty thousand. But the truth is, I didn't think I was really lending him the money. Now I think that you're always lending them the money. Whether it's holding it for five minutes, or can you just lemme hold some money till my wire transfer comes, or my friend gets here, or that guy pays me, or the bank opens, or I go to my box but my sister-in-law has the key so tomorrow night, c'mon. It's always lending, if they don't have it there then it's lending, and it's all the same.

Crazy Roger takes me aside and says, "Mickey, I know it's none of my business except I like you and don't want to see something bad happen to you, and I just thought you should know that John don't have such a great reputa-tion for paying people back. I talk to Iberville Tom a lot and he knows John from way back, and he won't lend him anymore, no more than two thousand. You do what you want with your own money, I'm just saying it ain't a particu-larly good spot, you know what I'm saying?"

And Brock calls me over where he's holding court as table captain in a 50–100 stud game. "How much you give Smiley?" he demands of me from be-hind his mirror sunglasses and drawing hard on his Camel straight. Like a fuckin' interrogator. Brock needs all the information, needs to know every-body's deal in the poker room so he can shoot all the angles. And maybe they all wanna understand it because I don't lend money, don't have a reputation for it. Say not much more than yes, and I guess it's a way to show that every leak, no matter how small, has the potential to break you.

You never know whether someone's good for the money. I mean you never know. John Smiley left town and he owed me fourteen thousand plus five thousand that I somehow got conned into giving Brock for the five thousand that John owed him. So John owed me nineteen thousand dollars, which I was kind of fine about until he left town and then I'm talking to people and they all say he's gonna stiff me and John says, check's in the mail. Sure enough, three days later three checks arrived in the mail for five thousand each—and they cleared.

John calls me at home and says, "If you're really in trouble I can get you the four thousand," and I just say, "No problem, John, give it to me when you get it and just try and get your shit sorted." Anyway, I'm more than happy for the fifteen thousand.

But you never know. There's this guy named Vic who appears in the high-limit games once every few weekends and he's a gentleman gambler and likes to gamble high and sometimes I see him busted on the rail and I always get on well with him and his wife who's super nice and always sits at an empty table nearby while he plays and gossips with everyone on the rail about her grandchildren.

So I've played 75–150 with Vic and 150–300 with him and one day I guess he's gone broke for the weekend, but I don't know his business—that's the whole point—and he comes up to me when I'm about to cash out one day and I got a whole lot of chips and he says, "Can I have a hundred bucks for a while?" and I say, "No, sorry." And he says okay and goes away but he's hurt and I feel bad about it, I mean a hundred bucks.

A few months later I'm in a poker room somewhere and Vic walks up to me and says, "Hey, Mickey, don't you know John Smiley pretty well?" And I say, "yeah," and he hands me two hundred dollars and says, "Could you give this back to him when you see him? I owed him this money." Now I just feel like an asshole. Now I feel like Bart.

It just goes to show you never know shit. But there are some people out there who think pride means something.

From Bob the Gambler

BY FREDERICK BARTHELME

Anton Chekhov has written that "the job of the artist is not to solve the problem, but to state it correctly." In the selection from *Bob the Gambler* (the title recalling the classic French film, *Bob le Flambeur*, 1955), Frederick Barthelme
shows us with a lightly dealt correctness a man who seems to have a problem.
Ray Kaiser has a good career as an architect and an understanding, supportive
family, yet he's tossing that security down the blackjack vortex one hand at a
time. He sits there, "frying," with even the dealers trying to hustle him out of
the casino, and yet he's never felt so alive. In presenting Ray unapologetically,
Barthelme explores risk, freedom, choice, and loss.

T
hursday before Thanksgiving we were settling in to watch *ER*
when I told Jewel I was feeling kind of lucky and was thinking of
stepping over to the Paradise. She shook her head and said, "Dangerous feeling."

"You want to go? We can tape this. Go for a while. We haven't been
much since Houston."

"We haven't lost any money since Houston either," Jewel said.

"You better stay home, Bob," RV said from the next room. "I think
that's what Mom's trying to tell you."

"Thanks, doll," I said over my shoulder. "I needed a clarification."

"You need something," Jewel said.

"Hey, don't worry. It's all right. I'll play a few hands and if nothing
magic happens I'll come home. I'll be back by midnight. You want to go?"

"Not me. Not tonight." She waved a hand. "Go. Go."

I felt guilty leaving the house, but then I was out and driving, and it was great to be alive—I felt free and young, the way I used to feel when I was eighteen, going on a date in my father's car. I stopped at a gas station, used one of the credit-card pumps, and watched the scattered rain pop the concrete. I got out on 90 and drove fast, the radio thumping. It was chilly out, colder than usual, and I had the heater on. I liked the way it smelled, liked the way it sounded. The windshield wipers clacked as I drove toward Gulfport, then made a U-turn on the highway, short of the Edgewater Mall, and drove back to the Paradise. I steered into the garage and pulled into a space on the first floor.

By the look of things, the number of cars, the place wasn't too crowded. I walked through the hollow-sounding garage and across the concrete bridge to the casino, rain tapping on the canvas awning over the entrance. Outside, I couldn't hear the slot machines at all, but as soon as I opened the door they were there in 3D Surround Sound. By the escalator there was a poster of a craps table with the headline "Winners Know When to Quit," slugged with a telephone number for Gamblers Anonymous. I stopped at the bar and got a beer, then walked past the craps tables and the roulette tables to the blackjack pits. I shook hands and watched the play at one table after another. Dealers and pit people asked where I'd been and I said I'd been practicing.

A dealer named Ed Romeo pointed to third base at his five-dollar table and nodded at me. "Take a seat," he said.

"Cards O.K.?" I said.

"I've seen worse," Ed Romeo said.

"I need to get a marker," I said.

Ed Romeo called over his shoulder to ask the pit person, a wiry woman in her forties who wore thick glasses and had mop-like red hair, if I could get a marker. She smiled, put an arm on my shoulder, kissed me on the cheek. "We can do whatever Raymond wants," she said, patting me.

"A thousand," I said. "I'll start with that."

She had a name tag with "Rebecca" on it in quarter-inch letters, and under that, where everyone else had "Trenton," or "Atlantic City," or "Reno," she had "Sunnybrook."

"Let's hope it's your only thousand for the night," she said. "Maybe you can turn it into five."

"Why stop there?" I said.

She went to the island behind the dealers and got on the phone, then went into a drawer and got some plastic buttons, two, each with "500" written on it. She brought the buttons out, put them on the side of the dealer's chip rack. "Give him a thousand," she told Ed Romeo. He pulled out five blacks and a tall stack of green chips.

"Half in green?" he said.

"Better give me some red," I said. "I'm starting slow."

"Sure," he said. He counted four hundred in green, pulled out some reds, counted a hundred in red, then lined up the black, green, and red stacks in front of him. "A thousand out," he said over his shoulder.

Rebecca looked up from where she was standing over the computer terminal. "Send it," she said.

He slid the chips across the tabletop to me, and I pulled the stacks back and to my left, then dropped ten dollars out on the spot in front of me. Ed Romeo had been changing decks when I arrived. Now he held the two decks out with a yellow card on top, pointed the cards at the player to my right, a crabby-faced Asian woman, quite short. She cut the cards. The guy on the other side of the table was playing two spots, a quarter each. There was a woman playing nickels next to him, then the Asian woman, then me.

"So what's been up?" I said.

"My wife got on as a dealer," Ed Romeo said. "She's working down here. It's her first night."

"You told me she was in school," I said.

"Yeah. She aced it. They wanted her out fast so they're starting her on single deck," he said.

The cards came and went. I raised my bet to a quarter and then was betting two spots. Money came, then went away, then came back. There wasn't any pattern to the way things were going.

Ed Romeo said, "I haven't seen you in a while. You been playing someplace else?"

"Out of town," I said. "My father died."

He made a face. "I'm sorry to hear that."

"Happens to everybody, doesn't it?"

"Sure does," he said. "Is Jewel with you?"

"She's at home watching *ER*," I said. "What time is it, anyway?"

He flipped his hands twice for the cameras, then looked at his watch. "Closing in on ten," he said.

Rebecca came back and stood at the edge of the table, putting her hand on my shoulder, watching me play. "How're we doing?"

"Same as ever," I said, showing her my cards.

"Oh, Mr. Thirteen," she said. "This doesn't look too promising. Maybe you ought to try Tanya over on two-oh-four. Her rack's low. I don't know if it's people buying and leaving, or if she's paying, but it's something."

I slid out two fifty-dollar bets. I'd lost a few hundred and change at the table and was getting ready to leave. When the cards came, I got a blackjack on one and a stiff on the other, hit the stiff and busted. I waited until the cards were played out for all the other players and shoved my chips back across the line toward Ed Romeo. "Color these, will you?" I said.

"Color coming in," the dealer said.

"Go," Rebecca said.

Ed Romeo matched up some new chips—a five hundred, a hundred, and three greens—alongside the chips I had given him. "Look right?" he said to Rebecca.

"Fine," she said, waving her pen toward me.

He pushed the chips across. Rebecca wrote something on the paper she had, which she had pulled out from behind the shuffle machine, then tucked the paper into her clipboard.

"You're going to Tanya?" she said.

"I thought I'd give her a try." I nodded at Ed Romeo and climbed off the stool.

I stopped to talk to another dealer I sometimes played with, a guy named Strobe, who was standing at the edge of the High Stakes Salon. He was red-faced and in his late thirties. His wife worked at the casino as a cocktail waitress and, according to him, made more than he did as a dealer. We were talking about Strobe's boat when a guy who looked like David Duke walked by with a young girl who had follow-the-bouncing-ball breasts.

"Is that him?" I said.

"Yep. Comes over all the time," Strobe said. He smoothed the front of his tux shirt. "Sometimes I wonder why somebody doesn't just pop him. He's a smug little son of a bitch."

"Not little," I said. "Looks like he's six two."

"He's little in the head," Strobe said. "Has that frail thing."

"Who's his friend?" I said.

"Never saw her before. She's got volatility there in the front, doesn't she?"

Tanya, the dealer I was going to play with, was a tall, thin blond woman in her late twenties. She walked by and rubbed the back of my arm. "Hi, sweetie," she said.

She had dark green metallic fingernails. I grabbed her hand for a closer look. "These are terrific," I said.

"Thanks. You're the only one who thinks so. Everybody else says they look slutty."

"Well?" I said.

"Yeah, that's what I say," Tanya said.

"I was coming to play with you. You're on break?"

"Coming back from break," she said. "Cards are pretty good tonight."

"Great. I'll be there in a minute. You can dump the rack. Hold third base, will you?"

"Sure thing," Tanya said.

Three Vietnamese women were talking loud and fast in Vietnamese at a table in front of us. "Look at this, will you?" Strobe said, twisting his neck as if he were trying to crack it. "I shouldn't say anything, never mind. I got no idea what they think they're doing. They win sometimes, but Jesus God, the way they play."

"I thought they were usually pretty good," I said.

"Some are," he said. "Not these three." He ran a finger around the inside of the collar of his tux shirt, adjusted his bow tie.

I patted his shoulder. "I'm going over here and steal some money from Tanya."

"Stay away from me," he said, jerking a thumb over his shoulder toward the salon. "I'm burning. Don't even come close."

"You're always burning."

"It's worse tonight. And it's not changing. Save yourself. Stay away."

We shook hands and I started around the cluster of blackjack tables toward 204.

The shift manager, Phil Post, was coming toward the blackjack pit from the main cashier's cage. He stopped. "How're things?" he said.

"Don't know yet," I said. "Got any advice?"

"Go home?" Phil said.

"Who you got dealing there?" I said.

Phil Post was always pleasant, always commiserating, urging us to leave when we were ahead or when we got even after a bad run of cards. He seemed genuinely friendly, but he worked for the Paradise, so who knew. He was paid to grease the skids, to shill, so it didn't matter whether he was friendly or not, because even if he was, even if everything he said to us and everybody else he dealt with was as genuine as the day was long, it still amounted to coaxing more money out of our pockets.

"Nobody's dealing there, that's the point," he said. "I'm trying to save you some money."

"I might win, though," I said.

"I might date Marilyn Monroe in the afterlife," Phil said. "But I'm not making book on it."

I caught the eye of a dealer named Hazel who I'd played with a number of times. I waved, she waved.

"Look," Phil said. "If the cards don't come, get up and leave. That's my advice."

"Will do," I said.

Phil rattled the papers he had in his hand. His eyes were watery, like he was stoned. "Got to take care of the guests," he said. "See you later?"

I played with Tanya until ten-thirty, playing fast, losing the thousand then winning half of it back. The cards were good, but my betting was erratic. I got hung out on a couple of big bets. Then I caught cards on a couple of small ones. I was five hundred down and that didn't seem too bad. I thought about going home, but decided to wait. I got a comp from Rebecca and went upstairs for a hamburger at the restaurant. I sat by a window overlooking the lighted piers in the shrimpers' marina behind the Paradise. There were people working out there, going back and forth, on and off the boats, making big gestures, tugging around on the nets. They were all bundled against the rain that slashed across the sky.

Shortly after eleven I was back at Ed Romeo's table, only Ed Romeo had taken off early, so I was playing with Tildra, a short, black-haired woman who told a lot of dirty jokes and more than most wanted her players to win. Like all dealers, she gave advice, but hers was book perfect. She'd been dealing for ten years, and she played at other casinos when she wasn't working. I went to hit fours against a five and she shook her head, refused to give me a card.

"What?" I said.

She pointed at the fours, wagging her forefinger.

"Split?"

"Against five and six," she said.

I put out another twenty-five-dollar chip to match my original bet. As it turned out, I lost both.

I won for the first hour. I was a thousand dollars ahead, then fifteen hundred. I was increasing my bets and winning. The cards were coming. Tildra and her relief were pleased for me. I tipped heavily when I was winning. If I bet a hundred, I tipped a quarter. The way the tips worked, if I won, the dealer won double what I bet for her. By midnight I was up two thousand dollars.

Tildra said, "Now you ought to go home."

"You think?" I said.

She rolled her eyes. "What do I have to do, come over there and slap you silly?"

"No, hey, I can take a hint," I said. I colored up and took my purple chips to the cashier's cage and got my money. Since they didn't have anything larger than hundred-dollar bills, the three thousand made a fair size wad that I couldn't easily get into my wallet. I put the money in my pants pocket, walked the length of the casino, and stood outside in the breezeway.

I was anxious to tell Jewel. I thought about calling her, then thought I'd better wait. It was rainy and pretty out there, and I was overwhelmed with my good fortune, and thought how much I loved Jewel and RV. Asian music came across the water from the fishing boats where the people worked. Shaded bulbs were strung from ropes that clanked against the masts. Water was cracking over rocks that ran alongside the jetty behind the casino hotel. Occasionally some fish disturbed the water and the surface opened and there was a splash.

The rain had slowed and there was fog gathering, though I could see high clouds moving fast. I watched them slide and wished Jewel was there to see. I was feeling lucky to have her, RV, the house, Frank—everything. I was in love with all of it. I pictured them in bed, asleep, Frank with RV. I had a perfect TV image of them. The bedroom just light enough to see their contented faces against the pillows. I stuck my hand down in my pocket and felt the thickness of the bills, and a chill caught my neck. I thought I'd get RV a Vespa of her own, an old one, silver, maybe blue, the kind that always showed up in French movies. I put my hands on the round steel railing, felt the cold wet metal, looked over the side at the debris floating in the water. There was a Styrofoam take-out box, there were cups, there was a plastic bottle. Midnight was a wonderful time. When the rain picked up I stepped back so that I was under the second-floor balcony between the casino and the hotel. The concrete in front of me was white with rain, reflecting the floodlights that shined on it. I dried my hands on my pants, listening to the water rush down the sides of the building. The pink and lime neon of the casino decoration was reflected in the rain. Upstairs, there were silhouettes of people inside, behind glass doors, looking out. Behind them, other people played slots.

I thought about what I was going to do next. I knew I should take the two thousand I was ahead and come another night, try to win another two.

That way, over time, I might win back what we'd lost. But I felt good and I knew I wasn't leaving. I was going to play. It was my casino, my night. If I didn't hit it at the tail end of swing, I'd get it on graveyard at three. That was my shift, anyway. The dealers were all friends, my people, and I would win, as if by magic. This time, this night. This was my moment. I had three thousand dollars. That was a stake. I was going to move to the salon, where there were twenty-five- and fifty-dollar tables, hundred-dollar tables if you wanted them, where the felt was blue and there were only five spots per table instead of seven.

Rain spattered the concrete, the steel railing, the otherwise serene water of the Mississippi Sound—a sweet static, hushed and reverent. Full of potential. I thought again of calling Jewel and telling her what I was going to do, but I knew that might break the spell. She might talk some sense into me, and the one thing I didn't want was sense. The one thing I didn't need, could not use, the one thing that would not help me, was sense.

The tall lights of the marina reflected in the water, shimmering, rippled strips that faded to nothing. There were half a dozen scrawny trees in large wooden planters on the walkway getting their fill of rain. I don't know how I knew this was my night, I just did. Risk everything. No losing.

A boat pulled out of the marina, its two bright searchlights swiveling past me as it turned to go out into the sound. Caught in the light, the rain looked as if it were hopping on the walk. I thought back over the past few months, the other times I'd played at the casino, the people I'd met, the winners, the losers. I remembered going to the men's room once and, while I was drying my hands, seeing a guy walk in counting a fistful of hundreds. The guy went into a toilet stall and went on counting. I could see his feet as he stood there and went through his stack of hundred-dollar bills. The bills made this flip flip flip sound as he counted.

I'd played enough at the casino to know that if I was going to win, I was going to have to push my luck. I wasn't going to outplay them, or outthink them, and I wasn't going to outwait them—they had too much money for that. If I was going to get them, I was going to get them by surprise. By the grace of God, good luck, and surprise. Nothing else. For some reason I *knew* it would work. I was certain. I was as sure of that as I was of anything in the world. All I had to do was go inside, pay attention, play crazy, and win very big.

It was an impulse I'd felt before, but never paid attention to. I usually got scared when the bets went up. At two hundred I was shaky, at five I was frying. Money moved fast when you played five hundred a hand. I'd gotten myself up six thousand one night, playing that way, before losing it. And when money moved fast, it could move either way. The key was picking the moment to bail. I hadn't done well with that, but there was always a first time.

The rain dropped off again and the surface of the sound went glazed, the lights suddenly focused, reflected, diving down into the water. I looked out at the foot of the marina and saw only tall columns of yellow and white light. It was my turn, my time. I laughed, scrubbed a palm over my forehead, and went inside.

I heard nothing. The rattling gibberish of the machines, the jackpots bonging off, the twirling reels and people shouting craps calls, the piped-in music, the change machines counting coins, the jabbering of the patrons—none of it registered. I went to the main cashier, took out a MasterCard, put it on the counter. "See if you can get me five thousand on this."

The cashier was a woman named Kathleen, with whom I usually joked about the small increments of my withdrawals. She looked at me and at the card as if we were both strangers. "Are you sure about this, Ray?" she said.

"Yep," I said. "And there's more where that came from. That card is blemish free."

The cashier area was like a bank, five or six teller windows and a couple of other areas with computers. Kathleen went to one of the computers, slipped my card through the reader, typed in my Paradise ID number. I watched her. She was a pleasant-looking woman in her forties—someone who would look out of place in the casino without the outfit.

In a minute she looked up from the computer and said, "Won't do it."

"What do you mean?"

"Won't give you five thousand. Says I have to call them," she said.

"Fine," I said. "While you're at it, try this one, too." I reached into my back pocket for my wallet, pulled out a second credit card, flipped that out onto the counter. "Five on this one as well, please."

"What are you going to do, break the bank?" She picked up the second card, fed it through the card reader, then got the phone to call Customer Service on the first card.

"They're just checking to make sure it's me," I said.

That's what it was. The Customer Service people had to speak to me, get some identification from me, get my mother's maiden name, and then they O.K.'d the deal. The second card didn't bother to ask. When Kathleen brought the two five-thousand-dollar checks for me to sign, she said, "You know, we can pick up the charges on these."

The charges amounted to more than three hundred dollars each, so I thanked her and said, "Please."

"I'll call shift," she said. "He's got to sign it." She took the two checks into the back, returned a minute later with signatures and two other sheets of paper for me to sign. I signed them, and she counted out ten thousand dollars. I tried to get her to leave the cash in its wraps, but she wouldn't do that. She had to count it, and she had to have two people stand there and verify the exchange. When she finally released the money to me, I stacked it up and folded it over, pulled the three thousand out of my pocket and wrapped it around the ten, then thanked Kathleen.

That's when Phil Post showed up. "What are you going to do with all this?" he said, signing the receipts for the casino to pay the freight for the cash advances.

"Play some blackjack. Do a little dance," I said.

"I don't know," he said. "You sure this is a good idea?"

"It's my night, Phil," I said. "I feel it. I'm already up. I'm going up more. All that money you guys have taken from me over the last couple of months? Coming home tonight."

"God, I hope so," he said. "Nothing would please me more than to see the nice guys like you and Jewel end up big winners. Where is she, anyway?"

"She's not playing tonight," I said. "She's resting on her laurels."

"She know you're playing this big?"

"She knows. She knows," I said.

Post laughed and clapped me on the shoulder. "Listen. If it starts going bad, you get out. You hear me? I don't want to see you coming back for more."

"Never happen," I said. "I'm only getting this so the stuff I take from you will have some company."

Phil Post laughed.

"Dream a little dream," I said, laughing at myself and trying to make sure that he knew that's what I was doing.

"You're in the salon?" Phil said.

"Yep," I said. "Going down there now. What time is it?"

"Twelve-thirty, twelve forty-five, something like that." He tapped the watch on his wrist. "This sucker isn't working the way it once did."

I had a table all to myself with a woman named Bambi dealing. That's what her name tag said, "Bambi." When I finally asked, she said it was real.

"Bambi what?" I said.

"Locks," she said. "Bambi Locks."

She was dealing a six-deck shoe. I got ten thousand dollars' worth of chips—five oranges, four grand in five-hundred-dollar chips, one in blacks, and started playing two hands at two hundred a hand. I went through my blacks right away, cashed another thousand for blacks, and started to go through that when I hit a run of cards. I got that thousand back, and the first thousand, and a thousand more. I was going two hands at five hundred now, and Bambi was dealing fast.

I moved to three hands at five and was hitting pretty good, winning two out of three, sometimes all three, doubling down and splitting when I had the cards. When I was up four thousand dollars, I bumped my bet to a thousand but played only two spots. The big orange chip looked small out on the betting circle compared to the stacks of blacks I'd been playing. I split a couple of hands like that, then jacked the bets up to two thousand on each of two spots. Bambi called out, "Orange in action," and dealt the cards. I dropped both of those bets and another pair like them. Then I pushed one and won one for three thousand. A quick check of the chips in front of me said I was down a grand.

"We have to do this?" I said, pointing at the table-limit card, which said that the maximum bet was three thousand.

"They'll raise it," Bambi said.

"Get them to make it five, will you?" I said.

She called the pit guy, spoke to him over her shoulder, and he nodded. "Fine," he said. He wrote something down on a pad.

I bet five thousand dollars on each of two spots, having to make up the second five with bills from my pocket. I got twenty on each hand and in my excitement kicked over my chair trying to slide out of it and stand at the table, waiting for Bambi to roll her down card. She'd dealt herself a nine up. I waved across the tops of both of my betting spots. When she flipped a queen I shouted and banged the foam-filled cushion around the edge of the table. The pit guy came out to get the chair as Bambi measured off my ten thousand.

"Great hit," she said.

"Thanks," I said. I pulled the money back away from the spots and grabbed my shoulders right at the neck, trying to loosen the knots. "Now what?" I said.

I put two thousand on each spot and the cards came out. Two more winners. Again, and again winners, and I spread my bets to three spots at a thousand. I lost a couple, won a double, lost a split. The hands were going by fast, the cards were pouring out of the shoe, and my betting and drawing off winnings, and Bambi's dealing and paying and sweeping lost bets synchronized like a perpetual-motion machine. We played this way for ten minutes or more—I wasn't tracking the time or how much I was ahead. I had ten-high stacks of five-hundred-dollar chips, lopsided stacks, some taller than others, four tall stacks of hundreds, and a single stack of the orange thousands. The cards were running so sweetly that I nursed my bets on the three spots back up to five thousand, then seven, after I got another increase in the table limit. I looked at my chips and knew that I could never lose them, there were too many stacks, the cards were too good. I bumped my three bets to ten thousand, scarcely believing it myself, and at the same time not at all nervous, not wary, just certain of the cards to come. And they did—two pair of faces, and a nineteen against a jack of spades that Bambi had up. I waved her off and she smiled happily, as if she knew I had her beaten. Casually she flipped her down card with the corner of the jack. Was an ace.

I felt that. An electric shock, a two-by-four brought down across my back. Thirty thousand dollars swept away. She didn't look up. Something forced me to bet five thousand on each of the three spots without pausing, and I got three stiff hands that I had to hit against a face card, and lost all three. That's when I stopped to count what was in front of me. Fifteen thousand three hundred.

"Can't win if you don't play," I said, sliding that out in three stacks. Five thousand on each spot with a hundred tip riding. That was it. No more chips. The cards came. Bambi's up card was an ace of diamonds. I quickly flipped my hands. I had seventeen, thirteen, and a pair of tens. She tucked her second card and asked if I wanted insurance. I was shocked. I held out both hands and said, "Wait a minute, please."

She stood across from me with one hand on the shoe and the other at her chest. "I'm not going anywhere," she said. "You take your time."

I stepped back from the table and ran my hands through my hair. Insurance was a sucker bet unless you were counting. I tried to call up some memory of how many of the ten-value cards were out. I looked to see where we were in the shoe. I'd have to get more money to insure the hands. The twenty might be worth insuring, the thirteen surely wasn't. I rubbed my eyes and rocked back from the table, sighed, finally cut my hand across the top of my betting spots to turn down the insurance. "No," I said. "I can't, no."

Bambi still didn't move. "You're sure?"

"Yes," I said, taking another deep breath, blowing it out in almost a whistle.

She leaned forward and slowly eased the corner of her cards into the peeper, built into the tabletop so dealers with aces up could check for blackjacks without lifting their down cards. Her shoulders sank and at the same time I saw her head begin to shake. She pushed the cards forward, turned over a bright-colored king.

I felt as if rows of needles were running along the tops of my shoulders and up both sides of my neck into the scalp behind my ears. Bambi pulled my three bets and the tips, and said, "Thanks for the try." Then she collected the cards.

I stood there watching her straighten the table. I'd been playing maybe twenty-five minutes. My ears were ringing. I couldn't quite figure out how much I'd bet, where I was. To lose thirty, fifteen, fifteen, I had to have been ahead fifty, plus the ten I started with.

"I bet thirty, then fifteen twice, right?"

"Yes," Bambi said.

Up fifty thousand dollars. The needles were spreading across my upper back. Phil Post came up with seven hundred that was the payback on the credit-card charges.

"What happened?" He clawed my shoulder.

"Don't know. I was great. I was killing you. Then—things turned."

Phil counted the seven hundred into my hand. "Maybe this will help a little. You got some of the ten left?"

"Sure, I got plenty," I said, folding one of the hundreds and handing it back to Post, who waved it off.

"Take me to dinner some night," he said.

"O.K.," I said.

I felt like a robot. I pulled the cash out of my pocket. I had two thousand. I gave it to Bambi, along with the money Post brought, and asked for black chips. I played one spot for a hundred. I did that for a while, playing automatically, not paying attention, winning and losing some, the cards going back and forth. My head was ringing. I wasn't really there. I was trying to get a grip. After a while I jumped my bet to two hundred, and then, when the cards weren't coming, I backed down to one.

A couple of college kids came up and started playing quarters. They were drinking and screwing around with a hundred dollars' worth of five-dollar chips. It was a quarter table, so they were betting piles of five, and the way the cards were running, they won as much as they lost, so their hundred kept them in.

When Bambi hit the cut card and started shuffling the six decks, the two kids headed off for the bathroom, and the pit guy, whose name was

Scooter and who looked like casino scum right out of the movies, slid around to my side of the table and said, "Want a hundred-dollar table?"

I shook my head. "No. They're fine with me. They don't bother me."

"I can do it if you want to," Scooter said. "They got no business over here anyway."

"None of us has any business over here, Scooter."

"You got that right," he said.

"Shuffle through," Bambi said, packing the cards back against the shoe, flipping the yellow cut card to me.

"Could we make this my special shoe?" I said to her as I cut the cards.

"I'm trying," Bambi said.

I slid five blacks into my circle and she dealt. I won a couple of quick hands, then lost one on which I'd split sixes and had to split a second time, dropping fifteen hundred on that hand. I only had about three hundred left in front of me. "Hold these, will you?" I said, pointing to my playing spots. "I'm going to the cage."

I got another five thousand dollars from Kathleen and played on that until two-thirty. Then I was busted.

I wouldn't let myself think of quitting, but things had moved much faster than I'd anticipated. I was in worse shape now than ever, liquidation country. Still I was excited, filled with a sense of abandon that I hadn't felt in so long that I couldn't remember when I *had* felt it.

Money had shot across the table. I was up, down, then up further ahead than I'd ever been, or thought of being, but I didn't notice, and dumped it all. I was down sixteen thousand for the night and wandering around the casino, figuring my next move. Down like that, another five thousand didn't make any difference. I had to try.

I went to the washroom upstairs, rinsed my hands, patted water on my face, dried off with a paper towel out of the dispenser. Some guy standing at a urinal was talking to his buddy about having lost three hundred dollars. The guy was really mad. I heard it in his voice, his anger echoing in the men's room. I swiped at the shoulders and lapels of my jacket, wondering why I wasn't mad.

As I went down the escalator and walked to the cashier, I thought about my father, about how he was a better gambler than I was. Of course, he would never have played for five hundred dollars a hand, let alone what I was doing. Money was still money to him. Tonight, for me, was a chance to play. The way I played was a kind of probable suicide, but there was always that one chance I'd catch a streak just right, get in and get out. I knew I was way out of my league, playing the way I was. Lots of people could afford it, I just wasn't one of them. But it didn't bother me that much, and I was surprised that it didn't, that I wasn't nervous when I'd been betting large every hand. I'd calmed down since the real big bets, and playing seemed comfortable, felt right. It was a joy to see the money move at a sedate pace back and forth across the table, as if it had a life of its own, or was reacting to my will, or the dealer's, or even the magic in the cards. It was thrilling to see stacks of blacks coming at me, to see purples in play, to watch my hands and the cards, and to be at the table when the cards turned perfect for a few hands, so that when I hit a sixteen I *knew* my next would be a four or five, when I doubled my elevens I was sure of getting the face.

I gave Kathleen another credit card and asked for five thousand. I had a walletful of cards. Two that were over limit now, the one Jewel had finished and the one I'd finished off tonight, one that was half done, two others that had two or three thousand apiece on them, with limits of ten.

I said to Kathleen, "I wonder if you can set me up with a line of credit, in case I have to write a check."

"I can do the paperwork tonight, but I can't set up the line. Takes twenty-four hours," she said.

I gave her a fatigued look. "C'mon," I said. "I've lost a bunch. Maybe you could do me a favor?"

"I wish I could. Really. Let me call the shift manager for you."

"Phil?" I said.

"Yes," she said. "He'll have to do it."

"O.K.," I said.

When Phil Post came, he said the same thing that Kathleen said, but then he sort of shrugged and said, "Well, maybe we can work something. How much do you want?"

"I don't know," I said. "Ten, maybe fifteen thousand."

He smiled a weak, sort of sad smile. "You don't want to do that, Ray. We're not going to be able to, anyway. I can tell you that. Let me look into it and see what I can do."

I put my hand on his shoulder. "Just so we're clear, Phil," I said. "I do want to do it, O.K.? If you can. Thanks."

"Don't thank me," Phil said. "My advice was go home. It's still go home." He said it in a way that made me both like him and despise him. It was the gentlest sentiment that could have been offered, and at the same time it was wholly ignorant of the condition I was in, it ignored everything—the losses, the excitement, the hope, the desperation, the high. All of it. It was nonsense, a Hallmark card.

I smiled at Phil Post.

We had to do the telephone business with the Customer Service people at another one of the card companies, but I finally got my money and left the receipt for Post to sign for the cashier. I went back down to the black-jack salon.

For a while I stood behind a Vietnamese guy who had two ten-thousand-dollar racks of hundred-dollar chips. The guy had a hundred-dollar table all to himself. He was playing three spots. I nodded at the dealer, a woman named Margie.

She said, "Hey, Ray. How you doing?"

"Hitting 'em hard," I said.

She smiled at that and kept on dealing, machine-line, to the Asian guy. I skirted the next table, said hello to Sharon, a dealer I never played with be-cause she always beat me. She smiled. There were two pit people, Claire and Coyle, working four tables open in the salon. I nodded at both of them as I took a seat with a favorite dealer, Lisette, who was dealing a two-deck pitch game. It was already a fifty-dollar table, and there was a heavyset gray-haired guy playing the last two spots. I dropped the five thousand in front of me and waited for Lisette to finish the deck. The guy was getting good cards, playing two spots at two hundred to five hundred each. He had what looked like seven or eight thousand in front of him.

After the shuffle, Lisette took my money and counted it out onto the tabletop, placing the bills in rows, one on top of the other, offset enough so that the camera in the ceiling could check her count.

"Purple and black?" she said.

"Right," I said. "You been O.K.?"

"Oh, sure," she said. "I've got trouble with my kid skipping school and getting caught, doing dope. You know, the usual." She finished stacking my chips, called them out and got them checked by the pit person, pushed them across to me. "I heard you were burning earlier."

"Yeah. It was amazing. I was up huge but it went out of control."

"Bambi told me. I'm sorry. Maybe we can turn it around," she said. "The cards are running." She introduced me to the guy playing third base. His name was Jack Delaplane.

I said hello when Lisette introduced us.

Delaplane said, "Why don't we play one and one? Two spots have been working."

"Fine by me," I said. "I'm looking for a slow start."

"How long have you been here?" Lisette said.

"Since about nine," I said. I put two black chips in my betting circle. Delaplane put out a five-hundred-dollar chip. The cards came.

A couple of hands later we forgot about the one and one, and each of us was playing two spots. Lisette dealt fast but funny, with the deck held back up at her chest and the cards shooting from there to our spots. The cards spun out, the way she dealt. Sometimes she counted my cards for me. She made jokes and chatted about how much she hated the drips who worked the pit. I'd caught her at the first of her shift, so we had forty minutes, and when she left to go on break, I had come back three thousand.

The relief dealer was a kid named Dave who I'd played with before, and when he took over the cards went cold. I got thirteens, fourteens, fifteens. In the twenty minutes Lisette was gone, I lost six thousand.

When she came back, I had a thousand dollars bet on each of two spots. She looked at this and did some kind of mock scream. "What are you doing? What happened to our chips?"

"Dave happened," I said.

"Why don't you get up and leave when he starts?" she said. "Mark and walk."

"Next time," I said. "I didn't plan to lose."

"Get those bets off there," she said, shooing them with her hand. "You're scaring the cards. Wait till I clean them up."

I withdrew my bets, leaving a hundred on each of the spots. The cards didn't change. I lost more, but I bet low until she shuffled. After that I had fifteen hundred dollars and bet three spots of five each. I lost two and won one, bet the thousand on one spot, and lost that. I shoved away from the table and asked Lisette to hold my place. She slid clear markers out onto the first two spots.

I was feeling crazy. I went back to Kathleen at the cashier's desk, pulled out the credit cards I thought I had money on, flipped them onto the granite countertop. "Start at five thousand on each of these, will you? Go down by five hundred until they give you something," I said.

"Are you sure about this?" she said. Kathleen seemed concerned for me.

"Yes, Kathleen. Thanks," I said.

She went to the computer and swiped the first card through. I reached into my pants pocket and pulled out a couple of hundreds I found there. The craps tables were close, so I went over there and put the two hundred down and asked for chips. "What're the dice doing?" I said to the stick man.

"They be sleepy," he said.

I put fifty dollars on the Don't Come. A cowboy at the other end of the table was in mid-roll. The point was four. His first roll after my bet was a seven.

"Bad timing," said the stick man.

"Now you tell me," I said. I put down fifty on the pass line and the guy came out with an eight. I put my last hundred behind in odds, and the guy threw seven.

The box man looked up at me and shrugged, as if to apologize. I smiled at him and shook my head. "It goes that way," I said.

"Sometimes," he said.

The guy working the stick said, "Cold wind. Sorry."

I patted his shoulder. "Don't worry."

I went back to the cashier. Kathleen said, "I got eight off of two cards. I didn't try the third one."

"Which is the third one?" When she waggled a gold Visa at me, I said, "Give me that. I'll keep that in reserve."

She finished the paperwork and signing and counted out the eight thousand.

"Oh, yeah," she said. "Phil Post said you could have two thousand as your line of credit, if you want it."

"I want it," I said.

"You want a marker or you want to write me a check?"

"I'll write you a check."

Lisette dealt good cards right off the bat, and soon I was betting a thousand dollars a hand, so I went up fast. Between four and four-forty, I ran the ten thousand to sixteen and change. Then I stayed out for Dave's relief and came back just after five.

The cards felt funny, stiff and plastic. I said, "What's this? New cards?"

"Yep. They made me do it," Lisette said, tossing her hair back. "I begged, but no good."

In the next forty minutes I lost the sixteen thousand I had on the table and another four I got from Kathleen off the last Visa card, putting me thirty-five and change down for the night. I'd tried to push it when I was winning, tried to get it back up to where it had been earlier. My largest bet was an eight-inch stack of hundred-dollar chips, four thousand, and I watched it walk. Lisette was doing everything she could to help me. Several times she ditched the deck because the cards were coming out bad. Once she went through a special shuffle she said ought to turn the cards around. She almost never let me take insurance, closing it fast so I wouldn't waver and take it when it was a bad bet. Still, I lost everything I looked at. At twenty minutes to six, when she was getting ready to go on break, I was alone at her table with no chips and no way to get any. My ears were ringing again. The bright lights in the ceiling focused on the tabletop, warmed the backs of my hands. All the pit people were going wide of the table. They always got scarce if you were taking a beating.

Lisette said, "Sorry, Ray. Jesus. This really pisses me off. They were going so good for a while."

"It's O.K.," I said, then laughed at that, laughed at hearing myself say it was O.K. I put my head down on the table. "You're going on break now?"

"Yeah," she said. "Can I get you something? You going to play more?"

"I don't think I can," I said. "Not until nine, anyway. I can go to the bank at nine."

"Opens eight-thirty," she said. "What bank?"

"First American," I said.

"Eight-thirty," she said.

I was trying to remember how much money I had in the bank. I didn't have much. I had a money-market checking account, so I could get money from that. I had a few grand there, in the account we'd started for RV's college. Short of selling things, that was all I could get my hands on. There was Jewel's salary, some in IRA and Keogh accounts. But with the cards loaded, I was close to the end of my easy-access bankroll.

I walked with Lisette down past the cashier's cage, where she turned off toward the elevator that went up to the break room. I went through the casino, out the side door by the parking garage. The concrete walk led down to the piers and the fishing boats. I wasn't sure what I wanted to do, so I went into the garage, opened the Explorer, climbed in, sat down, locked it up. I looked at my watch. I bent my head forward and rested it on the steering wheel. I tried to remember how I'd gotten into all this, how I'd gotten so far behind. I could see specific hands—the ten-thousand win, the big-bet losses, dealers drawing out on me, dramatic bets, double downs. I remembered being crushed by unexpected defeats—good cards beaten by better cards. Hands by the book and with the book going out the window. None of it accumulated in my head. It went through, each hand a snapshot, isolated. I knew how much I'd lost, but it was too ridiculous, too far-fetched to take seriously. People like me didn't lose thirty-five thousand dollars overnight—how had I even gotten my hands on that much? I was numb. I couldn't imagine what this would mean to our lives. It was crazy. What would Jewel say? What could she? I laughed when I thought of hiding it from her. Maybe we could get loans, remortgage, get work, who knew?

Suddenly I was the guy in the newspaper who loses everything at the casino. I sat in the car and looked across the garage. There were plenty of cars. It was dark. I had a headache, reached into the glove box for aspirin. There was a small bottle of isopropyl alcohol in the compartment, and I took that out, unscrewed the cap and set it on the dash. Then, carefully, I pooled a little alcohol in my palm and set the bottle down in the drink holder. I rubbed my hands together, then did their backs, the wrists, finally my face, wiping both hands over the forehead, down the nose, back across the cheeks, and under the chin to my neck. I breathed deeply so that the alcohol scorched my nostrils.

I wiped a spot that showed up under the cap on the dash, then screwed the cap on the bottle and put the alcohol away.

If I could win a couple thousand, maybe five, that would be a big improvement. That would be something. I could play conservatively, hundred-dollar bets, try to build it up over a long time. I'd done that. Or I could bet it all, win two hands and get out. I'd have to get some cash from the bank, but wasn't sure how I could do that—deposit a check from the money-market account, which was out of state, to cover some check I would write to the bank? That would work up to the amount I had in the money market, but that wasn't enough.

I sat in the car, staring out the windshield. My clothes reeked of smoke. I was wasted, my back ached, my arms ached, they were too heavy to lift. I thought about telling Jewel. I imagined myself on the side of our bed waking her up, her eyes squinting open, closing again as I told her about my night at the Paradise.

Slots *and* Thrall

BY FREDERICK AND STEVE BARTHELME

One way of looking at literature, and gambling literature in particular, is as a form of compensating for deficiencies or excesses, or as a way of recovering, recuperating, redeeming through words what one has done in life. This seems the case with the memoir Frederick Barthelme co-authored with his brother Steven, entitled *Double Down: Reflections on Gambling and Loss* (1999). With directness, wry self-awareness, and sadness, the book reflects on a stretch in their lives in which they went from "workaday English teachers to gambling junkies," in the process gambling away their inheritance. Yet the book exists because of their losses, and it is more and richer than a salvage operation. The smell of casinos, the slick of cards and chips, and the highs of gambling are shuffled into its correct expression. In the selections from that memoir the Barthelmes reflect precisely on "Thrall," the process of being drawn into addictive gambling, and on the lure and absurd logic and aura of "Slots" (by far the most popular game in casinos).

Slots

Two thousand dollars behind, Steve rests in a comped room, complete with Jacuzzi, then walks back into the casino near midnight. He's had one hour's sleep in two nights. On the down escalator to the blackjack tables, he floats in a suspended state, like a ghost, watching all the other people who seem to be there having a good time. It's like a step-framed film; they're moving in slow motion or something, x-ray vision. He wanders over to a slot machine that once, months before, hit five thousand dollars for him, and he puts a hundred dollars in and starts playing. The reels spin and the machine does it again: three red "sizzlin' sevens" with their backdrop lightning bolts fall into the three windows. It feels pleasantly terrifying. Better than drugs, if he remembers drugs accurately, which he probably doesn't, because that was a long time ago. He laughs. He checks the machine once more, touching the first window, the second, the third, to be absolutely certain that this has happened, then he hands an attendant his driver's license and goes looking for Melanie, his very occasional companion on these trips, because now, after forty-eight hours, they can leave.

Read almost any gambling book and, after a lengthy discussion of "random number generators" and a short history of the Bally Corporation, you will see this advice: "Slots are for suckers. Don't ever play slots." Then you'll see a second lengthy discussion, this one treating the "house edge," that laughably small percentage of each dollar, on average, the casino doesn't give you back, and pointing out that this edge is nine (or seven or five) percent on slot machines as against perhaps half a percent on a perfectly played game of blackjack. If this advice is absent, you have a bad gambling book; it might be a P.R. piece prepared at some casino's corporate headquarters, or one of those newsstand magazines whose fondest desire is to run such a P.R. piece, accompanied by a four-color, full-page paid advertisement.

Slots may be for chumps, but there are worse things to be. You could be someone who spends his time sifting out who's a chump and who isn't, a spiritual fraternity boy. You could do everything right, and be made gloriously happy thereby, but then, you wouldn't be in a casino.

We put nickels, quarters, and half dollars into the machines. We put in one-, five-, ten-, twenty-five-, and, a few times, for the sport, "to see what it feels like," hundred-dollar tokens. The cheaper slots are sometimes played with real coins, while the high-ticket slots are played with bills that the machine converts into tokens or credits. Put a hundred-dollar bill into a five-dollar slot and you have twenty credits; hit something and you might win fifty credits, or a hundred, or a thousand. A thousand credits on a five-dollar machine is five thousand dollars.

Sometimes you hit it. The first time might be at a twenty-five-cent draw-poker machine, betting five credits a hand, a dollar and a quarter. After being there for ten minutes or so, while you're pressing the worn and discolored buttons to make bets and other discolored buttons to hold cards and yet another button to make the draws, just casually you start thinking, in spite of all the common sense in the world, that this machine in front of you is a "good" machine, or maybe that it seems "hot," or even, after reading one of those P.R. pieces, that you have found that lost Atlantis of slot players, a "loose" machine. Sheer genius, that word.

"Loose," with all its implications of sin and imperfection and factory defect, its suggestion that the customarily tight mechanical fist holding all those coins deep inside the machine has been momentarily distracted, its hint that this son of a bitch is tired, worn out, relaxing into death, about to come completely unglued and just rain money, its threat that if you don't hurry, the management will discover this treasonous machine and fix—that is, *tighten*—it double-quick . . . well, someone dreamt that up. The word is a miracle, inspires awe.

Anyway, you've had a couple of flushes and a full house and some three-of-a-kinds, and your original twenty credits bought with a five-dollar bill is up to ninety-eight, and you're thinking maybe you've got a loose machine. That five dollars is now almost twenty-five dollars, and that's not much really, but you've been to the casino only a few times before, and it's not just twenty-five dollars, it's *ninety-eight credits*. So what happens now? You lose? No way. You're a beginner. You are just now contracting this disease. The next time you hit the dirty little lit-up Bet Five Credits button, the machine delivers a hand with two wild deuces and three low cards, so you hold the deuces and discard the others, punch Draw, and what shows up? Two more deuces. Four of a kind, deuces. Five of a kind, really, because they're wild, but on this machine four deuces is a bonus hand. It's not worth a few hundred credits; it's worth a thousand credits. A thousand.

You do the right thing: you hit the Cash Out button, and the quarters start clanking into the mailbox-size steel tray set below the video screen, and you start taking handfuls and tossing them into one of the big white plastic cups that are stacked around the rows of slots for this purpose. It's like those movie scenes in which people are throwing money into the air or running their hands through gold dust, letting it slip through their fingers back into the pile. It's a victory over money, the tyrant that has been pushing you around your whole life.

The quarters keep coming. And then they stop. But you are not paid off yet; the machine just ran out. It's exhausted. It needs a fill. You have broken the bank. A light on top of the machine goes on, and you start looking around for an attendant. Eventually she comes, looks, goes away, and then returns some time later lugging three chubby shrink-wrapped plastic bags of quarters, which she tears open and empties into the machine's hopper. She slams it closed, makes notations on a clipboard, says "Congratulations," and disappears.

In a room somewhere, somebody is thinking all this stuff up, choreographing it—the machine running out, the light on top, the jargon ("a fill"), just how to package the quarters, how the inside of the machine should look to the eager chump looking over the attendant's shoulder—you know all that, but it still works. You are stupid with joy. More quarters start clanging down into the tray. Eventually you have three full plastic buckets. You carry these to the "cage" to be turned into bills.

You're literally weaving around the machines, lights are glistening, everything's brighter than before. A thousand quarters is Publishers Clearing House. Uncle Scrooge. The Donald. Unbridled bliss. Free money, and an experience that seems foreordained, ultimate, perfect.

Two years later, at six-thirty in the morning, you will hit eight thousand dollars on a five-dollar slot machine. By that time, eight thousand dollars will be looking across the ledger at a figure ten times its size in the other column. You will stare at this machine, tired, quiet, and you will be . . . pleased.

Hitting a jackpot is ridiculous, a joke, sense in nonsense. When people hit jackpots, first they scream, then they laugh, then look around for someone else to laugh along. It's odd. You have just bet, say, ten dollars and get five thousand back—five hundred times your money. You just made two or three months' salary in a breath, so you laugh. It must be at least partly relief, but mostly you are laughing because this event is an echo of all that you know to be so but in your everyday life have set aside for the more efficient functioning of social, political, and economic systems and the greater psychological good of everybody. This money just fell on you and it makes no sense. It's as nonsensical as love or cancer.

It takes a while to get from the twenty-five-cent machine to the Slot Salon, where the five-, ten-, twenty-five-, and hundred-dollar machines are gathered like some East Egg picnic of folk in dandy white clothes. It's a progression. We started on quarter machines and in time were playing dollar machines and then we moved to five- and twenty-five-dollar machines. Rick made this whole progression in a couple of weeks; for Steve, it took longer. We play a little roulette, mini-baccarat, pai gow poker, some let it ride and hold 'em and craps, whatever the casino has to offer, but mostly it's slots and blackjack. Rick plays blackjack almost exclusively.

The high-ticket machines in the salon might look like people at a fashionable picnic, but the players do not. They're a grab bag. Once or twice a country music star with his name on his hat came to play at the little square island of twenty-five- and hundred-dollar machines and had himself roped off so he could play in peace—never mind that no one seemed to know he was famous until the velvet ropes went up. Even then, the only person who bothered

FREDERICK AND STEVE BARTHELME · **255**

him for an autograph was a cocktail waitress. "We're the people who buy his dumb records," she muttered afterward.

Another guy who played regularly came from Louisiana, someone said, and he always brought with him an enormous roll of hundred-dollar bills and three or four other people, one or two white guys and a very calm black man and his wry-looking wife, who played the machines in a desultory way while they attended Mr. Big. Sometimes they would just sit and smoke at a machine Mr. Big wasn't playing but might want to play later, or had played and intended coming back to.

There were a lot of women among the slot players—rich and poor, white, black, and Asian—more women than men, probably. Many gamblers look down on slot machines. It's partly a macho thing, because slots are favored by women, but it's also because the house edge is so high, because the machines are so simple and playing straight slots requires no skill at all. In contrast, table games require a belief in know-how, an expertise that is freely and sometimes loudly directed at players who hit hands when they shouldn't, or don't when they should, and are then held accountable for every evil turn the cards take thereafter.

This faith in know-how—based on books and laws of probability, diluted with savvy remarks by knowledgeable-looking people at some table you once played at ("First hand in the shoe is always the dealer's")—is not entirely illusory, but it's only part of the story. Playing the odds impeccably, one loses thousands. Splitting tens, one wins big. Sometimes. Nothing deserves one's faith more than the happy stupidity of luck. Which returns us to the much maligned but honest, honest slot machine. There's an essentialist argument for the simple slot: this is true gambling; place the bet, punch the button, win or lose. Repeat.

And it's mesmerizing. You're ready to leave and go look for your wife, find her sitting at a slot machine in a dark, smoky aisle several rows over. "Melanie," you say a little loudly, so as to be heard over the music of the machines, the bells ringing and horns tooting and quarters slapping down into the trays. She makes another bet, hits the button, spins the reels again. "Melanie," you say, still louder, a little closer to her ear, so close that you have to check whether it *is* Melanie, because if it isn't you're going to get arrested. Still nothing. She keeps playing the machine, winning, losing. You touch her shoulder, and she glances up in your direction, then quickly back at the machine in front of her, punches the Bet Max Coins button, and the wheels spin again. Finally, instead of out-and-out shouting, you get her attention by putting a hand between her and the buttons. Only then does she recognize you, with a slightly puzzled look, and return from wherever she has been. The same thing happens later, more often, a dozen times, in reverse: "We're going upstairs to dinner. You want to go?" she says. You wave at the air, oblivious.

Yes, only chumps play slot machines, but sometimes chumps make money. It comes as something of a shock that the machines really do pay off, and the shock tends to come when we start playing the expensive ones.

One night Rick feels bad because he has won and our friend Mary's along and she has lost, so they go over to the high-ticket slots and he takes out a hundred-dollar bill and sticks it in a twenty-five-dollar Wild Cherry machine. "We'll play the hundred for you," he says. She plays and right away wins two hundred and fifty dollars. She moves to cash out, but Rick shakes his head, so she goes on hitting buttons, pausing before each play, and nothing more happens for a while, until she has one credit left. On this last twenty-five-dollar pull, three wild cherries show up—five thousand dollars. Another time, Rick moseys over to where Steve is playing a five-dollar Double Diamond machine and sits on the next stool. Rick has lost a lot playing blackjack. He takes some of the five-dollar tokens that have collected in the tray of Steve's machine and starts idly dropping them into the machine in front of him. Steve has been at it for half an hour, an hour, all night maybe. Right away, Rick's machine tosses up three matching symbols that look like blue and white turtles. Four thousand dollars' worth.

Another time, Steve, playing a twenty-five-dollar Double Diamond machine, has hit a four-thousand-dollar jackpot, and one of the casino people has come with the W-2G form and a wad of hundreds to pay him. She gives him his four thousand, minus the state income tax they always deduct, and says, "We need you to play it off," meaning that he has to play the machine once more, so it won't be left showing a big jackpot, a common casino practice. This procedure is ostensibly intended to avoid frightening off potential players, but it also induces winners to keep at it and become losers again. Is it a plot? When you've just won four thousand dollars, you don't much care. Steve punches the button again, the wheels whirl around and around and settle, showing a Double Diamond, a red 7, and another Double Diamond. Oops. Eight thousand dollars, twelve for a total. He laughs and sits down.

These ridiculous moments tend to become the only ones we remember, so the recollection that one year Steve won $132,000 in slot machine jackpots and still lost money somehow decays in the mind. We remember the day and the minute when we won twelve thousand dollars in two pulls and forget the hours when nothing matching showed up in the little windows. We forget the time we were sitting at a machine, having won five thousand but lost half of it back, with the remaining twenty-five hundred-dollar bills in our hand, when one of us says to the other, "Whoa, let's rethink here." The winner, who still has fifty percent of his winnings, gets a real hard-eyed, made-for-TV-movie look on his face and says, "What's the point?" and feeds in the other twenty-odd bills as fast as they'll go. We forget what we know about pointlessness.

There is a perfect alignment or echo between our experience in gambling and our experience of the world, and it is in the big win—a slot machine jackpot or a successful thousand-dollar double down at the blackjack table— that this echo is most apparent. All the disorder, illogic, injustice, and pointlessness that we have spent our ordinary days ignoring and denying, pretending to see the same world our fellow citizens insist on seeing, trying to go along to get along, trying not to think too much about the implications, all of it flows forth in this confirmation of pointlessness—by luck. Yes, that is how it is, the funny blue thousand-dollar turtle-looking symbols say. And we laugh.

A gambler feels a powerful rush of vindication in winning, but it's not about beating the casino or the blackjack dealer or the slot machine, at least not principally. It's not even really about beating money. It's about beating *logic.* It's about chance confirming everything you knew but could make no place for in your life. Gambling is of course a very expensive way to beat reason. You can get pretty much the same thing by staying awake for a night and a day, or however long it takes you to get a little psychologically unhinged, destabilized, detached from whatever you believed the day before, and then staring at the cat, the dog, the stapler, the back of your hand, water. Most anything'll do it, once you've shed your silly confidence.

♣ ♦ ♥ ♠

Thrall

e had heard about gambling and addiction, about people who had lost their jobs, their houses, their cars, their families, their lives. We'd heard about people who got crosswise with a bookie or other unconventional lender. We had seen the gambling movies, Karel Reisz's *The Gambler,* Robert Altman's *California Split.* We had read Dostoyevsky's novella. We had read *Under the Volcano,* seen *The Lost Weekend* and *Days of Wine and Roses.* We wondered if that was us. Decided that it was.

We discussed addiction on those long drives down Highway 49. We were analytical about it, examined it in excruciating detail. We knew that your average psychologist would have said we were addicts in a minute. We knew the threatening jargon, that we were "enabling" each other, that we were a codependency case, and in the normal course of things, had we seen ourselves flying to the coast every four or five days for eighteen hours of blackjack and slot machines, we might have said we were addicts. But in the car headed down there this characterization seemed insufficient.

There was a catch: So what? Being an addict didn't mean anything. One of the virtues of having gambling as your vice—as opposed to sex, drugs, or alcohol—was that the disadvantages were felt only at the bank. As long as you had the bankroll, these disadvantages were only superficial wounds. At worst, we were in an early stage of addiction, before the wounds amounted to much, and the customary assumption (which all of the movies, books, and hand-wringing newspaper articles made) that the later, catastrophic stages were inevitable was something we didn't buy. We doubted it. We had been trained to doubt the omnipotent sway of psychology.

Ours was not a family brought up on psychology. In our father's view, the great seething life of feelings could be a damn nuisance. Father had more than a teaspoon of the Frank Bunker Gilbreth about him. Although the family did recognize the psychological dimension, pragmatism—some kind of physical pragmatism—superseded psychology when explanations or remedies were wanted.

Being good sons of our father, we rode to the coast night after night, streaming through the sweltering Mississippi heat, clouds of grasshoppers popping off the highway like a plague of sparks, humidity as thick as gravy, and when we said to each other that we were addicts, when we talked about being addicts, it was a joke—a joke with a nasty twist, but still a joke. Later, after we became accused felons, we would call each other Lyle and Erik, with the idea that a joke needs a Menendezian edge.

You're a gambling addict, so what? Have you got money in the bank? Yes? Go on being an addict. A part of the pleasure was being able to go over the top, way over the top, without any of the mess or travail associated with doing drugs or becoming alcoholics or cheating on our wives, which is not to say the wives approved. They did not. But neither did they react the way they might have had we become enmeshed in other vices.

Sometimes, at first, they went with us. Later, not. But even then, during our long gambling nights, we would call in, advise our spouses how we were doing, how far ahead or behind we were, tell them that we loved them. And we did love them, somehow more fiercely when we were at the coast, when we were free to go to the coast. Something about the intensity of the experience of gambling, of risking the money, of risking loss, made the security and solidity of the home front much more important, much more sweet. More than that, it was a detachment, the anesthetic clarity with which you sometimes saw things in the middle of a drunk. Once Rick stood at the bank of telephones downstairs at the Grand, leaning his forehead against the chrome surface of a wall phone, standing there after hanging up from a conversation with Rie. They had exchanged I love yous and suddenly, after the call, he felt that love with crippling intensity.

An addict is someone who "surrenders" to something, the dictionary will tell you, "habitually or obsessively." Most people are at least a little addicted to something—work, food, exercise, sex, watching sports on television, cooking, reading, the stock market. Some people are addicted to washing their hands. Some people trim their hedges from dawn to dusk. Some people play too much golf. Almost anything can be the object of addiction.

Whatever his pleasure, an addict usually knows he is, or may be, an addict, but inside the warmth of his addiction, the label seems secondary, does not signify, as we like to say over at the college. It's like telling a horse he's a horse. Take President Clinton, for example. When he was involved in certain activities, he must have known he was addicted to something; he just didn't care. We felt just like the president. We didn't care. We supposed, in our conversations, both in Hattiesburg and en route to the coast, that when the time came we would bail. We knew that push would come to shove at some point, and at that point we would get out of the game.

Steve, wisely but very late in all of this, bought a house with some of his inheritance. Made a down payment, got a low mortgage, *invested* in a home. Buying houses didn't come easy to us, in part because the house in which we had grown up was as much a cultural declaration as a dwelling, embodying ideas about design always to be defended against Philistines. Since we had left that house, we had lived in more or less ordinary houses for many years, but we had always rented. Buying an undistinguished house seemed like giving in, disloyalty. There were other reasons, of course. We had led unstable lives, so the idea of settling in the same place for thirty years had seemed laughable. Until Steve started teaching, and for some time afterward, he had never had the steady income to envision buying a house. Buying a house seemed rash when half one's worldly goods were in cardboard boxes awaiting the next move.

We admitted having "addictive personalities," but we *liked* our addiction, the object of our addiction. It wasn't so different from all the other things, large and small, that we had intense attachments to—Diet Coke and Russian writers, springer spaniels and computers, box wrenches and movies. From childhood we had been taught that the object of an addiction was secondary. It was the way in which you cared about something, the quality of your interest rather than its object, that mattered. The first measure of the quality of an interest was its intensity, its thoroughgoingness. Best was to surrender oneself to something habitually or obsessively. We had done that all our lives.

Now the important thing was gambling. The care and feeding of our addiction, the pleasure of our addiction. Gambling was a very cerebral, almost slow-motion activity, which made it easy to savor. It was markedly more satisfying because we were doing it together. As brothers, we shared all the surprise and exhilaration of a new and consuming interest, like any new hobby—skydiving, methamphetamine. Codependency has its good side. Both doing it, we were each part performer and part audience. Every gambling session wrote its own swift, strange story, filled with highs and lows, finely calibrated details ("she flipped another five . . .") and compelling nuances ("and I thought, 'Fuck, ace, next one's an ace,' and then, sure as shit . . ."). Gamblers want to talk. For us, there was always someone to tell, someone who knew in his blood what you were talking about. After a trip, our conversations went on for days, full of lurid, taunting laughter. The kind that revealed just how completely we were hooked on risk, on gambling.

We weren't measuring ourselves against the real daredevils of the culture; we were measuring ourselves against other normal people, middle-class people, good solid stock, people with jobs, families, houses, cars, and responsibilities that they dispatched in a workmanlike way. People like us. We told ourselves that betting a thousand dollars on a hand of blackjack might be stupid, but it wasn't as stupid as shooting yourself full of heroin or, as various members of our family had done for years, drinking yourself into oblivion by five o'clock in the afternoon—or better yet, doing it by noon, waking up at three and doing it again by five, having dinner and doing it again by nine. Maybe we were just looking for a way to keep up with the rest of the family, members of which had had their troubles with various forms of conspicuous consumption, of obsession, of, well, for lack of a better word, addiction. Yes, it ran in the family. From our father on down, maybe even from *his* father on down.

The only time you really think of yourself as an addict is when you want to stop. When it's time to stop. When you're in so much trouble that stopping is the only thing left. But we never got there. We could afford it. It was fun. It was a way to blow off steam. It took us out of ourselves in a way that we hadn't been taken out of ourselves by anything else.

We had had good luck with addictions in the past. Both of us had been drinkers and smokers. Rick had been a drunk in his early twenties, but had stopped dead after he moved to New York and discovered that getting drunk and waking up at four A.M. on a Lower East Side street was not healthy. Steve had long since given up heavy drinking for steady drinking, three drinks a day, give or take a couple, for the past thirty years. Both of us had had smoking habits—two or three packs a day—and while we'd tried to curb them, following the path of declining tar and nicotine, going from regular cigarettes to pretend cigarettes like True and Carlton, we'd had no intention of quitting until, as mentioned, our two older brothers were diagnosed with throat cancer, one within a month of the other.

We quit smoking.

But gambling wasn't producing a downside for us. Gambling was only producing the release, the euphoria, and the opportunity to behave bizarrely, just like—we imagined—ordinary, everyday people. We didn't think we were wild and crazy; we thought gambling made us regular guys.

It was an aesthetic thing too. Everywhere around us were writers and artists and professors, hard at work at what Ishmael Reed describes as "all wearing the same funny hat." It had long seemed obvious that the best course was the other direction. Neither of us had the customary late-twentieth-century middle-class phobia for people who were deemed ordinary. In fact, ordinary was what we both liked best.

What we didn't like about the academy was the falseness: conservative people presenting themselves in Che Guevara suits, digging hard for career advantage while settling hearty congratulations all around for assigning radical authors to their students to read, thus threatening the established order. Soon they would take their SUVs into the mountains.

This put a little extra heat under the affection we had for the ordinary people we imagined existed somewhere and for whom we felt a special kinship. It was ordinariness that we were extending with our gambling, by being addicted to it, by doing it to excess, by risking more money than made any sense at all, by telling ourselves that we were going to win, or that we might win, when we knew as surely as anybody else that the likelihood of that was slim. Still, you'd be surprised at how much positive thinking goes on on the highway at midnight.

You'd be surprised by how dearly the heart holds the idea that tonight you might actually win, that this two thousand dollars, the last two thousand you have in your bank account, will be the basis of your big comeback. Even in the heat of battle, down five or fifteen thousand in a night, the not particularly well heeled but still liquid blackjack loser can imagine winning it all back in a flash.

And he would not imagine it had he not already done it once or twice or maybe more. Had he not experienced that thrill of the cards having run against him all night, run against him for five consecutive hours and having in that time lost an enormous amount of money, gone to the cashier's cage again and again, new resources, the thrill that comes when the cards turn, when they become your cards, when they became his cards, not the casino's, when in the space of forty-five minutes you recognize that you're going to win whatever you bet. And if you recognize it soon enough, and if you're secure enough in the recognition, you can turn around the whole night, turn around five thousand dollars in twenty minutes. You can turn around fifteen thousand dollars in an hour.

It's a rare, even amazing experience. It almost makes gambling worthwhile. Everything you touch turns to gold. You bet five hundred dollars and you bet a thousand. You double down and you win. Your stacks of chips grow. Pretty soon they are paying you in hundreds, then five hundreds—the purple chips. You've got a stack of those in front of you. Then, if the going is really good, they start paying you in orange—the thousand-dollar chips. The thousand-dollar chips are slightly larger, a sixteenth of an inch larger in diameter than all the other chips. You stack them separately.

Your stack grows, and maybe you bet one of them or two of them on a hand. Or you play two hands. And still you win. Sure, this isn't Monte Carlo, you're not some duke or some heiress, and so you're not betting hundreds of thousands of dollars a hand, but that fact makes your betting and your winning just that much sweeter, because you have no business in the world betting a thousand dollars on a hand of blackjack, and you know it. You have no business in the world betting five thousand dollars on a hand of blackjack, and you know it. So when you do, and when the cards are coming your way, and when your five thousand turns to ten, your ten to twenty, it's mesmerizing. Suddenly that business they always say about feeling like you'll live forever becomes a little bit true, because you've crossed over some line, gone into some other territory, become somebody else.

You're part of the table, part of the machine that plays blackjack, part of the casino, part of the system. Only you're not the part that gives your money to them anymore, you're not the part you usually play: the mark, the bozo. You've skidded out onto the ice in the middle of the Olympics in a huge stadium filled with cheering people and swaying, lime-colored spotlights and, suddenly, inexplicably, you can skate like an angel.

From Oscar and Lucinda

BY PETER CAREY

In nineteenth-century English novels, aristocratic women are often seen playing cards, or sitting at roulette wheels, sometimes wagering sizeable sums; but they are rarely put into competitive gambling encounters with men. Peter Carey's presentation of Oscar and Lucinda in nineteenth-century Australia not only puts a man and a woman in head-to-head gambling, but makes that the center of their relationship. Oscar is a young English clergyman, Lucinda an heiress who bucks the expectations for women of the time. When the two meet on the passage to Australia, Lucinda invites him into her cabin to play poker, and they discover at once their shared passion for gambling. Basically, they'll both bet on anything. They separate, but after Oscar bumps into Lucinda in a Chinese gambling den, they are drawn into wagering their inheritances on whether Oscar can transport a glass cathedral across the Australian Outback. There are fine early sections in the novel in which Oscar discovers his love of gamble and must accommodate it into his religious thinking. The selection below suggests ways in which, in addition to drawing her together with Oscar, Lucinda's love of risk and gambling is a way, paradoxically, of achieving a sense of self-reliance and personal security. *Oscar and Lucinda* won a Booker Prize and was made into a film starring Ralph Fiennes and Cate Blanchett.

She came down the rutted track of the ridge. She was frightened again, to be out by herself. These fears came and went, like the cold pockets of air by creeks. She did not believe in ghosts, but now she was easily frightened and jumped three inches in her hard seat when someone in a long coat rushed across her path. She wished she were back home, and then she reminded herself what it was like to be home. She used her whip unsentimentally, drawing a deft flick along the gelding's flank. The flick produced a skip of rhythm, a toss of the head, and they set off at a brisker pace, following the slippery clay-white lines of the track round the shores of White Bay.

There were racing fools with no lanterns. A drunk wagoner with half his load tumbling off behind him. How cowardly Mr Hasset had been! To abandon her, here, when he did not even wish to go away.

She was angry, with Dennis Hasset, with the hallooing gallopers who rushed out of the dark, with the rutted track and the mud-churned soak where the drunken wagoner dropped a plank which almost jammed between her wheels.

Anger made her reckless. She drove fast. She was going for a trot. She went all the way into George Street although she did not like it at this time of night. She dared herself. She did not care. She brought her jinker up past the theatres. Her Majesty's. The Rappallo. Lyceum. The weather had not kept the crowds at home. The street was a river of wheels and horses, the banks awash with the flotsam and jetsam of men's hats.

There were gangs of larrikins afoot, up from The Rock with their hands boasting against their braces. She was afraid. Inside her big coat, she was small and white, soft-breasted, weak-armed, all soaked with sweat in the wind-cold night. A man spoke to her from a carriage. She put the tired gelding into a canter. There were shouts of, 'Gee-up, Nelly'. Laughter. She came in under the shadows of St Andrew's. The loathed St Andrew's. It stood grim and dark, the castle of Bishop Dancer. A crowd by the nave door announced not late service but a fight. Two policemen ran towards it, momentarily brilliant and livid-faced in the gaslight. She swung into Bathurst Street at the last moment, nearly colliding with one more unlit sulky. The sulky gave up a wail of silk-and-feathered screams. Lucinda felt contempt. It curdled in her jealousy. She struck her horse and followed the line of wide verandas as if she were going to see her dear friend in Woollahra. But there was nothing at Woollahra. There was a too-pretty child with a hoop who said the house was hers.

'I am going mad,' she said. She said it out loud. 'I am unlaced and not connected.' It was a frightful city in which to contemplate madness, all hard with eucalyptus, snapping sticks, sandstone rocks with fractured faces and cutting edges. You could not, not in Sydney, dear God, allow yourself to fall into such a weakened state.

'A mad woman,' she whispered. 'Trrrrot up.'

She was going for a trot. The horse knew this. He knew the destination. 'Not a mad woman,' she said, as they went down into the smoky dark of The Rocks. You could not see the fire so close. It was on the other side. The drains reeked. They reeked everywhere, but it was worse here towards the quay. Her nerves were on edge. 'Dear God, forgive me.'

She intended nothing more than a little Pak-Ah-Pu. This was a lottery run by the Chinese down at that end of George Street. It was dark down there, and dangerous. The front of the establishment had a candle burning—no gas— inside a glass lantern. There were men standing around in twos and threes. She could smell putrid meat but also liquor. These two smells were carried on the salty air of the harbour. The wind played on the rigging of the tall-masted ships. She tied the rein to the railing. Even before she betrayed her sex by the sound of her walk, the men around her were unnaturally silent. The big wet coat was an inadequate disguise. She affected a stiff-spined *haut froid*. She told herself this: 'You're the boss.'

The front room pretended to be a shop. Everyone knew this was not the case, even the policemen on the beat (who wore gold rings and heavy watches). Lucinda did not look at whatever dusty goods were displayed, but walked—she heard her boots echo on the wooden boards—towards the curtained doorway at the back. She could *hear* how small her feet were. She felt their unmaleness.

The truth is that she no longer wished merely for a Pak-Ah-Pu ticket. She was having a trot. There is nothing to Pak-Ah-Pu except a lottery. There is none of the sting (her term) you get in a good game. But she began, once she reached the table, as she had originally pretended. It was nearly half pst nine, time for the last draw of the day, and there was therefore quite a crowd standing around the table. Several of them were drunk, but they did not sway. They had that rather sullen stillness which is the mark of a betting shop late in the day. The floor was littered with crumpled paper, cigarette ends, matches broken nervously in three. The men had a look at once scuffed and glazed. She felt—or imagined—an anger, barely contained, but the anger may well have been her own.

She gave the Chinaman at the table her sixpence. She was given her ticket and she marked, quickly, urgently even, ten of the Chinese characters on the paper. There were eighty all told. She did not know what they meant. They were printed on coarse grey paper. Twice she pushed the unpleasant little chewed pencil stub (property of the house) through the paper. She wrote her name (not her real name) on the paper and gave it to the Chinaman who put it into a bowl, which appeared to be black but was probably a dark Chinese blue. The light was bad. She could see the squashed stub of a fat cigar near her foot. She tried to look at nothing while she waited for half past nine.

It took three and a half minutes. All this time she stood immobile. The air around her was still. Occasionally a man said something in a low voice. This would be followed by laughter. Once she heard a word she knew referred to copulation. She was quite drenched inside her oilskin coat. All this fear she felt, this hostility and danger, was but the aura surrounding something else, a larger body of feeling which was dense, compacted, a centre of pure will—Lucinda was willing herself to win. Her anger became as inconsequential as blue-flies, then less, like summer thrip.

Six correct marks would bring her ten shillings. Seven would deliver four pounds, eight shillings and eight pence. Eight good marks was twenty-three pounds, six shillings and eightpence. This was all written on the blackboard above the back wall. She was not silly enough to waste her will on ten. She decided on eight, imagining that this was within her limit. There was a smell of incense, another like wet dog, and that other smell—the bodies of men who work hard sweaty work and only bathe once a week. You can produce a similar smell by leaving damp cleaning rags in a bucket. Not an attractive smell, but Lucinda liked it. The cigar smoker had lit another cheroot and made the air slightly blue and streaky. Through all this there came the soft crying of a baby in another room. Many of the Chinese, she had been told, had European wives. It was said the Chinese men were kind to their women. These were fallen women, beyond the pale. It was said—the reverend friend had said so—that they were loved and found happiness. She tried to block out the sound. She shut a large and heavy door on it and pressed it—for it did not wish to go—firmly shut.

There was a movement now. A shoulder, blind of feeling, pressed against her. The men pushed, like fish feeding, or piglets rushing the teat—all feeling concentrated in the mouth, the rest of the body quite numb. There were eighty characters. They would put twenty in a bowl. Of these twenty, they would select ten. They were doing it now. She was crushed all about. The Celestial, one eye half-shut against his own cigarette smoke, drew out ten yellowed ivory counters and placed them on a little wooden tray.

She had been told that these characters represented virtues. She had trouble recognizing them in this light. There was the one with the roof, the one with the two Fs standing huffily back to back, the one with eyes like a cat staring from the grass, the one like a river, Jesus Christ Almighty, dear Lord forgive her, she had eight correct.

She felt light, high as a kite. The Chinaman gave her money but did not approve of her. She could not imagine him being kind to his wife. She did not give a damn what he thought. She was going for a trot. She was going to hell.

Don't think that!

She clenched all her muscles to resist the idea. Then, almost at once, she did not care. The punters saw the small woman in the big oilskin coat walk towards the door. She walked briskly and bossily towards it—not the door to the street, but the door in the back wall.

She was going for a trot.

The second room was where fan-tan was played. It was dark all round its edges, much darker than in the Pak-Ah-Pu room. But the light above the zinc-covered table was brighter and the zinc itself threw back a dull glow into the faces of the noisy players, making them look sickly, tinged with green. No one looked up when she entered. She stayed back for a moment in the cover of dark. She felt, suddenly, quite wonderful. She could not explain why this change should come, that she should move from blotchy-faced hell-fear to this odd electric ecstasy merely in the moving from one room to the next. She felt herself to be beyond salvation and did not care. She would not be loved, not be wife, not be mother.

She felt the perfect coldness known to climbers.

The croupier was thin, with gold in his mouth. She could smell the rancid oil from his pigtailed hair. All sorts of smells here. Sailor's oilskin, someone's newly polished shoes. The croupier made a small cry—probably English, although it sounded alien, mechanical, as if he were an extraordinary construction from the Paris exhibition. The dark enveloped her, warmed her like brandy. The croupier threw—such a *svelte* motion—the brass coins. They sounded, as they hit the zinc, both dull and sharp; light, of no substance, but also dead and heavy. It was lovely to watch, just as lovely as a good butcher cutting a carcass, the quick movement of knife, the softness and yielding of fat from around kidneys, the clean separation of flesh from bone. The croupier's tin cup covered some of the coins while his right hand swept the others away. She was a Christian. Her mind found the parallel— Judgement Day, saved coins, cast-out coins—without her seeking it. Sheep on the right. Goats on the left. She drew the curtains on the picture, turned her back, and concentrated all her attention on the heathen as he lifted the cup and set the coins—see how sweetly this is done, the suppleness of long fingers (three of them ringed, one of them with emerald)—and slid the coins into sets of four.

There was much barracking now. Cries of yes, it is, no, it's not, groans, and then an odd cheer, squeaky as a schoolboy's which attracted comments, not all of them good-natured.

'It's two.'

'Toe,' said the Celestial. 'Numma toe.'

He had placed all the coins in sets of four. There were two remaining. Anyone who had placed their stake on the side of the zinc designated '2' had trebled their money.

The Chinaman gave out the winnings. He slid out six coins across the zinc. Someone expressed a wish to pass water in an eccentric style. Another wind. There was laughter and crudity. Lucinda was not lonely. She pressed forward now, to make her bet, but also to reveal herself. They must know she was there. It was to prevent their embarrassment. She would rather she did not reveal herself, but she must not delay it. She did not look at the faces of the men as she pressed between them to reach the bright square of pitted zinc.

She said: 'Excuse me.'

It took longer to register than you might expect, partly because of the alcohol, which gave the air in the room its volatility, but also because of the intense focus created by the zinc square which, at the moment she chose, contained nothing of any significance except the red numerals (1, 2, 3, 4) which had become almost ghostly with the heavy traffic of coins across their painted surfaces.

At last they felt her otherness, her womanness. She felt the bodies move aside. Where there had been a hot press, she now experienced a distinct and definite cooling.

But she was not lonely, and she was not frightened or shy. She looked at the Chinaman—*he* was lonely, she saw, and very young—but she observed this in a way that did not involve her capacity for compassion or sympathy. What moved her were his ringed hands, the black metal cup, the brass coins, the red scratched numbers, and these things, being merely instruments, provided the anticipation of an intense, but none the less mechanical, pleasure.

She placed a florin against the four. This was soon joined by the more customary coppers. The '4' won. She felt herself liked. She felt the hot pulse of their approbation. They went from cold to hot. It was done as quickly as the cutting of a cockerel's throat. She did not acknowledge it, but she welcomed it. She was not lonely. She looked at no one. She played with inspired recklessness. She felt she could control the game with no other tool than her will.

4, 3, 2, 4, 4, 4, 4, 1, 4, 3, 3, 3, 4, 1.

She won until she touched the quicksand of the final '1'. Then she could not get the run of it again. She was out of step. There was a hidden beat she could not catch. The men stopped following her then. They no longer announced their bets as 'the same as the missus'. But they did not withdraw from her either. And when, at three o'clock in the morning, she snapped her purse shut, she had no more money than the poorest of them. The purse was empty, freed from all weight, contained nothing but clean, watered silk. She felt as light and clean as rice paper. She allowed herself to notice her companions. She felt limp as a rag doll, and perfectly safe.

From Four-and-Twenty Hours in the Life of a Woman

BY STEFAN ZWEIG

Among the hardest things to capture in writing about gambling are the interior, physiological sensations. It is as difficult to write about as it is to explain pain accurately to a doctor, where one falls back upon clumsy metaphors, such as "steaming," "icy," "tingling," "throbbing." Observant writers or players, however, can intuit what is going on inside gamblers from their body language. The great poker players can read the "tells" of their opponents, those tics that, at their most absurd, like John Malkovich in *Rounders* twisting Oreo cookies every time he's bluffing (yeah, right!), give away a hand.

In games where the gambler plays against the impassive House, information about the players may be irrelevant to the outcome, but they can be richly revealing of their characters. Gambling or risking something, perhaps to the degree to which the player is immersed, opens up personality. And those who watch games, participating vicariously, are in turn revealed by their responses to the joys and sufferings of others. One may try to close oneself off, disengage one's feelings, like the dealer in the film *Croupier*. Or one might become massively involved, like the elderly woman in the excerpt from Austrian writer Stefan Zweig's novella that follows, to whom a gambler's "hand blabs secrets shamelessly." Through her odd form of kibbitzing, the casino at Monte Carlo becomes visible, as do various physiological ways in which gamblers betray their lives.

♣ ♦ ♥ ♠

"Thenceforward, my life was meaningless and futile. The man with whom I had shared every hour and every thought for three-and-twenty years was dead. My children did not need me, and I was afraid of overshadowing their youth with my grief. For myself, I had no further desires. My first move was to Paris, where I bored myself with sight-seeing. Inanimate things did not interest me; and as for people, I found their company trying, for their polite sympathy at sight of my widow's weeds was intolerable to me. I can hardly tell you how I passed these first weary months of wandering. I only know that I longed for death, but lacked energy to quicken its coming.

"In the second year of my widowhood and the forty-fourth of my life, this flight from an existence which had become valueless but which I did not know how to escape, brought me towards the end of March to Monte Carlo. No doubt boredom directed my footsteps. I was suffering from that sense of vacancy in which the most trifling external stimuli may bring distraction. The less stir there was in my inner self, the more did I feel drawn to places where the whirl of life was swift. For one who is having no personal experience, the passionate disquiet of others is at any rate a titillation of the nerves, like seeing a play or listening to music.

"I often went, therefore, to the Casino. I liked to watch the waves of joy or despair flit across the faces of others, what time my own mind remained so horribly inert. Besides, my husband, though no gambler, had been fond of whiling away an hour in this place from time to time, and I was making a sort of cult of reviving all our joint experiences. Thus began the four-and-twenty hours which were far more exciting than any plunge at the gaming table.

"I had lunched with my relative the Duchess of M. After dinner I did not feel tired enough to go to bed. Instead, I went to the Casino, wandered up and down between the tables, and watched the gamesters in a peculiar fashion. Explicitly I say 'in a peculiar fashion,' one I had learned from my husband. This was when, weary of looking on, I had complained of the tedium of perpetually watching the same faces: the wrinkled old women who will sit for hours before they venture to stake a trifle; the professional gamblers and cocottes; the enigmatic and strangely compacted company which, as you know, is far less picturesque and romantic than novelists would have us believe, the novelists who tell us that the *'fleur d'élégance'* and the aristocracy of Europe assemble at Monte Carlo. Besides, this was the Casino of long ago, when there was plenty of money on the tables: rustling notes, golden napoleons, fat five-franc pieces—far more attractive than the modern gaming-house, fashionably re-built, where Cook's tourists tediously fritter away their insipid counters. But even in those days I was bored by the sameness of it all, until my husband, who had a passion for chiromancy, drew my attention to the possibility of a peculiar method of observation, which was certainly far more interesting, far more exciting, than idle contemplation of the spectacle. 'Don't bother about the faces,' he said. 'Look at the table; watch the players' hands; study the behaviour of their hands.'

"I wonder whether you yourself have ever concentrated your gaze on the table in this way, looking only at the green square of cloth, in the middle of which the ball is whirling from figure to figure as if drunk, while in the quadrangle notes and gold and silver coins are scattered like seed, which the croupier rakes in from the loser or shovels out to the winner. In such a view, the only things that really change are the hands—the pale, quickly moving or motionless hands round the green table; each one of them peeping forth from a cavern-like sleeve; each one of them a beast of prey crouching for the spring; all of them differently shaped and tinted; some of them bare, some of them decked with rings and clinking bracelets; some of them hairy like wild beasts, some of them damp and writhing like eels; all of them tense, pulsing with impatience. As I watch them I cannot but think of a race-course, where the horses waiting for the signal are reined in with difficulty lest they should make a false start; they tremble, rear, and prance in just the same fashion.

"All kinds of things can be inferred from these hands, from their attitude in repose and from the way in which they grasp the money or the counters. A clawlike hand betokens avarice; a loose hand, extravagance; a quiet one, calculation; a tremulous one, despair. A hundred characteristics are suddenly betrayed by the gesture with which the winnings are seized. One person will nervously crumple up the notes; another, overcome with lassitude, will leave everything where it lies while the ball starts on a new round. The gambler betrays himself in various ways. He has but to say a dozen words, and I know what he is; but his hands betray him even more effectually. For almost all gamesters learn to control their faces, wearing a mask of imperturbability, setting their features in a fixed expression, retaining their excitement within their clenched teeth, keeping the sparkle of excitement out of their eyes, assuming a pose of indifference. But, for the very reason that their attention is thus concentrated upon facial expression, they are apt to forget their hands, to forget that some are present who watch these hands, reading there everything which the forced smile and the impassive countenance are designed to conceal. The hand blabs secrets shamelessly. A moment inevitably comes when these laboriously controlled, apparently slumbering fingers, throw off their well-bred indifference in the tense instant when the roulette ball settles down into its little hollow and the winning number is proclaimed; then it is that these hundred or five hundred hands involuntarily make a movement which is the purely individual expression of primitive instinct. One who has learned, as I had learned under the guidance of my husband's hobby, to watch the arena of hands, finds the unexpected outbreak of temperament, varying from person to person, more interesting than any theatrical or musical performance. I cannot tell you how many thousand varieties of hands there are: wild beasts with hairy, crooked fingers, seizing the money as a spider seizes a fly; nervous and tremulous fingers, with pallid nails, scarcely venturing to grasp what has been won; noble and base, violent and timid, crafty and faltering; differing from person to person, each pair of hands giving expression to one particular life. The four or five pairs belonging to the croupiers can alone be excepted, for they are pure automata, doing their work with circumstantial, business-like, and utterly noncommittal precision, so that in contrast with the passionate liveliness of the gamblers' hands they seem as mechanical as a calculating machine. Yet in their very self-control, these hands of the croupiers produce a remarkable impression; they contrast so powerfully with their questing and passionate brethren. They are ranged in uniform, so to speak, like policemen in the midst of an agitated crowd.

"An additional charm in this method of observation is derived from the fact that after a few days the observer becomes personally acquainted with the habits and passions of particular hands. I myself got to know some of them intimately, feeling friendly or hostile as the case might be. Many of them were so repulsive in their greed that I would turn away from them when I caught sight of them, as if I had become the chance witness of some impropriety. But every new hand on the table was a stimulating experience, and an object for curious enquiry. Often I was so much interested that I forgot to look at the face to which it belonged, the face that rose imperturbably above a stiff-fronted shirt or a white bosom.

"One evening I entered the Casino, and made my way, past two crowded tables, to a third where there was still room. I was getting out some gold pieces for my own stake, during that pause in the game, that period of ominous silence, when the ball, wearied almost to death, is staggering from one number to the next. At this moment I heard a strange crackling noise. Looking to see whence it came, I was astonished, nay alarmed, to perceive two hands that were strange to me, a right and a left, grappling with one another like furious animals, seizing one another so convulsively that the finger-joints were cracking like nut-shells. These hands were singularly beautiful; long, slender, and yet tense with muscle; extremely white, with well-shaped, pearly nails. I watched them throughout the evening, these extraordinarily distinctive hands. What especially moved me was the passion they exhaled, and the convulsive way in which they gripped one another. They were the hands of some one (I realized this in a flash) who was forcing all the strength of his feelings into his finger-tips, lest their violence tear him to pieces. But at the moment when, with a dry sound, the ball fell into its socket, and the croupier called out the winning number, of a sudden the two hands fell apart like two animals hit by the same shot. They fell dead, as it were, and not merely exhausted. They showed a lassitude and a disillusionment, a sense that everything was at an end, which I feel it almost impossible to describe. Never before or since have I seen such expressive hands, hands whose every muscle was a mouth, whose every emotion exuded palpably through the pores. For a moment they lay on the green table like jellyfish cast up on the seashore, flat and dead. Then one of them, the right, began laboriously to move at the finger-tips. It trembled, drew back, rotated on its axis, rocked, circled, and at length nervously grasped a counter, which it rolled irresolutely like a little wheel between thumb and forefinger. Then, suddenly arching like a cat about to spring, it positively spewed the hundred-franc counter into the middle of the black field. Thereupon, as if a signal had been given, the left hand, which had hitherto been inactive, became a prey to excitement likewise. It crept towards its trembling brother, now exhausted by placing the stake; then the two hands lay shuddering side by side, the wrists beating noiselessly on the table, as the teeth chatter gently in the cold fit of a fever. Never, I repeat, had I seen such expressive hands, manifesting such spasmodic excitement and tension. Everything else in this vaulted room—the murmur of conversation, the calling of the croupiers, the to-and-fro movement of men and women, the circling of the ball which had again been launched upon its course—all this multiplicity of confusing impressions, now seemed to me lifeless when contrasted with these trembling, breathing, panting, expectant, freezing, shuddering, wellnigh incredible hands, at which, as if under a spell, I was forced to stare.

"At last, however, I could no longer refrain from looking at the face which belonged to these wonderful hands. I was anxious, exceedingly anxious, when I did this, for I was afraid of the hands! Slowly my gaze travelled up the arms, past the narrow shoulders, and reached the face. Once more I was seized with alarm, for the face spoke the same unrestrained, the same fantastic and extravagant language as the hands; like them, it was a terrible blend of moroseness with delicate, almost feminine, beauty. Such a face! Isolated there, detached from its surroundings, I had ample time to study it as if it were an eyeless mask. There were eyes, of course; but they stared straight forward, not turning for a moment either to right or to left. The pupils looked like black glass balls between the widely opened lids; they mirrored, as it were, that other mahogany-coloured globe which was wantonly spinning round the roulette table. Never, never in my life had I seen so tense a visage, one that exercised such a strange fascination. The man to whom it belonged was about four-and-twenty years of age. Like the hands, the face was rather that of a passionate boy, full of pranks, than of a grown man. All these details came under my notice later. For the nonce, the face was monopolized by an expression of greed and frenzy. The small mouth, being half open, gave a glimpse of the teeth. From where I was, ten paces away, I could see that they were tightly clenched, and that the parted lips were rigid. A lock of fair hair had fallen across the damp forehead. The nostrils were working with excitement, as if little waves were pulsating beneath the skin. The head was thrust forward, still further forward even as I watched, so that it seemed to me as if it were on the point of being involved in the whirling of the little ball. Now I understood why the hands were so convulsively pressed together. Only by such a convulsive effort could the balance of the whole body be retained.

"Yet again I must say that never before had I seen a human face in which passion was revealed with such animal frankness, such shameless nudity. I myself was no less enthralled by its aspect than the face itself was enthralled by the leaps and bounds of the circling ball. Thenceforward I paid no heed to anything else in the hall; the surroundings seemed to me dull, vague, and obscure in comparison with the ardour of this countenance. For a long while, an hour perhaps, I watched the man and his every gesture; watched the sparkle in his eyes, the tremulous and almost frantic movement of his hands, when the croupier shovelled out twenty gold pieces for their greedy grasp. When this happened, the face lighted up and looked quite young; the lines in it were smoothed away; the eyes shone; the body, which had been bent forward, straightened. Now my gamester sat easily in his chair, sustained by a sense of triumph; his fingers toyed affectionately with the coins, chinked them one against the other, danced them up and down. Then he restlessly turned his eyes back towards the green table; looked at it like a young hound which, with dilated nostrils, is eagerly snuffing a scent; and, with a quick movement, staked the whole pile of gold pieces on one of the squares. The tense watching was resumed. Again the lips twitched; again the hands were convulsively clasped; the boyish expression of countenance disappeared, to be replaced by a look of lustful expectation—till the tension lapsed into disappointment. Now the face grew pale and elderly; the fire in the eyes was quenched; and these changes took place in a twinkling, when the ball settled down upon the wrong number. He had lost. For a second or two he stared fixedly as if he had not understood. Then, at the strident call of the croupier, the fingers pushed forward two or three gold pieces. But he was no longer self-confident. First he staked his coins in one place; then, changing his mind, in another; finally, when the ball was already rolling, with tremulous hand and following a sudden impulse, he placed two crumpled notes in the same square as before.

"The quivering alternation of loss and gain went on for about an hour, during which my eyes were fixed on this face with its ebb and flow of passions; or upon the hands, those wonderful hands, whose movements reflected the whole gamut of emotion. Never, even in the theatre, have I gazed with such rapt attention at the face of an actor, as I now looked at this countenance across which the alternations of passion flitted incessantly like light and shade across an April landscape. Never had I shared so intimately in any game in which I myself had been a player, as I shared now in the reflexion of this stranger's excitement. Had any one been observing me at the time, he would have fancied me in a hypnotic trance. In very truth my absorption resembled hypnosis. I could not wrest my eyes away from this dumb show. Everything else in the room—the lights, the laughter, the glances—was for me but a formless haze, out of which the face flamed forth. I heard nothing, saw nothing, did not notice the people who passed by, paid no attention to the other hands extended like tentacles to clutch their winnings. I did not see the whirling ball, or heed the voice of the croupier. All that happened seemed nothing more than a dream, perceived as a magnified image in the concave mirror of these hands. I did not need to look at the ball in order to learn whether it settled down on red or on black. Every phase of loss or gain, expectation or disappointment, was instantly mirrored in the fleeting passions of this face.

"Then came a terrible moment, one which I had been dimly anticipating, one which had hung over my tense nerves like a threatening storm, and now suddenly burst upon them. Once more the ball was rattling round its course; once more the hundred players were holding their breath in suspense. The voice of the croupier, calling 'Zero,' broke through the silence, and, with his rake, he promptly gathered in all the clinking coins and rustling notes. At this instant, the convulsive hands made a peculiarly terrible movement, leaping up together as if to seize something which was not there, and then falling back on the table by their own weight as if utterly exhausted. Coming to life once more, they moved quickly back from the table to the body of their owner, scrambling like wildcats up and down, to right and to left, feeling in one pocket after another on the chance that a coin might have been overlooked. The search was fruitless, but was renewed, while the ball was spinning once again, and the other gamblers were clinking their money, moving in their chairs, and filling the room with the murmur of manifold noises. I trembled as I watched, so keen was my sympathy. The fingers, still desperately hunting for money in pocket after pocket, might have been my own! Now the man sprang to his feet, like one who rises when suddenly taken ill, and feels that he will choke if he remains sitting. His chair, overturned, crashed on the floor. Regardless of his neighbours (who drew back in consternation), he tottered, and groped his way from the table.

"I felt as if I had been turned to stone. I understood wither he was going; he was going to his death. One who stood up with such a gesture, had it not in mind to seek a hotel, a drinking booth, a woman, a railway carriage, or any form of life, but was about to hurl himself into the unknown. Even the most callous among those present in this hell must have realized that the man had nothing more to depend upon at home or in his bank or among relatives, but had been staking his last coins, and therefore his very life, and was now stumbling away to find an exit from that life. From the outset I had feared, had felt convinced, that something more was being hazarded than ordinary losses and gains; yet it came as a shock to me when I saw the life ooze out of his eyes, and death's visage peep forth from the face of one who still drew breath. Unwittingly mimicking the gestures I had been watching, I clasped my hands convulsively together while he staggered way; and the disorder of his movements affected me no less powerfully than the previous tension had done. Something irresistible drew me after him; my feet seemed to move without the instigation of my will. Thus, unconsciously as it were, and not of my own volition, I followed him through the door.

"He was at the window of the cloak-room, and the attendant had brought him his overcoat. His arms no longer obeyed him, and the servant had to help him on with his coat as sedulously as if he had been paralysed. Mechanically, he put his fingers into his waistcoat pocket, wishing to give the man a tip; but he found nothing there. This made him realize the situation anew. Stammering a word of apology, he gave fresh impetus to his limbs, and reeled down the steps of the Casino like a drunken man, the attendant watching him from the top, contemptuously at first, and then with a knowledgeable smile.

"The ruined gambler's gestures were so pitiful that I was ashamed of myself for spying upon them. I hesitated, vexed with myself for having pried into a stranger's despair as nonchalantly as if he had been an actor on the stage. Then, in spite of myself, anxiety drove me once more into ill-considered action. Quickly getting my own cloak, with no clear thought of what I was doing, mechanically and impulsively I hastened through the darkness in pursuit of the stranger."

Na Kupa Hati M'zuri

BY BERYL MARKHAM

Ernest Hemingway wrote that a real *aficionado* would consider betting on bull-fighting a dilution of the pleasure of viewing, suggesting that where the passion of spectatorship is sufficient gambling threatens to befoul the priorities of caring. I have felt this way on rare occasions about sporting events, like boxing, where I wouldn't want to root for my money over a fighter. What people feel too passionate about to gamble on is largely a personal affair. At the same time, you can bet that, no matter how sacred or trivial or monumental a thing may seem to you, there's someone somewhere betting on the outcome. Millions of pounds were bet in England on the outcome of the last episode of *Dallas.*

The selection below from Beryl Markham's *West With the Night* is a good example of that kind of story that, while involving gambling and vividly capturing a gambling event, is as invested in the personalities of the contenders (in this case two horses) as in the wagering that surrounds them. "Every horse has a story," says Brendan Boyd in *Racing Days,* and for passionate racetrackers those stories, the track itself, and the life, are a large part of the pleasure. "Inspiration," Boyd writes: "two indomitable horses battling nose to nose to the wire." 'Na Kupa Hati M'zuri' (I Bring You Good Fortune) was engraved in stone over the fireplace in Club Muthiaga in colonial Kenya where the inspired racing in this story is set. Of Markham's memoir (she flew a small plane all over the African continent), Hemingway wrote his editor, "She can write rings around all of us who consider ourselves writers."

'nd so,' says Eric Gooch, 'what are our chances?'
I frown and shake my head. 'Without Wrack to run against us, they would be perfect.'

What a thing to have to say! My own skill and labour have moulded every muscle on the hard, dynamic body of the chestnut colt. Wrack's prowess is the product of my own hands; he is far and away the favourite for the Leger—but he will run against me. Part of that conversation buzzing around these wide, white walls is gossip about Wrack—little words of speculation droning like bees in a bottle.

Eric and I think back.

Just twelve weeks ago Wrack had been taken from my stable at Nakuru by his owner and put into the care of another trainer—a man who knew a good thing when he saw it. In the year Wrack had been with me, he had developed from a leggy, headstrong colt into a full-formed race-horse, swift, haughty, and contemptuous of competition. Wrack could run and knew it. Nervously, his owner had listened to the argument that a girl of eighteen could not be entrusted with those precise finishing touches, that careful shading of muscle against bone, that almost sophistical task of persuading a horse that nothing in his own world of probabilities was so improbable as another horse's ability to beat him past the post. Wrack had been taken from me on the strength of the doubt, and my reputation as a trainer, which had only begun to take firm root, was hardly encouraged by the act.

But gossip has its better points. Whispers are not restricted to the bearing of bad news and there are men who smell injustice however softly it walks.

Eric Gooch had known that I would bring about fifteen horses to Nairobi for the big Race Meeting, and that some of these would win the lesser races. He had also known that, without Wrack, I had nothing to enter as a serious contender for the classic—the single race that really mattered. Eric had thought hard, and then he had come to my stable from his farm at Nyeri.

'I've worried about this thing,' he had said, 'but I don't know any way out. Wrack is already being backed to win, and, so far as I can see, there is nothing to stop him. Of course, there's Wise Child—but, hell, you know about Wise Child.'

Know about her? Like Pegasus, she had been born into my hands. Her Thoroughbred blood had filtered through twenty generations of winners. Hers was the metal to match the metal of Wrack. Only there was the question of legs.

Wise Child, as a two-year-old, had been mishandled by her first trainer. Her tendons had been concussed—jarred too early against too hard a track. With all that fire in her heart, all that energy in her tidy bay body, she could barely carry a man on her back. Would it be possible in twelve weeks' time to strengthen those willing but ailing legs—to build them up so that she could drive them a mile and three-quarters—and win?

Eric had thought not—but she was mine if I would have her.

Well, I would have her. It cost only work to try, but to watch Wrack, my own Wrack, sweep the field, bearing alien colours, would cost much more.

And so it had been settled. Wise Child of the gentle manner, the soft, kind eyes and the will to win (if only those legs could be strengthened again), had come into my care at Nakuru. Together we had worked and worried—Arab Ruta, myself, and the little bay filly; but at least we had been blessed with a world of our own to work in.

It was a world of absolutes. It held no intermediate shades, neither of sound nor of colour. There were no subtle strokes in the creation of Nakuru.

The shores of its lake are rich in silence, lonely with it, but the monotonous flats of sand and mud that circle the shallow water are relieved of dullness, not by only an occasional bird or a flock of birds or by a hundred birds; as long as the day lasts Nakuru is no lake at all, but a crucible of pink and crimson fire—each of its flames, its million flames, struck from the wings of a flamingo. Ten thousand birds of such exorbitant hue, caught in the scope of an eye, is a sight that loses credence in one's own mind years afterward. But ten thousand flamingos on Lake Nakuru would be a number startling in its insignificance, and a hundred thousand would barely begin the count.

Menegai Crater overlooks the township and the lake. In the time of man it has breathed no brimstone, and barely a wisp of smoke. But in the annals of the Rift Valley which contains all this as a sea contains a coral atoll or a desert a dune, the time of man is too brief a period to deserve more than incidental recording. Tomorrow, next day, or next year, Menegai may become again the brazier over which some passing Deity will, for a casual aeon or so, warm his omnipotent hands. But until then, one can stand safely on its edge, watching the lake of pink and scarlet wings, so far below—the lake that seems to have stolen for the moment, at least, all the mountain's fire.

This was the lavish background against which I worked my horses at Nakuru. My entrance with Arab Ruta and Wise Child on the flat shore each morning just after daylight must have been as anticlimactic as the spectacle of three mice crossing a stage gigantically set for the performance of a major Wagnerian opera. I used the shore because it was the only place soft and yielding enough for Wise Child's sensitive legs.

My quarters were hardly so elaborate as the hut at Molo had been. By day I lived in a stable I had renovated for my own use, and by night I slept at the very top of the modest little grandstand, built, as was the race-course, by stolidly British members of the district, who, like all the others of our immutable clan, were allergic to the absence of horses.

And each time I had watched Wise Child test her tendons on the moist ground while flamingos rose and settled on the surface of the lake or sluggard hippopotami waddled into it, I had thought of Wrack—disdainful Wrack. How well I knew him!

But the twelve weeks had hurried on, the work had been done as - skilfully as I could do it.

And now, at last, we are here. Now Eric fingers his glass and questions me hopefully, while the music of Muthaiga marches through our talk, and festive people clasp hands, revive old toasts—and make bets on tomorrow's Leger. One hundred pounds—two hundred pounds . . .

'Has the filly a chance?'

'Against Wrack? Of course not.'

'Don't be too sure . . . don't be too sure. Why, I remember . . .'

Well, that's what makes a horse-race.

Jockey: Sonny Bumpus.

What's in a name? At least there's no weight in this one. There's an airy insolence in it. Who would be so heedless as to run a horse against such a happily cocksure combination as—Sonny Bumpus on Wise Child?

And if this were not enough to ponder, what about Arab Ruta? Arab Ruta, the mystic, the conjurer, the wizard of Njoro?

'Ah-yey!' he says, as he grooms the filly with inspired hands, 'I will make these muscles like the muscles of a Murani ready for battle. I will make them tough as the bow of a Wandorobo. I will put my own strength into them!' He spits contempt. 'Wrack—I warn you! You are a colt, but God has given our filly the blade of a Nandi spear for a heart, and put the will of the wind in her lungs. You cannot win, Wrack. I, Arab Ruta, say so!'

He turns to me. He is solemn. 'It is settled, Memsahib. Wrack will lose.'

I look up from the plaiting of Wise Child's mane, and smile.

'There are times, Ruta, when you sound like Kibii.'

With hesitance my smile is returned. Ruta is thoughtful, but unchastened. 'No, Memsahib—it is only that I have the power to make truths of my beliefs. It is a thing only a Murani can do.'

We are in our stable at the race-track. Within two hours the Leger will be run. While Ruta grooms, I plait the silky mane and the blacksmith spreads out his tools to put on Wise Child's aluminum racing plates. The filly stands quiet as a nodding kitten, but she is not asleep. She knows. She is thinking. Per-haps she is wondering, as I am, about those weakened tendons. She cannot feel them; it is not a matter of pain. It is only a question of how long they will take the strain of speed, the piston-pounding of hooves against the hard track, the long way from that excited start to that distant finish.

She straightens at the touch of the blacksmith's hand, then yields a foot with graceful resignation. She will do whatever is asked of her, as she always has done. She turns her head, nudging me, speaking to me—do not worry; I will run. As long as these legs will bear me up, I will run. But have we long to wait?

Not long, Wise Child, not very long.

When the blacksmith is finished, I leave the stable, and, for a few min-utes, inspect the course again—as if I had not already done it a dozen time. Other trainers, and owners, stand alone or in pairs about the paddock gates or lean on the white rails that enclose the oval track. Syces are busy, a jockey wearing the colours of Lady MacMillan's stable scurries through the bustle—an important, a resplendent midget. Bookmakers tread on each other's toes, on mine, on anybody's, or stand flat-footed scowling at scraps of paper clutched like passports to El Dorado.

A cloud of people, growing darker, creeps over the course, across the grandstands, muffling in its billows the martial thunder of the K.A.R. Band.

To the north looms Mount Kenya, throne of the Kikuyu God, jew-elled in sunlight, cushioned in the ermine of lasting snow. And, to the north-east, lying lower, like a couch of royal purple awaiting the leisure of this same prodigious God, spread the Aberdares. Under the shadow of such sovereign furnishings sprawl the ignoble stamping grounds of little people—the Indian Bazaar, the Somali Village, Nairobi itself in its microcosmic majesty. And the in-habitants of these, coloured as variously as unsorted beads, stream through the open gates of the race-course, paying for passage, eager for pleasure.

I have wondered sometimes if it is the beauty of a running-horse that brings so many people of so many kinds to such a makeshift amphitheatre as this is, or if it is the magnetism of a crowd, or if it is only the banal hope of making an easy shilling? Perhaps it is none of these. Perhaps it is the unrecog-nized expectation of holding for an instant what primordial sensations can be born again in the free strength of flashing flanks and driving hooves beating a challenge against the ground.

A keeper of an Indian duka—a Government clerk—a Lord Delamere—an Eric Gooch, all cogs of a kind, in a life of a kind, have made for themselves here, and everywhere, places where they can sit with folded arms and pay regular tribute to an animal so humble that he can be bought for a banknote.

Yet I wonder if he is ever bought? I wonder if the spirit of Camciscan, the sturdy integrity of Pegasus, the wise and courageous heart of Wise Child can ever be bought?

Is this too much to say of horses?

I remember the things they did; I remember this Saint Leger.

In the large talk of Continental sweepstakes, it is a trivial thing. It is not trivial to Wrack, to Wise Child, to the eight other horses who will leave the starting post; it is not trivial to me as I make the final preparations.

I feel the filly's legs, a little puffy, but not feverish. I kneel down and strap the tendon boots on them, firmly, carefully. I slip on the light racing bridle with my blue-and-gold colours striping the forehead band; I put the martingale over her head, onto her neck.

Arab Ruta fixes the protective pad on her withers, the number cloth over that, and then the saddle. At last I tighten the girths. We do not talk very much. It is only a matter of minutes before the bell will ring calling the horses to the paddock.

Sonny Bumpus has had his instructions. The lean, dark-haired boy has listened earnestly to every word. He is a grand horseman, honest as daylight.

I have explained the strategy over and over: 'Lie two or three lengths behind Wrack for the first couple of furlongs—until the filly gets warmed up. Steady her round the first bend; if her legs are still standing after that, let her go on the far stretch. Get the lead—keep it. She's willing and fast. She'll stay forever. If Wrack challenges, don't worry—so long as her legs can take the drive she'll never quit. If they fail—well—it won't be your fault, but whatever happens don't use your whip. If you do, she'll stop in her tracks.'

That's all. That's all there can be. A bell rings and I nod to Ruta. He takes Wise Child's reins in his hands and leads her slowly toward the paddock. The small fleck of sweat on her flanks is the only indication that she shares with us our anxiety, our unmentioned fears, and our quiet hopes.

It is only coincidence that in the paddock she falls in line behind Wrack, giving me a chance to compare them closely. I do not even bother about the others—Lady MacMillan's entries, one of Delamere's, a couple entered by Spencer Tryon, one of the best of trainers. They are all good horses, but I admit none as a threat. Wise Child has but two threats—Wrack, and her own weak tendons.

Wrack is triumphant in advance of victory. He is a beautiful colt, sleek as speed itself, dancing like a boxer on quick, eager feet, flaunting his bright body in front of the steady and demure Wise Child. I look at him and take credit for that impressive form, but allow myself the comfort of small malice at the sight of too much sweat streaming from his chestnut coat—a coat that looks as if it might be otherwise a bit too dry under the touch of experienced fingers. Has Wrack been overtrained since he left me? Has someone been too anxious? Or am I smothering reason with a wish ...

I recognize Wrack's owner a few yards down the rail—at the elbow of the colt's new trainer. We nod to each other all around, with about the same warmth one might expect of so many robots. I can't help it. I'll be doubly damned if I will try to help it.

Eric Gooch touches my shoulder. 'I couldn't resist,' he says; 'the filly looks so good I've placed a bet on her for myself—and another for you. I won't have to mortgage the old homestead if she loses, but we'll both be a little richer if she wins. Will she?'

'Her legs are weak as oat straws, but she'll try.'

'Wrack's the horse!' A dogmatic gentleman next to me hurries off to place his bet on Wrack. I wince a little, but the man's no fool.

Comments are being made on the splendid condition of Wise Child, but the filly is as deaf to flattery as a hitching post. She's deaf to everything. She circles round the paddock before the critical gaze of five hundred pairs of eyes. She moves modestly, even shyly, as if her being there at all is a matter she can only hope will be regarded as an excusable error.

Suddenly the crowd mumbles and shifts, the paddock opening is cleared, and the lead horse—a black stallion—prances in pompous style toward the track. In a few minutes it will all be over.

Eric and I hurry through the grandstand into Delamere's box. We wait; we watch; we brace ourselves against the wooden ledge.

The horses canter briskly past the stands. Wise Child, with Sonny riding feather light, trips like a shy schoolgirl behind the others. She is without ego, but she can afford vanity. There's not a prettier one in the field—nor one more thoughtful. I strain forward, trying foolishly to make her aware of me, to make her feel somehow that the burden of her secret is a little shared—the secret of those smartly bound legs that may have to yield so soon.

'She's in wonderful shape!'

Eric is radiant, but there's no answer from me. I unbuckle my binocular case and find that my hands are shaking. She won't win; she can't win. I know Wrack's form. I try to be casual, nodding to my friends, fumbling my program as if I could really read it. But the pages are blank. I read nothing. I stand staring down at the little group of horses with humourless anxiety, not as if this were just a race held under the African sun in a noisy settlement between Lake Victoria and the Indian Ocean, but as if this were the greatest race of all time, held on the greatest course, with the world looking over my shoulder.

Incongruously the band blares out the nerve-tightening notes of 'Mandalay' and some of the crowd beat the floor boards in heavy time. I wish the band would stop—and I love bands. I wish people would stop humming that dreary tune—and I love the tune. I can see perfectly well without glasses, but I lift the binoculars to my eyes and watch.

They're at the post—some of them eager, some of them stubborn, some of them not quite sure. Atop their gleaming backs the jockeys look like gaudy baubles, secured with strings. They bob up and down, they rise, lean forward, then settle again. A horse rears, or whirls, striking plumes of dust from the track until the bright marionette he carries is swallowed in it, but appears again, transformed now—stubbornly human now, controlling, guiding, watching.

I find Wrack. Look at Wrack! He's fighting to run, dying to run. As always, he's impatient with delay. Arrogant devil—he wants it over with; it's his race and he wants to hammer it into our heads once and for all. Why the ceremony? Why the suspense? Let's run! He's doing a pirouette; he'll plunge if his boy can't hold him. Easy Wrack—quiet, you elegant fool!

The starter is ready, the crowd is ready, Eric and I are ready. The band has stopped and the grandstand is a tabernacle of silence. This is the moment— this should be the moment. Steady, Sonny—the end may hang on the beginning, you know. Steady, Wise Child. All right. Everybody on their feet; everybody crane their necks.

Beautiful line-up; their noses are even as buttons on a tape. Watch the flag. Watch . . .

No! False start. Wrack, you idiot; I'd hammer that out of you. I had it out of you once. You can't start that way; you've got to be calm. Don't you remember? You've got to . . .

'Be calm,' says Eric, 'you're trembling.'

So I am. Not quite like a leaf, but anyway like a branch. I don't see how I can help it much, but I turn to Eric and smile vacuously as if somebody just past eighty had asked me to dance.

When I turn again, they're off with Wrack in the lead. That's fine. That's what I expected. It's what the crowd expected too. Five thousand voices, each like a pipe in an immense, discordant organ, swell and roll over the single, valiant note of the trumpeter. They roll over me, but they sound like a whisper—a bit hoarse, but still like a whisper. I have stopped trembling, almost breathing, I think. I am calm now—wholly composed. They're off, they're on their way, swinging down the long course, leaving behind their heels a ripple of thunder.

How can I compare a race like this to music? Or how can I not? Will some perfectionist snug in the arms of his chair under the marble eyes of Beethoven shudder at the thought? I suppose so, but if there's a fledgling juggler of notes and cadences, less loyal to the stolid past, who seeks a new theme for at least a rhapsody, he may buy a ticket at any gate and see how they run. He will do what I cannot. He will transpose and change and re-create the sound of hooves that pelt like rain, or come like a rolling storm, or taper like the rataplan of fading tympani. He will find instruments to fit the bellow of a crowd and notes to voice its silence; he will find rhythm in disorder, and build a crescendo from a sigh. He will find a place for heroic measures if he watches well, and build his climax to a wild beat and weave the music of excitement in his overtones.

A race is not a simple thing. This one is not. There are not just ten horses down there, galloping as fast as they can. Skill and reason and chance run with them. Courage runs with them—and strategy.

You do not watch a race; you read it. There is cause in every flux and change—jockeys have ability or they haven't; they bungle or they don't. A horse has a heart of he lacks it.

Questions must be answered before the rap of one hoof follows another—when to hold back, when to coax, when to manoeuvre. More speed? All right, but will he last?

Who can tell? A good boy—a sound judge of speed can tell. Slow pace, medium pace, fast pace—which is it? Don't let a second-rater snatch the race! Sonny shouldn't; he's sensitive as a stop-watch. But he might.

What's that behind—trick or challenge? Don't be fooled, don't be rattled, don't be hurried. Mile and three-quarters, you know—with ten in the field, and every one a winner until you prove he's not. There's time, there's time! There's too much time—time for errors, time for a lead to be stolen, time for strength and breath to vanish, time to lose, with the staccato insistence of forty hooves telling you so. Eyes open—watch the score!

Wrack's first, then the black stallion pulling hard. A brown horse with more style than speed clings to a precarious third. It's Wise Child at his flank, on the rails. She's smooth. She's leopard smooth.

'God, she's going well!' Eric yells it, and I smile. 'Be calm—you're trembling.'

He isn't, perhaps, but he's hopping up and down as if he'd won the race, and he hasn't. He hasn't won anything yet. Tendons. Tendons—remember the tendons! Of course she's going well, but . . .

'Come on, Wrack!'

Support for the enemy, unidentified. I snort and mumble in my mind. Silly man, don't yell—watch. They're in the far stretch now. My jockey's no fool—Sonny's no fool. See that? See Wise Child easing up, gliding up? Where's your Wrack now? Don't yell—watch. She's catching him, isn't she? She's closing in, isn't she?

She is; she does. The crowd stirs, forgetting bets, and roars for blood. They get it too. Wrack is a picture of driving power—Wise Child a study in coordination of muscle and bone and nerve. She's fast, she's smooth. She's smooth as a blade. She cuts the daylight between Wrack and herself to a hand's breadth—to a hair's breadth—to nothing.

'Come on, Wrack!'

A diehard, eh? All right, roar again—howl again, but bet again if you can!

The filly streaks past the colt like a dust devil past a stone, like a cheetah past a hound. Poor Wrack. It will break his heart.

But it doesn't—not Wrack's heart! His head is up a little and I know he's giving all he has, but he gives more. He's a stallion, and the male ego kindles a courage that smothers the pain of his burning muscles. He forgets himself, his jockey, everything but his goal. He lowers his head and thunders after the filly.

Without seeing, I know that Eric gives me a quick glance, but I cannot return it. I can only watch the battle. I am not yet so callous that the gallantry of Wrack seems less than magnificent.

Gallop, Wrack!—faster than you can, harder than you can. My own Wrack—my stubborn Wrack—six lengths behind.

But for how long? Wise Child's still against the rails—a small shadow against the rails, moving like a shadow, swift as a shadow—determined, quiet, steady. My glasses are on her. Thousands of eyes are on her when she sways.

She sways, and the groan from the crowd absorbs my own. The filly swings from the rails and falters. Her legs are going, her speed is going, her race is going!

Wrack's jockey sees it. Wrack sees it. The whip smarts against his quarters, but he needs no whip. He closes fast, narrowing the distance—length by length.

'Come on, Wrack!' The cry is almost barbaric now, and it comes from a hundred places.

Scream—yell! Cheer him on! Can't you see her legs are going? Can't you see she's running only on her heart? Let him have the race—let him win. Don't push her, Sonny. Don't touch her, Sonny . . .

'Eric . . .'

But he's gone. He's jumped over the box and run down to the rails. For myself, I can't move. I exist in a cauldron of screams and cheers and waving arms. Wrack and the filly are down the last stretch now, and he's on her flank, overtaking her, passing her, shaming her—while she breaks.

My glasses dangle on their strap. I bend over the edge of the box, clamping my fingers on the wooden ledge. I can't shout, or think. I know this is only a horse-race. I know that tomorrow will be the same as yesterday, whoever loses. I know the world won't turn a hair, whoever wins—but it seems so hard to believe.

I suppose for an instant I'm in a trance. My eyes see everything, but register nothing. Not a noise, but the sudden hush of the crowd jars me to consciousness again. How long is an instant? Could it be long enough for this?

I see it happen—clearly, sharply, as a camera must see things happen. I am as cold and as bloodless As rigid too, I think.

I see Wise Child falter once more, and then straighten. I see her transformed from the shadow she was to a small, swift flame of valour that throws my doubt in my teeth. I see her scorn the threat of Wrack and cram the cheers for his supporters back in their throats. I see her sweep the final furlong on swollen legs, forging ahead, feeding him the dust of her hooves.

And I hear the crowd find its voice again, hurling her past the winning post in a towering roar of tribute.

And then it's over. Then it's silent, as if somebody closed the door on Babel.

I feel my way down to the unsaddling enclosure. A grey mass of people clings to the rails—a foggy, but articulate jungle of arms, heads, and shoulders surrounding the winner—chanting, mumbling, shifting. They stare, but I think they see nothing. They see only a bay filly, standing quietly with quiet eyes—and that is nothing. That is ordinary; it can be seen anywhere—a bay filly that won a race.

The crowd dwindles as I talk to Eric, to Sonny, to Arab Ruta, and stroke the still sweating neck of Wise Child. The movement of my hand is mechanical, almost senseless.

'She didn't just win,' Eric says; 'she broke the Leger record.'

I nod without saying anything, and Eric looks at me with kindly impatience.

Weighing out of the jockeys is finished; everything is over and the last notes of the band have whimpered into silence. All the people press toward the gates, the emblems of their holiday litter the course, or scamper in a listless dance before the wind. Half the grandstand lies in a shadow, and the other half is lit with the sun. It is like a pod emptied of its seeds. Eric takes me by the arm and we jostle toward the exit with the rest.

'She broke the record—and with those legs!' says Eric.

'I know. You told me.'

'So I did.' He walks along, scuffing the ground, and scratches his chin in a masculine effort not to look sentimental—a futile effort, but at least he can inject a note of gruffness into his voice.

'Maybe it's silly,' he says, 'but I know you'll agree that no matter how much money we could make with Wise Child, she deserves never to race again.'

And she never does.

Things I Have Learned Playing
Poker on the Hill

BY DAVID MAMET

Gambling types tend to believe, at some level, that their fortunes at the table are connected to forces of luck or "fate" outside of themselves. For some, to win is to feel smiled on by fortune, while to lose is to feel metaphysically afflicted. In other words, while gambling is logically a thing of edges and percentages, few gamblers accept the idea of outcomes as purely mathematical. This poetic aspect of the gambler's outlook has venerable roots. Within the Judeo-Christian tradition, for instance, gambling began as a way of knowing God's will, as "sortilege" or divination by lots.

The idea was that when critical decisions had to be made that couldn't be trusted to logic, chance events would absolve humans of responsibility, letting "fate" decide. Thus starving castaways agree to draw lots, passing the choice of menu to the powers that be. The most famous fictional version of this kind of "gambling" is Shirley Jackson's "The Lottery," in which a community chooses its sacrifice through a lottery, the "winner" of which is stoned to death by the vicious town. This sense of intervention by a higher power is observable at gambling tables in unorthodox rituals.

In the short essay that follows, playwright David Mamet philosophizes about how the interaction of chance and what gamblers interpret as "fate" enables insights into character. In another poker essay, "Black as the Ace of Spades," Mamet writes:

> The game is not about money. The game is about love, and divine intervention. The money is a propitiatory gift to the Gods. It is the equivalent of Fasting and Prayer: it is to gain God's attention, and to put the supplicant in the properly humbled frame of mind to receive any information which might be coming.

♣ ♦ ♥ ♠

I n twenty years of playing poker, I have seen very few poor losers.

Poker is a game of skill and chance. Playing poker is also a masculine ritual, and, most times, losers feel either sufficiently chagrined or sufficiently reflective to retire, if not with grace, at least with alacrity.

I have seen many poor winners. Most are eventually brought back to reality. The game itself will reveal to them that they are the victim of an essential error: they have attributed their success to divine intervention.

The poor winner is celebrating either God's good sense in sending him down lucky cards, or God's wisdom in making him, the lucky winner, technically superior to the others at the table. In the first case, the cards will eventually begin to even out and the player will lose; in the second case, both the Deity and the players will tire of being patronized. The Deity will respond how he may, but the players will either drop out of the game or improve. In either case the poor winner will lose, and pride, once again, will go before a fall.

Speaking of luck: is there such a thing as luck? Yes. There is such a thing as luck. There is such a thing as a *run of luck*. This is an instructive insight I have gained from poker—that all things have a rhythm, even the most seemingly inanimate of statistics.

Any mathematician will tell you that the cards at the poker table are distributed randomly, that we remember the remarkable and forget the mundane, and that "luck" is an illusion.

Any poker player knows—to the contrary—that there are phenomenal runs of luck which defy any mathematical explanation—there are periods in which one cannot catch a hand, and periods in which one cannot *not* catch a hand, and that there *is* such a thing as absolute premonition of cards: the rock-bottom *surety* of what will happen next. These things happen in contravention of scientific wisdom and common sense. The poker player learns that sometimes both science and common sense are wrong; that the bumblebee *can* fly; that, perhaps, one should never trust an expert; that there are more things in heaven and earth than are dreamt of by those with an academic bent.

It is comforting to know that luck exists, that there is a time to push your luck and a time to gracefully retire, that all roads have a turning.

What do you do when you are pushing your luck beyond its limits? You must behave like a good philosopher and ask what axiom you must infer that you are acting under. Having determined that, you ask if this axiom, in the long run, will leave you a winner. (You are drawing to a flush. You have a 1-in-4½ chance. The pot is offering you money odds of 5 to 1. It seems a close thing, but if you did it all day, you must receive a 10 percent return.)

If the axiom which you are acting under is not designed to make you money, you may find that your real objective at the game is something else: you may be trying to prove yourself beloved of God.

You then must ask yourself if—financially and emotionally—you can afford the potential rejection. For the first will certainly and the second will most probably ensue.

Poker is boring. If you sit down at the table to experience excitement, you will consciously and subconsciously do those things to make the game exciting; you will take long-odds chances and you will create emergencies. They will lose you money. If your aim, on the other hand, is to win money, you will watch the game and wait for the good cards, and play the odds-on chance, and, in the long run, you must be a winner. And when you do *not* win, you can still go home without mumbling, for, as Woodrow Wilson said: "I would rather lose in a cause which will eventually prevail than triumph in a cause doomed to failure." (I'll bet that most of you didn't even know he was a poker player.)

Playing poker you must treat each hand, as Epictetus says, as a visit to the Olympic Games, each hand offering you the chance to excel in your particular event—betting, checking, managing your money, observing the players, and, most often, waiting.

The poker players I admire most are indeed like that wise old owl who sat on the oak and who kept his mouth shut and his eye on the action.

As for observation, Confucius said man cannot hide himself—look what he smiles at, look what he frowns at. The inability to hide is especially true of men under pressure, which is to say, gamblers. This is another reason for stoic and correct play.

When you are proud of having made the correct decision (that is, the decision which, in the long run, *must* eventually make you a winner), you are inclined to look forward to the results of that decision with some degree of impassivity. When you are so resolved, you become less fearful and more calm. You are less interested in yourself and more naturally interested in the other players: now *they* begin to reveal themselves. Is their nervousness feigned? Is their hand made already? Are they bluffing? These elections are impossible to make when you are afraid, but become easier the more content you are with your own actions. And, yes, sometimes you lose, but differences of opinion make both horse races and religious intolerance, and if you don't like to take a sporting chance, you don't have to play poker.

Poker will also reveal to the frank observer something else of import—it will teach him about his own nature.

Many bad players will not improve because they cannot bear self-knowledge. Finally, they cannot bear the notion that everything they do is done for a reason. The bad player will not deign to determine what he thinks by watching what he does. To do so might, and frequently would, reveal a need to be abused (in calling what must be a superior hand); a need to be loved (in staying for "that one magic card"); a need to have Daddy relent (in trying to bluff out the obvious best hand); et cetera.

It is painful to observe this sort of thing about ourself. Many times we'd rather suffer on than fix it. It's not easy to face that, rather than playing cards in spite of our losses, we are playing cards because of them.

But poker is a game played among folks made equal by their money. Each player uses it to buy his time at the table, and, while there, is entitled to whatever kind and length of enjoyment that money will buy.

The pain of losing is diverting. So is the thrill of winning. Winning, however, is lonelier, as those you've taken money from are not likely to commiserate with you. Winning takes some getting used to.

Many of us, and most of us from time to time, try to escape a blunt fact which may not tally with our self-image. When we are depressed, we re-create the world around us to rationalize our mood. We are then likely to overlook or misinterpret happy circumstances. At the poker table, this can be expensive, for opportunity may knock, but it seldom nags. Which brings us to a crass thought many genteel players cannot grasp: poker is about money.

The ability of a poker player is judged solely by the difference between his stack when he sat down and his stack when he got up. The point is not to win the most hands, the point is not even to win in the most games. The point is to *win the most money*. This probably means playing less hands than the guy who has just come for the action; it means not giving your fellow players a break because you value their feelings; it means not giving some back at the end of the night because you feel embarrassed by winning; it means taking those steps and creating those habits of thought and action which, in the long run, must prevail.

The long run for me—to date—has been a period of twenty years.

One day in college I promoted myself from the dormitory game to the *big* poker game. Up on the Hill in town.

After graduation I would, occasionally, come back to the area to visit. I told myself my visits were to renew friendships, to use the library, to see the leaves. But I was really coming back to play in the Hill game.

Last September one of the players pointed out that five of us at the table that night had been doing this for two decades.

As a group, we have all improved. Some of us have improved drastically. As the facts, the statistics, the tactics are known to all, and as we are men of equal intelligence, that improvement can be due to only one thing: to character, which, as I *finally* begin to improve a bit myself, I see that the game of poker is all about.

Five-Card Draw, Jacks or Better

BY HERBERT O. YARDLEY

In Yardley's poker classic, *The Education of a Poker Player*, an education in cards is both rite-of-passage and an education for life. To learn poker for Yardley is to learn about personality, and to develop a range of knowledges and skills—as well as a control over one's face—that will stand one well in a variety of contexts. Many businessmen and politicians—some professed readers of Yardley—have received crucial early training in their local chapters of Monty's poker room, which functions something like Melville described a whaleship—as his "Harvard and Yale College." About Yardley's book, British scholar and poker writer A. Alvarez wrote, "When I first picked it up I was ignorant not only in the ways of poker. I also had the deep ignorance which goes with excessive education." In an age of poker printouts and computer analysis, Yardley's entertaining, earthy book remains one of the best manuals for lessening poker ignorance. Each dramatic scene is followed with a technical analysis of the hands described in the story that goes with it, making the book as valuable for its practical poker lessons as it is entertaining. In the first selection below, Yardley—who later served in the East as a newsman and cryptologist—describes how, through breaking the code of card-room owner Monty's play, he acquired a mentor. Monty is a fabulous, bruising raconteur, with a code of honor that manages to remain a code of honor at the same time that it almost invariably leads to his own enrichment. In the second selection, we see a dramatic instance of Monty's ability to recognize the main chance in what is one of the more memorable showdown hands in the annals of poker.

Out of seven saloons which ran poker games, Monty's Place was the only clean one. The poker room itself was at the rear of the saloon and was about twenty feet square with two barred windows high above the ground and an iron wood stove at the end kept polished by the town idiot, called Dummy. The windows had dark, drawn curtains. The walls were unplastered brick, the woodwork painted white, and the floor scrubbed. In the center was a large round table covered with green billiard cloth and surrounded by seven cane chairs. Others, for loafers and kibitzers, were scattered here and there or were grouped around the stove when the weather was cold. The table was lighted by a single bulb, extended to the center by a cord from the ceiling and shaded against the eyes of the players. At the side of each chair was a spittoon; others were at convenient spots.

While the game was in progress, the door was barred with the usual sliding window and guarded by Runt, the bouncer, so named because of his size. Strangers were welcome after being frisked for weapons by Runt.

Monty had trouble with players looking at the discards after they were tossed face down to the player to the left of the dealer, whose chore it was to gather them up and shuffle after the show-down was over. Finally Monty put up a sign for everyone to see upon entering the poker room. It read:

Please Don't

FRIG

with the Discards

Penalty $20

Then under this sign he had impishly written,

Vulgar Language Forbidden

MONTY'S CLUB

Beneath the poster he had signed his own name with a flourish,

James Montgomery.

When I began to play poker I guessed Monty to be around thirty-five. He could have posed as Gentleman Jim Corbett in height, weight and looks, and judging from occasional fights that he got into to keep the peace, he was almost as good with his fists. Rumor had it that he had killed a man in New York who was fooling around with his wife. No one knew why he picked our town to settle in, though it was wealthy enough to satiate even a gambler's greed. He was definitely a man's man, but from the side glances he received in the streets from young girls and married women, he was not without attraction to them, though it might have been that they attached a certain glamour to him because he was a successful gambler who had killed a man.

My mother died when I was sixteen years old, and thereafter I did pretty much as I pleased. I inherited two hundred dollars from her and with this, together with the money I had saved from odd jobs, I made my first venture at poker. The take-out was twenty dollars in chips but a player could play open; that is, he could play with the twenty dollars in chips plus whatever he had in his pocket. Aside from cash in the pocket, many played open by backing their play with real property—cattle, farms, grain and the like. The player was never asked how much he played open, but if he was bet more than the chips he had in front of him, he was required to put up the difference in acceptable IOU's, and if he didn't have all the difference he played for the pot while the other players, if they wished to continue the betting, bet on the side. After a man went broke he was permitted to play one round without any money and if he won the antes he had another start.

Three games were played at Monty's—stud, draw and deuces wild. In the first the dealer anted two dollars. In draw and deuces each player anted fifty cents. Not more than seven were permitted to play, because in draw and deuces so many stayed that the game was slowed up by shuffling the discards to fill out the draw, and a slow game works against the house, which in this case took a fifty-cent cut per game.

The first night I played I think my heart never left my mouth—in any case it all seemed like a bad dream the next morning. I didn't lose much, because to my way of thinking I played conservatively—but the going was rough. It is one thing to face eleven football opponents when you have ten men with you, but to face six hungry wolves alone is something else indeed.

The next few days I watched the game to get over my fear, then I tried it again. And I lost. The alternate observation and play went on until I was down to my last fifty dollars. Then I made a discovery. It all happened one night when I suddenly woke up in a sweat. I had been playing cards in my nightmares but for the moment couldn't recover the details.

I could see Monty, his face clouded in anger over some argument by the players, yelling, "Deal! Goddammit, deal!" Then he pounded his right fist on the table.

His *right* fist! That rang a bell. But what bell? Then quickly I knew. Monty was left-handed. When excited he pounded on the table with his *right* fist. Yes, I must be right. At times-it must have been because of tension—he bet with his *right* hand. Of course. When he was bluffing, he shifted his cards from the right hand to the left and bet with the right. I could see him now. When he bet he came charging like a wild buffalo. He grabbed just the right amount of chips from his stack, and *bang!*—he bet. If his opponent wasn't scared to death, he was at least confused. Monty had come at me like that every night I had played. No wonder I was afraid. I knew every move he made now. And why he made each move. Now I could see that he was dealing every time he made this fierce move at me. And every time he made this particular play he was dealing draw.

What a sucker I had been! It was too late to do anything about what was done but I might just as well go to see if they were still playing, for I couldn't sleep. I tossed in bed for an hour or so and finally put on my clothes and got my remaining cash from its hiding place and went to the back of Monty's Place. The windows were shaded but I could see a fringe of light around the drawn curtains and knew that a game was still in progress.

I pounded on the back door and was let in by Runt. When I entered the poker room the game was at full tilt, with a half dozen loafers either drunk or asleep in the chairs. By good luck there was a vacancy at the table—not exactly a vacancy, but one of the house men was playing and at the direction of Monty he was ordered to give up his seat to me—a live fish. I bought $50 in chips, leaving myself only a few dollars in cash.

When it came time for Monty to deal he took out the joker and said, "This is straight draw," which at that time meant what is now known as jacks or better. This means that the pot cannot be opened unless the opener has at least two jacks. The joker was restored to the deck if they played deuces wild.

Monty dealt skillfully, a diamond as large as his thumbnail on his little finger sparkling in the artificial light.

I had deduced Monty's trick. Someone else on whom Monty had played his trick too often opened the pot, so Monty didn't stay. On his third deal I opened for $5, the usual opening, on a pair of aces. I was sitting just to his right. He raised me $15. I stayed and drew three cards.

Monty's poker face turned into a wicked smile. He said, "I play these." I didn't help the aces. I knew what was coming but I didn't know how much he would bet. He glanced at my chips, calculating how much I had left.

Wham! His right fist hit the center of the table. He had bet $30. I pretended to hesitate, then nervously put down my hand and counted out $30, about all I had.

"I call," I said and spread my hand face up, showing two aces. Monty could not conceal a look of utter disbelief. "Well, I'll be a son-of-a-bitch," he said and threw his hand face down in the discards. "Didn't you know I stood pat?" he said in disgust. "How can you call a pat hand on two aces?"

I grinned at him. "You wiggled your ears," I said.

"Fresh kid," he grumbled. "Beats anything I ever saw."

Someone opened the window to let out the smoke. It was daylight. I ought to get some sleep before school, I thought. But the time went on. I had confidence now and was winning a bit.

It must have been after eight in the morning when a fat little drummer called Jake Moses came in. He had just got off the morning train.

"Hello, sucker," Monty greeted him. "Take a seat." Jake smiled back good-naturedly.

There was another vacant chair so I got up from Monty's side and took the other seat. It caused no comment, for players are always changing places at the least opportunity, especially when losing. I knew Monty was going to pick on the drummer and I wanted to be in a strategic position to win when he did.

Round after round passed before my opportunity came. I was sitting to Monty's left, the sucker to be fleeced to his right. "Let's play draw," said Monty and took out the joker and dealt.

I passed. The next four players passed, making five in all. The drummer, the sixth player, opened with a $5 bet. Monty came out roaring with a $15 raise. I called. Monty showed no signs of annoyance though I know he hadn't planned for more than one player to draw against him. The drummer called, which was according to Monty's plan.

I drew one card. "Flushing, kid?" Monty said pleasantly.

I didn't answer. I never talked while playing poker except to announce my bet and the showdown. I was afraid that my voice would crack; in this case, I was sure it would if I opened my mouth.

The drummer took three cards.

Monty said, "I play these," meaning he was standing pat.

The drummer, after a peek at his cards, checked.

Without a moment's hesitation Monty bet $50—but not as boldly, I thought, as before. It was obvious to him that I had backed in the pot and was drawing to a straight or a flush. He was certainly taking me for a sucker. I had learned early never to risk money drawing one card to a straight or a flush unless there was in the pot at least five times the amount of the bet.

When Monty bet $50 I raised him $100. I didn't have a thing but I was playing it safe, I thought, with Monty betting right-handed. I felt sure he was standing pat on a bust. I wasn't concerned too much about the drummer who had checked. Even if he had helped his hand, he would hesitate to call, with me taking one card and raising.

The drummer showed his openers of two kings and folded.

Monty shook his head sadly. "You lucky little bastard," he said, and threw in his hand. "Imagine drawing one card with all that money at stake."

I tossed my hand in the discards and drew in the pot with trembling hands. I got up and cashed in. I had more than my original stake of $250.

I was shivering with excitement, and I huddled around the fire which Dummy had lighted in the early hours as if the warmth of the stove would stop the shivers. It was too late to go to school so I sat down to watch the play. I had fallen asleep when I heard Monty's fist bang the table. Here he goes again, I thought, but when I looked, I saw him using his left hand to bet. He wasn't bluffing this time, I reflected.

As the play was recaptured later, Monty had used the same tactics on the drummer he had tried on me and then later on both me and the drummer—raising and standing pat. But now the circumstances were different. Monty was betting with his left hand.

It seems that the drummer had opened with the usual bet and Monty raised with the drummer staying and drawing three cards. Monty, as before, stood pat. The drummer made aces up and checked to trap Monty, for experience told him that Monty could not have a pat hand as often as he bet.

Much to my surprise Monty bet $500 on his pat hand.

"You can't have a pat hand all the time," the drummer said, grinning.

"You son-of-a-bitch, you'll never know unless you call," Monty cried back.

"I call," said the drummer. He was about out of chips.

"With what?" asked Monty.

"Ain't my credit good?"

"Not for five hundred."

"How much?"

Monty thought a moment. Then his face broke out in a mischievous grin. "How much are those ten trunks you carry around full of shoes worth?"

"Several thousand."

"Give me a bill of sale and I'll lend you five hundred. Deliver the trunks here and I'll let you redeem them when you fork up the five hundred."

"Jesus Christ, Monty, you're tough."

"I have to be," said Monty.

The drummer scribbled out a bill of sale which Monty handed to him, and threw it in the pot. He spread his hand. "Aces up," he said.

"Well, I'll be a son-of-a-bitch!" Monty laughed. "You mean you called a pat hand on aces up?"

"You can't bluff me. You don't have a pat hand."

"No, I don't," Monty said, spreading his hand. "I only have three tens."

You could have heard a pin drop as Monty raked in the pot. He had tricked the drummer by not drawing cards.

At last the drummer gathered his wits together. He said, "Now, Monty, I can't work without those trunks and you can't use all those shoes."

"That's a fact. But you can redeem them at any time by paying me five hundred."

"I can't write a check. My wife would know if I drew out five hundred from the bank."

"Then telegraph your manufacturer. You're a sucker for cards and must have got in trouble before. It's around ten o'clock. Telegraph your people and say you need five hundred."

The drummer looked dejected but followed Monty's advice. He had the money from Indianapolis by noon, and Monty released his trunks.

Right after this play the game broke up and Monty asked me to come to his study, which was next to the card room. When he turned on the study light a dark-blue rug was revealed covering the floor. In the center of the room was a flat-topped mahogany desk, and at the end, two deep chairs and a huge sofa covered in leather faced the fireplace. One entire wall was adorned with rows of books. The others were bare except for autographed pictures of Teddy Roosevelt, Jim Corbett and Diamond Jim Brady. He did not offer to tell me how he came into possession of them and I did not ask.

He fixed drinks from a private stock and bade me sit down.

"Kid," Monty said, "that was a smart call you made last night and even a smarter raise. Now I'm not dumb enough to believe you engineered those two plays just on your own judgment. I know I did something that tipped my hand. I don't ask what it was but I'll think twice before betting you again."

I was now at ease. I said, "I told you you wiggled your ears."

"That's good enough for me. How would you like to work for me? Loggy Flick, one of my housemen, is quitting. He's cost me too much money. He plays a poor game of poker and I think he steals from me. When he's running the game he cuts every pot fifty cents, which runs into about ten dollars an hour. He can easily steal two dollars an hour from me without my knowing it. After school and up to bedtime when I'm not playing I'd want you to cut the pots. You can play at the same time you cut."

Monty paused, and when I said nothing, continued. "I'll tell you what I'll do. I'll back you up to two hundred dollars and you give me one half of what you win. I'll stand the losses if any. You keep one half of the cut. Is that fair?"

"More than fair," I said. "But I couldn't let you back me unless I knew more about the game. I'll cut the pot for twenty-five per cent of the cut and will back myself if you will give me lessons in play. When you think I am good enough to risk your money I'll accept your offer."

"It's a deal, kid," he said, shaking hands.

"Monty, I want to tell you how I knew you were bluffing," I said.

"That's your secret, kid."

"No, I want to tell you. After all, if I'm an apt student we will be partners." I paused to frame my words. "Monty, you are left-handed and ordinarily hold your cards in your right hand and bet with your left. Under stress you switch your cards to your left hand and bet with your right. That's how I knew."

"Well, I'll be a son-of-a-bitch," he said, and got as red as a beet. "And you changed seats just to get on my left so that when I raised the shoe drummer you could back in and draw one card. You'll do. You make some bad plays but I can correct that. By the way, what did you have when you drew one card?"

"The same as you—nothing. That's the reason I had to raise."

"Well, I'll be a son-of-a-bitch!"

I was eating prairie chicken at ten cents a chicken at Monty's bar about ten days later when Jack came in to tell me that he wanted relief and that he had left a vacant seat.

"Is Monty playing?"

"Yes. It's eight o'clock now. I'll be back at 2 A.M."

I went in and sat down in the chair vacated by Jack. There were two new faces. I had seen the two hanging around the tent show where they featured such plays as *Ten Nights in a Barroom, Uncle Tom's Cabin, Dr. Jekyll and Mr. Hyde,* and the like.

"Kid, you know Tom Lawrence and Pete Hunter, leading man and producer," Monty said with a sweep of his hand.

I nodded the introduction. The handsome chap sitting at Monty's left I judged to be the leading man; the other, sitting next to the actor, looked for all the world like a producer. He was chewing at a dry cigar and he grinned constantly, showing yellow teeth filled with gold inlays which glistened in the lamplight.

I sat next, then Chic the chicken picker, Doc and then Bones Alverson, the farmer, his leatherlike face beaten from exposure. I knew he had lost most of his farm at poker. Rumor had it that he had hocked everything to Bert Willis, the land speculator, known to be a ruthless and shrewd operator.

I turned to Chic. He had several stacks in front of him. "You must have sold some more dead chickens," I said in a low voice. Chic was a notoriously poor poker player and when he wasn't taking live chickens to New York he picked them dry at the poultry house for three cents a head.

He gave me a sour look. "Keep your mouth shut, you little shrimp," he warned.

The game progressed as usual—some winning, some losing. I was trying to remember all that Monty had told me, and played carefully.

Monty looked bored. Doc Prittle nodded in his seat between deals, his head resting on his double chin. Bones Alverson was getting some good hands and was winning consistently. The actor and his backer seemed alert and were holding their own.

The game droned on. I got up and stretched my legs to relieve my nervousness. I don't know what it was but I had a feeling of impending tragedy. And it wasn't long in coming.

Doc Prittle was fumbling with the deck. He had put in the joker preparatory to dealing deuces wild and was awkwardly reshuffling the cards.

Monty watched him in disgust. "Deal, goddammit, Doc."

Startled, Doc yelled back, "Hold your horses," then, after taking his time, began to deal five-card draw deuces wild.

Bones, the farmer, skinned back his cards in his gnarled hands. I imagined I saw a flicker in his eyes. Anyway he made an unusual opening bet. He bet $50 right under the gun.

Monty, sitting next, studied Bones for a fleeting moment, then folded. He later told me he held a jack full.

The actor tossed his hand in the discards in disgust.

But his producer was grinning impishly. "I raise one hundred," he said and tossed in the chips.

I threw my hand in the discards, as did also Chic and Doc, the dealer. Looks like those two had all the wild cards, I reflected.

Bones pretended to study a moment, then counted out a big stack of chips, for he had been winning. "I up you five hundred," he said, his voice quivering.

Bones had a mouthful of tobacco juice and was watching the producer intently. I could see he was afraid to turn his head to spit. He made the motion to do so, but changed his mind and swallowed tobacco cud, juice and all. He choked a bit, and pulled out a red handkerchief and wiped his mouth.

Monty, seeing the play, cried the usual "I'll be a son-of-a-bitch."

Bones choked again. "Well," he said to the grinning producer, "what the hell you going to do?"

The producer took out a sheaf of hundred-dollar bills. "I'm just going to raise you five hundred."

"Raise you five hundred more," Bones quivered, "you city prick." He turned to Monty. "Put in one thousand, Monty," he said. Monty demurred. "You've never seen me welch on a bet," Bones pleaded.

"No, I never did," said Monty thoughtfully. "But you used to have a farm. Do you have one now?"

"I'll tell you the God's own truth, Monty," he said. "I've got the farm, stock and implements plastered to Bert Willis for fifteen thousand. Bert offered me twenty thousand. So I have five thousand equity."

Monty shook his head sadly. "Bones, let me give you some friendly advice. Just call him. I'll lend you money for that."

"Call, hell!" exclaimed Bones. "This is a chance of a lifetime. Loan me the thousand. I want to raise the bastard."

"I can't understand you, Bones. You've lost three-fourths of your farm and now you want to bet the last fourth."

"Goddammit, yes. I might just as well be broke as to try to pay ten per cent interest on fifteen thousand to that goddamned bloodsucker."

"Jesus," said Monty. "I don't mind risking the thousand but—"

"You ain't risking nothing, goddammit. I've got him beat."

"All right. But just give me first chance to buy the farm if you do lose." Monty tossed two five-hundred-dollar bills in the pot and took Bones's IOU.

The producer had lost his grin. Even the unlighted cigar had disappeared somehow. He reached for his purse and spread five hundred-dollar bills and pushed them in the pot.

He said in a subdued voice. "There's my five hundred and I raise two thousand. I'll have to give you an IOU."

"You will in a pig's ass. Go get it."

"How can I? The banks are closed."

"You ain't got no two thousand in the bank. Put up or shut up," said Bones.

"Monty, will you take my IOU?" asked the producer.

"Let me tell you bastards something," Monty replied. "I'm not financing this poker game. I'm just playing in it. If I'd wanted to stay I'd have stayed and financed myself if I got in trouble. And another thing. You bastards slow up a game. I only get fifty cents cut. This one I should cut five hundred."

No one offered to agree to this but I had a sneaking feeling that Monty was going to profit in this transaction somehow.

The producer placed some chips on his cards resting on the table and got up and pulled along the actor with him. They went in the other end of the room and I couldn't hear what they said, but the actor was protesting and the producer was really telling it to him. Finally, they both sat down.

The producer addressed Monty. "You know my reputation. You know I own three other tent shows and I can tell you I don't owe a dime on them. My leading man here owns one-third of this show. I'd like to own that farm even if it is mortgaged."

"Well," said Monty, "what's your proposition?"

"This farmer gave you an IOU for one thousand. Put it in the pot and take out one thousand in cash. That makes you square. I'll make out a bill of sale for my show for two thousand, if this farmer will make out a bill of sale for his farm for three thousand. The extra thousand covers the money you take from the pot."

"Bones, do you understand the deal?" asked Monty.

"Is the show worth two thousand?"

"I'd like to own it for that."

"But I'm pledging three thousand and my equity is five thousand."

"You'll get the difference if you lose."

"Goddammit, I'm not going to lose. I'd like to own a show. More money in it than following a plow around a field, I reckon."

"It's your funeral," said Monty prophetically, and directed Runt to bring in bills of sale, pen and ink. When Monty looked over the papers he pointed out that the producer's bill of sale needed the actor's signature because of a one-third interest. He put Bones's IOU in the pot and took out a thousand according to the agreement.

"Just a minute, Monty. I didn't pledge my prize bull. Nobody's going to plaster him with a mortgage."

"He'll get plastered if you fill your hand," Monty laughed. "How many cards you want, Bones? You take cards first."

"I want one," Bones said and tossed his discard toward Doc.

Doc was so nervous he could scarcely get a card off the top of the deck. Monty didn't help much by yelling at him. Doc finally flicked a card face down toward Bones. It touched Bones's hand, bounced; then turned over, exposed. I looked at it horror-stricken, for I had said a little prayer for Bones.

It was the joker.

"I'm sorry, Bones," said Doc.

Bones opened his mouth as if to protest, but no sound came. He just sat there fascinated and stared at the joker who, I thought, stared impishly back at him. Then a deep pallor began to creep slowly over Bones's weather-beaten face.

"What'll I do, Monty? Can't Bones take the joker?"

"No. If you'd read the rules you'd know he can't. They're all printed and framed on the wall behind you. You deal whatever cards the producer wants to him, then Bones gets the next card. Tough luck, Bones."

The pallor had spread over Bones's face. His eyes looked glazed. Suddenly he fell over the table, clutching the cards in his heavy fist.

At this Doc jumped up, handing me the deck. He examined Bones for several seconds. At last he said, "He's dead, boys."

An air of disbelief settled over the players. Even Monty was speechless for the moment, then, "You're sure, Doc?" he asked.

"Yes, I'm sure. His heart stopped. Too much excitement. I guess I killed him."

The producer made a pass at the pot, starting to rake it in. Monty's fist reached out and nearly broke the showman's wrist. "Hands off!" Monty snarled.

"It's mine," protested the producer.

"Not yet, my friend," Monty said softly. "I think he had you beat. He didn't need the joker."

"Well, I don't think so, and I demand to draw to my hand," said the producer.

"Kid," asked Monty, "has the deck been disturbed?"

"No. Doc handed it to me."

"Well, I'm going to write a new rule that Hoyle didn't cover. If you fellows agree, I'll rule we let our producer draw to his hand, then take Bones's cards from his fist and add the next card to it." They all nodded agreement except the producer, who protested feebly.

"How many cards you want?" asked Monty.

"One," said the producer.

"Kid, give him a card."

The producer threw me the discard and I gave him one, face down.

By that time Doc had pried Bones's cards from his huge fist, so I slipped Doc a card to fill out the hand.

"Now wait a moment, boys," said Monty. "Who wants to bet on the winning hand?"

The actor was the only one to answer. "I've got five hundred that says my producer wins."

"Covered," said Monty, tossing the money on the table. The producer spread his hand. He held Q K K K 2. "Four Kings," said Monty.

Doc turned over Bones's cards one at a time, calling them out as he did so. "Ace, ace, ace, jack, deuce—four aces."

"You ran second," Monty said to the producer. "That's irony for you. A man dies holding the winning hand—" and he picked up the actor's bet. Then he began to rake in the pot. "I'll take this to Bones's widow. She'll probably grieve a couple of days, then be relieved that he's dead. At least he can't gamble the farm away now."

The producer said, "I'll redeem that bill of sale, Monty, when the banks open."

"You will like hell," said Monty. "I'll redeem it myself if the widow consents. I've always wanted to go into show business."

From Billy Phelan's Greatest Game

BY WILLIAM KENNEDY

The selection that follows is the opening scene of the second volume of William Kennedy's "Albany Cycle," the third of which, *Ironweed,* is one of my favorite contemporary novels. (Jack Nicholson, Meryl Streep, and Tom Waits starred in the film version.) A long-time resident and historian of Albany, New York, Kennedy masterfully captures the place of gambling in the texture or "mix" of a neighborhood. Finely tuned to the mystery and limits of talent, the relation of its expression to personality, and its effects in reputation-building within a community, Kennedy presents the manner in which his characters gamble as complex indexes into their ways of being in the world. Contests between gamblers in skill games can become charged matches of style, will, and personality—with much more at stake for the gamblers than the game. The live performance moment becomes one through which characters learn about themselves. Nested inside of the tense bowling match, with its swelling crowd of onlookers and side bettors, a private pursuit of excellence unfolds within Billy Phelan, who has been up to that point a "low-level maestro," "generalist," or "man in need of the sweetness of miscellany." His private drama against the limits of the game becomes an image of his larger potential, and raises the questions, "Is Billy Phelan ready for perfection? Can you handle it, kid? What will you do with it if you get it?"

M artin Daugherty, age fifty and now the scorekeeper, observed it all as Billy Phelan, working on a perfect game, walked with the arrogance of a young, untried eagle toward the ball return, scooped up his black, two-finger ball, tossed it like a juggler from right to left hand, then held it in his left palm, weightlessly. Billy rubbed his right palm and fingers on the hollow cone of chalk in the brass dish atop the ball rack, wiped off the excess with a pull-stroke of the towel. He faced the pins, eyed his spot down where the wood of the alley changed color, at a point seven boards in from the right edge. And then, looking to Martin like pure energy in shoes, he shuffled: left foot, right foot, left-right-left and slide, right hand pushing out, then back, like a pendulum, as he moved, wrist turning slightly at the back of the arc. His arm, pure control in shirtsleeves to Martin, swung forward, and the ball glided almost silently down the polished alley, rolled through the seventh board's darkness, curving minimally as it moved, curving more sharply as it neared the pins, and struck solidly between the headpin and the three pin, scattering all in a jamboree of spins and jigs.

"Attaway, Billy," said his backer, Morrie Berman, clapping twice. "Lotta mix, lotta mix."

"Ball is working all right," Billy said.

Billy stood long-legged and thin, waiting for Bugs, the cross-eyed pin-boy, to send back the ball. When it snapped up from underneath the curved wooden ball return, Billy lifted it off, faced the fresh setup on alley nine, shuffled, thrust, and threw yet another strike: eight in a row now.

Martin Daugherty noted the strike on the scoresheet, which showed no numbers, only the eight strike marks: bad luck to fill in the score while a man is still striking. Martin was already thinking of writing his next column about this game, provided Billy carried it off. He would point out how some men moved through the daily sludge of their lives and then, with a stroke, cut away the sludge and transformed themselves. Yet what they became was not the result of a sudden act, but the culmination of all they had ever done: a triumph for self-development, the end of something general, the beginning of something specific.

To Martin, Billy Phelan, on an early Thursday morning in late October, 1938, already seemed more specific than most men. Billy seemed fully defined at thirty-one (the age when Martin had been advised by his father that he was a failure).

Billy was not a half-bad bowler: 185 average in the K. of C. league, where Martin bowled with him Thursday nights. But he was not a serious match for Scotty Streck, who led the City League, the fastest league in town, with a 206 average. Scotty lived with his bowling ball as if it were a third testicle, and when he found Billy and Martin playing eight ball at a pool table in the Downtown Health and Amusement Club, the city's only twenty-four-hour gamester's palace, no women, no mixed leagues, please, beer on tap till 4:00 A.M., maybe 5:00, but no whiskey on premises, why then Scotty's question was: Wanna bowl some jackpots, Billy? Sure, with a twenty-pin spot, Billy said. Give you fifty-five for three games, offered the Scotcheroo. Not enough, but all right, said Billy, five bucks? Five bucks fine, said Scotty.

And so it was on, with the loser to pay for the bowling, twenty cents a game. Scotty's first game was 212. Billy turned in a sad 143, with five splits, too heavy on the headpin, putting him sixty-nine pins down, his spot eliminated.

Billy found the pocket in the second game and rolled 226. But Scotty had also discovered where the pocket lurked, and threw 236 to increase his lead to seventy-nine pins. Now in the eighth frame of the final game, the match was evening out, Scotty steady with spares and doubles, but his lead fading fast in front of Billy's homestretch run toward perfection.

Word of a possible 300 game with a bet on it drew the bar stragglers, the fag-end bowlers, the night manager, the all-night pinboys, even the sweeper, to alleys nine and ten in the cavernous old room, spectators at the wonder. No one spoke to Billy about the unbroken string of strikes, also bad luck. But it was legitimate to talk of the bet: two hundred dollars, between Morrie Berman and Charlie Boy McCall, the significance being in the sanctified presence of Charlie Boy, a soft, likeable kid gone to early bloat, but nevertheless the most powerful young man in town, son of the man who controlled all the gambling, all of it, in the city of Albany, and nephew of the two politicians who ran the city itself, all of it, and Albany County, all of that too: Irish-American potentates of the night and the day.

Martin knew all the McCall brothers, had gone to school with them, saw them grow up in the world and take power over it. They all, including young Charlie Boy, the only heir, still lived on Colonie Street in Arbor Hill, where Martin and his father used to live, where Billy Phelan used to live. There was nothing that Charlie Boy could not get, any time, any place in this town; and when he came into the old Downtown alleys with Scotty, and when Scotty quickly found Billy to play with, Charlie just as quickly found Morrie Berman, a swarthy ex-pimp and gambler who would bet on the behavior of bumblebees. A week ago Martin had seen Morrie open a welsher's forehead with a shotglass at Brockley's bar on Broadway over a three-hundred-dollar dart game: heavy bettor, Morrie, but he paid when he lost and he demanded the same from others. Martin knew Morrie's reputation better than he knew the man: a fellow who used to drink around town with Legs Diamond and had hoodlums for pals. But Morrie wasn't quite a hoodlum himself, as far as Martin could tell. He was the son of a politically radical Jew, grandson of a superb old Sheridan Avenue tailor. In Morrie the worthy Berman family strain had gone slightly askew.

The bet between Charlie Boy and Morrie had begun at one hundred dollars and stayed there for two games, with Martin holding the money. But when Morrie saw that Billy had unquestionably found the pocket at the windup of the second game, he offered to raise the ante another hundred; folly, perhaps, for his boy Billy was seventy-nine pins down. Well yes, but that was really only twenty-four down with the fifty-five-pin spot, and you go with the hot instrument. Charlie Boy quickly agreed to the raise, what's another hundred, and Billy then stood up and rolled his eight strikes, striking somberness into Charlie Boy's mood, and vengeance into Scotty's educated right hand.

Martin knew Scotty Streck and admired his talent without liking him. Scotty worked in the West Albany railroad shops, a short, muscular, brush-cut, bandy-legged native of the West End German neighborhood of Cabbagetown. He was twenty-six and had been bowling since he was old enough to lift a duckpin ball. At age sixteen he was a precociously unreal star with a 195 average. He bowled now almost every night of his life, bowled in matches all over the country and clearly coveted a national reputation. But to Martin he lacked champion style: a hothead, generous neither with himself nor with others. He'd been nicknamed Scotty for his closeness with money, never known to bet more than five dollars on himself. Yet he thrived on competition and traveled with a backer, who, as often as not, was his childhood pal, Charlie McCall. No matter what he did or didn't do, Scotty was still the best bowler in town, and bowling freaks, who abounded in Albany, gathered round to watch when he came out to play.

The freaks now sat on folding chairs and benches behind the only game in process in the old alleys, alleys which had been housed in two other buildings and moved twice before being installed here on State Street, just up from Broadway in an old dancing academy. They were venerable, quirky boards, whose history now spoke to Martin. He looked the crowd over: men sitting among unswept papers, dust, and cigar butts, bathing in the raw incandescence of naked bulbs, surrounded by spittoons; a nocturnal bunch in shirtsleeves and baggy clothes, their hands full of meaningful drink, fixated on an ancient game with origins in Christian ritual, a game brought to this city centuries ago by nameless old Dutchmen and now a captive of the indoor sports of the city. The game abided in such windowless, smoky lofts as this one, which smelled of beer, cigar smoke and alley wax, an unhealthy ambience which nevertheless nourished exquisite nighttime skills.

These men, part of Broadway's action-easy, gray-vested sporting mob, carefully studied such artists of the game as Scotty, with his high-level consistency, and Billy, who might achieve perfection tonight through a burst of accuracy, and converted them into objects of community affection. The mob would make these artists sports-page heroes, enter them into the hall of small fame that existed only in the mob mind, which venerated all winners.

After Billy rolled his eighth strike, Scotty stood, danced his bob and weave toward the foul line, and threw the ball with a corkscrewed arm, sent it spinning and hooking toward the one-three pocket. It was a perfect hit, but a dead one somehow, and he left the eight and ten pins perversely standing: the strike split, all but impossible to make.

"Dirty son of a biiiiiitch!" Scotty screamed at the pair of uncooperative pins, silencing all hubbub behind him, sending waves of uh-oh through the spectators, who knew very well how it went when a man began to fall apart at the elbow.

"You think maybe I'm getting to him?" Billy whispered to Martin.

"He can't even stand to lose a fiver, can he?"

Scotty tried for the split, ticking the eight, leaving the ten.

"Let's *get* it now, Scotty," Charlie Boy McCall said. "In there, buddy."

Scotty nodded at Charlie Boy, retrieved his ball and faced the new setup, bobbed, weaved, corkscrewed, and crossed over to the one-two pocket, Jersey hit, leaving the five pin. He made the spare easily, but sparing is not how you pick up pinnage against the hottest of the hot.

Billy might have been hot every night if he'd been as single-minded as Scotty about the game. But Martin knew Billy to be a generalist, a man in need of the sweetness of miscellany. Billy's best game was pool, but he'd never be anything like a national champion at that either, didn't think that way, didn't have the need that comes with obsessive specialization. Billy roamed through the grandness of all games, yeoman here, journeyman there, low-level maestro unlikely to transcend, either as gambler, card dealer, dice or pool shooter. He'd been a decent shortstop in the city wide Twilight League as a young man. He was a champion drinker who could go for three days on the sauce and not yield to sleep, a double-twenty specialist at the dart board, a chancy, small-time bookie, and so on and so on and so on, and why, Martin Daugherty, are you so obsessed with Billy Phelan? Why make a heroic *picaro* out of a simple chump?

Well, says Martin, haven't I known him since he was a sausage? Haven't I seen him grow stridently into young manhood while I slip and slide softly into moribund middle age? Why, I knew him when he had a father, knew his father too, knew him when that father abdicated, and I ached for the boy then and have ever since, for I know how it is to live in the inescapable presence of the absence of the father.

Martin had watched Billy move into street-corner life after his father left, saw him hanging around Ronan's clubroom, saw him organize the Sunday morning crap game in Bohen's barn after nine o'clock mass, saw him become a pinboy at the K. of C. to earn some change. That was where the boy learned how to bowl, sneaking free games after Duffy, the custodian, went off to the movies.

Martin was there the afternoon the pinboys went wild and rolled balls up and down the middle of the alleys at one another, reveling in a boyish exuberance that went bad when Billy tried to scoop up one of those missiles like a hot grounder and smashed his third finger between that onrushing ball and another one lying loose on the runway. Smash and blood, and Martin moved in and took him (he was fourteen, the same age as Martin's own son is this early morning) over to the Homeopathic Hospital on North Pearl Street and saw to it that the intern called a surgeon, who came and sewed up the smash, but never splinted it, just wrapped it with its stitches and taped it to Billy's pinky and said: That's the best anybody can do with this mess; nothing left there to splint. And Billy healed, crediting it to the influence of the healthy pinky. The nail and some bone grew back crookedly, and Martin can now see the twist and puff of Billy's memorable deformity. But what does a sassy fellow like Billy need with a perfectly formed third finger? The twist lends character to the hand that holds the deck, that palms the two-finger ball, that holds the stick at the crap table, that builds the cockeyed bridge for the educated cue.

If Martin had his way, he would infuse a little of Billy's scarred sassiness into his own son's manner, a boy too tame, too subservient to the priests. Martin might even profit by injecting some sass into his own acquiescent life.

Consider that: a sassy Martin Daugherty.

Well, that may not be all that likely, really. Difficult to acquire such things.

Billy's native arrogance might well have been a gift of miffed genes, then come to splendid definition through the tests to which a street like Broadway puts a young man on the make: tests designed to refine a breed, enforce a code, exclude all simps and gumps, and deliver into the city's life a man worthy of functioning in the age of nocturnal supremacy. Men like Billy Phelan, forged in the brass of Broadway, send, in the time of their splendor, telegraphic statements of mission: I, you bums, am a winner. And that message, however devoid of Christ-like other-cheekery, dooms the faint-hearted Scottys of the night, who must sludge along, never knowing how it feels to spill over with the small change of sassiness, how it feels to leave the spillover there on the floor, more where that came from, pal. Leave it for the sweeper.

Billy went for his ball, kissed it once, massaged it, chalked and toweled his right hand, spat in the spittoon to lighten his burden, bent slightly at the waist, shuffled and slid, and bazoo-bazoo, boys threw another strike: not *just* another strike, but a titanic blast this time which sent all pins flying pitward, the cleanest of clean hits, perfection unto tidiness, bespeaking power battening on power, control escalating.

Billy looked at no one.

Nine in a row, but still nobody said anything except hey, and yeah-yeah, with a bit more applause offered up. Billy waited for the ball to come back, rubbing his feet on the floor dirt just beyond the runway, dusting his soles with slide insurance, then picked up the ball and sidled back to the runway of alley nine for his last frame. And then he rolled it, folks, and boom-boom went the pins, zot-zot, you sons of bitches, ten in a row now, and a cheer went up, but still no comment, ten straight and his score (even though Martin hadn't filled in any numbers yet) is 280, with two more balls yet to come, twenty more pins to go. Is Billy Phelan ready for perfection? Can you handle it, kid? What will you do with it if you get it?

Billy had already won the match; no way for Scotty to catch him, given that spot. But now it looked as if Billy would beat Scotty without the spot, and, tied to a perfect game, the win would surely make the sports pages later in the week.

Scotty stood up and walked to the end of the ball return to wait. He chalked his hands, rubbed them together, played with the towel, as Billy bent over to pick up his ball.

"You ever throw three hundred anyplace before?" Scotty asked.

"I ain't thrown it *here* yet," Billy sid.

So he did it, Martin thought. Scotty's chin trembled as he watched Billy. Scotty, the nervous sportsman. Did saying what he had just said mean that the man lacked all character? Did only relentless winning define his being? Was the fear of losing sufficient cause for him to try to foul another man's luck? Why of course it was, Martin. Of course it was.

Billy threw, but it was a Jersey hit, his first crossover in the game. The ball's mixing power overcame imprecision, however, and the pins spun and rolled, toppling the stubborn ten pin, and giving Billy his eleventh strike. Scotty pulled at the towel and sat down.

"You prick," Morrie Berman said to him. "What'd you say that to him for?"

"Say what?"

"No class," said Morrie. "Class'll tell in the shit house, and you got no class."

Billy picked up his ball and faced the pins for the last act. He called out to Bugs, the pinboy: "Four pin is off the spot," and he pointed to it. Martin saw he was right, and Bugs moved the pin back into proper position. Billy kissed the ball, shuffled and threw, and the ball went elegantly forward, perfect line, perfect break, perfect one-three pocket hit. Nine pins flew away. The four pin never moved.

"Two-ninety-nine," Martin said out loud, and the mob gave its full yell and applause and then stood up to rubberneck at the scoresheet, which Martin was filling in at last, thirty pins a frame, twenty-nine in the last one. He put down the crayon to shake hands with Billy, who stood over the table, ogling his own nifty numbers.

"Some performance, Billy," said Charlie Boy McCall, standing to stretch his babyfat. "I should learn not to bet against you. You remember the last time?"

"Pool match at the K. of C."

"I bet twenty bucks on some other guy."

"Live and learn, Charlie, live and learn."

"You were always good at everything," Charlie said. "How do you explain that?"

"I say my prayers and vote the right ticket."

"That ain't enough in this town," Charlie said.

"I come from Colonie Street."

"That says it," said Charlie, who still lived on Colonie Street.

"Scotty still has to finish two frames," Martin announced to all; for Scotty was already at alley ten, facing down the burden of second best. The crowd politely sat and watched him throw a strike. He moved to alley nine and with a Jersey hit left the baby split. He cursed inaudibly, then made the split. With his one remaining ball he threw a perfect strike for a game of 219, a total of 667. Billy's total was 668.

"Billy Phelan wins the match by one pin, without using any of the spot," Martin was delighted to announce, and he read aloud the game scores and totals of both men. Then he handed the bet money to Morrie Berman.

"I don't even feel bad," Charlie Boy said. "That was a hell of a thing to watch. When you got to lose, it's nice to lose to somebody who knows what he's doing."

"Yeah, you were hot all right," Scotty said, handing Billy a five-dollar bill. "Really hot."

"Hot, my ass," Morrie Berman said to Scotty. "You hexed him, you bastard. He might've gone all the way if you didn't say anything, but you hexed him, talking about it."

The crowd was already moving away, back to the bar, the sweeper confronting those cigar butts at last. New people were arriving, waiters and bartenders who would roll in the Nighthawk League, which started at 3:00 A.M. It was now two-thirty in the morning.

"Listen, you mocky bastard," Scotty said, "I don't have to take any noise from you." Scotty's fists were doubled, his face flushed, his chin in vigorous tremolo. Martin's later vision of Scotty's coloration and form at this moment was that of a large, crimson firecracker.

"Hold on here, hold on," Charlie McCall said. "Cool down, Scotty. No damage done. Cool down, no trouble now." Charlie was about eight feet away from the two men when he spoke, too far to do anything when Morrie started his lunge. But Martin saw it coming and jumped between the two, throwing his full weight into Morrie, his junior by thirty pounds, and knocking him backward into a folding chair, on which he sat without deliberation. Others sealed off Scotty from further attack and Billy held Morrie fast in the chair with two hands.

"Easy does it, man," Billy said. "I don't give a damn what he did."

"The cheap fink," Morrie said. "He wouldn't give a sick whore a hairpin."

Martin laughed at the line. Others laughed. Morrie smiled. Here was a line for the Broadway annals. Epitaph for the Scotcheroo: It was reliably reported during his lifetime that he would not give a sick whore a hairpin. Perhaps this enhanced ignominy was also entering Scotty's head after the laughter, or perhaps it was the result of *his* genetic gift, or simply the losing, and the unbearable self-laceration that went with it. Whatever it was, Scotty doubled up, gasping, burping. He threw his arms around his own chest, wobbled, took short step, and fell forward, gashing his left cheek on a spittoon. He rolled onto his side, arms still aclutch, eyes squeezing out the agony in his chest.

The mob gawked and Morrie stood up to look. Martin bent over the fallen man, then lifted him up from the floor and stretched him out on the bench from which he had risen to hex Billy. Martin blotted the gash with Scotty's own shirttail, and then opened his left eyelid. Martin looked up at the awestruck mob and asked: "Anybody here a doctor?" And he answered himself: "No, of course not," and looked then at the night manager and said, "Call an ambulance, Al," even though he knew Scotty was already beyond help. Scotty: Game over.

How odd to Martin, seeing a champion die in the embrace of shame, egotism, and fear of failure. Martin trembled at a potential vision of himself also prostrate before such forces, done in by a shame too great to endure, and so now is the time to double up and die. Martin saw his own father curdled by shame, his mother crippled by it twice: her own and her husband's. And Martin himself had been bewildered and thrust into silence and timidity by it (but was that the true cause?). Jesus, man, pay attention here. Somebody lies dead in front of you and you're busy exploring the origins of your own timidity. Martin, as was said of your famous father, your sense of priority is bowlegged.

Martin straightened Scotty's arm along his side, stared at the closed right eye, the half-open left eye, and sat down in the scorekeeper's chair to search pointlessly for vital signs in this dead hero of very recent yore. Finally, he closed the left eye with his thumb.

"He's really gone," he told everybody, and they all seemed to wheeze inwardly. Then they really did disperse until only Charlie Boy McCall, face gone white, sat down at Scotty's feet and stared fully at the end of something. And he said, in his native way, "Holy Mother of God, that was a quick decision."

"Somebody we should call, Charlie?" Martin asked the shocked young man.

"His wife," said Charlie. "He's got two kids."

"Very tough. Very. Anybody else? What about his father?"

"Dead," said Charlie. "His mother's in Florida. His wife's the one."

"I'll be glad to call her," Martin said. "But then again maybe you ought to do that, Charlie. You're so much closer."

"I'll take care of it, Martin."

And Martin nodded and moved away from dead Scotty, who was true to the end to the insulting intent of his public name: tightwad of heart, parsimonious dwarf of soul.

"I never bowled a guy to death before," Billy said.

Penny Ante

BY EDWARD ALLEN

Dostoevsky wrote, "Can one even as much as touch a gaming table without becoming immediately infected with superstition?" Purely a rhetorical question.

I knew a guy who always wore two hats, one on top of the other, whenever he gambled. It looked a little funny, but it was none of my business. Maybe his head was cold. Maybe it gave him some kind of edge. We've all got our own ways of coaxing chance into going our way, things which might be signs of nothing to others taken for personal omens. Some people like the lights to be all green on the way to the casino. It makes them think things are going their way. Edward Allen's essay below combines a comic portrayal of his own superstitions and rituals with an essayist's thoughtful reflection on the sense of "what does not make sense." "Penny Ante" originally appeared in *Gentleman's Quarterly,* and was reprinted in *Literary Las Vegas,* edited by Nicholas Tronnes. Allen has authored a novel, *Mustang Sally,* in which gambling figures prominently.

I can't understand it. I've done everything right all day: left my ill-starred blue shirt home, brought along the sunglasses that have been so good to me, avoided abbreviating any of the items on my grocery list. And, of course, I have labored carefully over the exact placement of that certain hidden object, which I have pinned with much seriousness beneath my clothes.

What's more, I have been a careful driver, covering the fifty miles between my house and town without causing a single Toyota to honk at me angrily. I have taken care to be equally well-mannered with my shopping cart, there in the corridors of the bag-it-yourself discount warehouse, where love songs, nothing but love songs, filter down all afternoon, soft as asbestos, from the barnlike ceiling. Those tender lyrics, mostly about individuals learning to live with or without someone else's precious love, still echo through my head as I wheel my week's groceries through the parking lot, wandering in search of my car through the vague, frostless chill of a winter night in Las Vegas.

Now, with shopping over, half my supper eaten and the other half doggie-bagged, an inconclusive fortune-cookie chit folded in my shirt pocket and a clump of third-rate Mongolian beef sitting heavy on my stomach, I am an unhappy man. I am unhappy in that crushed and chastised way of a student who has been yelled at unfairly in front of the class. I can feel my face flush with the shame of it—the shame of someone who has no reason to deserve the kind of humiliation I see laid out on the table in front of me, hand after hand, here in a room where all the other blackjack players and crapshooters and roulette-wheel watchers seem, from their buzz and clamor, to be getting as rich as sweepstakes millionaire David Brumbalow.

I want to tell you that these are the thoughts of a man who prides himself on his common sense, who likes the efficiency of combining this weekly Las Vegas shopping trip with a quick and strictly budgeted run at the casino tables, a man who answers no chain letters nor dreams of buying real estate for no money down, someone to whom Nostradamus is nothing, someone who will never call in to Time-Life Books to order its *Illustrated Encyclopedia of Spooky Noises.* In short, I am a reasonable American, registered to vote, sitting at a blackjack table, losing, with a $2 bill safety-pinned to the front of my underpants.

What I like most about gambling is that it does not make sense. I find it comforting that in pursuit of its admittedly fraudulent promises, I don't have to pretend to make sense myself. The hobby of gambling, even at my wimpish betting level, allows me to believe things that I know are not true. It lets me be a devotional weirdo, without requiring me to dress funny. It gives me a chance to apply the most-Byzantine rules and structures to my most ordinary actions, all in search of that compelling fiction known as luck.

In short, gambling invites me to take an hour's recess from adulthood, to play in a well-demarked sandbox of irrationality and to look at the world as a magical place, which, of course, it is when the light hits it at the right angle. Those people who stubbornly remain adults and who look upon gambling's happy meaninglessness from within the logic of the real world will see something quite different. They will see a phalanx of games controlled by the indomitable law of averages, games that from an adult's wintry perspective you cannot hope to master. Those adults will see me, and the people sitting next to me, giving our money away week after week to people who do not love us.

One reason it's so hard to keep from getting angry tonight is that this casino has been very good to me on occasion. I do not believe in telling you the name of this establishment or how well I have done before, but I will say that in the past, on a summer night, I have stepped out onto the Las Vegas Strip with a smile on my face that you couldn't have wiped off with a shovel. I have walked past where the Caesars Palace loudspeakers blend flutes and drums to produce what I guess is supposed to sound like Cecil B. De Mille slave sacrifice music, have walked with the kind of stride that can only indicate the presence of multiple hundreds in the wallet. If I were a mugger, I would pay close attention to the way people walk.

But tonight, everything is terrible. The air is thick with carpet shampoo and cigarettes; the happy voices around me seem as empty and shrill as untrained parrots. Nothing falls together right. I chose this dealer for her kind face, yet there seems a ferocious hopelessness to the cards she tosses me. As she deals me a jack to bust another hand, I can hear, at the far end of the casino from beyond a bank of slot machines, the strains of "I've Got to Be Me" in the amplified voice of a lounge singer who I'm sure would rather be almost anybody else. Everything around this little $5 blackjack table seems wounded, like a country that has just devalued its currency.

One of the reasons I find gambling so much fun is that the adventure is not limited to the times when you are doing it. In fact, the moments when you are actually doing it will frequently stink, as they do tonight. For me, the subsidiary thrill is just as important, as well as much less expensive.

The surrounding excitement can stretch out in either direction. For hours before, on a Las Vegas shopping day, as the time draws near for me to leave my house in the desert and drive into town, I find an almost-religious excitement in the preparation for a session, complete with my own private rules, rituals, prohibitions. And coming home, blessed or wounded, I am allowed to wrestle again with the mystery of what I did wrong and what I did right; I must also try once more to find some way to recognize the difference in advance.

One of the things I know, though it doesn't matter on these local trips, is that I must never again permit myself to drive through another state and out again without stepping on the ground of that state. This is a superstition that I developed on my own, and I am rather proud of it. Somehow it seems right, a mandate for some kind of geographical integrity. I would be even prouder of it if it worked.

Particularly important in the moments of preparation is to avoid putting on any article of clothing in which I have had a bad night in the past. Unfortunately, a too-strict observance of this rule always leads to a problem with shoes because I have only a limited number, and I've had terrible nights in every pair I own. The best I can do, as a sort of nervous compromise, is always keep a second pair in the car so that if I get hurt in one casino, at least I can change shoes before trying the next.

Do I really believe any of this stuff? I do, in the sense that within the skewed world of gambling it is no crazier to believe it than not to. And at the purest level, the irrationality is its own payoff. I don't know if anybody in the world shares this feeling, but for me, to walk around in a place as public as a casino with a $2 bill fastened to the front of my shorts is an unqualified pleasure, whether it works or not. (It doesn't work. I will be honest now and admit that this account is narrated retrospectively and that I have since retired the $2 bill, which is the only reason I'm willing to mention it. That bill let me down one too many times—meaning somehow that it must have lost the power I knew it never possessed. I am trying to be scientific about these things. As I said, I pride myself on my rationality.)

So here I am, delivering more of my money to the absentee investors in a casino I won't name, on a night I could be reading a good book or maybe writing one. Why do I bother? This question always comes up when I talk to non-gamblers, and I never have a decent answer. Why is an activity with so little to offer so appealing to so many people, enough to make it one of the few growth industries in a retreating economy? Why should so many people fly so many thousands of miles to stay in rooms where the drapes never quite come together in the middle, and drop so many thousands of dollars at games that really aren't very interesting, all in pursuit of a chance that anybody with more brains than a state lottery player knows is mathematically remote?

In my experience, what makes it worthwhile is the idea that something as tyannical as the law of averages can be turned upside down, if only for an hour or a weekend, and that what does not make sense can be forced to make sense. That logical turnabout is in itself a pleasure worthy of any number of spongy hotel mattresses. Deep down we all know, unless we are of the intellectual caste who smoke cigarettes but find airplanes too dangerous, that we are suckers. But that's okay; we're in good company, and we're here to have fun. All day and night, the law of averages grinds away at our frail chances, immutable in its pronouncement that if you keep playing long enough at a game that has a negative expectation built into it, you will have to lose.

In other words, you can't even break even. But we also know that people have been known to have astonishingly good nights, even when they are playing like idiots. And the best players can, and will, get slapped in the face. It's not fair. That's another thing I like about gambling. It's value-free. You'll have a great night sometime, and the greatest thing about that night will be that you did nothing to deserve it.

I suppose that when I described some of my own private superstitions, I might have sounded like someone who has forgotten to take his medication. But I think I can demonstrate that such craziness makes at least some kind of sense.

Superstitious gambling behavior makes sense because even the smallest and most meaningless actions can be shown to affect, in some way, the random interconnectedness of all physical processes. By this logic, everything you do can be said to transform the world. If I cough once at the card table, or lean back in my chair, or audibly riffle my chips, I may distract the dealer during that magically important process of shuffling the cards. The outcome of the game will thus be changed completely—every hand, every possibility, turned upside down.

The example I use in my forthcoming novel has to do with what will happen if you bend down to pick up a penny as you are walking into a crowded casino.

The first thing that will happen is that you will get to the crap table a few seconds later than you would have without having bothered with the penny. A man who walked in the door before you, who would have been behind you if you had left that penny alone, will now get where he's going a few seconds earlier. The shooter about to roll the dice at your table will see you out of the corner of his eye and will shake the dice in his fist one less time, and the throw will come out showing a different number.

Because of that last throw, or because of all the throws following it, which have been changed as well, somebody will eventually leave your table. And it is a physical law that whenever someone leaves one place, he or she has to move to another place. When that happens, the progress of the game at whatever table that person ends up at will be changed utterly. Because of that change, a few who would otherwise have left their tables will stay, and others who might have stayed will leave. Where will they go? It doesn't matter. Wherever they go to will never be the same.

In time, every game in the whole casino will be changed utterly, because of that penny. The change will be so pervasive that eventually a man who would otherwise have been lavishly in the money will get discouraged and grab a taxi downtown (and, of course, the interference of that cab in traffic will delay by a few seconds another cabload of gamblers bound for Caesars, whose night, now, will never be the same, and they will never know it).

Thus, when our discouraged man gets downtown, Binion's Horseshoe Casino will be transformed by his effect on the games he buys into there, which effect again will multiply from table to table in a chain reaction, a process something like that film they played for us in elementary school to illustrate atomic fission, showing a floor covered with thousands of mousetraps armed with Ping-Pong balls, onto which one triggering ball (the neutron?) is dropped. Those people cashed out of Binion's by the change this man has caused will wander around Fremont Street, extending the process you have begun, carrying it from street to street, mousetrap to mousetrap, from Pioneer to Golden Nugget to Four Queens.

When you look around town a few hours after picking up that earth-shaking penny, everything will seem normal. But I believe that if you were able to go back, like George Bailey in *It's a Wonderful Life,* and see both worlds, with penny and without penny, the Strip would be a different place. People would still walk in and out of the same doors, but they would not all be the same people, cars gliding up and down the Strip would catch the traffic lights in a different sequence. Those two possibilities of the Strip would look much alike, but they would in reality be as different from each other as Jimmy Stewart's old Bedford Falls was from the soulless alternate reality of Pottersville. (Actually, I have to admit that I've always liked Pottersville better; every time I see that movie I wish I could drop into the Indian Club for a Christmas Eve martini.)

And more: I suspect that in one of these casinos there is a man who because of that penny will have the luck of his life. This guy will end up with so much money that he will choose to spend some of it on a young woman who is not his wife. If the girl does not turn out to be a police decoy, this man's casino session will culminate in her arms, with the result that later, on the too-soft Beautyrest, he will disappoint his wife by turning over and going to sleep—which means that the baby who would otherwise have been conceived that night will never be born to fulfill his appointed destiny, whether that be to develop sugar-free cotton candy or to blow up the world. That child's existence is now canceled, as thoroughly as all the other Pottersvillean ghosts have been canceled by all the other people who have bent down to pick up pennies in front of all the other casinos.

Like many other trains of thought, this one takes us to only a limited number of terminals. As crazy and metaphysical as the idea of interconnected events is, there's not much you can do with it, mostly because we can't ever see the alternative possibilities that our actions have preempted. All we can do is pay attention, go on with our strategies, not worry too much about what could have been and try to play as intelligently as we can. We will find, among other things, that intelligence does not help us.

Although the mathematics are pretty clear, any psychological observations I can make about the gambling will be almost as shaky as the hands of a poker novice holding the first full house of his life. The reason I know so little about anybody else's gambling experiences is that, even though it doesn't look that way, gambling is a profoundly solitary activity. In the crush around the casino tables, surrounded by the high spirits and camaraderie of players, one is really walking among thousands of strictly personal experiences. When I mention the irrational (or maybe I can be fancy and say *pararational*) behavior that I have no idea if it applies to anybody else. It's not the sort of thing we talk about.

I feel the same ignorance whenever I get into a discussion about the phenomenon of the compulsive gambler. From within my minimum-risk style, the cruelty of that disease seems incomprehensible. And although I don't think I'm likely to end up like that, the picture frightens me. Among those who consider ourselves noncompulsive, the specter of the toxic gambler, the driven and tortured person we have seen on television, with his face hidden from the interview camera, and who deep down we all fear we could turn into, waits at the edge of every table, his flamboyant sickness looming over our careful play the way the shadow of alcoholism hovers over the early social drinking of every young man with a family history.

Whenever the subject of compulsive gambling comes up, it is usual for someone to cite the many sources who believe that what the compulsive gambler really wants to do is to lose, that he is trying to reconnect with a distant parent, who will comfort him in his hour of loss and take him in. I don't know. I wonder if in some cases, the problem has more to do with rationality.

My admittedly unstudied theory is this: If "healthy" gambling is in part a vacation from rationality, then perhaps sick gambling is for some a failure to escape that rationality. Perhaps, the sick gambler suffers from bringing too much rational baggage along, into a part of the world where it does not work. I am thinking in particular of the principle of fair play, the idea that there exists some sort of moral balance sheet between getting and deserving

A normal gambler knows the dice and the cards and the wheels and the video chips will play anything but fair; cards will fall (as they have been falling for me on this rotten night) in a sequence that only a malevolent deity (or the always-suspected, but highly unlikely, crooked casino) could have engineered.

The healthy gambler winces, gets disgusted and finally writes it off, knowing the universe is unfair. I think some compulsive gamblers fail to understand this. The compulsive, frantic on a losing night, seems to believe both in fair play and in the inherently balanced nature of the universe—and so goes on losing disastrously, laboring under the conviction that the universe will relent, will show just a touch of human decency and will force the cards to pay the wronged player back for all those previous acts of cruelty.

I suspect also that some compulsives are simply drawn into their illness by the pure sensuality of the betting moment. When we see the misery that the compulsive gambler brings down upon himself, it is natural to imagine him the worst of masochists. But just because he almost always ends up ruined doesn't mean that the ruin itself is what he sought. To use an example from another illness: If we were examining the case of an alcoholic who every night gets so drunk that he throws up, we probably would not be taken seriously if we concluded that this person's real problem is that he's addicted to vomiting.

Instead of being a masochist, perhaps the compulsive gambler loses control because he is enjoying himself so much. Even if he seems miserable most of the time, there is something very powerful about the instant the dice are thrown, the second the deciding card is turned over, the moment the little ball takes its last spastic bounce into the numbered slot.

In my own timed experience, I've felt something of that thrill a few times. On those rare occasions, when a series of successful blackjack hands has allowed me to increase my bet to the grand total of, say, $30, the moment when the card comes down, while everything hangs in the balance—that's where the thrill is. It is a neurological jolt made up of greed, lust and excitement mixed together with a strong dose of fear. Whenever my game gets raised to such a level, then I can feel myself coming alive in a wy that seems to redeem all those previous hemorrhogenic hours I have spent on those stools, busting sixteens.

There is another thing that attracts me to casinos, and it may help explain why it felt so appropriate for me to pin that $2 bill to my shorts. For many people, and on many levels, gambling is strongly associated with sex.

On one level, it's easy to understand why that should be so: Money gained through the accident of luck comes with few restrictions on how it is to be spent. And even though Las Vegas is trying to put on a clean face for the benefit of its most profitable tourists (meaning the retirees and the young parents, devoted slot-players all), there remain plenty of young women ready to provide more-traditional forms of entertainment—after they have checked your ID and asked you all sorts of questions to make sure that you are not a cop.

But even for those players who would never call the Room-Service Showgirls escort agency nor board the free limousine that ferries patrons to the out-of-town, legal brothels, something of the old sexiness still hangs in the air above the real games, the ones still played on green felt instead of video terminals. I'm sure it is no accident that the prettiest employees in a casino are always the women who bring gamblers their free cocktails, encouraging them, without saying a word, to drink more, bet more, lose more.

Although the narrow-tied swagger of the Rat Pack is long forgotten down the endless corridors of Circus Circus RV Park, although the city seems determined to insulate the "slots-and-tots" crowd from any disturbing memories of how sexy this place used to be, although the public-relations industry seems bent on changing the symbol of Las Vegas from the painted showgirl to the painted clown—still, something filters through here and there, in the agitated light of the Strip when it catches your eye from an unexpected direction, in the climactic squeal of a Chicago secretary blessed with beginner's luck as she rolls another winning number.

And then there is the ubiquitous $100 bill, the controlling scrip against which all clattering chips and wrinkled twenties are measured. It is the only piece of American currency that cannot be called ugly. The reverse side is especially attractive, with its leafy green and that sort of Frederick's of Hollywood laciness in the scrollwork around the edges.

Even the most uxorious conventioneer knows that if an escort-agency transaction ever should occur, it would involve bills of this denomination. To handle one bill is perhaps to be remotely involved in all the adventures that that bill has helped to capitalize. That moment at the casino cage, as the cashier counts your chips and crisply deals out the stacked hundreds, remains, I think, an erotically charged moment—no matter that you have already earmarked that money to resurface your driveway.

Three Cushions

BY DAN MCGOORTY AS TOLD TO ROBERT BYRNE

from McGoorty: Confessions of a Billiard Bum

McGoorty's rowdy narrative was recorded by Robert Byrne, perhaps the pre-mier authority on writing about pool and billiards, and a fine writer-cueman himself. About his frank, sometimes bitter stories, McGoorty told Byrne, "If what I told you got published they'd lock us up for life. I tell the truth you know." McGoorty's story is a road trip through a generation of pool rooms, rich in detail about places and periods, particularly vivid about the experience of an often down-and-out, drunk pool bum during the Depression.

Whatever kind of pool hustler he was, McGoorty's a straight-shooter as a talker, steeped in the game's argots—a fluency in what boxing announcers call "the official particulars" of his game. He is gifted with the denigrating wit of a Minnesota Fats, though rawer and with more of the streets in him, and priceless in his descriptions of fellow gamblers. Several such profiles of characters—a sta-ple in the literature of poolrooms—are included below, after a selection in which McGoorty describes his education as a billiards player, pictured dead-pan as anal-ogous to stepping up in "class," becoming a gentleman of the poolroom.

Bums play pool, gentlemen play billiards. It was as true fifty years ago as it is today. Walk in any room that has both pool and billiard tables and look at the difference between the players. All of the jerks, drifters, bums, hoodlums, loudmouths, and pimps will be playing pool. The guys playing billiards will be a different sort entirely, doctors and dentists, business-men, professional people, serious-minded types. Sure, you can find college pro-fessors playing pool and cornholers playing billiards, but I am talking about the average. Why is this? The way I figure it, billiards is a tougher game . . . you have to be a good pool player to even think about playing billiards, so only those with some staying power get from one game to the other. And there is something about the games themselves that sorts people out. Pool is so obvious. Just knock the fucking ball in the hole—any idiot can see it. But in three-cushion billiards, where there are no holes, where you have to map out inside your skull the path the balls have to take around the table . . . well, there you have something that takes some brains. You can study three-cushion for a lifetime and learn tricks and variations right up to the end. I've been studying it for fifty years, and I've learned probably fifty new shots in the last five years alone.

Bums play pool, gentlemen play billiards. I noticed it the minute I lit in Chicago. The pool tables were either in the back of the room, or in the basement, so that the pool players wouldn't bother the billiard players. If you walked in a joint needing a shave, they would escort you right to the back, where the rest of the bums were. There was always a sign over the pool tables: "No loud talking. No swearing. No gambling. No massé shots." When one of the players missed a massé shot for some money, he might holler, "Goddam sonofoabitching motherfucker!" and the house man would shout, "Shuddup, you stupid cocksucker! Can't you read?"

They didn't need signs like that for the billiard players, because they weren't the type of people who hollered and cussed; they were allowed to shoot massé shots because they knew what they were doing.

I was a no-good, useless, drunken bum, but I wanted to be a gentleman. The only way open to me was to take up billiards. I didn't think of it that way at the time . . . Christ, I didn't think much about anything. I was just trying to get through each day as best I could. All I knew was that there was something *important* about billiards, something high class. All the billiard players seemed to have made something of themselves. Playing billiards was like belonging to a private club. Willie Hoppe, Welker Cochran, Jake Schaefer, they were players famous all over the world and they played billiards, not pool. When they saw a pool table they got sick to their stomachs.

When I arrived on the scene, straight billiards—where all you have to do to score a point is make the cueball hit the two other balls—was already in limbo. Jake Schaefer's father had killed it as a spectator sport. That old codger would get the balls trapped against the rail or in a corner and run thousands of points. The only way to stop him from scoring was hit him on the head with a club. When the game was over the ushers would have to slap the spectators in the faces to wake them up.

Something had to be done to make the game tougher. One of the ideas was to make the player hit a rail before hitting the second object ball, or hit the red ball first. Another idea was balkline, where they divided the table up with chalk lines. You couldn't make more than one or two points of straight billiards in any area without driving at least one of the balls into a different area. Things settled down finally to 18.2 balkline, where the lines are drawn eighteen inches from the rails, and you are allowed two points before you have to drive a ball out.

The record book shows that the first big balkline tournament was held in 1903 in Paris. Maurice Vigneaux, a frog, was the winner. I never saw the guy, but I know they called him The Lion because he had a big head of hair. He was the one Hoppe beat in 1906 to win the world title at the age of eighteen. It was a sensation at the time—front-page news, not sports-page news—and from then on you always had to pay money to see Hoppe play.

The first balkline tournament I saw was held in 1921 in the Grand Ballroom of the Congress Hotel in Chicago and was considered a very important event for the whole town. The *Chicago Daily News,* the *Herald Examiner,* the *Tribune,* those papers wrote it up as if the Prince of Wales was playing polo on Michigan Boulevard. The spectators had to be very well dressed to get in, and the players wore tuxedos. No kids allowed. No screening meemies in mothers' arms. The room was plush, with big chandeliers, private boxes all around at the balcony level, a brass rail between the audience and the arena, gold drapes. Just one table. That shit about having more than one table at a time got started much later. I can remember looking up at the ladies in the boxes, watching the game through opera glasses, and wondering if they knew what the hell was going on. Everything was so lavish . . . God, they did things up big then. They packed the people in . . . for an attraction that wouldn't draw flies today. Of course, billiards was a very big sport. In the Loop, at that time, there were at least five hundred billiard tables, and in the middle of the afternoon every one was busy.

The same thing killed balkline that killed straight rail: the players got so good they were boring to watch for the general public. They kept the balls in a little cluster and made cozy shots about an inch long that you couldn't see unless you were kneeling on the table. When a ball had to be driven to the other end of the table, it always came to the cluster as if it was tied to a long rubber band. If Hoppe or Cochran or Schaefer got the balls straddling a chalk line they kept making points until somebody turned out the lights or sprayed them with a hose. Cochran made one run of 684. To wake the audience up after that they had to shoot off a cannon.

Three-cushion—where the cueball has to hit at lest three rails and one ball, in any order, before it hits the second ball—is a better spectator sport so it has stayed alive. In three-cushion the shots are big—even the spectators in the cheap seats can see them. Sometimes in order to score you have to drive the cueball forty feet, or twice around the table. The game is so tough it is impossible to really master it. If you make a run of fifteen points in a row you get a standing ovation.

At Bensinger's in Chicago, the billiard tables were on one floor and the pool tables on another. The elevator was an open wrought-iron cage, and I could see the billiard games as I rode up to join the hoodlums on the next floor. After getting hoisted through that billiard atmosphere a thousand times, I decided to get off and see what it was all about. I have never been the same since.

When I stepped off the elevator a broad was right there to take my coat. Thank God I was well dressed that day. She led me to a table covered with beautiful new green cloth . . . Number One Simonis from Belgium, naturally. The best. She spilled out the three balls—clear heart ivory from Zanzibar. Lately we have been running out of elephants, so most billiards today is played with plastic balls, which is not too bad, but nothing like good ivory. The sound ivory balls make when they click together, the way they hesitate before the English takes, the way they hold the spin off the third rail—you just can't beat it. The girl asked me what weight cue I wanted, and when I told her twenty ounces with a twelve-millimeter tip she brought me one that was a dream— two-piece bird's-eye maple, brass joint, inlaid butt, ivory ferrule. I wanted somebody to play with, so she put up a little sign next to the table that said "Three-cushion player wanted." In other words, she treated me as if I *was* somebody, somebody special, when, as I said, I was nothing but a no-good, useless, drunken fucking bum.

It was quiet as a library in that billiard room. All you could hear was the clicking of the ivory and the bump of the balls against the rubber. If you shouted or swore they were liable to bar you for life. Even if you coughed a little they might ask you to step outside till you got control of yourself. Nothing was allowed that might be the least bit distracting. It almost makes me cry to remember the respect they used to have for billiard players.

A fellow showed up to play me. He was probably a corporation lawyer or a Superior Court judge, for all I know. At least a bail bondsman. He tried to get me to play for a little something, but I ducked that. He beat me without any trouble, but I enjoyed it, enjoyed the atmosphere. When you get beat at something and enjoy it, you've got to like it.

What makes three-cushion a great game is that every move you make is half offense and half defense. Like chess. I don't play chess myself, but that is what chess players tell me. When you study a three-cushion shot you have to estimate the odds of making it, the odds of leaving your opponent a tough shot if you miss, or yourself an easy one if you score. There are damned few really easy shots, but some are easier than others. If you can score one point an inning, on the average—one point each time you get a turn at the table—you are in the world-championship class. In rack pool the top players average about fifteen points an inning, in balkline about thirty-five.

The shots in three-cushion are so tough it is a pleasure when you make one. And it is a pleasure to watch the cueball do what you want it to do—slow down, speed up, curve. When you know what you are doing you can make that cueball act as if it had a mind of its own.

After that afternoon in Bensinger's, I was hooked, and I played three-cushion almost every day from then on. I was hungry for knowledge, and I drove some of the older players nuts with questions. It wasn't long before I was making people sit up and take notice. In 1924 something happened that sealed my fate as billiard bum for life: I won the Chicago Junior Amateur Tournament. There were twenty-four players in it, some of them very good, but all of them fairly young and green. We played twenty-five points of three-cushion in a different place every night—Rogers Park, Evanston, Arlington, all over. My record was 23–1, and for a while there I was the toast of the town. Well, housewives weren't hoisting glasses to me, but I was big in the Loop poolrooms. Up-and-coming young player, and all that.

I was introduced to Willie Hoppe and I almost pissed my pants. You can't believe what an honor it was to shake his hand—it was like meeting Babe Ruth. The fans wanted to see how I would do against various people, so some matches were arranged. I played Alfredo De Oro, who already was pretty old, maybe sixty, and got beat, but I dumped Leon Magnus, who was so old he shook like a leaf. Magnus had won the first three-cushion tournament ever held—in 1878. I'll bet I'm the only guy that has played him, the first champ, and Ceulemans, the current one. In fact, I've played almost all the champs in between, too.

Augie Kieckhefer set up a match for me against Johnny Layton, who was the reigning three-cushion king at the time. He went right through me, but he was a hell of a nice guy and I didn't mind too much. Not on the outside, anyway. Underneath, I promised myself I would learn how he made it look so easy, and why it was when I stepped to the table I never seemed to have anything to shoot at.

A fellow by the name of Dick Adams took me under his wing and was a big help to me. He ran a billiard room on 63rd between University and

Woodlawn. According to him I had a perfect billiard stroke and could go all the way to the top if I would quit drinking and learn to control my speed and how to lock up my short-angle shots. What I had to do, he said, was play balk-line, and play it, play it, play it. So we played, he and I did, at his place every morning for a year. Every morning it was 200 points of 18.2, and I hated it. It was too small a game for me; I wanted to let my stroke out and see those balls *move.* Adams taught me the massé, the dead-ball draw, how to kill the speed of the cueball with reverse English off the rail, how to spread the balls so the next shot brought them back together, a hundred things like that. There is no question that learning balkline helped me. There's nothing like it for short shots, speed, and position. Every three-cushion player should practice balkline once in a while. I tell all my students to do it, but few of them do. I can tell by the way they look at me what they are thinking. They are thinking: "What the fuck does that old fart know about it?"

Next time the Junior Amateur came around, in 1925, I was barred. I *gambled,* the other players said. I hung around with people like Bad Eye and Scarface Foreaker and The Eagle, they said. I was not the clean-cut type of youngster the amateur billiard program was designed to promote, or some such shit, they said. The other players just wanted me out, that's all. I was plenty clean-cut enough when they thought they could beat me. So I learned another important lesson: The better you get the bigger prick you become. You don't really change, but you do in the eyes of your competition. Everybody loves you as long as they can beat your brains out.

Sure, I hung around with Bad Eye and Scarface. I had to win a match with Scarface, in fact, to get that game with Layton. I've heard people whisper about Scarface, but he is a perfectly fine guy in my book. Last time I saw him was in Sacramento, California. He was running down a sidewalk, going so fast his raincoat was standing straight out behind him. I didn't find out what he had done because I couldn't catch him. All I know is that he was getting *lost.*

The best three-cushion players in the world were concentrated in Chicago during the 1920's, and I watched them whenever I could. It was in 1923 that the Interstate League started, which really put three-cushion on the map and killed balkline. The Interstate League started out with about a dozen players, each one sponsored by a room in a different town. Every guy had to play every other guy two matches, one at home and one away . . . a double round robin for the championship of the world. They charged $1.10 for front-row seats at the matches, and the rooms were always packed to the rafters. My God, the players . . . the players were the best in the world: Johnny Layton out of Sedalia, Missouri, Tiff Denton playing for Kling and Allen in Kansas City,

Augie Kieckhefer representing himself, Bob Cannafax out of Detroit, Gus Copulus playing for the Euclid Arcade in Cleveland, Otto Reiselt for Allinger's in Philadelphia—that gives you an idea of the caliber of play. Hoppe, Cochran, and Schaefer weren't in it. They were opposed to three-cushion. They had balkline locked up—nobody could come close to them—so they fought against three-cushion and didn't take it up until balkline died completely in the 1930's.

There were always at least two of the league players in Chicago, and they kept an open game going in the back room of Kieckhefer's most of the day. Seven points for two dollars. Anybody could play, but you got no spot. There were no spectators allowed . . . this was strictly a players' game. I got in and played with them every chance I could, and it was like going through a meat grinder. If there were, say, six players in the game, you never got more than two or three shots. Somebody would run seven and out, or a four and a three. For a year and a half I played, and one day I broke even. Broke even! I went right out and got drunk, I was so happy.

But it was the best training I could have got. If I became some kind of half-ass billiard player, I owe it to playing in those pot games. It cost me at least ten bucks a day, but it was priceless experience. Cheaper than taking lessons. They didn't mind me, so long as I brought my money and didn't ask for a spot. If I had asked for a spot, they would have said, "Don't let the door hit you in the ass." When they had picked me clean I would race out to Dick Adams's joint and set up shots I had seen played, particularly by Reiselt, who was terrific, and I would talk them over with Dick. "Why did he play it off the white instead of the red? Why did he elevate his cue a little? Why did he bank for this one instead of going cross table? Why did he slow the ball down?" Between the two of us we would figure out the answers. To beat a kiss. To drop the red into the opposite corner. To leave a tough shot. To drive a ball five rails for position.

I didn't quit playing pool entirely, because I had to hustle pool here and there to make a living between jobs, but three-cushion was what I enjoyed doing most. Besides, it is a big help to a hustler to know all games. After beating a guy in rotation it is nice to have him propose a little game of billiards for higher stakes.

I used to make swings through Indiana and Ohio, hustling both pool and billiards, whichever presented itself. One night I was lining up a shot, looking down my cue toward the front door, when I saw a police car pull up in front of the joint. The house man said to me, "Look, kid, I'm going to do you a favor. I called the cops on you. How am I going to make any money off my customers if you get it all? Now beat it out the back way."

He had a point, and I thanked him as I disappeared.

It is much nicer to hustle three-cushion instead of pool, because you rob a more refined type of person. In three-cushion, the worst that can happen is to have the guy ask you if you will take a check. But you beat a guy out of a few bucks in a pool game and he might pick up the cueball and knock your teeth out.

I have never taken a ball in the teeth, but I have taken checks. I was working for Cliquot Club as a salesman. One morning after the daily sales meeting, the pep talk—"Get out there and *sell* . . ." and so on—I ducked into 18 East Randolph Street. It was winter, the air was full of those white flies, the streets were a mess of dirty slush. I wanted to play billiards, I didn't want to get out there and sell. I got a set of balls and was knocking them here and there when a very solid citizen type asked me if I wanted to indulge in a little game.

"Why not?" I said. "I have to wait here until my secretary calls, anyway."

The guy had a big stickpin in his tie with a headlight on it, and another flasher on his ring. "Care to make it interesting?" he said while he chalked his cue.

"Anything you say, pal." I had plenty of money. I was doing well enough hustling so that my commissions from Cliquot Club were going right in the bank.

We decided on ten points for two dollars. After the first few shots I saw that the guy couldn't even *spell* billiards. We played six games and he never got more than five points.

When we quit he went up to the desk and paid the time with a bill he peeled off a roll he could hardly get his fingers around. Then to me he said, "I trust you will accept a check?"

"Holy shit," I said, "you got a roll you couldn't flush down a toilet and you want to give me a check?"

"I assure you the check is good. Furthermore, I enjoyed playing with you and I would like to meet you here next Friday at the same time for another session, and the Friday after that."

Talk about the soft con! But there was something solid about him. I took a chance.

The check was on the LaSalle Trust and Savings at LaSalle and Monroe, where I happened to know a teller by the name of Shorty Hackman. I busted over there through the slush.

"Say, Shorty, how good is this check?"

"Just a minute and I'll tell you if it is any good at all." He looked something up. "The check is good."

"Shorty, how good is it?"

"Danny, my friend, you could sign a long string of zeros on the end of it."

At 9:30 next Friday morning I came out of the sales meeting at Cliquot Club. It was a beautiful day—no slush, no white flies. A good day to call on my accounts and try to work up some new business. But it was the appointed hour, so I ducked into Kieckhefer's. There were fifty-five tables on one floor . . . forty billiards in front and fifteen pockets in the back. At that time of day there was nothing doing but one snooker game way in the corner. I hung around the top of the stairs, and sure enough, here came my opponent through the door. I raced to the back of the room and slumped into a chair and pretended to be watching the snooker game. He looked around, spotted me, walked back to where I was sitting, and tapped me on the shoulder.

"Well, hello!" I said.

"Shall we play?" he said.

We played every Friday for six weeks. He never won a game and his checks never bounced. I could count on twelve bucks a week like clockwork. Plenty of my so-called friends tried to get him away from me, but he wasn't interested. He had taken a liking to me, or some damned thing. I was supposed to be a killer, but I got to feeling a little sorry for this particular guy. One day I showed up half drunk after being out all night. As we were lagging for the break I turned to him and said, "Listen, why don't you smarten up? You won't beat me in a thousand years."

What he said to me made me feel about an inch tall. He said, "I know that, Dan, but don't you think I'm improving?"

A couple of Fridays later he didn't show up. I figured he was sick, and I half expected him to phone in or send a note. When he didn't show the next week either, or the week after, I went over to see Shorty at the bank.

"Hey, what happened to my meal ticket?"

Shorty looked in a few filing cabinets. "Danny, he's moved his account to Boston. He's gone."

"Who the hell was he, anyway?"

"You didn't know? He's the vice president of the Metropolitan Life Insurance Company?"

"The vice *president?*"

"That's right. One of the richest legitimate guys in the country. He probably paid you by check so he could deduct you from his income tax or put you on his expense account."

I've often wondered how he handled that, how he accounted for all those "Pay to the order of Danny McGoorty . . . $12.00." Maybe he put me down as a consulting engineer. Or a ballet teacher.

Horses

"What do you mean, 'How do I want it'?" I didn't know how the fuck I wanted it.

"Well, I mean do you want it on the snout, or what?"

"Yeah, that's it. On the snout."

He gave me a ticket and we sat back and waited. Pretty soon they were announcing the race. "At the quarter it is Mazzola and Appleknocker. . . . At the half it is Whozit. . . ." No mention of Lucky Dan at all, and I am catching daggers from the two Irishmen. "They are turning into the stretch . . . into the straightaway . . . they are in a bunch at the wire . . . it is a blanket finish." Then came the first mention of our horse. "The winner is Lucky Dan." That goddam horse paid $68.40! Jesus Christ Almighty. We were all so happy I talked them into giving me half the winnings.

That night my aunts heard the heavy jingle in my pockets and noticed my devil-may-care attitude. They asked me where I got the money and said that they would be able to tell if I was lying. So I confessed to having won it in a crap game and promised never to do it again. That satisfied them. Dice and cards, for some reason, didn't upset them as much as horses.

For a while my friends asked me to pick winners for them. I thought I had a special touch myself, but my reputation didn't last very long.

I want to get one thing across about horse racing, which is something I know quite a bit about. Well, actually, I know very little about it. All I know is that picking winners is a matter of sheer, dumb luck. I went back to that book every day for a month until I could read the racing form pretty good . . . how much the horse carries, what he did last year, how he finished a week ago Tuesday. Racing forms in those days were much more detailed than they are now because there weren't as many horses to cover. You could find out all kinds of facts. I found out that Lucky Dan hadn't been in the money for four years and that he was ten years old. That shows how lucky you have to be.

Winning a bet on a horse at an early age is one of the worst things that can happen to you. It was an accident that I didn't get bit by the bug worse than I did, for which I can thank Augie Kieckhefer. He made me forget about horse racing altogether for a number of years. Augie owned not only the big room in the Loop but a big billiard chalk business that his father left him, and was worth hundreds of thousands of dollars. He kept two phones at his desk so he could call his book and his book could call him. He lost the whole works, every fucking nickel his father left him, over those horses.

A few years later I got stung again. I was picking winners like mad, but losing money because I didn't know how to bet, didn't know how to manage my taw. Once I picked four winners out of eight races and lost nine hundred dollars. So I quit that sport again. It is a bad deal because you don't have any personal control over what is happening. You never know when the nags are doped or the jockeys have something cooked up.

Jockeys can do all sorts of things. Two or three can gang up on the favorite and box him in, make sure he doesn't win. Hell, I've had jockeys stand up in the stirrups in the stretch and haul back on the reins just to beat me out of the money. Before cameras came in it was hard to catch these things, hard to prove anything. Now they keep a camera on everybody from the front, back, side, everywhere, and they have to keep pretty much in line. One thing they still do is let some other jockey have it right in the teeth with a whip, which sort of throws the man off stride.

But it is hard to resist going to the track when there is nothing doing at a billiard room. You have got to have something working for you at all times, otherwise you stand no chance of making any kind of a score. So I keep finding myself at horse races with guys who are worse idiots than I am. As long as I keep thinking of Augie, though, I am all right.

Bob Cannafax

There are a lot of ways to win without actually cheating, more ways in billiards than in most games because it is played in silence, with time between shots for studying and aiming. That gives the man in the chair a chance to sneeze, go to the can, knock over a chair, and so on. It is what is called the psychological hustle. In the plain ordinary hustle you hide your true speed; in the psychological hustle you try to drive your opponent out of his fucking skull. Make him nervous, at least.

There are many things you can do. Bob Cannafax, one of the great billiard players of the 1920's, used to pretend that something was wrong with his eyes. He squinted and blinked and seemed to be suffering. When he sat down in the player's chair after his inning he threw his head back and with a lot of showmanship put drops in his eyes, acting like he might go blind at any minute. The idea was to make it just a little harder for the other guy to concentrate on the game.

Cannafax had a wooden leg, and when he limped around the table he would slip a little and examine the floor and complain that there were some slick spots. That made the whole audience nervous, not just his opponent, because nobody wants to see a handicapped person fall on his ass.

Cannafax had a quick temper, too, and he made sure his opponent knew it. Once he was scheduled to play an exhibition game and a few hours beforehand he went to the room to look at the table. He didn't like the condition of the cloth and demanded that a new one be put on. The proprietor said he wouldn't do it. So Cannafax took out a penknife and ripped the cloth from one end to another. They *had* to change it, then. It was all part of his general hustle. When you played him you had to worry about his eyes, his leg, and his temper.

There is a small-time pool player in San Francisco called Snakeface who pretends that if he gets beat he might go crazy or get a heart attack. He's no youngster, but when he misses a shot or gets a bad break he jumps back, swings his cue in a circle, cusses with all his strength, and turns beet red. Years ago he used to put his head down and run himself into the wall, but he gave that up. This act puts quite a bit of pressure on the guy he is playing, who may not want to kill an old man for two dollars.

Alfredo De Oro

The all-time master of the psychological hustle was a Cuban: Alfredo De Oro. He was a foreigner, but he spoke fine English—not with a limp like so many of them. When I first saw him in 1920 he was already way over sixty years old, maybe over seventy. Because he had lost some of his skill he had learned every possible way to irritate the other fellow and throw him off his game.

In his time he was quite a player. The record book shows that he won the world's title in pool in 1887 and won it fifteen more times after that. He won the three-cushion title at least six times, back around the turn of the century.

I met a lot of the old-timers in 1923 when I won the Chicago Junior Amateur—Hoppe, Emmet Blankenship, Buffalo Dowd. Nobody ever heard of Buffalo Dowd today, but at one time he was one of the biggest thieves in the country. I played exhibitions against most of them—the young against the old.

In the 1920's De Oro was past his prime and getting hunchbacked. He couldn't shoot well anymore, but he won games with sheer orneriness. He was old, with a big soup-strainer mustache, but he wasn't feeble. You could tell he had played before, but you always knew in advance what shot he would shoot. He would go outside the first ball, dropping it against the end rail, and bring the cueball up to the other end near the red ball. Strictly run and hide. One and duck. Stall safeties. He averaged close to nothing but he never left anything to shoot at.

He complained constantly. He objected to the referee's calls. He went to the can and stayed there forever, but if the other guy took a quick piss he raised the roof and demanded the game by forfeit. He shot deliberate safeties and then argued that he had tried to score, walking around the arena looking into the audience for support. "Is there a man here who can honestly say I didn't try to make that shot?"

He was a rib artist with a million irritating remarks. If you ignored what he said to you, then he would mutter to himself on the sidelines. While his opponent was trying to shoot, Alfredo was polishing his cue, or chalking it with loud squeaks, or filing the tip, or dropping it on the floor, or coughing, or sending up clouds of talcum powder. If the referee told him to stop doing those things, he would start doing a whole raft of *other* things. I've seen him change shafts just for one shot, taking all day about it.

You see players today whipping out a handkerchief just when the man at the table is about to shoot, but you should have seen the way Alfredo did it. It was masterful. He kept his handkerchief folded like an accordion, with the tip sticking out so he could grab it without fumbling. It was big, a big brilliant white handkerchief. When he snaked it out of his pocket he always sort of shook it to the right and left like a long scarf before putting it to his nose and honking.

And the way he lit a cigar in the other guy's line of sight! His timing on striking the match was terrific. I used to sit in the stands trying to second-guess him. The man at the table would be stroking, just about ready to pull the trigger. Alfredo watched him like a hawk, holding a big kitchen match against a box ready to strike it. "Now!" I would think to myself, leaning forward, anticipating him, but he would wait. "Now!" Not yet. Alfredo waited, watching the man stroke, studying him, then suddenly he would strike the match just as the guy was bringing his cue forward to hit the cueball. It was beautiful.

He played defense at the table and offense on the sidelines, and the fans crowded in to watch his antics.

Once he managed to claw and scratch his way to win over Cochran in the days when Cochran could shoot the lights out. That crusty, bent old man won a game from the great Cochran, who was one of the flashiest, most brilliant players of all time. It was a sensation when it happened, and old-timers still talk about it. Cochran had an excuse, though, that has never been put in print before. He told it only to the members of his immediate family.

Here is what Welker said:

"I knew the old man would have to take at least six piss breaks during the game. I couldn't complain about it because of his age, and I wasn't going to let it bother me if he took a lot of time. Halfway through the game he hadn't yet asked for permission to leave the table, and I started worrying about him. Started worrying about his bladder. After an hour he still hadn't gone to the can. Was he all right? Was he going to go in his pants? Was he in pain trying to hold it back? I got so worried about his bladder I couldn't concentrate on what I was doing. That old man did not take one piss the whole game, and that is what beat me."

The Talisman

BY HONORE DE BALZAC

Gambling was rampant among all classes throughout eighteenth- and nineteenth-century Europe, and countries influenced by European ways, and there is hardly a major novelist of the period who doesn't at some point refer to gambling. Particularly memorable are scenes in Tobias Smollett's *Count Ferdinand Fathom,* William Thackery's *Barry Lyndon,* and Leo Tolstoy's *War and Peace,* in which the directions of lives are changed at the gaming tables. In the American context, there is the story that Edgar Allan Poe might have had a career in the military if he hadn't lost all his money gambling while in school. (This might be considered an example of what philosophers call "moral luck," in which a bad event produces a good result.)

The great French novelist Balzac once proclaimed, "The world is mine because I understand it." The driving force of his "Human Comedy," consisting of over 90 novels written largely at night over strong coffee, is the attempt to represent and understand human passions. In the following selection, the opening of *The Wild Asses Skin,* Balzac deftly sketches the gambling dens of 1830s Paris as the backdrop against which a young man ventures his desperate wager. The short, devastating scene concentrates on the hardened sizing up of the man by onlookers as his personal drama unfolds.

T owards the end of October 1830 a young man entered the Palais-Royal just as the gambling-houses were opening in conformity with the law which protects an essentially taxable passion. Without too much hesitation he walked up the staircase of the gambling-den designated as No. 36

'Your hat, sir, if you please!' This cry, ejaculated in a sharp and scolding voice, came from a small, pallid old man squatting in the shadow behind a barrier, who suddenly rose to his feet and displayed a very ignoble type of countenance.

When you enter a gambling-house, the first thing the law does is to deprive you of your hat. Is this as it were a parable from the Gospel or a providential warning? Or is it not rather a way of concluding an infernal pact with you by exacting a sort of pledge? Might it not be devised in order to force you to show due respect to those who are about to win your money from you? Or do the police, lurking near every social sewer, insist on knowing the name of your hatter or your own if you have written it on the lining? Or indeed is it their purpose to take the measure of your skull and to draw up illuminating statistics on the cerebral capacity of gamblers? Administrative authorities remain completely silent on this point. But make no mistake about this: scarcely have you taken one step towards the green table before your hat no longer belongs to you any more than you belong to yourself: you are yourself at stake—you, your fortune, your headgear, your cane and your cloak. When you go out, the Spirit of Gaming will show you, by putting an atrocious epigram into action, that it is still leaving you something by restoring your personal belongings. But if your hat happens to be a new one, you will learn to your cost that if you go gambling, you need to dress the part.

The young man's astonishment as he received a numbered ticket in exchange for his hat, of which the brim was luckily slightly shabby, was proof that he was still innocent of soul; reason enough for the little old man, who no doubt had wallowed since youth in the scalding pleasures of a gamester's life, to give him a lack-lustre, lukewarm glance into which a thinking man might well have read the sufferings of doss-house inmates, the vagrancy of down-and-outs, the inquests held on innumerable charcoal-fume fatalities, sentences to penal servitude and transportation to overseas colonies. This man, who to judge by his haggard white face lived on nothing more nourishing than the gelatinous soups provided by popular caterers, offered the pale image of passion reduced to its simplest terms. Old torments had left their mark in the wrinkles on his brow: obviously he was in the habit of staking his meagre wages the very day he drew them. Like jaded horses no longer responsive to the whip, he was impervious to any thrill: the muffled groans of ruined gamesters, their mute imprecations, their vacant stares made no impression on him at all. He was the very incarnation of the gaming table. If the young man had paused to contemplate this dreary-looking Cerberus, he might perhaps have told himself: 'Nothing but a pack of cards is left in that man's heart!'

But the young stranger paid no heed to this warning in human guise, placed there no doubt by the same Providence which has set the seal of disgust over the threshold of all disorderly houses. He stepped boldly into the gaming-room in which the chink of gold coins was exercising its dazzling fascination over the senses driven by the desire for gain. The young man had probably come here in obedience to the most logical and most eloquently expressed of Jean-Jacques Rousseau's thoughts—a sad one. 'Yes, I can understand a man taking to gambling, but only when he can no longer see anything but one last florin between him and death.'

In the evenings, gaming-houses have but a commonplace poetry about them, even though the effect of it is as assured as that of a gory melodrama. The various salons are teeming with spectators and players; indigent old men who shuffle along there to find warmth; tormented faces belonging to those whose orgies began in wine and will end up in the Seine. Though there is passion in abundance, the multitude of actors prevents you from staring the demon of gambling full in the face. The evening session is a genuine concert-piece to which the entire company contributes, in which every orchestral instrument has its phrase to execute. You may well see many respectable people who come there for distraction and pay for it jus a they would pay for the pleasure of an evening at the theatre or that of a lavish meal, or just as they might climb up to a garret to buy on the cheap three months of sharp regret. But can you realize what delirium, what frenzy possesses the mind of a man impatiently waiting for a gambling-den to open? Between the evening and the morning gambler the same difference exists as between the nonchalant husband and the ecstatic lover waiting under his mistress's window. It is only in the morning that quivering passion and stark need manifest themselves in all their horror. At that time of day you may stare in wonderment at the true gambler who has not eaten or slept, lived or thought, so cruelly has he been scourged by the scorpion of his vice, so sorely has he been itching to make his throw at *trente-et-quarante*. At that baleful hour you will meet with eyes whose steady calm is frightening, with faces that hold you spellbound; you will intercept gazes which lift the cards and greedily peer beneath them.

Gaming-houses then reach sublimity only at opening time. Spain has its bull-fights, Rome had its gladiators. But Paris takes pride in its Palais-Royal, whose teasing roulette wheels afford spectators in the pit the pleasure of seeing blood flow freely without running the risk of their feet slithering in it. Cast a furtive glance into this arena! Venture down into it! . . . How bare it all is! The walls, covered with greasy wallpaper up to head height, show nothing that might refresh the spirit. There is not even a nail there to make it easier to hang oneself. The floor is worn and dirty. An oblong table occupies the middle of the room. The plainness of the straw-bottomed chairs crowded round the baize cloth, worn threadbare by the raking-in of gold coins, bespeaks a strange indifference to luxury in people who come there to perish in their quest of the fortune that can buy luxury.

This very human contradiction may be discovered wherever the soul reacts powerfully on itself. A man in love wants to clothe his mistress in silk, drape her in a soft, oriental gauze. Yet, most of the time, he makes love to her on a truckle-bed. The ambitious man dreams that he is at the pinnacle of power while he is still grovelling in the mire of servility. The tradesman vegetates in the depths of a damp unhealthy shop while he builds a huge mansion from which his son, having taken premature possession, will be ousted by fraternal litigation. But, when all is said and done, does anything less pleasureable exist than a 'house of pleasure'? A singular problem! Man, always at war with himself, finding his hopes cheated by his present ills and cheating his present ills with hopes for a future over which he has no control, imprints all his actions with the stamp of inconsistency and feebleness. Here below only calamity is ever complete.

At the moment when the young man entered the *salon de jeu* a few gamblers were already there. Three bald-headed old men were nonchalantly sitting round the green cloth; their plaster-white faces, as impassive as those of diplomats, betokened jaded souls and hearts which long since had forgotten how to beat even after they had staked not only their own, but also their wives', personal property. A young black-haired olive-skinned Italian was placidly leaning his elbows on the end of the table and appeared to be listening to that inner voice which gives prophetic warning to gamblers: 'Yes!—No!' His southerner's head was breathing fire and dreaming gold. Seven or eight onlookers were standing round in anticipation of the dramatic scenes which were being prepared by the vagaries of chance, the expressiveness of the gamblers' faces and the to-and-fro movement of coins under the croupier's rake. They stood idly by, silent and motionless, as watchful as a crowd gathered on the Place de Grève to see an execution.

A tall, spare man in a threadbare coat was holding a register in one hand and in the other a pin for pricking off the sequences of Red and Black. He was like a modern Tantalus, one of those men who live just out of reach of the enjoyment of their times, a miser with no store of coins, one who can only lay imaginary stakes: a kind of reasoning madman who consoled himself for his poverty by nursing a chimæra, who in fact dallied with vice and hazard as young priests do with the sacred elements when they are rehearsing for their first Mass. Sitting opposite the bank were one or two of those shrewd punters, expert in gambling odds and very like hardened convicts no longer afraid of the hulks, who had come there to risk three throws and carry off on the spot their likely winnings which were what they lived on. Two elderly attendants were walking unconcernedly up and down with arms crossed, and every now and then they stood at the windows overlooking the gardens as if to exhibit their featureless faces to passers-by as a sort of shop-sign.

The banker and the croupier had just cast on the punters their characteristically ashen and chilling glance and were uttering their high-pitched call: 'Lay your stakes!' when the young man opened the door. The silence grew somewhat more profound and heads were turned towards the newcomer. Wonder of wonders, the old men with dulled senses, the stony-faced attendants, the onlookers, and even the single-minded Italian, the whole assembly in fact, when they saw the stranger appear, experienced an appalling kind of emotion. Must not a man be inordinately unhappy to awaken pity, extremely enfeebled to excite sympathy, or else very sinister-looking to cause a shudder to pass through those who frequent such a den as this where grief has to be muted, where indigence must pretend to be gay, where even despair must behave in a seemly fashion? Such factors did indeed enter into the unprecedented sensation which stirred these icy hearts when the young man stepped in. But have not even executioners been moved to tears over maidens whose fair heads were about to be severed at the bidding of the Revolution?

At their first glance the gamblers were able to read some horrible mystery in the newcomer's face. His youthful features were stamped with a clouded grace and the look in his eyes bore witness to efforts betrayed and to a thousand hopes deceived. The gloomy passivity of intended suicide imparted to his brow a dull, unhealthy pallor, a bitter smile drew creases round the corners of his mouth, and his whole physiognomy expressed a resignation which was distressing to behold.

Some spark of undiscovered genius flashed deep down in those eyes, upon which pleasure perhaps had cast a veil of fatigue. Was it debauchery that had put its noisome seal upon that noble face, once bright and innocent, but now degraded? Doctors would no doubt have attributed to lesions of heart or lungs the yellow ring around the eyelids and the hectic flush on the cheeks, whereas poets would have discerned in these signs the ravages of knowledge, the traces of nights spent under the gleam of the student's lamp. But a passion more fatal than disease, a disease more pitiless than study and genius were robbing this young head of its beauty, contracting those still vigorous muscles, wringing the heart as yet only lightly touched by orgy, illness and the pursuit of knowledge. Just as, when a famous criminal arrives at the galleys he is respectfully welcomed by the convicts, so all these human demons, well-versed in torture, acclaimed an exorbitant sorrow and a wound whose depths their gaze could probe; they acknowledged him as a prince of their tribe thanks to the majesty of his mute irony and the elegant shabbiness of his attire.

Admittedly the young man had a stylish evening coat, but the junction of his waistcoat and cravat was too carefully preserved for one to suppose that he was wearing linen underneath. His hands, as dainty as a woman's, were none too clean; in fact, for the last two days he had worn no gloves. If the banker and his assistants shuddered, it was because some vestiges of the charm of innocence still bloomed in his slender, delicate proportions, his sparse, fair and naturally curly hair. He still had the face of a young man of twenty-five, and vice looked only to have touched it lightly. The vitality of youth was still warring with the enervating effects of dissipation; the struggle between light and darkness, between the forces of death and those of life gave an impression of grace as well as horror. The young man was standing there like an angel stripped of his halo, one who had strayed from his path. And so each of those emeritus professors of vice and infamy, like toothless old women seized with pity at the sight of a beautiful girl offering herself up to corruption, was ready to call out to the novice: 'Leave this place!' But the young man walked straight up to the table, remained standing, and blindly threw on to the cloth a gold coin he had been holding. It rolled on to black. Then, with the fortitude of such souls as abhor pettifogging uncertainties, he looked at the banker with a glance which was at once turbulent and calm.

This throw aroused such great interest that the old men laid no stake. But the Italian, in passionate single-mindedness, seized on an idea which took his fancy: he laid his pile of gold on the red in opposition to the stranger's play. The banker forgot to utter the conventional phrases which by dint of repetition have degenerated into a raucous and unintelligible cry:

'Place your bets!'

'The bets are placed!'

'Betting is closed!'

The dealer spread out the cards and seemed to be wishing good luck to the latest arrival, indifferent as he was to the loss or gain sustained by those addicted to those sombre pleasures. All the watchers guessed that the melodramatic closing scene of a noble life hung on the fate of that one gold coin; their eyes glittered as they studied the fateful scraps of pasteboard. And yet, in spite of the intentness with which they scrutinized turn by turn the young man and the cards, they could perceive no sign of emotion on his cold, resigned face.

'Red wins,' the dealer proclaimed. 'And even numbers over eighteen.'

A strange, muffled rattle issued from the Italian's throat as he saw the crumpled bank-notes falling one by one as the banker threw them down to him. As for the young man, he did not realize he had lost until the croupier stretched out his rake to pull in his last napoleon. The ivory hit the gold with a sharp click and the coin, fast as an arrow, shot across the table to join the pile of gold spread out in front of the bank. The stranger gently closed his eyes and the colour faded from his lips. But he soon lifted his eyelids again, his mouth regained its coral redness, he put on the air of an Englishman who sees no further mystery in life, and disappeared without even one of those pleading looks which despairing gamblers often cast around the ring of bystanders, hoping for some consolation. How many events can be crowded into the space of a second! How much depends on the throw of a dice!

'I bet that was the last shot in his locker!' the croupier said with a grin, after a moment's silence while he held the gold coin between his forefinger and thumb to show it to the assembled company.

'A young idiot who's going to jump into the river!' said an old *habitué*, looking round him at the gamblers, who all knew one another.

'Likely enough!' exclaimed an attendant as he took a pinch of snuff.

'If only we had followed that gentleman's example!' one of the old men said to his cronies as he pointed to the Italian.

All eyes were turned to the lucky gambler, whose hands shook as he counted his bank-notes.

'I heard,' he said, 'a voice crying in my ear: "The Game will get the better of that young man's despair."'

'He's no gambler,' the banker responded. 'Otherwise he would have divided his money into three lots to stand a better chance.'

The young man was leaving without claiming his hat, but the old watchdog, having noticed its battered condition, returned it to him without a word. The young gamester automatically gave up the check and went downstairs whistling *Di tanto palpiti* so softly that he himself could scarcely hear its charming notes.

High Stakes

BY P. G. WODEHOUSE

Growing up a city kid, golf seemed to me an improbable gambling game, because I associated gambling with smoky, seedy, indoor spaces (if outdoors, a crap game against a building wall), and golf with pastoral landscape and manicured grass. Because of the exclusivity of its clubs, and its preppified outfits, it was difficult for me to think of golf as a game on which people might bet their bottom dollar—more a thing in which the whitest of gentleman used money as symbolic currency for the bragging rights really at stake. At its most entertaining golf gambling was James Bond outcheating Auric Goldfinger for a bar of gold. This was, of course, in the days before Tiger Woods, Michael Jordan, and Charles Barkley began to change the game's public complexion.

Of course these prejudices of mine against golf as a gambling game were wrong. People of every sort gamble on golf, which, as a combination of finesse and athleticism, played on a moderately level field, offers extraordinary opportunities for hustle. The golf hustles of the legendary Titanic Thompson, who claimed he never beat anyone by more than a stroke because it might hurt their feelings, make up some of the great gambling lore.

The British humorist P. G. Wodehouse, known to his fans as "Plum," wrote about one hundred volumes, including novels, story collections, and poetry. His most memorable character, Jeeves, is a valet, or gentleman's personal gentleman, like the one who appears in the selection that follows, in which debonair golf buffoons try to con each other out of what each holds most dear. Wodehouse's golf stories are collected in *The Golf Omnibus*.

The summer day was drawing to a close. Over the terrace outside the club-house the chestnut trees threw long shadows, and such bees as still lingered in the flower-beds had the air of tired business men who are about ready to shut up the office and go off to dinner and a musical comedy. The Oldest Member, stirring in his favourite chair, glanced at his watch and yawned.

As he did so, from the neighbourhood of the eighteenth green, hidden from his view by the slope of the ground, there came suddenly a medley of shrill animal cries, and he deduced that some belated match must just have reached a finish. His surmise was correct. The babble of voices drew nearer, and over the brow of the hill came a little group of men. Two, who appeared to be the ringleaders in the affair, were short and stout. One was cheerful and the other dejected. The rest of the company consisted of friends and adherents; and one of these, a young man who seemed to be amused, strolled to where the Oldest Member sat.

"What," inquired the Sage, "was all the shouting for?"

The young man sank into a chair and lighted a cigarette.

"Perkins and Broster," he said, "were all square at the seventeenth, and they raised the stakes to fifty pounds. They were both on the green in seven, and Perkins had a two-foot putt to halve the match. He missed it by six inches. They play pretty high, those two."

"It is a curious thing," said the Oldest Member, "that men whose golf is of a kind that makes hardened caddies wince always do. The more competent a player, the smaller the stake that contents him. It is only when you get down into the submerged tenth of the golfing world that you find the big gambling. However, I would not call fifty pounds anything sensational in the case of two men like Perkins and Broster. They are both well provided with the world's goods. If you would care to hear the story—"

The young man's jaw fell a couple of notches.

"I had no idea it was so late," he bleated. "I ought to be—"

"—of a man who played for really high stakes—"

"I promised to—"

"—I will tell it to you," said the Sage.

"Look here," said the young man, sullenly, "it isn't one of those stories about two men who fall in love with the same girl and play a match to decide which is to marry her, is it? Because if so—"

"The stake to which I allude," said the Oldest Member, "was something far higher and bigger than a woman's love. Shall I proceed?"

"All right," said the young man, resignedly. "Snap into it."

It has been well said—I think by the man who wrote the sub-titles for "Cage-Birds of Society" (began the Oldest Member)—that wealth does not always bring happiness. It was so with Bradbury Fisher, the hero of the story which I am about to relate. One of America's most prominent tainted million-aires, he had two sorrows in life—his handicap refused to stir from twenty-four and his wife disapproved of his collection of famous golf relics. Once, finding him crooning over the trousers in which Ouimet had won his historic replay against Vardon and Ray in the American Open, she had asked him why he did not collect something worth while, like Old Masters or first editions.

Worth while! Bradbury had forgiven, for he loved the woman, but he could not forget.

For Bradbury Fisher, like so many men who have taken to the game in middle age, after a youth misspent in the pursuits of commerce, was no half-hearted enthusiast. Although he still occasionally descended on Wall Street in order to prise the small investor loose from another couple of million, what he really lived for now was golf and his collection. He had begun the collection in his first year as a golfer, and he prized it dearly. And when he reflected that his wife had stopped him purchasing J. H. Taylor's shirt-stud, which he could have had for a few hundred pounds, the iron seemed to enter into his soul.

The distressing episode had occurred in London, and he was now on his way back to New York, having left his wife to continue her holiday in England. All through the voyage he remained moody and distrait; and at the ship's concert, at which he was forced to take the chair, he was heard to observe to the purser that if the alleged soprano who had just sung "My Little Grey Home in the West" had the immortal gall to take a second encore he hoped that she would trip over a high note and dislocate her neck.

Such was Bradbury Fisher's mood throughout the ocean journey, and it remained constant until he arrived at his palatial home at Goldenville, Long Island, where, as he sat smoking a moody after-dinner cigar in the Versailles drawing room, Blizzard, his English butler, informed him that Mr. Gladstone Bott desired to speak to him on the telephone.

"Tell him to go and boil himself," said Bradbury.

"Very good, sir."

"No, I'll tell him myself," said Bradbury. He strode to the telephone. "Hullo!" he said, curtly.

He was not fond of this Bott. There are certain men who seem fated to go through life as rivals. It was so with Bradbury Fisher and J. Gladstone Bott. Born in the same town within a few days of one another, they had come to New York in the same week, and from that moment their careers had run side by side. Fisher had made his first million two days before Bott, but Bott's first divorce had got half a column and two sticks more publicity than Fisher's.

At Sing-Sing, where each had spent several happy years of early manhood, they had run neck and neck for the prizes which that institution has to offer. Fisher secured the position of catcher on the baseball nine in preference to Bott, but Bott just nosed Fisher out when it came to the choice of a tenor for the glee club. Bott was selected for the debating contest against Auburn, but Fisher got the last place on the crossword puzzle team, with Bott merely first reserve.

They had taken up golf simultaneously, and their handicaps had remained level ever since. Between such men it is not surprising that there was little love lost.

"Hullo!" said Gladstone Bott. "So you're back? Say, listen, Fisher. I think I've got something that'll interest you. Something you'll be glad to have in your golf collection."

Bradbury Fisher's mood softened. He disliked Bott, but that was no reason for not doing business with him. And though he had little faith in the man's judgment it might be that he had stumbled upon some valuable antique. There crossed his mind the comforting thought that his wife was three thousand miles away and that he was no longer under her penetrating eye—that eye which, so to speak, was always "about his bath and about his bed and spying out all his ways".

"I've just returned from a trip down South," proceeded Bott, "and I have secured the authentic baffy used by Bobby Jones in his first important contest—the Infants' All-In Championship of Atlanta, Georgia, open to those of both sexes not yet having finished teething."

Bradbury gasped. He had heard rumours that this treasure was in existence, but he had never credited them.

"You're sure?" he cried. "You're positive it's genuine?"

"I have a written guarantee from Mr. Jones, Mrs. Jones, and the nurse."

"How much, Bott, old man?" stammered Bradbury. "How much do you want for it, Gladstone, old top? I'll give you a hundred thousand dollars."

"Ha!"

"Five hundred thousand."

"Ha, ha!"

"A million."

"Ha, ha, ha!"

"Two million."

"Ha, ha, ha, ha!"

Bradbury Fisher's strong face twisted like that of a tortured fiend. He registered in quick succession rage, despair, hate, fury, anguish, pique, and resentment. But when he spoke again his voice was soft and gentle.

"Gladdy, old socks," he said, "we have been friends for years."

"No, we haven't," said Gladstone Bott.

"Yes, we have."

"No, we haven't."

"Well, anyway, what about two million five hundred?"

"Nothing doing. Say, listen. Do you really want that baffy?"

"I do, Botty, old egg, I do indeed."

"Then listen. I'll exchange it for Blizzard."

"For Blizzard?" quavered Fisher.

"For Blizzard."

It occurs to me that, when describing the closeness of the rivalry between these two men, I may have conveyed the impression that in no department of life could either claim a definite advantage over the other. If that is so, I erred. It is true that in a general way, whatever one had, the other had something equally good to counterbalance it; but in just one matter Bradbury Fisher had triumphed completely over Gladstone Bott. Bradbury Fisher had the finest English butler on Long Island.

Blizzard stood alone. There is a regrettable tendency on the part of English butlers today to deviate more and more from the type which made their species famous. The modern butler has a nasty knack of being a lissom young man in perfect condition who looks like the son of the house. But Blizzard was of the fine old school. Before coming to the Fisher home he had been for fifteen years in the service of an earl, and his appearance suggested that throughout those fifteen years he had not let a day pass without its pint of port. He radiated port and popeyed dignity. He had splay feet and three chins, and when he walked his curving waistcoat preceded him like the advance guard of some royal procession.

From the first, Bradbury had been perfectly aware that Bott coveted Blizzard, and the knowledge had sweetened his life. But this was the first time he had come out into the open and admitted it.

"Blizzard?" whispered Fisher.

"Blizzard," said Bott firmly. "It's my wife's birthday next week, and I've been wondering what to give her."

Bradbury Fisher shuddered from head to foot, and his legs wobbled like asparagus stalks. Beads of perspiration stood out on his forehead. The serpent was tempting him—tempting him grievously.

"You're sure you won't take three million—or four—or something like that?"

"No; I want Blizzard."

Bradbury Fisher passed his handkerchief over his streaming brow. "So be it," he said in a low voice.

The Jones baffy arrived that night, and for some hours Bradbury Fisher gloated over it with the unmixed joy of a collector who has secured the prize of a lifetime. Then, stealing gradually over him, came the realization of what he had done.

He was thinking of his wife and what she would say when she heard of this. Blizzard was Mrs. Fisher's pride and joy. She had never, like the poet, rear'd a young gazelle, but, had she done so, her attitude towards it would have been identical with her attitude towards Blizzard. Although so far away, it was plain that her thoughts still lingered with the pleasure she had left at home, for on his arrival Bradbury had found three cables awaiting him.

The first ran:
"How is Blizzard? Reply."

The second:
"How is Blizzard's sciatica? Reply."

The third:
   "Blizzard's hiccups. How are they? Suggest Doctor Murphy's Tonic Swamp-Juice. Highly spoken of. Three times a day after meals. Try for week and cable result."

It did not require a clairvoyant to tell Bradbury that, if on her return she found that he had disposed of Blizzard in exchange for a child's cut-down baffy, she would certainly sue for divorce. And there was not a jury in America that would not give their verdict in her favour without a dissentient voice. His first wife, he recalled, had divorced him on far flimsier grounds. So had his second, third, and fourth. And Bradbury loved his wife. There had been a time in his life when, if he lost a wife, he had felt philosophically that there would be another along in a minute; but, as a man grows older, he tends to become set in his habits, and he could not contemplate existence without the company of the present incumbent.

What, therefore, to do? What, when you came right down to it, to do?

There seemed no way out of the dilemma. If he kept the Jones baffy, no other price would satisfy Bott's jealous greed. And to part with the baffy, now that it was actually in his possession, was unthinkable.

And then, in the small hours of the morning, as he tossed sleeplessly on is Louis Quinze bed, his giant brain conceived a plan.

On the following afternoon he made his way to the club-house, and was informed that Bott was out playing around with another millionaire of his acquaintance. Bradbury waited, and presently his rival appeared.

"Hey!" said Gladstone Bott, in his abrupt uncouth way. "When are you going to deliver that butler?"

"I will make the shipment at the earliest date," said Bradbury.

"I was expecting him last night."

"You shall have him shortly."

"What do you feed him on?" asked Gladstone Bott.

"Oh, anything you have yourselves. Put sulphur in his port in the hot weather. Tell me, how did your match go?"

"He beat me. I had rotten luck."

Bradbury Fisher's eyes gleamed. His moment had come.

"Luck?" he said. "What do you mean, luck? Luck has nothing to do with it. You're always beefing about your luck. The trouble with you is that you play rottenly."

"What!"

"It is no use trying to play golf unless you learn the first principles and do it properly. Look at the way you drive."

"What's wrong with my driving?"

"Nothing, except that you don't do anything right. In driving, as the club comes back in the swing, the weight should be shifted by degrees, quietly and gradually, until, when the club has reached its topmost point, the whole weight of the body is supported by the right leg, the left foot being turned at the time and the left knee bent in towards the right leg. But, regardless of how much you perfect your style, you cannot develop any method which will not require you to keep your head still so that you can see your ball clearly."

"Hey!"

"It is obvious that it is impossible to introduce a jerk or a sudden violent effort into any part of the swing without disturbing the balance or moving the head. I want to drive home the fact that it is absolutely essential to——"

"Hey!" cried Gladstone Bott.

The man was shaken to the core. From the local pro, and from scratch men of his acquaintance, he would gladly have listened to this sort of thing by the hour, but to hear these words from Bradbury Fisher, whose handicap was the same as his own, and out of whom it was his imperishable conviction that he could hammer the tar any time he got him out on the links, was too much.

"Where do you get off," he demanded, heatedly, "trying to teach me golf?"

Bradbury Fisher chuckled to himself. Everything was working out as his subtle mind had foreseen.

"My dear fellow," he said, "I was only speaking for your good."

"I like your nerve! I can lick you any time we start."

"It's easy enough to talk."

"I trimmed you twice the week before you sailed to England."

"Naturally," said Bradbury Fisher, "in a friendly round, with only a few thousand dollars on the match, a man does not extend himself. You wouldn't dare to play me for anything that really mattered."

"I'll play you when you like for anything you like."

"Very well. I'll play you for Blizzard."

"Against what?"

"Oh, anything you please. How about a couple of railroads?"

"Make it three."

"Very well."

"Next Friday suit you?"

"Sure," said Bradbury Fisher.

It seemed to him that his troubles were over. Like all twenty-four-handicap men, he had the most perfect confidence in his ability to beat all other twenty-four-handicap men. As for Gladstone Bott, he knew that he could disembowel him at any time he was able to lure him out of the club-house.

Nevertheless, as he breakfasted on the morning of the fateful match, Bradbury Fisher was conscious of an unwonted nervousness. He was no weakling. In Wall Street his phlegm in moments of stress was a byword. On the famous occasion when the B. and G. crowd had attacked C. and D., and in order to keep control of L. and M. he had been compelled to buy so largely of S. and T., he had not turned a hair. And yet this morning, in endeavouring to prong up segments of bacon, he twice missed the plate altogether and on a third occasion speared himself in the cheek with his fork. The spectacle of Blizzard, so calm, so competent, so supremely the perfect butler, unnerved him.

"I am jumpy today, Blizzard," he said, forcing a laugh.

"Yes, sir. You do, indeed, appear to have the willies."

"Yes. I am playing a very important golf-match this morning."

"Indeed, sir?"

"I must pull myself together, Blizzard."

"Yes, sir. And, if I may respectfully make the suggestion, you should endeavour, when in action, to keep the head down and the eye rigidly upon the ball."

"I will, Blizzard, I will," said Bradbury Fisher, his keen eyes clouding under a sudden mist of tears. "Thank you, Blizzard, for the advice."

"Not at all, sir."

"How is your sciatica, Blizzard?"

"A trifle improved, I thank you, sir."

"And your hiccups?"

"I am conscious of a slight though possibly only a temporary relief, sir."

"Good," said Bradbury Fisher.

He left the room with a firm step and, proceeding to his library, read for a while portions of that grand chapter in James Braid's *Advanced Golf* which dealt with driving into the wind. It was a fair and cloudless morning, but it was as well to be prepared for emergencies. Then, feeling that he had done all that could be done, he ordered the car and was taken to the links.

Gladstone Bott was awaiting him on the first tee, in company with two caddies. A curt greeting, a spin of the coin, and Gladstone Bott, securing the honour, stepped out to begin the contest.

Although there are, of course, endless sub-species in their ranks, not all of which have yet been classified by science, twenty-four-handicap golfers may be stated broadly to fall into two classes, the dashing and the cautious—those, that is to say, who endeavour to do every hole in a brilliant one and those who are content to win with a steady nine. Gladstone Bott was one of the cautious brigade. He fussed about for a few moments like a hen scratching gravel, then with a stiff quarter-swing sent his ball straight down the fairway for a matter of seventy yards, and it was Bradbury Fisher's turn to drive.

Now, normally, Bradbury Fisher was essentially a dasher. It was his habit, as a rule, to raise his left foot some six inches from the ground and, having swayed forcefully back on to his right leg, to sway sharply forward again and lash out with sickening violence in the general direction of the ball. It was a method which at times produced excellent results, though it had the flaw that it was somewhat uncertain. Bradbury Fisher was the only member of the club, with the exception of the club champion, who had ever carried the second green with his drive; but, on the other hand, he was also the only member who had ever laid his drive on the eleventh dead to the pin of the sixteenth.

But today the magnitude of the issues at stake had wrought a change in him. Planted firmly on both feet, he fiddled at the ball in the manner of one playing spillikens. When he swung, it was with a swing resembling that of Gladstone Bott; and, like Bott, he achieved a nice, steady, rainbow-shaped drive of some seventy yards straight down the middle. Bott replied with an eighty-yard brassie shot. Bradbury held him with another. And so, working their way cautiously across the prairie, they came to the green, where Bradbury, laying his third putt dead, halved the hole.

The second was a repetition of the first, the third and fourth repetitions of the second. But on the fifth green the fortunes of the match began to change. Here Gladstone Bott, faced with a fifteen-foot putt to win, smote his ball firmly off the line, as had been his practice at each of the preceding holes, and the ball, hitting a worm-cast and bounding off to the left, ran on a couple of yards, hit another worm-cast, bounded to the right, and finally, bumping into a twig, leaped to the left again and clattered into the tin.

"One up," said Gladstone Bott. "Tricky, some of these greens are. You have to gauge the angles to a nicety."

At the sixth a donkey in an adjoining field uttered a raucous bray just as Bott was addressing his ball with a mashie-niblick on the edge of the green. He started violently and, jerking his club with a spasmodic reflex action of the forearm, holed out.

"Nice work," said Gladstone Bott.

The seventh was a short hole, guarded by two large bunkers between which ran a narrow footpath of turf. Gladstone Bott's mashie-shot, falling short, ran over the rough, peered for a moment into the depths to the left, then, winding up the path, trickled on to the green, struck a fortunate slope, acquired momentum, ran on, and dropped into the hole.

"Nearly missed it," said Gladstone Bott, drawing a deep breath.

Bradbury Fisher looked out upon a world that swam and danced before his eyes. He had not been prepared for this sort of thing. The way things were shaping, he felt that it would hardly surprise him now if the cups were to start jumping up and snapping at Bott's ball like starving dogs.

"Three up," said Gladstone Bott.

With a strong effort Bradbury Fisher mastered his feelings. His mouth set grimly. Matters, he perceived, had reached a crisis. He saw now that he had made a mistake in allowing himself to be intimidated by the importance of the occasion into being scientific. Nature had never intended him for a scientific golfer, and up till now he had been behaving like an animated illustration out of a book by Vardon. He had taken his club back along and near the turf, allowing it to trend around the legs as far as was permitted by the movement of the arms. He had kept his right elbow close to the side, this action coming into operation before the club was allowed to describe a section of a circle in an upward direction, whence it was carried by means of a slow, steady, swinging movement. He had pivoted, he had pronated the wrists, and he had been careful about the lateral hip-shift.

And it had been all wrong. That sort of stuff might suit some people, but not him. He was a biffer, a swatter, and a slosher; and it flashed upon him now that only by biffing, swatting, and sloshing as he had never biffed, swatted, and sloshed before could he hope to recover the ground he had lost.

Gladstone Bott was not one of those players who grow careless with success. His drive at the eighth was just as steady and short as ever. But this time Bradbury Fisher made no attempt to imitate him. For seven holes he had been checking his natural instincts and now he drove with all the banked-up fury that comes with release from long suppression.

For an instant he remained poised on one leg like a stork; then there was a whistle and a crack, and the ball, smitten squarely in the midriff, flew down the course and, soaring over the bunkers, hit the turf and gambolled to within twenty yards of the green.

He straightened out the kinks in his spine with a grim smile. Allowing himself the regulation three putts, he would be down in five, and only a miracle could give Gladstone Bott anything better than a seven.

"Two down," he said some minutes later, and Gladstone Bott nodded sullenly.

It was not often that Bradbury Fisher kept on the fairway with two consecutive drives, but strange things were happening today. Not only was his drive at the ninth a full two hundred and forty yards, but it was also perfectly straight.

"One down," said Bradbury Fisher, and Bott nodded even more sullenly than before.

There are few things more demoralizing than to be consistently outdriven; and when he is outdriven by a hundred and seventy yards at two consecutive holes the bravest man is apt to be shaken. Gladstone Bott was only human. It was with a sinking heart that he watched his opponent heave and sway on the tenth tee; and when the ball once more flew straight and far down the course a strange weakness seemed to come over him. For the first time he lost his morale and topped. The ball trickled into the long grass, and after three fruitless stabs at it with a niblick he picked up, and the match was squared.

At the eleventh Bradbury Fisher also topped, and his tee-shot, though nice and straight, travelled only a couple of feet. He had to scramble to halve in eight.

The twelfth was another short hole; and Bradbury, unable to curb the fine, careless rapture which had crept into his game, had the misfortune to overshoot the green by some sixty yards, thus enabling his opponent to take the lead once more.

The thirteenth and fourteenth were halved, but Bradbury, driving another long ball, won the fifteenth, squaring the match.

It seemed to Bradbury Fisher, as he took his stand on the sixteenth tee, that he now had the situation well in hand. At the thirteenth and fourteenth his drive had flickered, but on the fifteenth it had come back in all its glorious vigour and there appeared to be no reason to suppose that it had not come to stay. He recollected exactly how he had done that last colossal slosh, and he now prepared to reproduce the movements precisely as before. The great thing to remember was to hold the breath on the back-swing and not to release it before the moment of impact. Also, the eyes should not be closed until late in the down-swing. All great golfers have their little secrets, and that was Bradbury's.

With these aids to success firmly fixed in his mind, Bradbury Fisher prepared to give the ball the nastiest bang that a golf-ball had ever had since Edward Blackwell was in his prime. He drew in his breath and, with lungs expanded to their fullest capacity, heaved back on to his large, flat right foot. Then, clenching his teeth, he lashed out.

When he opened his eyes, they fell upon a horrid spectacle. Either he had closed those eyes too soon or else he had breathed too precipitately—whatever the cause, the ball, which should have gone due south, was travelling with great speed sou'-sou'-east. And, even as he gazed, it curved to earth and fell into as uninviting a bit of rough as he had ever penetrated. And he was a man who had spent much time in many roughs.

Leaving Gladstone Bott to continue his imitation of a spavined octogenarian rolling peanuts with a toothpick, Bradbury Fisher, followed by his caddie, set out on the long trail into the jungle.

Hope did not altogether desert him as he walked. In spite of its erratic direction, the ball had been so shrewdly smitten that it was not far from the green. Provided luck was with him and the lie not too desperate, a mashie would put him on the carpet. It was only when he reached the rough and saw what had happened that his heart sank. There the ball lay, half hidden in the grass, while above it waved the straggling tentacle of some tough-looking shrub. Behind it was a stone, and behind the stone, at just the elevation required to catch the back-swing of the club, was a tree. And, by an ironical stroke of fate which drew from Bradbury a hollow, bitter laugh, only a few feet to the right was a beautiful smooth piece of turf from which it would have been a pleasure to play one's second.

Dully, Bradbury looked to see how Bott was getting on. And then suddenly, as he found that Bott was completely invisible behind the belt of bushes through which he had just passed, a voice seemed to whisper to him, "Why not?"

Bradbury Fisher, remember, had spent thirty years in Wall Street.

It was at this moment that he realized that he was not alone. His caddie was standing at his side.

Bradbury Fisher gazed upon the caddie, whom until now he had not had any occasion to observe with any closeness.

The caddie was not a boy. He was a man, apparently in the middle forties, with bushy eyebrows and a walrus moustache; and there was something about his appearance which suggested to Bradbury that here was a kindred spirit. He reminded Bradbury a little of Spike Huggins, the safe-blower, who had been a fresher with him at Sing-Sing. It seemed to him that this caddie could be trusted in a delicate matter involving secrecy and silence. Had he been some babbling urchin, the risk might have been too great.

"Caddie," said Bradbury.

"Sir?" said the caddie.

"Yours is an ill-paid job," said Bradbury.

"It is, indeed, sir," said the caddie.

"Would you like to earn fifty dollars?"

"I would prefer to earn a hundred."

"I meant a hundred," said Bradbury.

He produced a roll of bills from his pocket, and peeled off one of that value. Then, stooping, he picked up his ball and placed it on the little oasis of turf. The caddie bowed intelligently.

"You mean to say," cried Gladstone Bott, a few moments later, "that you were out with your second? With your second!"

"I had a stroke of luck."

"You're sure it wasn't about six strokes of luck?"

"My ball was right out in the open in an excellent lie."

"Oh!" said Gladstone Bott, shortly.

"I have four for it, I think."

"One down," said Gladstone Bott.

"And two to play," trilled Bradbury.

It was with a light heart that Bradbury Fisher teed up on the seventeenth. The match, he felt, was as good as over. The whole essence of golf is to discover a way of getting out of the rough without losing strokes; and with this sensible, broad-minded man of the world caddying for him he seemed to have discovered the ideal way. It cost him scarcely a pang when he saw his drive slice away into a tangle of long grass, but for the sake of appearances he affected a little chagrin.

"Tut, tut!" he said.

"I shouldn't worry," said Gladstone Bott. "You will probably find it sitting upon an india-rubber tee which someone has dropped there."

He spoke sardonically, and Bradbury did not like his manner. But then he never had liked Gladstone Bott's manner, so what of that? He made his way to where the ball had fallen. It was lying under a bush.

"Caddie," said Bradbury.

"Sir?" said the caddie.

"A hundred?"

"And fifty."

"And fifty," said Bradbury Fisher.

Gladstone Bott was still toiling along the fairway when Bradbury reached the green.

"How many?" he asked, eventually winning to the goal.

"On in two," said Bradbury. "And you?"

"Playing seven."

"Then let me see. If you take two putts, which is most unlikely, I shall have six for the hole and match."

A minute later Bradbury had picked up his ball out of the cup. He stood there, basking in the sunshine, his heart glowing with quiet happiness. It seemed to him that he had never seen the countryside looking so beautiful. The birds appeared to be singing as they had never sung before. The trees and the rolling turf had taken on a charm beyond anything he had ever encountered. Even Gladstone Bott looked almost bearable.

"A very pleasant match," he said, cordially, "conducted throughout in the most sporting spirit. At one time I thought you were going to pull it off, old man, but there—class will tell."

"I will now make my report," said the caddie with the walrus moustache.

"Do so," said Gladstone Bott, briefly.

Bradbury Fisher stared at the man with blanched cheeks. The sun had ceased to shine, the birds had stopped stinging. The trees and the rolling turf looked pretty rotten, and Gladstone Bott perfectly foul. His heart was leaden with a hideous dread.

"Your report? Your—your report? What do you mean?"

"You don't suppose," said Gladstone Bott, "that I would play you an important match unless I had detectives watching you, do you? This gentleman is from the Quick Results Agency. What have you to report?" he said, turning to the caddie.

The caddie removed his bushy eyebrows, and with a quick gesture swept off his moustache.

"On the twelfth inst.," he began in a monotonous, sing-song voice, "acting upon instructions received, I made my way to the Goldenville Golf Links in order to observe the movements of the man Fisher. I had adopted for the occasion the Number Three disguise and—"

"All right, all right," said Gladstone Bott, impatiently. "You can skip all that. Come down to what happened at the sixteenth."

The caddie looked wounded, but bowed deferentially.

"At the sixteenth hole the man Fisher moved his ball into what—from his actions and furtive manner—I deduced to be a more favourable position."

"Ah!" said Gladstone Bott.

"On the seventeenth the man Fisher picked up his ball and threw it with a movement of the wrist on to the green."

"It's a lie. A foul and contemptible lie," shouted Bradbury Fisher.

"Realizing that the man Fisher might adopt this attitude, sir," said the caddie, "I took the precaution of snapshotting him in the act with my miniature wrist-watch camera, the detective's best friend."

Bradbury Fisher covered his face with his hands and uttered a hollow groan.

"My match," said Gladstone Bott, with vindictive triumph. "I'll trouble you to deliver that butler to me f.o.b. at my residence not later than noon tomorrow. Oh yes, and I was forgetting. You owe me three railroads."

Blizzard, dignified but kindly, met Bradbury in the Byzantine hall on his return home.

"I trust your golf-match terminated satisfactorily, sir?" said the butler.

A pang, almost too poignant to be borne, shot through Bradbury.

"No, Blizzard," he said. "No. Thank you for your kind inquiry, but I was not in luck."

"Too bad, sir," said Blizzard, sympathetically. "I trust the prize at stake was not excessive?"

"Well—er—well, it was rather big. I should like to speak to you about that a little later, Blizzard."

"At any time that is suitable to you, sir. If you will ring for one of the assistant-under-footmen when you desire to see me, sir, he will find me in my pantry. Meanwhile, sir, this cable arrived for you a short while back."

Bradbury took the envelope listlessly. He had been expecting a communication from his London agents announcing that they had bought Kent and Sussex, for which he had instructed them to make a firm offer just before he left England. No doubt this was their cable.

He opened the envelope, and started as if it had contained a scorpion. It was from his wife.

"Returning immediately. 'Aquitania'," (it ran). *"Docking Friday night. Meet without fail."*

Bradbury stared at the words, frozen to the marrow. Although he had been in a sort of trance ever since that dreadful moment on the seventeenth green, his great brain had not altogether ceased to function; and, while driving home in the car, he had sketched out roughly a plan of action which, he felt, might meet the crisis. Assuming that Mrs. Fisher was to remain abroad for another month, he had practically decided to buy a daily paper, insert in it a front-page story announcing the death of Blizzard, forward the clipping to his wife, and then sell his house, and move to another neighbourhood. In this way it might be that she would never learn of what had occurred.

But if she was due back next Friday, the scheme fell through and exposure was inevitable.

He wondered dully what had caused her change of plans, and came to the conclusion that some feminine sixth sense must have warned her of peril threatening Blizzard. With a good deal of peevishness he wished that Providence had never endowed women with this sixth sense. A woman with merely five took quite enough handling.

"Sweet suffering soup-spoons!" groaned Bradbury.

"Sir?" said Blizzard.

"Nothing," said Bradbury.

"Very good, sir," said Blizzard.

For a man with anything on his mind, any little trouble calculated to affect the *joie de vivre,* there are few spots less cheering than the Customs sheds of New York. Draughts whistle dismally there—now to, now fro. Strange noises are heard. Customs officials chew gum and lurk grimly in the shadows, like tigers awaiting the luncheon-gong. It is not surprising that Bradbury's spirits, low when he reached the place, should have sunk to zero long before the gangplank was lowered and the passengers began to stream down it.

His wife was among the first to land. How beautiful she looked, thought Bradbury, as he watched her. And, alas, how intimidating. His tastes had always lain in the direction of spirited women. His first wife had been spirited. So had his second, third, and fourth. And the one at the moment of holding office was perhaps the most spirited of the whole platoon. For one long instant, as he went to meet her, Bradbury Fisher was conscious of a regret that he had not married one of those meek, mild girls who suffer uncomplainingly at their husband's hands in the more hectic type of feminine novel. What he felt he could have done with at the moment was the sort of wife who thinks herself dashed lucky if the other half of the sketch does not drag her round the billiard-room by her hair, kicking her the while with spiked shoes.

Three conversational openings presented themselves to him as he approached her.

"Darling, there is something I want to tell you—"

"Dearest, I have a small confession to make—"

"Sweetheart, I don't know if by any chance you remember Blizzard, our butler. Well, it's like this—"

But, in the event, it was she who spoke first.

"Oh, Bradbury," she cried, rushing into his arms. "I've done the most awful thing, and you must try to forgive me!"

Bradbury blinked. He had never seen her in this strange mood before. As she clung to him, she seemed timid, fluttering, and—although a woman who weighed a full hundred and fifty-seven pounds—almost fragile.

"What is it?" he inquired, tenderly. "Has somebody stolen your jewels?"

"No, no."

"Have you been losing money at bridge?"

"No, no. Worse than that."

Bradbury started.

"You didn't sing 'My Little Grey Home in the West' at the ship's concert?" he demanded, eyeing her closely.

"No, no! Ah, how can I tell you? Bradbury, look! You see that man over there?"

Bradbury followed her pointing finger. Standing in an attitude of negligent dignity beside a pile of trunks under the letter V was a tall, stout, ambassadorial man, at the very sight of whom, even at this distance, Bradbury Fisher felt an odd sense of inferiority. His pendulous cheeks, his curving waistcoat, his protruding eyes, and the sequence of rolling chins combined to produce in Bradbury that instinctive feeling of being in the presence of a superior which we experience when meeting scratch golfers, head-waiters of fashionable restaurants, and traffic-policemen. A sudden pang of suspicion pierced him.

"Well?" he said, hoarsely. "What of him?"

"Bradbury, you must not judge me too harshly. We were thrown together and I was tempted—"

"Woman," thundered Bradbury Fisher, "who is this man?"

"His name is Vosper."

"And what is there between you and him, and when did it start, and why and how and where?"

Mrs. Fisher dabbed at her eyes with her handkerchief.

"It was at the Duke of Bootle's, Bradbury. I was invited there for the week-end."

"And this man was there?"

"Yes."

"Ha! Proceed!"

"The moment I set eyes on him, something seemed to go all over me."

"Indeed!"

"At first it was his mere appearance. I felt that I had dreamed of such a man all my life, and that for all these wasted years I had been putting up with the second-best."

"Oh, you did, eh? Really? Is that so? You did, did you?" snorted Bradbury Fisher.

"I couldn't help it, Bradbury. I know I have always seemed so devoted to Blizzard, and so I was. But, honestly, there is no comparison between them—really there isn't. You should see the way Vosper stood behind the Duke's chair. Like a high priest presiding over some mystic religious ceremony. And his voice when he asks you if you will have sherry or hock! Like the music of some wonderful organ. I couldn't resist him. I approached him delicately, and found that he was willing to come to America. He had been eighteen years with the Duke, and he told me he couldn't stand the sight of the back of his head any longer. So—"

Bradbury Fisher reeled.

"This man—this Vosper. Who is he?"

"Why, I'm telling you, honey. He was the Duke's butler, and now he's ours. Oh, you know how impulsive I am. Honestly, it wasn't till we were half-way across the Atlantic that I suddenly said to myself, 'What about Blizzard?' What am I to do, Bradbury? I simply haven't the nerve to fire Blizzard. And yet what will happen when he walks into his pantry and finds Vosper there? Oh, think, Bradbury, think!"

Bradbury Fisher was thinking—and for the first time in a week with-out agony.

"Evangeline," he said, gravely, "this is awkward."

"I know."

"Extremely awkward."

"I know, I know. But surely you can think of some way out of the muddle?"

"I may, I cannot promise, but I may." He pondered deeply. "Ha! I have it! It is just possible I may be able to induce Gladstone Bott to take on Blizzard."

"Do you really think he would?"

"He may—if I play my cards carefully. At any rate, I will try to per-suade him. For the moment you and Vosper had better remain in New York, while I go home and put the negotiations in train. If I am successful, I will let you know."

"Do try your very hardest."

"I think I shall be able to manage it. Gladstone and I are old friends, and he would stretch a point to oblige me. But let this be a lesson to you, Evangeline.

"Oh, I will."

"By the way," said Bradbury Fisher, "I am cabling my London agents today to instruct them to buy J. H. Taylor's shirt-stud for my collection."

"Quite right, Bradbury, darling. And anything else you want in that way you will get, won't you?"

"I will," said Bradbury Fisher.

A Story Goes With It

Dubbed the "Official Diarist of New York after Dark," Runyon created a style—Runyonese—for the several decades that, according to Jimmy Breslin, Runyon "practically invented." His cast of soft-boiled criminals, figures like Nicely-Nicely Johnson, Last Card Louie, and Lemon Drop Kid, are part of the permanent folklore of Broadway. Runyon's own life was worthy of his characters—full of boozing, philandering, and improbable benevolence (for instance, he sponsored and later consorted with an orphan girl he'd met in a racetrack box shard by the bandit Pancho Villa and a group of American gamblers). Runyon is best remembered for the stories that inspired *Guys and Dolls* (the name of the poolroom where I received my own early gambling education, along with invaluable lessons in ethics and other subjects). *Guys and Dolls* ran for years on Broadway, and was later made into a film starring Marlon Brando as Sky Masterson (Brando sings "Luck be a Lady") and Frank Sinatra as Nathan Detroit. Other classic Runyon-inspired films include *Little Miss Marker* (Shirley Temple) and *The Lemon Drop Kid* (Bob Hope).

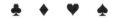

One night I am in a gambling joint in Miami watching the crap game and thinking what a nice thing it is, indeed, to be able to shoot craps without having to worry about losing your potatoes. Many of the high shots from New York and Detroit and St. Louis and other cities are around the table, and there is quite some action in spite of the hard times. In fact, there is so much action that a guy with only a few bobs on him, such as me, will be considered very impolite to be pushing into this game, because they are packed in very tight around the table.

I am maybe three guys back from the table, and I am watching the game by standing on tiptoe peeking over their shoulders, and all I can hear is Goldie, the stick man, hollering money-money-money every time some guy makes a number, so I can see the dice are very warm indeed, and that the right betters are doing first-rate.

By and by a guy by the name of Guinea Joe, out of Trenton, picks up the dice and starts making numbers right and left, and I know enough about this Guinea Joe to know that when he starts making numbers anybody will be very foolish indeed not to follow his hand, although personally I am generally a wrong better against the dice, if I bet at all.

Now all I have in my pocket is a sawbuck, and the hotel stakes are coming up on me the next day, and I need this saw, but with Guinea Joe hotter than a forty-five it will be overlooking a big opportunity not to go along with him, so when he comes out on an eight, which is a very easy number for Joe to make when he is hot, I dig up my sawbuck, and slide it past the three guys in front of me to the table, and I say to Lefty Park, who is laying against the dice, as follows:

"I will take the odds, Lefty."

Well, Lefty looks at my sawbuck and nods his head, for Lefty is not such a guy as will refuse any bet, even though it is as modest as mine, and right away Goldie yells money-money-money, so there I am with twenty-two dollars.

Next Guinea Joe comes out on a nine, and naturally I take thirty to twenty for my sugar, because nine is nothing for Joe to make when he is hot. He makes the nine just as I figure, and I take two to one for my half a yard when he starts looking for a ten, and when he makes the ten I am right up against the table, because I am now a guy with means.

Well, the upshot of the whole business is that I finally find myself with three hundred bucks, and when it looks as if the dice are cooling off, I take out and back off from the table, and while I am backing off I am trying to look like a guy who loses all his potatoes, because there are always many wolves waiting around crap games and one thing and another in Miami this season, and what they are waiting for is to put the bite on anybody who happens to make a little scratch.

In fact, nobody can remember when the bite is as painful as it is in Miami this season, what with the unemployment situation among many citizens who come to Miami expecting to find work in the gambling joints, or around the race track. But almost as soon as these citizens arrive, the gambling joints are all turned off, except in spots, and the bookmakers are chased off the track and the mutuels put in, and the consequences are the suffering is most intense. It is not only intense among the visiting citizens, but it is quite intense among the Miami landlords, because naturally if a citizen is not working, nobody can expect him to pay any room rent, but the Miami landlords do not seem to understand this situation, and are very unreasonable about their room rent.

Anyway, I back through quite a crowd without anybody biting me, and I am commencing to figure I may escape altogether and get to my hotel and hide my dough before the news gets around that I win about five *G's,* which is what my winning is sure to amount to by the time the rumor reaches all quarters of the city.

Then, just as I am thinking I am safe, I find I am looking a guy by the name of Hot Horse Herbie in the face, and I can tell from Hot Horse Herbie's expression that he is standing there watching me for some time, so there is no use in telling him I am washed out in the game. In fact, I cannot think of much of anything to tell Hot Horse Herbie that may keep him from putting the bite on me for at least a few bobs, and I am greatly astonished when he does not offer to bite me at all, but says to me like this:

"Well," he says, "I am certainly glad to see you make such a nice score. I will be looking for you tomorrow at the track, and will have some big news for you."

Then he walks away from me and I stand there with my mouth open looking at him, as it is certainly a most unusual way for Herbie to act. It is the first time I ever knew Herbie to walk away from a chance to bite somebody, and I can scarcely understand such actions, for Herbie is such a guy as will not miss a bite, even if he does not need it.

He is a tall, thin guy, with a sad face and a long chin, and he is called Hot Horse Herbie because he nearly always has a very hot horse to tell you about. He nearly always has a horse that is so hot it is fairly smoking, a hot horse being a horse that cannot possibly lose a race unless it falls down dead, and while Herbie's hot horses often lose without falling down dead, this does not keep Herbie from coming up with others just as hot.

In fact, Hot Horse Herbie is what is called a hustler around the race tracks, and his business is to learn about these hot horses, or even just suspect about them, and then get somebody to bet on them, which is a very legitimate business indeed, as Herbie only collects a commission if the hot horses win, and if they do not win Herbie just keeps out of sight awhile from whoever he gets to bet on the hot horses. There are very few guys in this world who can keep out of sight better than Hot Horse Herbie, and especially from old Cap

Duhaine, of the Pinkertons, who is always around pouring cold water on hot horses.

In fact, Cap Duhaine, of the Pinkertons, claims that guys such as Hot Horse Herbie are nothing but touts, and sometimes he heaves them off the race track altogether, but of course Cap Duhaine is a very unsentimental old guy and cannot see how such characters as Hot Horse Herbie add to the romance of the turf.

Anyway, I escape from the gambling joint with all my scratch on me, and hurry to my room and lock myself in for the night, and I do not show up in public until along about noon the next day, when it is time to go over to the coffee shop for my java. And of course by this time the news of my score is all over town, and many guys are taking dead aim at me.

But naturally I am now able to explain to them that I have to wire most of the three yards I win to Nebraska to save my father's farm from being seized by the sheriff, and while everybody knows I do not have a father, and that if I do have a father I will not be sending him money for such a thing as saving his farm, with times what they are in Miami, nobody is impolite enough to doubt my word except a guy by the name of Pottsville Legs, who wishes to see my receipts from the telegraph office when I explain to him why I cannot stake him to a double sawbuck.

I do not see Hot Horse Herbie until I get to the track, and he is waiting for me right inside the grand-stand gate, and as soon as I show up he motions me off to one side and says to me like this:

"Now," Herbie says, "I am very smart indeed about a certain race today. In fact," he says, "if any guy knowing what I know does not bet all he can rake and scrape together on a certain horse, such a guy ought to cut his own throat and get himself out of the way forever. What I know," Herbie says, "is enough to shake the foundations of this country if it gets out. Do not ask any questions," he says, "but get ready to bet all the sugar you win last night on this horse I am going to mention to you, and all I ask you in return is to bet fifty on me. And," Herbie says, "kindly do not tell me you leave your money in your other pants, because I know you do not have any other pants."

"Now, Herbie," I say, "I do not doubt your information, because I know you will not give out information unless it is well founded. But," I say, "I seldom stand for a tip, and as for betting fifty for you, you know I will not bet fifty even for myself if somebody guarantees me a winner. So I thank you, Herbie, just the same," I say, "but I must do without your tip," and with this I start walking away.

"Now," Herbie says, "wait a minute. A story goes with it," he says.

Well, of course this is a different matter entirely. I am such a guy as will always listen to a tip on a horse if a story goes with the tip. In fact, I will not give you a nickel for a tip without a story, but it must be a first-class story, and most horse players are the same way. In fact, there are very few horse players who will not listen to a tip if a story goes with it, for this is the way human nature is. So I turn and walk back to Hot Horse Herbie, and say to him like this:

"Well," I say, "let me hear the story, Herbie."

"Now," Herbie says, dropping his voice away down low, in case old Cap Duhaine may be around somewhere listening, "it is the third race, and the horse is a horse by the name of Never Despair. It is a boat race," Herbie says. "They are going to shoo in Never Despair. Everything else in the race is a cooler," he says.

"Well," I say, "this is just an idea, Herbie, and not a story."

"Wait a minute," Herbie says. "The story that goes with it is a very strange story indeed. In fact," he says, "it is such a story as I can scarcely believe myself, and I will generally believe almost any story, including," he says, "the ones I make up out of my own head. Anyway, the story is as follows:

"Never Despair is owned by an old guy by the name of Seed Mercer," Herbie says. "Maybe you remember seeing him around. He always wears a black slouch hat and gray whiskers," Herbie says, "and he is maybe a hundred years old, and his horses are very terrible horses indeed. In fact," Herbie says, "I do not remember seeing any more terrible horses in all the years I am around the track, and," Herbie says, "I wish to say I see some very terrible horses indeed.

"Now," Herbie says, "old Mercer has a granddaughter who is maybe sixteen years old, come next grass, by the name of Lame Louise, and she is called Lame Louise because she is all crippled up from childhood by infantile what-is-this, and can scarcely navigate, and," Herbie says, "her being crippled up in such a way makes old Mercer feel very sad, for she is all he has in the world, except these terrible horses."

"It is a very long story, Herbie," I say, "and I wish to see Moe Shapoff about a very good thing in the first race."

"Never mind Moe Shapoff," Herbie says. "He will only tell you about a bum by the name of Zachary in the first race, and Zachary has no chance whatever. I make Your John a stand-out in the first," he says.

"Well," I say, "let us forget the first and go on with your story, although it is commencing to sound all mixed up to me."

"Now," Herbie says, "it not only makes old man Mercer very sad because Lame Louise is all crippled up, but," he says, "it makes many of the jockeys and other guys around the race track very sad, because," he says, "they know Lame Louise since she is so high, and she always has a smile for them, and especially for Jockey Scroon. In fact," Herbie says, "Jockey Scroon is even more sad about Lame Louise than old man Mercer, because Jockey Scroon loves Lame Louise."

"Why," I say, very indignant, "Jockey Scroon is nothing but a little burglar. Why," I say, "I see Jockey Scroon do things to horses I bet on that he will have to answer for on the Judgment Day, if there is any justice at such a time. Why," I say, "Jockey Scroon is nothing but a Gerald Chapman in his heart, and so are all other jockeys."

"Yes," Hot Horse Herbie says, "what you say is very, very true, and I am personally in favor of the electric chair for all jockeys, but," he says, "Jockey Scroon loves Lame Louise just the same, and is figuring on making her his ever-loving wife when he gets a few bobs together, which," Herbie says, "makes Louise eight to five in my line to be an old maid. Jockey Scroon rooms with me downtown," Herbie says, "and he speaks freely to me about his love for Louise. Furthermore," Herbie says, "Jockey Scroon is personally not a bad little guy, at that, although of course being a jockey he is sometimes greatly misunderstood by the public.

"Anyway," Hot Horse Herbie says, "I happen to go home early last night before I see you at the gambling joint, and I hear voices coming out of my room, and naturally I pause outside the door to listen, because for all I know it may be the landlord speaking about the room rent, although," Herbie says, "I do not figure my landlord to be much worried at this time because I see him sneak into my room a few days before and take a lift at my trunk to make sure I have belongings in the same, and it happens I nail the trunk to the floor beforehand, so not being able to lift it, the landlord is bound to figure me a guy with property.

"These voices," Herbie says, "are mainly soprano voices, and at first I think Jockey Scroon is in there with some dolls, which is by no means permissible in my hotel, but, after listening awhile, I discover they are the voices of young boys, and I make out that these boys are nothing but jockeys, and they are the six jockeys who are riding in the third race, and they are fixing up this race to be a boat race, and to shoo in Never Despair, which Jockey Scroon is riding.

"And," Hot Horse Herbie says, "the reason they are fixing up this boat race is the strangest part of the story. It seems," he says, "that Jockey Scroon hears old man Mercer talking about a great surgeon from Europe who is a shark on patching up cripples such as Lame Louise, and who just arrives at

Palm Beach to spend the winter, and old man Mercer is saying how he wishes he has dough enough to take Lame Louise to this guy so he can operate on her, and maybe make her walk good again.

"But of course," Herbie says, "it is well known to one and all that old man Mercer does not have a quarter, and that he has no way of getting a quarter unless one of his terrible horses accidentally wins a purse. So," Herbie says, "it seems these jockeys get to talking it over among themselves, and they figure it will be a nice thing to let old man Mercer win a purse such as the thousand bucks that goes with the third race to-day, so he can take Lame Louise to Palm Beach, and now you have a rough idea of what is coming off.

"Furthermore," Herbie says, "these jockeys wind up their meeting by taking a big oath among themselves that they will not tell a living soul what is doing so nobody will bet on Never Despair, because," he says, "these little guys are smart enough to see if there is any betting on such a horse there may be a very large squawk afterwards. And," he says, "I judge they keep their oath because Never Despair is twenty to one in the morning line, and I do not hear a whisper about him, and you have the tip all to yourself."

"Well," I say, "so what?" For this story is now commencing to make me a little tired, especially as I hear the bell for the first race, and I must see Moe Shapoff.

"Why," Hot Horse Herbie says, "so you bet every nickel you can rake and scrape together on Never Despair, including the twenty you are to bet for me for giving you this tip and the story that goes with it."

"Herbie," I say, "it is a very interesting story indeed, and also very sad, but," I say, "I am sorry it is about a horse Jockey Scroon is to ride, because I do not think I will ever bet on anything Jockey Scroon rides if they pay off in advance. And," I say, "I am certainly not going to bet twenty for you or anybody else."

"Well," Hot Horse Herbie says, "I will compromise with you for a pound note, because I must have something going for me on this boat race."

So I give Herbie a fiver, and the chances are this is about as strong as he figures from the start, and I forget all about his tip and the story that goes with it, because while I enjoy a story with a tip, I feel that Herbie overdoes this one.

Anyway, no handicapper alive can make Never Despair win the third race off the form, because this race is at six furlongs, and there is a barrel of speed in it, and anybody can see that old man Mercer's horse is away over his head. In fact, The Dancer tells me that any one of the other five horses in this race can beat Never Despair doing anything from playing hockey to putting the shot, and everybody else must think the same thing because Never Despair goes to forty to one.

Personally, I like a horse by the name of Loose Living, which is a horse owned by a guy by the name of Bill Howard, and I hear Bill Howard is betting plenty away on his horse, and any time Bill Howard is betting away on his horse a guy will be out of his mind not to bet on this horse, too, as Bill Howard is very smart indeed. Loose Living is two to one in the first line, but by and by I judge the money Bill Howard bets away commences to come back to the track, and Loose Living winds up seven to ten, and while I am generally not a seven-to-ten guy, I can see that here is a proposition I cannot overlook.

So, naturally, I step up to the mutuel window and invest in Loose Living. In fact, I invest everything I have on me in the way of scratch, amounting to a hundred and ten bucks, which is all I have left after taking myself out of the hotel stakes and giving Hot Horse Herbie the finnif, and listening to what Moe Shapoff has to say about the first race, and also getting beat a snoot in the second.

When I first step up to the window, I have no idea of betting all my scratch on Loose Living, but while waiting in line there I get to thinking what a cinch Loose Living is, and how seldom such an opportunity comes into a guy's life, so I just naturally set it all in.

Well, this is a race which will be remembered by one and all to their dying day, as Loose Living beats the barrier a step, and is two lengths in front before you can say Jack Robinson, with a thing by the name of Callipers second by maybe half a length, and with the others bunched except Never Despair, and where is Never Despair but last, where he figures.

Now any time Loose Living busts on top there is no need worrying any more about him, and I am thinking I better get in line at the pay-off window right away, so I will not have to wait long to collect my sugar. But I figure I may as well stay and watch the race, although personally I am never much interested in watching races. I am interested only in how a race comes out.

As the horses hit the turn into the stretch, Loose Living is just breezing, and anybody can see that he is going to laugh his way home from there. Callipers is still second, and a thing called Goose Pimples is third, and I am surprised to see that Never Despair now struggles up to fourth with Jockey Scroon belting away at him with his bat quite earnestly. Furthermore, Never Despair seems to be running very fast, though afterwards I figure this may be because the others are commencing to run very slow.

Anyway, a very strange spectacle now takes place in the stretch, as all of a sudden Loose Living seems to be stopping, as if he is waiting for a street car, and what is all the more remarkable Callipers and Goose Pimples also seem to be hanging back, and the next thing anybody knows, here comes Jockey Scroon on Never Despair sneaking through on the rail, and personally it looks to me as if the jock on Callipers moves over to give Jockey Scroon plenty of elbow room, but of course the jock on Callipers may figure Jockey Scroon has diphtheria, and does not wish to catch it.

Loose Living is out in the middle of the track, anyway, so he does not have to move over. All Loose Living has to do is to keep on running backwards as he seems to be doing from the top of the stretch, to let Jockey Scroon go past on Never Despair to win the heat by a length.

Well, the race is practically supernatural in many respects, and the judges are all upset over it, and they haul all the jocks up in the stand and ask them many questions, and not being altogether satisfied with the answers, they ask these questions over several times. But all the jocks will say is that Never Despair sneaks past them very unexpectedly indeed, while Jockey Scroon, who is a pretty fresh duck at that, wishes to know if he is supposed to blow a horn when he is slipping through a lot of guys sound asleep.

But the judges are still not satisfied, so they go prowling around investigating the betting, because naturally when a boat race comes up there is apt to be some reason for it, such as the betting, but it seems that all the judges find is that one five-dollar win ticket is sold on Never Despair in the mutuels, and they cannot learn of a dime being bet away on the horse. So there is nothing much the judges can do about the proposition, except give the jocks many hard looks, and the jocks are accustomed to hard looks from the judges, anyway.

Personally, I am greatly upset by this business, especially when I see that Never Despair pays $86.34, and for two cents I will go right up in the stand and start hollering copper on these little Jesse Jameses for putting on such a boat race and taking all my hard-earned potatoes away from me, but before I have time to do this, I run into The Dancer, and he tells me that Dedicate in the next race is the surest thing that ever goes to the post, and at five to one, at that. So I have to forget everything while I bustle about to dig up a few bobs to bet on Dedicate, and when Dedicate is beat a whisker, I have to do some more bustling to dig up a few bobs to bet on Vesta in the fifth, and by this time the third race is such ancient history that nobody cares what happens in it.

It is nearly a week before I see Hot Horse Herbie again, and I figure he is hiding out on everybody because he has this dough he wins off the fiver I give him, and personally I consider him a guy with no manners not to be kicking back the fin, at least. But before I can mention the fin, Herbie gives me a big hello, and says to me like this:

"Well," he says, "I just see Jockey Scroon, and Jockey Scroon just comes back from Palm Beach, and the operation is a big success, and Lame Louise will walk as good as anybody again, and old Mercer is tickled silly. But," Herbie says, "do not say anything out loud, because the judges may still be trying to find out what comes off in the race."

"Herbie," I say, very serious, "do you mean to say the story you tell me about Lame Louise, and all this and that, the other day is on the level?"

"Why," Herbie says, "certainly it is on the level, and I am sorry to hear you do not take advantage of my information. But," he says, "I do not blame you for not believing my story, because it is a very long story for anybody to believe. It is not such a story," Herbie says, "as I will tell to any one if I expect them to believe it. In fact," he says, "it is so long a story that I do not have the heart to tell it to anybody else but you, or maybe I will have something running for me on the race.

"But," Herbie says, "never mind all this. I will be plenty smart about a race to-morrow. Yes," Herbie says, "I will be wiser than a treeful of owls, so be sure and see me if you happen to have any coconuts."

"There is no danger of me seeing you," I say, very sad, because I am all sorrowed up to think that the story he tells me is really true. "Things are very terrible with me at this time," I say, "and I am thinking maybe you can hand me back my finnif, because you must do all right for yourself with the fiver you have on Never Despair at such a price."

Now a very strange look comes over Hot Horse Herbie's face, and he raises his right hand, and says to me like this:

"I hope and trust I drop down dead right there in front of you," Herbie says, "if I bet a quarter on the horse. It is true," he says, "I am up at the window to buy a ticket on Never Despair, but the guy who is selling the tickets is a friend of mine by the name of Heeby Rosenbloom, and Heeby whispers to me that Big Joe Gompers, the guy who owns Callipers, just bets half a hundred on his horse, and," Herbie says, "I know Joe Gompers is such a guy as will not bet half a hundred on anything he does not get a Federal Reserve guarantee with it.

"Anyway," Herbie says, "I get to thinking about what a bad jockey this Jockey Scroon is, which is very bad indeed, and," he says, "I figure that even if it is a boat race it is no even-money race they can shoo him in, so I buy a ticket on Callipers."

"Well," I say, "somebody buys one five-dollar ticket on Never Despair, and I figure it can be nobody but you."

"Why," Hot Horse Herbie says, "do you not hear about this? Why," he says, "Cap Duhaine, of the Pinkertons, traces this ticket and finds it is bought by a guy by the name of Steve Harter, and the way this guy Harter comes to buy it is very astounding. It seems," Herbie says, "that this Harter is a tourist out of Indiana who comes to Miami for the sunshine, and who loses all his dough but six bucks against the faro bank at Hollywood.

"At the same time," Herbie says, "the poor guy gets a telegram from his ever-loving doll back in Indiana saying she no longer wishes any part of him.

"Well," Herbie says, "between losing his dough and his doll, the poor guy is practically out of his mind, and he figures there is nothing left for him to do but knock himself off.

"So," Herbie says, "this Harter spends one of his six bucks to get to the track, figuring to throw himself under the feet of the horses in the first race and let them kick him to a jelly. But he does not get there until just as the third race is coming up and," Herbie says, "he sees this name 'Never Despair,' and he figures it may be a hunch, so he buys himself a ticket with his last fiver. Well, naturally," Herbie says, "when Never Despair pops down, the guy forgets about letting the horses kick him to a jelly, and he keeps sending his dough along until he runs nothing but a nubbin into six G's on the day.

"Then," Herbie says, "Cap Duhaine finds out that the guy, still thinking of Never Despair, calls his ever-loving doll on the phone, and finds she is very sorry she sends him the wire and that she really loves him more than somewhat, especially," Herbie says, "when she finds out about the six G's. And the last anybody hears of the matter, this Harter is on his way home to get married, so Never Despair does quite some good in this wicked old world, after all.

"But," Herbie says, "let us forget all this, because to-morrow is another day. To-morrow," he says, "I will tell you about a thing that goes in the fourth which is just the same as wheat in the bin. In fact," Hot Horse Herbie says, "if it does not win, you can never speak to me again."

"Well," I say, as I start to walk away, "I am not interested in any tip at this time."

"Now," Herbie says, "wait a minute. A story goes with it."

"Well," I say, coming back to him, "let me hear the story."

A Day at the Races

JANE SMILEY

A passionate horseback rider herself, who owns sixteen horses, Jane Smiley heard some racetrack expressions on the radio while driving home one day and was drawn to the language. The resulting novel, *Horse Heaven,* shows an immersion in that language, and in the many layers of the racing world, which is depicted with great exuberance and detail. Winner of the Pulitzer Prize for *A Thousand Acres* (later a film starring Michelle Pfeiffer), Smiley writes particularly well in the chapter from *Horse Heaven* that follows about the ritual of visiting the racetrack shared by a father and son.

First they stopped by the liquor store his dad owned, and Jesse got a candy bar out of the cabinet while his dad opened the register and took out a handful of money. He didn't even count it, but just shoved it in his pocket. After they got in the car, Jesse surreptitiously looked down at his father's socks. They matched, plain gray. They also matched his pants. That was a relief. They traveled in silence for a while, and Jesse stared out the window. He rather liked the drive out to Santa Anita. It was long and sunny. Along about the time they were passing under Highway 5, his dad piped up: "Ah, Jesse! Look at that tree, there. That's a beautiful tree. You know, that tree's been sitting by the side of this road for fifty years, I'll bet, and I never noticed it before. You go through life, and you travel the same road over and over, and all of a sudden you notice something. That's a gift. That tree tells me something. That tree tells me we're going to have a good day. Don'tcha think?"

"I hope so, Pop."

"I got my lucky socks on. You got your lucky socks on?"

"We hit that daily double that time when I had these socks on."

"Your mom wash 'em since?"

"Well, yeah."

They pondered this together, then Leo said, "Well, maybe that doesn't matter."

"Dad, I've worn them a lot of times since. We hit that daily double last summer."

"But not to the track?"

"Not to the track."

"This is the first time you've worn them to the track since then?"

"Yeah."

"Okay, then."

Jesse let out his breath.

Leo began to sing. Then they pulled off the highway and drove into the parking lot—on a lucky day they always parked in preferred parking, so they wouldn't have to walk so far. That was five dollars. That was a part of your overhead, which you wanted to keep as low as possible. They parked, got out of the car, and locked it. There were two things his father never looked at at Santa Anita—the shopping mall next door and any Mercedes Benz automobiles that might be parked between him and the gate. It was okay if Jesse looked at them; in fact, it was better if Jesse spied them and reported them. Today there weren't many, and Leo managed to keep his head down. He counted the money, too: $278.32, with the $.87 Jesse had in his pocket. They had to combine their money. That was lucky, too.

They were almost to the gate, and no Mercedes, when disaster struck. "Ah, fuck," said Leo, softly and seriously. Jesse knew he shouldn't, but he did it anyway. He said, "What's the matter, Pop?"

"I looked at a fucking nun."

"What?"

"I can't believe I looked at a fucking nun. There she was, and I looked at her!"

Looking at a nun was the worst thing you could do, Jesse knew. Now they might as well go home. He looked around, though. Nothing. He proffered, "I don't see any, Pop."

"Over there." Leo gestured toward the west without daring to look. Still Jesse saw no nuns, not even any women. But Jesse knew better than to argue. After a moment, he said, "Do you want to go home, then?"

Leo stopped walking and turned to Jesse. He had a very serious look on his face, and he put a hand on each of Jesse's shoulders. Jesse lifted his face and looked his father right in the eye, as he had been told to do many times.

"Jesse," Leo said. "Jesse, son. On the one hand, we've got the, uh, you know." Yes, the nun. "And on the other, we've got the socks, two pairs, the tree, no Mercedes, no shopping mall, and almost three hundred bucks. I'll tell you what. Here's the *Racing Form*." He pulled it out of his pocket and opened it to the first race. "Read those starters." Leo threw back his head and closed his eyes, listening.

Jesse read, "Lonesome Jones, Howdy Babe, Hickey's Prince, Gottalottayotta, Prigogine, Sandtrap, Baby Max, and Holy Mackerel."

Leo remained silent, mulling, for a long moment, and then said, "Don't you have a friend named Max?"

"No," said Jesse. "No Maxes."

Leo threw up his arms. "Okay, then! Let's go! That may just turn the trick. Let's go look at some horses, boy!"

They passed through the gate, where the woman smiled and said, "Hi, Leo! Have a good day, now," then went through the betting hall and out again, onto the tiled apron that sloped down to the homestretch, the finish line, and the winner's circle. It was a sunny, clear day, a good March day, and the arc of the mountains was dark green against the blue sky. Since it was Wednesday, there weren't many people in the stands yet, and so Leo staked out his spot— he had his *Racing Form,* covered with the notations he'd made after dinner the night before, his seat cushion, which he always brought but never sat on, his binoculars, his thermos of coffee, and his extra pens for making more notations on the *Racing Form* if he had to. He was smiling. He ruffled Jesse's hair and said, "Well! Got here! Good deal! Really, this is the best place in the world, don't you think? Hard work, harder than standing around the liquor store, but better, in the end." Leo took a deep breath and threw his shoulders back, looked around his personal domain, and then said, "Okay, boy! Better get to work, there's money to be made."

In the first race, a thirty-thousand-dollar claiming race of seven furlongs, for three-year-olds and up, they boxed Lonesome Jones and Sandtrap in the exacta. Sandtrap was the favorite, but Leo thought he was coming down from his peak form. Lonesome Jones, however, had had a bad trip in his last race, his first start after a six-week layoff. He'd been bumped in the backstretch and gone wide on the turn as a result, but still come in third by only a head. His speed ratings in his previous starts had been at or close to the top for the horses in this race, and Leo thought, as a three-year-old, the animal could still manage a jump. Best of all, he was a good bet—the morning line of ten-to-one had dropped, but not very far, only to eight-to-one. Sandtrap was clearly the class of the field. Even coming off his best form, he was a contender, and the bettors were backing him heavily. Leo also boxed the two horses with a horse he liked in the second race, See Me Now, for the daily double. After placing his bets, he was very calm, and stood with Jesse in the grandstand to watch the horses make their way to the gate, which was positioned in the chute, as far away from the grandstand as possible. The announcer, whose pronunciation was clarion-crisp, said, "The horses are approaching the starting gate. The horses have reached the starting gate. We have Lonesome Jones in. Now Howdy Babe," and on down the line, to Holy Mackerel. There was a pause, then a clang, and the gates were open and the horses were away. Leo's binoculars were pressed to his head, and he was deadly silent. Jesse could see only the colors of the jockeys' silks, but he knew that Lonesome Jones was in purple, and that purple was trailing by open lengths. The favorite was one of two horses in yellow. One of the two was in the lead. "All right!" breathed Leo, as the purple horse began to pass the others. And the announcer said, "And we have the number-one horse, Lonesome Jones, now passing Howdy Babe and Prigogine. Still on the lead is Sandtrap, the favorite." Leo began to get more agitated as the horses came around the turn, bouncing up and down on his toes. Jesse could see them clearly now, from the front, their heads down, their feet up, the tiny rounds of their toes reaching up and forward, echoing the tiny rounds of their flared nostrils. Then they came into the homestretch, and the angle was different. They were horses now, pulled out like rubber bands from their noses to their tails, with the jockeys on top, also pulled out, hands, arms, heads, backs, and then the curl into their legs. Some of the jockeys' colored arms were rising and falling, another stretched-out thing, a shoulder, an elbow, an arm, a hand, a whip. Behind Jesse was a lot of yelling, and beside him, too, from his father, because there came Lonesome Jones on the rail, finding a hole and slipping through it, eating up the track. By contrast, the red horse fell back, the green horse fell back, the blue and the black-and-tan horses fell back. Leo's hand was on his head, and suddenly pressed down as the horses crossed the finish line. In a moment, the tote board flashed "Photo Finish," and they had to wait. But Leo was sure. "They did it! They did it! I knew it! Perfect pick! One and six. That's always been a great pick for me, because I dated this girl when I was sixteen, her name was Peggy Sue! It really was, and that song was such a great hit that my statistical average with one and six over the years has been way out of the normal range! Now, you've got to have the information to back it up—only losers just bet patterns—"

The results flashed, and the winner was the number-seven horse, Baby Max, by a head. Lonesome Jones and Sandtrap were second and third.

"God damn!" said Leo.

That meant that all bets were off, the exacta, the daily double. Sixty dollars, Jesse thought, gone already. He said, "Hey, Pop, let's go home."

Leo was staring at Baby Max, who was being led into the winner's circle, but he shook himself and looked down at Jesse and smiled. "Nah, nah. We're here. We've just got to work a little harder. Here, here's ten bucks for something to eat. Go away and leave me alone for a while, I got to concentrate and you're a little distracting. It isn't your fault. I just have to get into a zone, you know. That's a good boy."

Jesse took the ten and followed Baby Max and his associates as they walked under the stands and out into the open air. The jockey and the trainer were smiling, but professionally so. This was only the first race of many today for the jockey. Jesse liked looking at him. He was, in fact, about Jesse's height, but he walked like a man, and a very self-confident one, at that. When he looked up at the trainer to tell him about the race, he didn't seem to be looking up, but to be looking down. Jesse liked looking at jockeys, and always tried to do so. They had different stomachs and backs from anyone at the track, strong, straight, supple, powerful. Something in their stomachs, as far as Jesse could see, was the thing that made them able to hold those horses. Leo didn't pay much attention to jockeys, and had advised Jesse not to. "A winner never bets the jockey," he said, but Jesse always thought that if he could get what the jockey had in his stomach into his own stomach other things would go away—butterflies, gas pains, that feeling that all his insides were dropping.

Out in the open air, he saw that the horses for the second race were leaving the saddling enclosure to go to the paddock.

Leo didn't like watching the horses get saddled, or the paddock parade. He said it was too confusing, and that you ended up betting hunches when you should be betting form, numbers, past performances. Watching the horses in the saddling enclosure was like tempting yourself to fall in love at first sight, and if you couldn't control yourself, then you had to control your circumstances, which Leo did by staying inside the track. Jesse liked the preliminaries the best, though. It allowed him to think that horse racing wasn't really about betting, but about looking at the animals. The coolest thing about them was that they were all different. For example, in the second race, for maiden two-year-old fillies, there were six entries idling with their connections. Of all the fillies, only one was calm. She was a chestnut, number two. She stood quietly with her head up and her ears pricked while her trainer smoothed the number-cloth over her back.

"That's Buddy Crawford, the trainer," said a woman standing next to Jesse. "He's won a lot of races. They say he's kind of a crook."

Jesse liked the horse, though. He looked at the program. Her name was "Residual." Jesse leaned on the barrier to get a better look at the filly. The people around the filly put the saddle on her, then did the girths. They petted her a lot, and Jesse could see why. She was very shiny, but even apart from that, something about her made you want to pet her. He wanted to pet her himself. Around her, all of the other fillies were doing something—twisting their necks or jumping around. One stood there rigid with tension, lifting one foreleg and curling it under herself, then putting it down and lifting the other. The only thing Residual did was rub the side of her nose gently on the sleeve of her groom one time, as if, Jesse thought, she was reassuring him. Now the number-one filly headed out, and Residual followed her. Behind them, the last four fillies made a ruckus, but Residual only looked at the fans lining the rail of the walking ring, and when she came to the spot where she was supposed to receive her jockey, she stopped and stood. Jesse took one last look, and ran under the grandstand. Leo was sitting on the concrete steps, still studying his form. Jesse went up to him. As Residual walked onto the track, he exclaimed, "Look at number two, Dad! You've got to bet on her."

"I never bet maiden two-year-old fillies," said Leo. "That's like playing the lottery."

Jesse looked up at the tote. He said, "Her odds are six to one. That's good odds."

"Those are good odds, yes. But I have standards, Jesse."

Jesse said, "It's Pincay, Dad."

"Even so." He put his hand on Jesse's shoulder and looked him in the eye, then said in a very serious voice, "Jesse, son, these little girls don't know a thing about racing. The gate is going to open, and they are going to be wondering what to do next. Anything can happen—"

"But that's good, Dad."

"Well, that is good in a larger sense, in a, let's say, universal sense, in the sense that if you spend your life drawing a weekly paycheck, and that's what you know you're going to get every Friday for the rest of your life, unless the boss decides to give you a two-percent raise one of these years, and you know the wife is going to spend so much for food and so much for rent and everything, well, some people like to live like that, and some don't. So, in that sense, the idea that anything can happen is a liberating idea. But in this sense, in this race, the things that can happen aren't good in that way—"

"I've got ten dollars at home. I would give it to you if you would bet that on her now."

"Jesse, the thing is, I want you to benefit from my experience. Now, my dad, he would bet on any race, but I've—"Then he stopped. Then he said, "Well, you've got to learn sooner or later. Okay. How do you want to bet your ten dollars?"

The horses were jogging. Residual continued to ease along. Pincay, the strongest jockey, the oldest jockey, the most amazing jockey, sat calmly atop her. Three times, he reached down and stroked her neck, slowly, not as if reassuring her, but just as if he enjoyed it. Jesse said, "Two across the board. Two more to win, and two more to place. The odds are at eight to one, now, Dad. I think she's way undervalued."

"Okay, son. If you can use the word 'undervalued' and know what it means, I suppose you're ready to make up your own mind."

The lines at the betting windows were short, so they got back out to the rail in time to see the horses begin to jog and then canter past the stands on their way to the gate in the chute. The number-five filly was nearly climbing her pony, she was so ready to lose it at the noise and turmoil of the fans in the stands. None of the others liked it, either—even Residual looked—but soon enough they had all been led away from the noise, little suspecting that they would have to run back into it before long. Jesse held his tickets in his hand. He knew the fillies had to go through this—a time or two and they would be like the horses in the first race, ready, and even eager for this pandemonium—those in the first race that didn't prance at least perked up. But these fillies skittered and jumped and the pony riders held them close. They disappeared after the turn, and only by putting his hand up and squinting could Jesse see the gate at the front of the chute. After a bit, the first horse and pony approached it. That filly shied and backed. The pony went with her for a step, then stood until the filly came back up to it. A man standing next to them said to his friend, "All them jocks is prayin' right now."

The friend nodded.

"You know," the man went on, "there's culling takes place in everything, but horse racin's the only thing where they cull the ones that ain't gonna cut it right in front of ya."

"Football."

"Now, there's a difference right there. You let a kid come to practice month after month and then warm the bench all season, and pretty soon he gets the idea that he's no good, and he goes off. But horses, they don't get to warm no bench. They got to try it all equal with each other. They're more equal in these maiden races than they'll ever be again."

"Yup," said the friend.

"Culls 'em. Breaks 'em down."

"Yup," said the friend. "Who ya got?"

"Well, I got a pick three that's still got a breath of life in it. I did a five-five-five this time."

"Hell, that's a crazy bet. I know a guy who did this thing for a year. He played the horses that he liked best across the board, and also the longest shot in the race. He did it for a year, and even though he ended up with a lot of favorites, those eighty- or a-hundred-to-one shots came in just often enough to put him in the black for the year. I always thought it was a good system."

"Why don't you use it, then?"

"Ah, it was his system. I got one of my own."

"Don't we all."

"Jesse," said Leo. He had the binoculars to his eyes. Jesse said, "Are they in?" Leo, for the first time ever, handed him the glasses.

The bell clanged and the gates opened. Residual, of course, was in the second hole. The thing was, when the gates opened in a normal race, a line of horses leapt forth. A good start was a nice thing to see, everyone doing the same thing for a moment, then, boom, everyone different. But this was a bad start. Residual leapt forth, but the filly in the number-one slot stood for a moment, and the filly in the number-four spot jumped out, then stopped dead in her tracks. The outside filly crossed to the rail, not as if her jockey was taking her there, but as if she was out of control. And the number-three filly reared up and dumped her jockey. Jesse took the glasses down from his eyes and looked up at Leo, who was shaking his head. But there was no time for that. Now the field organized itself tentatively. Residual and the number-six horse were in front, but right behind them was the riderless filly, her reins dangling. The number-one filly was out now, but fighting her jockey. She and the other two had at least four lengths of daylight between them and the first group. Jesse focused the glasses on Residual. As she disappeared behind the stuff in the infield that hid everything from the gaze of the fans, she looked awkwardly boxed in. The filly with the jockey seemed to be pressing against her where she was on the rail, and the riderless filly was right on her heels. But she floated, that's what Jesse thought, she floated.

He set the glasses on the beginning of the turn and waited. When they came into his view, things had changed. Now all six horses were strung out along the rail, nose to tail. The number-six filly, whose jockey had a white cap, was first, the riderless filly was second, Residual was third, the number-one filly was fourth, the number-four filly, the one that had stopped dead, was fifth, and galloping along behind was number five. They came around the turn in just this order, as if they were a merry-go-round. Jesse heard Leo say "Shit!" with a certain amount of surprise in his voice, more than he normally cared to allow. As they entered the stretch, Jesse could see some of the jockeys begin to do stuff. The leading jockey glanced back, and then went to his whip; the last two pulled to the outside. The horse behind Residual simply ran out of steam, and disappeared from Jesse's view. Pincay did nothing for a moment, then he simply moved his hands up the filly's neck and seemed to lift himself off her. How he could do this, Jesse could not say, but, then, Leo always said that Pincay could do anything. Residual continued to float. She floated around the riderless filly, who, as they came under the stands, threw her head in fear at the noise everyone was making. She floated away from the fillies behind her, and she floated right up to the lead filly, seemed to encompass her and then to overtake her. They crossed the finish line. "Photo" once again flashed on the tote. Jesse handed the glasses to Leo, and Leo said, "Well, maiden fillies is maiden fillies, is what my dad used to say. There's never been a man in the world who could see into the heart of a maiden filly."

"Residual was perfect, Dad."

"She ran a pretty good race, son. She kept out of trouble, but I don't think she won."

"Nothing bothered her, Dad. All that stuff was all right with her. She didn't even notice it."

"Son, from the perspective of the bettor, perfect is a win. The other stuff is just nice."

The results came up. Residual had not won. But she had come in second. Jesse pulled his tickets from his pocket. He still had two place bets and one show bet. He looked at the tote and added them up. Then he said, "I still get thirty-five dollars, Dad, plus my original ten. That's forty-five dollars. That's good investing."

Leo ruffled his hair and said, "Yes it is, son."

Jesse noticed that, when the grooms went out to retrieve their horses, Residual came up to her groom and nosed him on the arm. After Pincay took off his saddle but before he turned to walk away, he gave the filly a long stroke and she gave him a look. Pincay laughed. Jesse heard him say to the groom, "Nice girl, this one." Then Buddy Crawford was there, and he and Pincay talked. Pincay was nodding and smiling. Buddy Crawford was shaking his head. Then Pincay laughed, one of those laughs you saw sometimes, where you realized that the person laughing just knew everything was fine, and he was right. Your dad could say this, and your mom could say that, and the trainer could be mad about some little thing, and maybe not everything went your way, but if you saw how there could be floating in spite of all that, then everything was fine anyway.

Leo, who had gone to cash the tickets, came back with the money and put it in Jesse's hand. Jesse looked at it. Leo was smiling, but it seemed strange to him. He wondered if he would ever know the same things that other people knew, ever look at something as simple as money and know anything simple about it. Even the numbers in the corners seemed mysterious. His dad was always telling him things, always pointing out what it was that going to the track taught you about, like life and the president and how you should be and stuff. What the track taught you was very detailed, and there was a lot to remember, and his dad knew all about it. But his dad hadn't seen how the filly floated. Maybe no one else had seen that, either, maybe only he and Pincay had noticed that. Pincay had noticed it, Jesse knew from the pat he gave her when he got off. She was a nice girl, that filly.

His dad was bouncing up and down on the balls of his feet with his hands in his pockets. It was the third race. He and his dad always got to this point at about the third race, where Leo had to go off by himself and do his thinking alone. Without being told, Jesse went to one of the benches by the walking ring and sat down. He pulled out the comic book that he had in his back pocket.

Then the fourth race.

Then the fifth race. Even if you won one, Jesse thought, a day at the races was a long day.

Then the sixth race. When they came out for the sixth race, Jesse realized that he must have dropped off to sleep, because a black lady with a big sunhat on was poking him. He sat up and said, "Oh, I'm sorry," thinking that he had maybe fallen over on her, but she was saying, "Honey, look at this. I got these two in this race. Here's Easy Pieces, he's that big chestnut, he's by Sea Hero, you know who that was, and here's Boraboola. He's a Pleasant Colony." Jesse gazed at the giant animal, nearly black, with one white sock. "Now, which one do you like? Here's my thinking. This race is a mile and a sixteenth on the turf. This Boraboola horse is a distance horse, maybe. He's got the breeding and the bone, and he's been pretty lightly raced, like they're saving him. Those Pleasant Colony horses tend to develop late. Now, Sea Hero was a great racehorse, but he hasn't proved himself as a sire, so you don't really know how to judge his get, you know. But this chestnut, now, to my mind, he's built."

Jesse said, "What's his form?"

"Honey, I don't look at the form, I look at the horse."

"Me, too," said Jesse.

"I don't know," said the lady. "I just don't know."

"I like the black horse."

"Well, he's not black, but almost. They say no Thoroughbreds are black, but I've seen one or two, you ask me."

"He's the one I like. He's very proud of himself today."

"Okay, then."

The lady got up and walked off toward the betting windows, and Jesse thought about going to watch the race, but he really didn't want to, because he might run into his father, and that might be too much. If his father wanted him, he would find him. He felt the money in his pocket, and remembered he was hungry.

They ran the race while he was eating his burger and onion rings. He saw it on the monitor. Boraboola won by a length. The chestnut was third. Jesse felt a very private sense of pleasure descend upon him, from wherever it came from. He hadn't bet, of course, no nine-year-old could bet alone, but he had picked a winner. He knew he would think about that tonight in bed, then tomorrow, when he got up and went to school. It would be a good thing to think about over and over.

Lots of people, of course, left during the ninth race, just to miss the rush hour, or to get away, or because they were tired, but for Leo, leaving before the end of the day was not a possibility. Leo always promoted hard work and doing a good job. But the ninth race could be a killer, Jesse knew. The eighth race was the feature—it always had a name, good money was attached, and the best horses and trainers competed. The ninth race was what Leo called the dogfood run, lots of old geldings or mares who'd seen better days, nothing that could go to the breeding shed, and probably too unsound to be sold off, so their trainers and owners were extracting the last drops of their investment before sending the animals away.

"Where?" Jesse asked once.

"Where do you think, son?"

Jesse knew. And Jesse knew cattle went here, hogs went there, sheep went there, chickens and turkeys went there. Why not horses? But if he tried to imagine, let's say, Residual or Boraboola or Easy Pieces going there, it made him anxious again.

The reason the ninth race might be a killer was that, if his dad had had a winning day, and had parlayed all his bets, then he could lose it all in a matter of moments. If he'd had a losing day, then he might keep betting to get the money back. Theoretically, he could win it all in a matter of moments, too, but that was less likely. And the horses, being unsound, old, unpredictable, were harder to bet, and his dad would be tired, too. Jesse decided to find Leo, though. The fact was, he missed him, and his desire to know how he was doing suddenly outweighed his fear of knowing the same thing. He came out in front of the stands and saw Leo right away, stock-still, binoculars to his face, staring at the line of horses approaching the starting gate, which was out at the chute. This was a six-furlong race, quick, at least. It was impossible to tell from a distance whether Leo was winning or losing, he was so still. When Jesse went up to him, just as the horses left the gate, Leo dropped his hand on his head to keep him quiet. The race had a small field, only five. A man standing nearby said, "Look at these plugs. This is gonna take till midnight. That number-four horse looks like she has to remember how to move her feet."

The five mares and fillies came around the turn. Leo's hand pressed Jesse a little harder. When the horses crossed the finish line, the number-two horse first, the hand lifted, and after a moment, Leo said the magic words, "All right!" Jesse looked up at him. He was smiling. Leo had had a winning day. He said, "Just had a little bet on that sweetie-mare, but let's cash it anyway. Goosey Lucy. What a name! I love how they name these Thoroughbreds. That's a poem in itself. You know, sometimes you read down the program, and it's a song, or a poem, or something like that. Goosey Lucy. Well, sweetie, you made me a winner today."

Goosey Lucy had gone off at four-to-one, so Leo walked away from the window with twenty-two dollars, which he arranged carefully in his wallet with the rest of the money. Dollars weren't falling out of his pockets the way they did once in a while, when Leo hit a big exotic bet, but there was a thick wad in the wallet that would make for a nice evening.

On the way home, with the sun setting over the 210 and all of Los Angeles displayed before them, Leo sang his usual hymn. Jesse liked to hear it. "There's no place like the racetrack, son. Everyone of every sort is there. No one is excluded at the racetrack. Blacks, Jews, Hispanics, Chinese. Koreans love the racetrack. Kids play there. People picnic there. Families break bread together at the racetrack. Rich, poor, and everything in between. It doesn't matter what you do in your life, son, the richest man you will ever see will be someone you saw at the track, walking along, holding his tickets just like you. And probably the poorest man you ever see will be at the track, too, because there's always somebody, every day, who managed to wipe out all his assets at the betting windows. A beggar on the street with a sawbuck in his hat is richer than that man. Now, that's just the socio-economic aspect, which I appreciate, but which is just an aspect. These jocks are great athletes. Now, some say they're crooked, but I don't say that, I just say they're great athletes. If you blew up a jock's body to the size of a basketball player's, the jock would be stronger, more muscled, more coordinated, more you name it. Jock just is. They've done studies. So you get to see that. But the other thing is, and the thing I love the most is, every single horse race is something that can't be understood. Eight or nine times a day, day after day, men and horses go out and line up and start running, and the next thing you know, you are in mystery-land. Which horse has a hairline fracture, which horse sees something funny, which horse is feeling especially good, which jock pushes which other jock. It's a mystery that can't be plumbed by the form, by the theories, by any known science, and it happens every day, for me to look at. And, then, it's a story, too. Every horse, every jock, every owner, every trainer, every bettor, every race. A football game is one story, one day a week. That's boring. A day at the races is thousands of stories, with grass around, trees around, a breeze, some mountains in the background. You know, in the summer, we'll go to a real horse heaven. We'll get out to Del Mar."

Permissions Acknowledgments